WILEY

Federal Government Auditing

Laws, Regulations, Standards, Practices, & Sarbanes-Oxley

WILEY

Federal Government Auditing

Laws, Regulations, Standards, Practices, & Sarbanes-Oxley

Edward F. Kearney   Jeffrey W. Green

Roldan Fernandez   Cornelius E. Tierney

WILEY

JOHN WILEY & SONS, INC.

For general information on our other products and services, please contact our Customer Care Department within the US at 800-762-2974, outside the US at 317-572-3993 or fax 317-572-4002.

Wiley also publishes its books in a variety of electronic formats. Some content that appears in print may not be available in electronic books.

Library of Congress Cataloging-in-Publication Data:

Kearney & Company.
   Federal Government Auditing: Laws, Regulations, Standards, Practices & Sarbanes/Oxley / Kearney & Company.
       p. cm.
   Includes index.
   ISBN 13: 978-0-471-74048-3 (pbk.)
   ISBN 10: 0-471-74048-9 (pbk.)
   1. Finance, Public—Auditing—Law and legislation—United States. 2. Finance, Public—United States—Auditing. 3. Finance, Public—United States—Accounting. 4. Government purchasing—United States—Auditing. I. Kearney & Company (Alexandria, VA)
   KF6235.F43 2006
   343.73'034—dc22   200511179

Printed in the United States of America

10 9 8 7 6 5 4 3 2 1

CONTENTS

PREFACE

Auditing within the federal government has been evolving since the 1950s, and until 1972, had primarily consisted of reviews of a federal department by its internal audit staff, and of audits of government contracts and grantees by internal auditors charged with conducting "external" audits. *Auditing in the Federal Government: Laws, Regulations, Standards, and Practices* is directed to all auditors of federal agencies and programs and those who may be subject to audits by the federal government. The book provides essential knowledge for all who audit the federal government, its programs, contractors, and grantees, including many who are affected by, or should have some knowledge of, the impact of a federal audit.

As of 2005, federal audit and internal control criteria and requirements consist of a "patchwork" of laws enacted by Congress; regulations and rules issued by the Federal Office of Management and Budget; rules and procedures required by the council of Federal Inspectors General; the *Government Auditing Standards* of the GAO (updated and revised several times since issuance in 1972); and, where applicable, appropriate, or mandated, various aspects or portions of the *generally accepted auditing standards* of the American Institute of Certified Public Accountants (AICPA). In 2002, the passing of the Sarbanes-Oxley Act required management of all public companies to annually assess and then have independent audits made of the companies' internal controls over financial reporting. Whether Sarbanes-Oxley will lead to additional legislation/regulations affecting the federal government remains to be seen, but warrants close monitoring by those interested in federal auditing and internal controls.

Federal auditing is not typically a course found in a college curriculum, and coverage of the subject is absent in writings and publications from academe. Federal laws and regulations highlight the government's needs, objectives, and requirements, but detailed guidance on what, why, how, and by whom federal audits should be made is sparse.

This book, *Auditing in the Federal Government: Laws, Regulations, Standards, and Practices*, by Kearney & Company, P.C., is intended to serve as a single-source informative guide through the "patchwork" of criteria for performing audits unique to federal departments and agencies, as well as federal audits made of contractors and grantees, universities, and other non-profits. Kearney & Company is a regional certified public accounting firm founded in 1985 that specializes in providing auditing, accounting, and information technology services to the federal government's executive, legislative, regulatory departments, and agencies, and other organizations doing business with the federal government. Additional details on the firm can be found on the Web at www.kearneyco.com.

This book has been written in a manner which endeavors to assist professionals and non-professionals employed by the federal government or other organizations—performing internal and external audits for governmental entities, inspectors general, independent public accountants, military comptrollers, legislators, staffs of legislators, state and local government officials, financial managers, budget officers, program and financial analysts, attorneys, systems designers, and systems experts—in short, anyone having an interest in or repeated financial dealings with the federal government. The book is divided into several parts in an attempt to better address the interests of this diverse constituency, some sections with more detail, and some with less.

Part I—Background of Federal Auditing consists of four chapters that highlight the evolution of federal accounting and auditing—the laws, regulations, rules, standards, and other requirements that form the criteria for audits of federal departments and agencies, and of the countless organizations that do business with the federal government, principally through federally funded contracts and grants. Part I also includes a chapter on the implications of Sarbanes-Oxley and concludes with a chapter on auditors of federal agencies.

Part II—Federal Budgeting, Accounting, and Financial Statements includes two chapters, both in nontechnical language, on budgeting, accounting, and financial reporting of the receipts, expenditures, and application of federal monies. The first chapter outlines the federal budget process and the life cycle of federal accounting transactions, while the second chapter describes the package of the annual financial statements required of federal departments and agencies.

Part III—Auditing in the Federal Government consists of several chapters that describe the scope and work performed to audit federal departments and agencies. These chapters provide an overview of the specific phases of an audit: (1) The federal audit model, (2) planning the audit, (3) documenting internal controls, (4) assessing and evaluating control risk, (5) testing controls, transactions, and accounts, and (6) closing procedures, quality control, and reporting (including the form of required reporting).

Part IV—Nature of Selected Federal Audits highlights the audit objectives, issues, tasks, and concerns of other audits and examinations of federal funds, in addition to annual financial statement audits. These audits and examinations are more limited in scope, and include audits performed under the Single Audit Act, performance audits, contract audits, and grant audits. The specialized or expert knowledge required to plan, design, and execute a methodology for selected, specialized reviews appears in this section.

This book is the result of numerous consultations over many years with accountants, auditors, financial managers, and systems consultants specializing in the financial management issues of the federal government. In addition, reliance has been placed on the bodies of knowledge created by Congress, the Office of Management and Budget, the Government Accountability Office (formerly the General Accounting Office),[1] the American Institute of Certified Public Accountants, the Public Company Accounting Oversight Board, the Federal Accounting Standards Advisory Board, the Chief Financial Officers Council, and Offices of Inspectors General. Promulgations of all of these organizations have contributed to the body of knowledge one must possess to conduct an audit of any organization responsible for receiving and dispensing federal monies.

---

[1] *In 2004, GAO, the General Accounting Office, changed its name to the Government Accountability Office. This new agency name is used throughout the text.*

WILEY

Federal Government Auditing

Laws, Regulations, Standards, Practices, & Sarbanes-Oxley

PART I
Background of Federal Auditing

1 BACKGROUND OF FEDERAL AUDITING

EVOLUTION, STANDARD SETTERS, RESPONSIBILITIES, AUDIT TYPES

The financial impact of government in America is enormous. The economic impact of the federal government alone overshadows any state, local government, or private sector entity, not to mention the governments of other countries. The United States federal government employs millions, owns billions, and spends trillions each year. For fiscal year 2006 (ending at midnight on September 30, 2006), the receipts of the federal government are budgeted at $2.177 trillion; federal outlays are budgeted at $2.539 trillion. And these are merely the "budgeted" amounts. Not included are the "off-budget" expenditures and contingent liabilities of independent agencies, government-sponsored enterprises, government corporations, and other federal entities that comprise additional trillions of dollars.

EVOLUTION OF GOVERNMENTAL AUDITING

The roots of governmental auditing can be traced back to the conception of the Constitution. The following sections will trace and summarize highlights in the evolution of governmental auditing.

Federal Financial Management: Frustrations and Discontent

Authors of the Constitution vested responsibility for the financial affairs of the federal government in the legislative branch, giving Congress exclusive power to levy and collect taxes, borrow on the credit of the United States, and coin money. Very early in 1789, with the passage of the Treasury Act, Congress provided for an auditor and a comptroller in the Department of the Treasury. At the same time, Congress placed reliance on the discretion of departmental accounting officers to enforce legislative provisions related to expenditures of public funds. The next 150 years were overshadowed by the frustration of part-time Congresses, with few senators and representatives, and minimal professional assistance. The legislative history of the times, as recorded in congressional committee hearings and enacted financial management legislation, documented discontent with inconsistencies in executive branch accounting practices, the credibility of financial reporting by agencies, and repeated lapses in controls over federal financial reporting.[1]

One hundred years later, by the Dockery Act of 1894, Congress attempted to streamline the federal financial system and formally institute fiscal reforms: an Office of Comptroller of the Treasury was created. Six auditors were assigned depart-

---

[1] *U.S. Senate, Committee on Government Operations,* **Financial Management in the Federal Government: A Comprehensive Analysis of Existing and Proposed Legislation including Financial Management Improvements Made on a Government-wide Basis**, *Washington, DC, 1961.*

mental audit responsibilities and were required to certify to the balances of agency accounts that underwent mandated examinations; and individual federal departments were charged with the responsibility to make administrative examinations of their accounts before submission to the auditors. Because the comptroller and auditors were officials in the executive branch, congressional frustration continued over the legality and propriety of expenditures by the executive branch.

With the Budget and Accounting Act of 1921, Congress instituted numerous financial management improvements, many of which remain to this day. Two among several, which are discussed later in this chapter and in other chapters, were the establishment of the Bureau of Budget in the Department of Treasury and the General Accounting Office in the legislative branch, with government-wide responsibilities for accounting and auditing. Throughout the twentieth century, congressional discontent and frustration over the inadequate methods of federal financial practices continued. In fact, in the decade of the 1990s alone, Congress passed more financial management legislation than in any decade in the country's history.

Auditing and Government

The practice of auditing dates back millennia; its roots are more in the public sector than in the private sector. Interestingly, these earlier audits were not merely fiscal or financial in nature, but often addressed broader accountability, stewardship of assets, and legal compliance with respect to the receipts, disbursements, and uses of funds. Frequently, the sovereign or government's assets, administered by agents, were the impetus for periodic audits. In America, however, it was the government's treasury and finances that were of concern to citizens and legislators. The priorities of colonial auditors closely paralleled those of today: conformance to budgets, completeness of reported receipts, appropriateness of expenditures, application or use of tax monies, and compliance with laws.[2]

Over the course of two centuries, the practices and ongoing problems of auditing perplexed many, confounded multitudes, and seemed to be the source of never-ending legal suits, trials, and judgments. Not the federal government, the courts, the public, or the accounting profession had definitive views on what constituted an acceptable audit. Many attempts were made to set auditing standards and mandate specific auditing practices, and generally, these promulgations were appropriate and applied. But in many instances, when it was not possible to anticipate or provide for all of the circumstances and conditions that might be encountered in an audit, legislators, regulators, and standard setters told the auditor to "use judgment." At times, the judgment exercised was in conflict with or challenged by regulators, recipients, and other users of auditor reports. This was evident in the print and electronic media coverage of the 1990s and early 2000s on numerous accounting, financial, and audit inadequacies. In many instances, the contested audit practices involved publicly traded corporations. Reviews of court dockets and governmental administrative law courts disclose similar disputes involving the federal and other governments.

---

[2] *William Holmes, Linda H. Kistler, and Louis S. Corsini, **Three Centuries of Accounting in Massachusetts** (New York: Arno Press, 1978).*

Auditing: Issues Continue

To this day, the auditing issues continue. What is an appropriate audit scope? What transactions should be audited, how many, and for which fiscal periods? What type of audit report should be issued? And, who says so? Editions of *The Accountant* document a contradiction of views. Consider the audit expectations of the 1880s:[3]

> *The auditor's task is compared to judge and jury; for some outstanding matters, estimation must be introduced; but the auditor should not indulge in forecasts or expressions of feeling; rather the auditor should adhere to only the facts—the hard, dry, realities.*

Of course, most people outside the accountancy profession do not subscribe to such a restricted scope for financial reporting and auditing. The audit determination of an entity's financial position, whether profits in the case of companies or fund balances in the case of governments, is replete with exercises of auditor judgment, which cannot be avoided. With the possible exception of the cash account balance, all balances in a financial statement are the product of some level of estimation, and even forecasting or projection. Clearly, adhering only to the facts— "the hard, dry, realities" —was never an option.

Independent accountants first attained visibility and national recognition through work in the governmental sector, a sector that generally lacked internal auditors. Teaming with progressive reformers and governmental "do-gooders" of the late 1800s, accounting practitioners highlighted the relationships between the corruption and inefficiency of government to the prevailing social ills of public sector governance. The absence of uniform accounting, minimal or inadequate financial reporting, and no requirement for periodic independent audits were significant contributors to the disclosed problems.[4]

Standards for audits of federal entities are similar to those applied in audits of private sector organizations. Like private sector audits, federal audits must satisfy several constituencies: legislative overseers, federal regulatory agencies, the rules of other federal departments, and a host of accounting and auditing standard developers. The result is that the practice of federal auditing must conform to a blend of laws, regulations, rules, customs, and practices, enunciated by a patchwork of congressional committees, governmental agencies, offices, and boards and by nongovernmental groups.

Congress is cognizant of the need to clarify current guidance. As this book is being written, the House Government Reform Subcommittee on Government Management, Finance and Accountability is seeking ways to hold federal executives more accountable for their behavior. Representative Todd Russell Platts (R-Pa), subcommittee chairman, is holding hearings regarding how to continue to improve financial management in the federal government, and two of the writers of this book testified in the initial hearing held by Representative Platts. One area of emphasis is

---

[3] *The Accountant was the professional periodical of the predecessor to the American Accounting Association, which today is the national organization of accounting professors in the United States.*

[4] *Gary John Previts and Barbara Dubis Merino, **A History of Accountancy in the United States**, (Columbus: Ohio State University Press, 1997), Chapter 5.*

the possible consolidation and, to the extent possible, simplification of the many federal financial management laws which have been passed over the years (a discussion of several of these laws appears in Chapter 2).

AUDITING THE FEDERAL GOVERNMENT: DEFINITION AND SCOPE

In the 1970s, the General Accounting Office (now, and hereon, the Government Accountability Office [GAO]) declared that audits of government needed to be different and more comprehensive and would require, if not entirely different audit standards, then the application of additional standards. These standards would address issues beyond the financial that are important to accountability in the federal government and by state and local governments, organizations, entities, and others involved with, or benefiting from, federal financial assistance. Thus, GAO's generally accepted *Government Auditing Standards* defined an *audit* as:

> *A term used to describe, not only work done by accountants in examining financial statements, but also work done in reviewing (1) compliance with laws and regulations, (2) economy and efficiency operations, and (3) effectiveness in achieving program results. The objective of such an examination includes an expression of the fairness of presentation of an entity's financial statements, but additionally a reporting, or an audit opinion if sufficient audit work was performed, on the nature of tests made and results of those tests with respect to an entity's system of internal controls and its compliance with laws and regulations and provisions of contract and grant agreements.*

In 2005, the focus of federal audits not only includes audits of an organization's financial statements, but may include concurrent assessments and attestations relating to an organization's performance, management, compliance with laws and regulations, and effectiveness of financial controls. The premise is that financial statement audits are important and will continue to be so, but audits of only financial data, as of a specific point in time, provide limited information as to whether an organization is economical or efficient, or if its operations even approach operational objectives defined in enabling legislation.

In the most recent edition of *Government Auditing Standards*, dated June 2003 (and effective for financial audits and attestation engagements on or after January 1, 2004, and for performance audits beginning on or after January 1, 2004), the current Comptroller General declared:

> *The concept of accountability for public resources is key to our nation's governing process and a critical element for a healthy democracy. Legislators, government officials, and the public want to know whether government services are being provided efficiently, effectively, economically, and in compliance with laws and regulations. They also want to know whether government programs are achieving their objectives and desired outcomes, and at what cost.*
>
> *Government managers are accountable to legislative bodies and the public for their activities and related results. Government auditing is a key element in fulfilling the government's duty to be accountable to the people. Auditing allows those parties and other stakeholders to have confidence in the reported information on the results of programs or operations, as well as in related systems of internal control.*

Beginning in the mid-1980s, congressional interest, special investigations, hearings, and new laws created significant audit opportunities for more frequent and better audits of federal activities. By the late 1990s, the significance of governmental auditing increased and the number of governments undergoing annual audits rose enormously. These laws mandated better audits: audits that focused on the broader issues of federal government, were more informative and of greater use to Congress and executive managers, and provided financial and operational perspectives to federal overseers.

FEDERAL AUDITING: WHO SETS THE STANDARDS?

Several organizations, both governmental and nongovernmental, by law or otherwise, have accrued significant statutory and other authority to prescribe standards for audits of federal agencies and of financial assistance provided to nonfederal entities through contracts, grants, and other agreements. In addition to laws of Congress establishing overall federal audit policy, other organizations, in and out of the federal government, have been instrumental in defining or impacting the scope of federal audits. These organizations include the American Institute of Certified Public Accountants (AICPA), GAO, the Office of Management and Budget (OMB), federal Inspectors General, the Securities and Exchange Commission (SEC), and the Public Company Accounting Oversight Board (PCAOB). These organizations are discussed in more detail in the following sections.

American Institute of Certified Public Accountants

At this time, the American Institute of Certified Public Accountants prescribes the generally accepted auditing standards (GAAS) that form the underlying foundation of the *Government Auditing Standards* used by all auditors when auditing any federal entity or recipient of federal financial assistance. Federal audits must satisfy the GAAS of the AICPA, which include general, fieldwork, and reporting standards, plus the AICPA's Statements on Auditing Standards (SAS).

The federal government's reliance on the AICPA's GAAS was noted in the initial issuance of *Government Auditing Standards* in 1972 and confirmed in its 1988, 1994, and 2003 revisions. In various sections, GAO stated that *Government Auditing Standards* incorporate all of the AICPA's fieldwork standards and reporting standards for audits and its Statements on Auditing Standards, unless the Comptroller General (who heads GAO) excludes such standards by formal announcement. To date, no Comptroller General has excluded any AICPA fieldwork, reporting standards, or Statement on Auditing Standards.

US Government Accountability Office

GAO, a federal agency in the legislative branch, was established by Congress in 1921 to be its audit, evaluation, and investigative arm. Its founding legislation, the Budget and Accounting Act, provided that a core responsibility of GAO was to investigate, at the seat of government or elsewhere, the *receipt*, *disbursement*, and *application* of public funds and to report annually to Congress on its work and its recommendations for needed legislation. GAO, completely independent of the executive branch and accountable only to Congress, is headed by the Comptroller General. The Comptroller General is appointed by the President and serves with the advice and consent of Congress for a 15-year term of office. The Comptroller General cannot be reappointed and can be removed from office only by way of formal impeachment proceedings by Congress.

In 1972, GAO issued the initial edition of the *Standards for Audit of Governmental Organizations, Programs, Activities, and Functions*, a title that was shortened in later editions to the *Government Auditing Standards* and is popularly referred to as the "yellow book," a reference to the cover's color. *Government Auditing Standards* states that audits involving public funds, federal, and other public monies, may not be limited to those financial statement audits annually made by CPAs and other auditors. The *Government Auditing Standards* govern audits of financial statements, assessments, and attestations with respect to an entity's compliance with laws and regulations and controls over financial reporting, as well as performance audits. In its *Government Auditing Standards*, GAO categorizes audits into three categories:[5]

1. Audits of financial statements at the conclusion of which the auditor provides an opinion
2. Financial related reviews for which the auditor might provide written assurances or attestations other than an audit opinion
3. Performance audits, the scopes of which encompass assessments of program effectiveness and results, economy and efficiency, internal control, and legal compliance

US Office of Management and Budget

The Office of Management and Budget, an agency in the federal government's executive branch and within the Executive Office of the President, has the primary responsibility of assisting the President with development and implementation of the federal government's budget, providing management policy guidance, and generally overseeing the performance of federal cabinet departments and other agencies, boards, and commissions. OMB was organized in 1970, but its predecessor, the Bureau of the Budget, dates back to the 1940s. Earlier, the Budget and Accounting Act of 1921, which established GAO, also established a federal budget office within the US Treasury Department.

In legislation such as the Chief Financial Officers Act of 1990 and other laws of the 1990s relating to financial management, Congress delegated responsibilities to OMB for federal accounting, auditing, systems oversight, and other financial management tasks. In exercising these responsibilities, OMB prescribed detailed policies and procedures to be applied in audits of federal executive branch departments, agencies, and their activities. The policy announcements appear in series referred to as OMB circulars and OMB bulletins, which are executive branch government-wide

---

[5] *Unless otherwise noted, all references to, or citations of **Government Auditing Standards** or generally accepted government auditing standards relate to the guidance provided by GAO in the 2003 revision, **Government Auditing Standards**.*

regulations and directives detailing how federal departments and agencies are to implement laws of Congress.

OMB Circulars and Bulletins

OMB circulars are issued when the nature of a subject is of continuing effect and remains in force until rescinded or superceded. Circulars are identified by the prefix "A" and a number. For example, OMB Circular A-133, titled *Audits of States, Local Governments, and Non-Profit Organizations*, sets forth the federal audit policy, regulations, standards, and, in some instances, detailed audit procedures that must be employed when auditing recipients of federal financial assistance. OMB bulletins are used either when the nature of the subject requires a single or ad hoc action by federal departments and agencies or the issue is transitory in nature. The last two numerals of the fiscal year are used to indicate the annual series of bulletins and the sequential number of the specific subject matter. For example, OMB bulletins affecting federal audits: OMB Bulletin No. 01-02, *Audit Requirements for Federal Financial Statements* (issued on October 16, 2000, in the fiscal year 2001). Note that the federal government's fiscal year begins on October 1 of one calendar year and ends on September 30 of the succeeding calendar year.

Offices of Federal Inspectors General

Within the executive branch, there exist councils of federal Inspectors General established by presidential executive order to address integrity, economy, and effectiveness issues that transcend individual government agencies. A major function of these councils is to conduct intra-agency and intra-entity audit, inspection, and investigation projects to promote economy and efficiency in federal programs and operations, and to address government-wide issues of fraud, waste, and abuse more effectively. Collectively, Inspectors General develop audit and investigation policies, standards, and approaches, and issue mandatory audit guidance relating to audits of federal departments and agencies, as well as audits of nonfederal entities receiving varying forms of federal financial assistance.

The passage of the Inspector General Act of 1978 created, in the larger federal agencies, an Office of Inspector General with the responsibility to conduct and supervise audits and investigations of their respective agencies. The law provided that these Inspectors General would be appointed by the President and serve with the counsel and consent of Congress. Although Inspectors General may be removed from office by the President, the President must communicate the reason for the removal to Congress. In these agencies, the law required that there be an assistant Inspector General for auditing responsible for supervising performance of all auditing activities relating to the agency's programs and operations.

Securities and Exchange Commission and Public Company Accounting Oversight Board

The Sarbanes-Oxley law, passed by Congress in 2002, required changes to, and elimination of, some existing corporate governance practices of publicly listed companies. Additionally, this law created PCAOB, endowed with the authority to set reporting and auditing standards that must be used by registered public accounting firms in the preparation and issuance of audit reports related to financial statements of publicly traded companies. However, Sarbanes-Oxley requirements might soon be imposed on the federal financial management community, as the essence of the Act is already de facto federal financial management policy. For example:

- A government-wide federal policy relative to internal controls over financial reporting preceded and addressed the same issues as the Sarbanes-Oxley Act. This earlier internal controls policy arose as a result of actions taken over the years by: Congress in enacting earlier laws; OMB in its implementation of policy circulars and bulletins that prescribed regulations closely aligned with this new act; federal departments and agencies that for some years have been adapting systems of accounting, controls, financial management, and auditing guidance to the same subjects as the new act; and corrective and follow-up actions taken by federal agencies pursuant to recommendations of federal Inspectors General and GAO that are quite similar to those practices prescribed in the new act.
- Section 404 of the 2002 Sarbanes-Oxley Act requires that managements of public companies make assessments of the effectiveness of their internal controls based on a "suitable, recognized control framework established by a body of experts that followed due process procedures to develop the framework," specifically citing the *Internal Control–Integrated Framework* (the *Framework*) developed by the Committee of Sponsoring Organizations (COSO) of the Treadway Commission in 1992. Since the 1990s, OMB and GAO have encouraged adoption of the COSO *Framework* as the standard for federal agencies.

Thus, the essence or substance of these requirements by Sarbanes-Oxley would appear to be the same or quite similar to laws and federal policies of the 1990s directed toward improving the accounting and controls within federal agencies. GAO, in 2004 public forums, announced that as PCAOB promulgates auditing standards, GAO will refine its *Government Auditing Standards* to clarify any new guidance desired for federal audits.

TYPES OF GOVERNMENTAL AUDITS

When applied to corporate entities, the term *audit* is used primarily in reference to financial statement audits. Such audits are annually made of each required federal department and agency.[6] Additionally, however, during the course of a fiscal year, a far greater number of audits are made under other descriptors, such as *internal audits, functional audits, contract and grant audits,* and *performance audits*, to note a few. These special-focus audits are, for the most part, done by auditors of Inspectors General staffs, but a smaller number are also done by independent certified public accountants under contract to federal agencies. All of these audits are in conformance with GAO's *Government Auditing Standards*, applicable OMB circulars and

---

[6] *Includes the 24 CFO Act agencies and agencies subject to the Accountability of Tax Dollars Act of 2002, as documented by OMB.*

bulletins, and rules promulgated by Inspectors General either for their individual agency or collectively for the federal government. This section highlights a few such audits that are described with more detail in other chapters.

Financial Statement Audits

Financial statement audits are audits primarily concerned with providing reasonable assurance as to whether the annual financial statements of federal departments and agencies are presented fairly in all material respects in conformity with generally accepted accounting principles or *another comprehensive basis of accounting.*[7] For financial statement audits, an auditor would render an audit opinion or a disclaimer of opinion, depending on the results of the audit of the federal entity's financial statements. Such audits would have to conform to the *Government Auditing Standards* issued by GAO.

Nonstatement Financial Audits, Reviews, and Examinations

Nonstatement audits may have a variety of audit scopes, objectives, and purposes that differ from financial statement audits. These nonstatement audits could include an audit opinion on a scope of less than an entity's entire financial statement, or the auditor's reporting could be in the form of a written assurance or attestation with respect to the audit work performed and the results of the audit.

If the audit objective is to express an opinion on financial statements, selected chapters of the *Government Auditing Standards* for financial statement audits apply. Of the eight chapters of guidance in the "yellow book," three chapters apply directly to financial audits: Chapter 3, General Standards, applies to both financial and performance audits; Chapter 4, Fieldwork Standards for Financial Audits, and Chapter 5, Reporting Standards for Financial Audits, both pertain to financial audits.

Chapter 6, General, Fieldwork, and Reporting Standards for Attestation Engagements, pertains to attestation audits; Chapter 7, Fieldwork Standards for Performance Audits, and Chapter 8, Reporting Standards for Performance Audits, pertain to performance audits.

Performance Audits

The term *performance auditing* evolved during the 1950s and, in practice, connotes types of reviews other than financial statement audits. Other descriptors for performance audits include *management evaluations, operational reviews, comprehensive audits,* and *compliance examinations.* Defined by GAO, a *performance audit* entails:

> *An objective and systematic examination of evidence to provide an independent assessment of the performance and management of a program against objective crite-*

---

[7] *Only three authoritative organizations may establish generally accepted accounting principles for governments: the Governmental Accounting Standards Board (GASB; for state and local governmental units), the Federal Accounting Standards Advisory Board (for federal departments, agencies, commissions, offices), and the Financial Accounting Standards Board (for state and local governmental units, but only on specific recognition by GASB).*

ria as well as assessments that provide a prospective focus or that synthesize infor-mation on best practices or cross-cutting issues.

Thus, GAO views a performance audit as one with audit objectives related to: assessing a program's effectiveness, program results, or achievements; relative economy and efficiency with which an activity is operated; internal or management controls; value-for-money audits; or an entity's compliance with laws and regula-tions. Because these audits may address a variety of objectives, it follows that they must be performed to different criteria. Each performance audit is unique with varying scopes of work and usually will result in a report in which the auditor sets forth the audit findings, conclusions, and recommendations. The Government Au-diting Standards do not mandate a specific or described audit report for performance audits. Rather, they state that the form of a performance audit report should be ap-propriate for its intended use and be written or in some other retrievable form con-sidering the users' needs, likely demand, and distribution.

Three chapters of the *Government Auditing Standards* apply directly to perfor-mance audits, whether such audits are performed by staffs of Inspectors General or independent accountants under contract to a federal agency: Chapter 3, General Standards, would apply to both financial and performance audits; Chapter 7, Field-work Standards for Performance Audits, and Chapter 8, Reporting Standards for Performance Audits, apply to performance audits.

In many instances, the objectives of performance audits are exclusively financial in nature, but can assess operational performance, compliance with laws and regula-tions, effectiveness of managerial controls, or other scopes, limited only by those requiring auditor assistance. The automatic application of performance auditing standards to financial audits, or vice versa, is not appropriate and may be prohibited by federal legislation.

Other Federal Audits

An almost inexhaustible variety of audits take place within the federal arena. Examples and summaries of some of the more common types are provided next.

Settlement audits. The term *settlement audit* could refer to any number of ex-aminations and reviews that are unique to the public sector. Other descriptors in-clude: *turnover audits, transition audits, discharge audits, year-end encumbrance/ obligation audits,* and *carry-forward audits.* All are examinations or reviews with the objective of determining year-end account cutoff balances and amounts that could be due to or from *accountable officers.*

Settlement or discharge audits of accountable officers have a long precedence in the United States, dating to the 17th century. At the conclusion of these earlier set-tlement audits, the auditor was required to read the account to an audit committee of peers who concluded on the reasonableness of the accounting, after which the report probably would be submitted to the governing court.[8] Settlement audits are not full-scope financial statement audits, but are more often an examination of the receipts,

---

[8] *William Holmes, Linda Kistler, and Louis Corsini,* **Three Centuries of Accounting in Massachu-setts.**

disbursements, and the propriety of the cutoff or "turnover" balance of an official's "account." In the federal government, there are several thousand *accountable officers* (e.g., collection officers, disbursing officers, cash custodians, and, in some cases, certifying officers).[9] GAO is authorized by law to perform a settlement audit of the final financial reporting of these executives.

Financial-related audits. Tens of thousands of audits are performed annually by other than independent CPAs, for scopes of audits that do not include a financial statement, and the auditor's report may or may not contain an auditor's opinion. These audits might be generically referred to as *financial-related audits*. Financial-related audits, routinely performed by the internal auditors of governments, significantly outnumber annual financial statement audits.

Financial-related audits have several common features:

- The audit scopes of these audits will differ from those of the annual statement audits performed in accordance with GAAS.
- The auditor's report will most often be in narrative form (e.g., detailing what was audited, what was found, the auditor's recommendations) in contrast to the financial statement short-form opinion-type reporting, wherein the auditor states: "In our opinion…."
- In the vast majority of instances, these audits are performed by thousands of internal auditors employed by tens of thousands of governments.

A description of some types of financial-related audits follows.

- *Payroll and personnel audits* are regularly performed, often premised on the fact that these expenditures are the most significant budgeted item by most governments. Often these costs—salaries, benefits, vacations, sick leave, overtime, and so on—can be 75 to 80%, or more, of a government's expenditures. The scope of such audits is directed toward assessing compliance with voluminous laws, regulations, and rules controlling appointments, hiring, promoting, paying, transferring, vacationing, terminating, and retiring government employees.
- *Contract and grant audits* are generally directed to assessing costs and/or performance by a government's contractors and grantees. With respect to costs, a common concern is compliance with the contract or grant financial budget and adherence to any allowable, unallowable, and indirect or overhead criteria. To a lesser extent, but still common, these audits will evaluate the performance of a contractor or grantee in relation to cost expended or accomplishment of predetermined objectives in relation to elapsed time budgets.
- *Property and fixed asset audits* are assessments of embedded or sunk costs of property and fixed assets in possession of governments or government contractors and grantees that are valued in the trillions of dollars. Such audits could cover all or a portion of the life cycle of these assets, with the audit scope addressing the adequacy of or compliance with a government's fixed as-

---

[9] *The Federal Joint Financial Management Improvement Program statistic appears in a study of accountable officers and the effectiveness of disbursement control procedures.*

set policies, procedures, and practices over the purchase, receipt, accounting, storage, use, safeguarding, disposing, inventorying, and reporting of capital items such as buildings, equipment, furniture, fixtures, and, at times, infrastructure assets.

- *Systems audits,* in contrast to common perception, are not part of the annual financial statement audits. When an auditor opines, *"In our opinion, the financial statements present fairly, in all material respects...,"* this opinion provides minimal or no solace with respect to the adequacy or inadequacy of an entity's cost accounting, managerial competence, or effectiveness of control systems. A systems audit requires an audit scope specifically designed to assess the adequacy of account structure and data hierarchy, or the degree to which systems are accurately and timely capturing, compiling, and reporting financial and nonfinancial data relevant to the critical decisions being made by management or, increasingly, the extent, appropriateness, and effectiveness of automation.

- *Imprest/petty cash audits* are routinely made by governmental internal auditors of imprest fund and petty cash fund receipts, disbursements, and end-of-period balances. As is the case with corporate entities, these funds are widely utilized by governments to promote and simplify the cash disbursement process and reduce administrative costs. These audits typically are made on a surprise basis. The scope of such reviews includes an examination of support documents, tests for compliance with fund policies and procedures, assessing the appropriateness of fund balances, and determining the frequency of fund balance turnover.

AUDITING THE FEDERAL GOVERNMENT

Every day, thousands of professionals are involved with auditing and reporting on the activities of the federal government. Although many of these professionals are employed by the government, many others are employed by independent accounting firms to conduct audits under contracts from federal agencies. Little, though, has been published about these audits, which involve some of the largest professional audit organizations, nationally or internationally, in or out of government. Even less is taught about this branch of accountancy. A more complicating factor is that the form of federal financial statements, the applied federal accounting principles, and the mandated federal audit standards are not those applied to private sector or nonprofit sector entities or to state and local governmental units.

The practice of federal auditing encompasses those systems of controls, accounting, and financial reporting required by federal laws and government regulations that impact federal agencies and the hundreds of federal financial assistance programs in whatever form (e.g., federal subsidies, contracts and grants, loan and loan guarantees, settlement overruns and overhead disputes, and resolution of allowable, unallowable costs, and indirect cost issues). Knowledge of what federal financial executives must do to "keep the books straight" is information vital to all who do business with the federal government and all recipients benefiting from a federal assistance program. Knowing the issues of concern to federal financial managers, what will be audited, and how, provides insight into federal financial decisions pertaining to settlement of disagreements concerning legality or propriety of disbursed federal monies, settlement of disputes, and payment of claimed contract and grant costs.

The federal government, like other organizations and industries, has generated a jargon, a financial management language, of its own. Many of these terms, which permeate laws, policy, procedures, and practices that impact federal financial management, accounting, reporting, and auditing, are defined and illustrated in this book. An effort has been made to avoid altogether the journal entries and "T-accounts" so dear to accountants and auditors. The focus of this book, instead, is the professional and nonprofessional, in and out of government, academics and students, who have a need or desire to be better informed about their dealings with federal agencies and federal financial assistance programs. The book is divided into four parts to address interests of a diverse constituency that, at times, might well include legislators and their staffs, federal state and local governmental program managers and analysts, financial managers and accountants who must regularly undergo audit, and those doing business with the government.

Part I: Background of Federal Auditing

Part I consists of four chapters that provide a foundation for understanding the general nature of a federal audit, the legal mandates, and the types of audit organizations that have authority and responsibility to conduct federal audits and the conditions and restraints of such audits.

Chapter 1 highlights some of the history of auditing in the federal government, provides a description of auditing as practiced by federal agencies, and identifies the laws requiring the various types of audits conducted involving federal agency operations and financial assistance provided to nonfederal entities.

Chapter 2 identifies several laws that, over the past 200 years, have been the legal basis and precedent for audits historically and currently made of federal agencies, federal programs, and the government's contractors, grantees, borrowers, and those benefiting from any of many loan guarantee programs.

Chapter 3 describes the implications of the Sarbanes-Oxley Act of 2002. This act reordered the audit priorities of the past with respect to the controls over financial reporting of publicly listed companies. It mandated that managements must now assess the effectiveness of internal controls and have those controls independently audited; an audit report must be made of the effectiveness of controls in conjunction with the audit of an entity's financial statements.

Chapter 4 notes some shortcomings of past federal audits, discusses the roles and methods by which OMB, Inspectors General, and GAO oversee the practice of federal auditing, and describes organizations that audit the federal government and its national and international programs.

Part II: Federal Budgeting, Accounting, and Financial Statements

Part II describes, in summary, the accounting and audit significance of the federal budget, the economic events for which there must be an accounting and reporting, and an example of the financial statements required to make that accounting and reporting.

Chapter 5 describes, in general terms, the federal budget process and its participants, budgetary events requiring an accounting and reporting, plus an overview of the accounting life cycle of federal financial transactions.

Chapter 6 illustrates the form and content of several federal financial statements and describes the purpose or objective of each statement and the compilation process necessary to meet the advanced, accelerated federal reporting mandates.

Part III: Auditing in the Federal Government

Part III describes, overall and by specific phases, the process for planning, conducting, reviewing, and the ultimate reporting of a financial statement audit of a federal agency.

Chapter 7 provides an overview of the financial audit and briefly describes the processes, phases, and selected steps of an optimal plan for conducting the annual financial statement audit of a federal agency.

Chapter 8 discusses initial audit planning, including the development of an audit plan, and emphasizes the need to reassess plans as the audit progresses and new facts develop.

Chapter 9 outlines an approach and procedures for documenting the auditor's understanding of an agency's internal controls over financial reporting.

Chapter 10 provides an overview of the development of an audit approach and audit procedures based on the auditors' evaluation of internal control and assessment of control risk.

Chapter 11 identifies audit procedures relevant to conducting tests of internal controls, transactions, accounts, account groupings, and line items of an agency's financial statements.

Chapter 12 discusses certain end-of-audit concerns, considerations, and audit close-out tasks, and illustrates the types and content of auditor reporting that must be made to conform to Government Auditing Standards, including examples of audit reports.

Part IV: Nature of Selected Federal Audits

Part IV describes types of audits made annually or periodically by federal and other auditors of federal agencies, their contractors and grantees, and other organizations that are recipients of federal financial assistance. Also included is an overview schematic of suggested chronology and sequencing of the audit procedures and tasks for the more common audits.

Chapter 13 provides, in summary, a description of a methodology for audits made pursuant to the Single Audit Act, identifying requirements of the Act and pertinent OMB regulations and guidance.

Chapter 14 defines performance auditing, identifies types of these audits, explains who conducts them, and provides a suggested audit methodology for such examinations.

Chapter 15 highlights audit concerns and audit procedures that typically might be employed in an examination or audit of a federal agency's procurement and contracts function.

Chapter 16 highlights audit concerns and audit procedures that typically might be employed in an examination or audit of a federal agency's grants administration function.

2 FEDERAL AUDIT CRITERIA: LAWS, REGULATIONS, AUDIT STANDARDS

The federal government and its constituent departments and agencies generally earn no income and have no profitability concerns. The federal government can, however, print money, write checks, borrow money, and spend. By law, federal agency executives are responsible for the accurate and timely accounting, controlling, and reporting of the receipts, disbursement, and application of public monies. For over 200 years, Congress, by legislation, has attempted to control these financial activities through a process that includes authorizing, appropriating, and budgeting authority approvals relating to raising and spending federal funds. Other laws offer criteria directing federal departments and agencies to better plan, manage, and monitor their operations, and to do so in a more economical, efficient, and effective manner. These responsibilities lead to peculiarities and variations for federal entities that are not the same for private sector organizations.

The financial management laws of direct concern to federal financial executives and auditors of federal operations and activities are listed in Exhibit 2.1 and described in more detail in this chapter. The provisions of these laws establish the financial and operational criteria that must be subjected to scrutiny during the annual independent audit of an agency's financial statements. Selected provisions of several of these laws and regulations are of direct concern to those conducting federal audits. A close review of each law, in its entirety, is a condition precedent to developing an effective plan to audit a federal department's financial statements, operations, activities, functions, and awarded contracts and grants-in-aid.[1]

Exhibit 2.1: Major legislation to establish federal financial management policy

Current Guidance

- The Constitution of the United States
- Anti-Deficiency Act of 1870
- Budget and Accounting Act of 1921
- Budget and Accounting Procedures Act of 1950
- Supplemental Appropriations Act of 1955
- Impoundment Control Act of 1974
- Inspector General Act of 1978
- Federal Managers' Financial Integrity Act of 1982
- Single Audit Act of 1984 (amended in 1996)
- Federal Credit Reform Act of 1990
- Chief Financial Officers Act of 1990

---

[1] *An excellent reference source for many of these laws is the report, "Laws Related to Federal Financial Management," by the House of Representatives' Committee on Government Reform and Oversight, Washington, DC, August 1996.*

- Government Management and Reform Act of 1994 and Accountability of Tax Dollars Act of 2002
- Government Performance and Results Act of 1993
- Federal Financial Management Improvement Act of 1996

Developing Guidance

- Sarbanes-Oxley Act of 2002
- Congressional Subcommittee on Government Management, Finance, and Accountability

THE CONSTITUTION: "THE POWER OF THE PURSE"

All fiscal, financial, and operational responsibility is vested in the United States Congress under the Constitution. Over the years and through various laws, Congress has delegated aspects of that responsibility to selected central agencies (e.g., OMB,[2] GAO, the Department of the Treasury, the General Services Administration [GSA], and the Office of Personnel Management [OPM]). These central agencies, in turn, publish more detailed government-wide regulations to implement the laws. Additionally, Congress grants broad discretion to the heads of each federal agency to determine appropriate managerial, accounting, systems, and controls over financial reporting, and to establish the procedures and practices needed to effectively, efficiently, and economically manage the individual agency's operations, programs, and activities.

Constitutional Financial Authority

The first and most basic financial management legislation referring to federal revenues, disbursements, and the use of public monies appears in the Constitution itself. Portions of Article 1, Sections 8 and 9, outline what powers the drafters vested with Congress; for example:

- Section 8, Clause 1: "The Congress shall have the power to lay and collect taxes, duties, imposts, and excises to pay the debt and provide for the common defense and general welfare of the United States…"
- Section 8, Clause 2: "To borrow money on the credit of the United States…"
- Section 9, Clause 7: "No money shall be drawn from the Treasury, but in consequence of appropriations made by law; and a regular statement and account of receipts and expenditures of all public money shall be published from time to time."

This constitutional provision provides Congress with the "power of the purse." No agency, program, activity, or function can be initiated, nor can federal monies be expended by the President, without an earlier legal action by the Congress (i.e., the enactment of an authorization, appropriation, or budgetary authority, described in the following sections).

---

[2] *Throughout this book, reference is made to OMB with the recognition that laws and regulations prior to 1974 make reference to the Office of Management and Budget and other descriptors earlier in the country's history.*

Each year, much is made of a President's State of the Union address, and his budget is a key aspect of this annual speech. More accurately, though, the annual message is the President's *proposed* budget for the federal government. Unless both houses of Congress agree with the President—and seldom are all of the President's proposals accepted without change—there will be no budget; thus, the cliché: "The President proposes, Congress disposes." When serious disagreements arise between the President's and Congress's views on the federal budget for any fiscal year, the ramifications are significant. If Congress refuses to conclude on a budget for the federal government, the federal government shuts down, as in the government closures in 1996.

The Federal Budget Defined

The *federal budget* is the legal mandate of Congress to the President and heads of federal departments and agencies to tax, collect, borrow, obligate, and expend money in the manner, only for the purposes, at the rate, and within the time period prescribed by Congress. The federal budget, approved by both houses of Congress, is, at one and the same time:

- A listing of national priorities, as determined by Congress, for the next year and, in some cases, the next several years
- Permission or direction to the executive branch to commence, continue, or cease operating specific governmental agencies, programs, and activities
- The legal authority to collect revenues, incur and pay financial obligations, and borrow on the credit of the federal government
- The financial plan for managing the federal government during the next fiscal year
- The financial management policy dictating acceptable accounting, financial reporting, and audit policies and, at times, detailed procedures and prohibitions

Congressional Authorizing Legislation

Congress does not approve the President's requested budget as a single amount. Instead, the amount requested by the President is broken down and analyzed by several congressional committees and subcommittees that may approve, change, or disapprove of the President's proposal or even approve budget authority that was never sought by the President. During the legislative review phase, Congress will initiate committee hearings and, at times, turn budget issues into matters of considerable public prominence, widely reported in the news and electronic media.

By law, Congress must complete its appropriation process and approve a budget for the overall federal government by October 1 of each year. In recent years, many appropriations have not been made final by Congress until well after the new fiscal year has begun. The failure to pass a federal budget results in Congress having to give temporary operational and spending authority to the executive branch; this legislation is referred to as a *continuing resolution*. The approved financial budget or authority takes the form of several pieces of legislation—that is, several individual *appropriations*—which, when summed, become the federal government's legal budget or financial plan for the fiscal year. Once passed by Congress, the individual appropriation laws, if not vetoed by the President, become the budget and spending authority, which is closely managed, monitored, accounted for, reported on, and audited by federal departments and agencies. Deviations from the provisions of authorization and appropriation legislation are statutory violations for which there must be a reporting to the OMB, President, and Congress.

ANTI-DEFICIENCY ACT: CANNOT SPEND MORE THAN CONGRESS PROVIDES

Since the country's founding, Congress has battled the executive branch over fiscal excesses, perceived waste and mismanagement, and failures to adhere to spending laws. An objective of the Anti-Deficiency Act of 1870 was to prevent federal executive departments from spending more than was appropriated by Congress. Later amendments to this law mandated specific procedural practices, such as requiring that federal agencies obtain formal approval from OMB of all funds appropriated by Congress. This OMB approval is referred to as an apportionment. An *apportionment* constitutes the authorization by OMB to a federal agency citing the amounts, purposes, and rates at which an agency may spend the funds appearing in its appropriation law. And, of course, no apportionment of funds by OMB can exceed the ceiling set by Congress in the appropriation.

"Section 3679" Audit Considerations

Within the federal financial management community, probably the most quoted and most closely monitored legislation includes provisions of the Anti-Deficiency Act, referred to by accountants and auditors as Section 3679 Audits (of the Revised Statutes). Some of the key provisions having audit implications include:

- OMB is required to apportion or reapportion appropriated funds, in writing, either by

  - Months, calendar quarters, operating seasons, or other time periods
  - Activities, functions, projects, or objects
  - Some combination thereof

- No apportionment is permitted that would necessitate a deficiency or supplemental appropriation estimate unless such an action is required because of: (1) laws of Congress passed after the appropriation law that require additional expenditures; (2) emergencies involving safety of human life, protection of property, or immediate welfare of individuals, where an appropriation requires sums to be paid to such individuals.

- An officer of the government with administrative control of an appropriation is required to prescribe, by regulation, a system of administrative controls designed to: (1) restrict obligations or expenditures against each appropriation to the amount of the apportionment; and (2) enable such officer or agency head to fix responsibility for creation of any obligations or make an expenditure in excess of an apportionment or reapportionment.[3]

Other provisions of the Revised Statutes of concern to federal auditors provide that no federal officer or employee shall:

- Make or authorize an expenditure from, or create or authorize an obligation under, any appropriation or fund in excess of an amount available therein
- Involve the government in any contract or obligation for payment of money for any purpose, in advance of an appropriation made for that purpose, unless such contract or obligation is authorized by law
- Accept voluntary service for the United States or employ personal services in excess of that authorized by law, except in cases of emergency involving the safety of human life or the protection of property
- Authorize or create any obligation or make expenditures in excess of an apportionment or reapportionment, or in excess of the amount permitted by agency regulations prescribed and approved pursuant to law.

Noncompliance Consequences

Violation of any of these prohibitions requires that a federal employee be subject to appropriate administrative discipline that could include suspension without pay or removal from office. The willful or knowing violation, upon conviction, may result in a fine of not more than $5,000, imprisonment for up to two years, or both.

BUDGET AND ACCOUNTING ACT OF 1921

The Budget and Accounting Act of 1921 led to some important improvements and changes in federal financial management:

- A government-wide budget system was established, and the Bureau of the Budget, the predecessor to OMB within the Department of the Treasury, was established.
- The General Accounting Office (renamed the Government Accountability Office in 2004) was created as an independent agency in the legislative branch, headed by the Comptroller General, and accountable only to Congress.
- The powers earlier held by the comptroller of the treasury and the six auditors of Treasury with respect to prescribing fiscal practices, forms and procedures for administrative control, and accounting for appropriated funds were vested in GAO.
- Amendments later gave GAO the authority to settle and adjust all claims and demands by or against the government.

Although revised, in part, by subsequent legislation, the Budget and Accounting Act of 1921 required the Comptroller General to prescribe forms, systems, and fund accounting for all federal departments and establishments and to examine fiscal officer accounts and claims against the United States.

---

[3] *These federal executives, one or more of whom reside in every federal agency, are referred to as accountable officers.*

Audit and Examinations of the Government and Others

GAO was given the responsibility of examining fiscal officers' accounts and claims against the government and for investigating, "at the seat of government and elsewhere," all matters relating to the receipt, disbursement, and application of federal funds. To fulfill these responsibilities, Congress provided GAO with the right to access and examine any books, documents, papers, or records of federal departments or establishments. This right was later expanded to include the right to access and examine records and documents of federal contractors and grantees insofar as those records related to the expenditure of federal monies.

BUDGET AND ACCOUNTING PROCEDURES ACT OF 1950

With the implementation of the Budget and Accounting Procedures Act of 1950, Congress attempted to amend provisions of the Budget and Accounting Act of 1921 and impose improvements requiring that:

- Federal accounting provide full disclosure of results of financial operations, adequate financial information needed in management of operations and formulation and execution of the budget, and effective control over income, expenditures, funds, property, and other assets.
- Full consideration be given to the needs and responsibilities of both the legislative and executive branches in establishing accounting and reporting systems requirements.
- The maintenance of accounting systems and the production of financial reports, with respect to operations of executive agencies that compiled and disclosed information of the government as a whole that will be the responsibility of the executive branch.
- Auditing of the federal government will be conducted by the Comptroller General as an agent of Congress and is to be directed at determining: the extent to which accounting and related financial reporting are for the purposes specified in law; financial transactions have been consummated in accordance with laws, regulations, and other legal requirements; and adequate internal financial control over operations is exercised and affords an effective basis for settlement of and accounts of accountable officers.
- The Comptroller General, the Secretary of Treasury, and the Bureau of the Budget conduct a continuous program for improvement of accounting and financial reporting, a responsibility that continues to this day under the auspices of the Joint Financial Management Improvement Program.

Audit Principles and Standards

Regarding GAO's new auditing responsibilities, the Budget and Accounting Procedures Act of 1950 stated that GAO's audits should include, but are not to be limited to, the accounts of accountable officers. *Accountable officers* are specially designated federal executives who reside in all federal agencies. Further, the act stated that the GAO audit was to be conducted in accordance with the principles and standards prescribed by the Comptroller General. The audit and examination procedures were to give due regard to generally accepted "principles" of auditing, including consideration of the effectiveness of accounting organizations and systems, internal audit and control, and related administrative practices of federal agencies. To this day, GAO continues to prescribe audit standards, to wit: the *Government Auditing Standards,* the 2003 edition being the latest revision.

SUPPLEMENTAL APPROPRIATIONS ACT OF 1955

The Supplemental Appropriations Act of 1955 statutorily established the criteria for valid obligations and claims for payment under federal appropriations. If a claim fails to conform to the criteria in this act, the claim is not a valid obligation of the United States and cannot be paid.

According to Section 1311 of this act, no amount shall be recorded as an obligation of the government unless it is supported by one of the eight prescribed forms of documentary evidence. Congress intended that these eight forms of documentary evidence (defined in more detail in Chapter 5) encompass the full range of the types of obligations that could be legally incurred by an agency in the course of its operations.

The Supplemental Appropriations Act requires that every agency report at year-end, for each appropriation and budget authority, the unliquidated obligations and remaining unobligated appropriation balances. This report must be certified by those agency officials formally designated as having the responsibility for recording and monitoring obligations. This reporting also initiates a special federal year-end audit known government-wide as a 1311, or year-end or unliquidated obligations audit.

IMPOUNDMENT CONTROL ACT OF 1974

The need for the Impoundment Control Act arose as a result of a financial dispute between the Office of the President and Congress over the expenditure of congressionally appropriated monies. Although earlier congressional concerns were focused primarily on the potential overexpenditure of appropriated funds, this particular instance focused on the President's decision *not* to spend appropriated funds in an attempt to reduce federal expenditures. The issue was that the President desired to spend less money than Congress had appropriated. Thus, the Office of the President "impounded," restricted, reserved, froze, or otherwise reduced spending by federal agencies to amounts below those appropriated by Congress. The Impoundment Control Act, with few exceptions, prohibited future "impoundments" of appropriated monies. If an impoundment of appropriated funds was requested, advanced notification had to be provided to Congress and fully disclosed to the public. Except as otherwise authorized in the act, Congress stated that no reserves of an appropriation shall be established.

Other Provisions

For years preceding the passage of the Impoundment Control Act of 1974, Congress had been in violation of its own laws, as well as the Constitution, with respect to budgeting and financial accountability. The 1974 act established a new budget process, attempted to impose more control over the financial activities of the executive branch, and brought greater discipline to Congress itself.

In subsequent years, however, Congress, more so than the executive branch, was in violation of the Impoundment Control Act. For example, by the 1974 Act, Congress:

- Established a new budget process for itself, which included, among other items, setting up a Committee of the Budget in each house of Congress to force the many committees to coordinate and agree on revenue and expenditure levels in advance. This was done to impose fiscal and operational controls over the members and to impose a discipline of appropriation on other congressional committees with respect to planned expenditures and growing deficits.

    The committees of the budget may not always have been ignored by members of Congress, but they were never among the stronger of congressional committees and often were not particularly instrumental or successful in the enforcement of budget discipline.

- Established the Congressional Budget Office (CBO) to provide Congress with a professional counterweight to challenge and otherwise critique the budget data provided to it by OMB and agencies of the executive branch. CBO has since provided that service and has also acquired a reputation, among the general public, of being an independent and honest broker of calculations, forecasts, and estimates of budget data.

    At times, to the chagrin of Congress, the President, and OMB, CBO publicly pointed out where Congress, the President, or OMB may not have always provided the public with the fullest, clearest explanations or the full impact of details embedded in the trillion-dollar budget of the federal government.

- Mandated a new fiscal year for the federal government, changing it from July 1 of each year to October 1. The reason for the change was viewed, at the time, as specious and considerably more expensive than the benefit alleged by Congress. For many years, Congress had been remiss in providing an approved budget (i.e., enacting of all required appropriation laws) for the federal government to be effective on July 1, the first day of the government's fiscal year since the country's founding. By changing the fiscal year, Congress bought itself another three months in the single year of transition.

    But, in the years following passage of this act, Congress repeatedly failed to complete its budget work by the newly established deadline. This was the case on October 1, 2004, the first day of fiscal year 2005. To avoid an indefinite shutdown of the government, Congress provided temporary financing to federal agencies (referred to as a *continuing resolution*). This funding could have continued for weeks, even several months, into the new fiscal year.

This act, the budget process, budget cycle, and some of the budget strategies applied or used in the federal government are discussed in more detail in Chapter 5.

INSPECTOR GENERAL ACT OF 1978

The Inspector General Act of 1978 created independent and objective units within departments and agencies to conduct and supervise audits and investigations. It is the intent of Congress that federal Inspectors General provide leadership and coordination in preventing fraud and promoting economy, efficiency, and effectiveness. In addition, Inspectors General are expected to keep Congress, the President, and top agency executives abreast of important developments within their individual agencies.

FEDERAL MANAGERS' FINANCIAL INTEGRITY ACT OF 1982

The Federal Managers' Financial Integrity Act of 1982 (FMFIA) displayed Congress's continuing concern over the financial management practices of the federal government. FMFIA required that systems of accounting and administrative controls be established and that each agency annually conduct an evaluation and report to the President and Congress on the adequacy of these systems.

Selected provisions of the act that could impact the nature of tests made when conducting a federal audit might be those provisions that require each executive agency to provide reasonable assurances that:

- Systems of internal accounting and administrative controls are in accordance with standards prescribed by the Comptroller General.
- All obligations and costs of a federal agency comply with applicable laws.
- All federal funds, property, and other assets are safeguarded against waste, loss, unauthorized use, or misappropriation.
- Revenues and expenditures of agency operations are properly recorded and accounted for to allow preparation of accounts and reliable financial and statistical reports, and to maintain accountability over assets and other resources.
- Heads of federal agencies shall evaluate, prepare, and submit a statement to the President affirming that the agency's systems of internal accounting and administrative controls fully comply with the guidelines established by the Comptroller General in consultation with OMB, pursuant to this act.
- The President, in submitting the budget request to Congress, shall include a separate report on whether the agency's accounting system conforms to the principles, standards, and related requirements prescribed by the Comptroller General.

Agencies continue to conduct reviews of their systems of accounting and administrative controls and make reportings pursuant to the FMFIA of 1982 and later legislation.

FEDERAL CREDIT REFORM ACT OF 1990

The Federal Credit Reform Act of 1990 is not well known because few federal agencies are authorized to make loans or enter into loan guarantee transactions. In addition, upon its original passage into law, this act was part of the federal government's general Omnibus Reconciliation Act of 1990. But the Federal Credit Reform Act significantly changed financing, accounting, and reporting for federal loans and loan guarantees. These financial assistance programs included some of the more popular of the government, including farmers' home loans, small business loans, veterans' mortgage loans, and student loans.

The Federal Credit Reform Act required, for the first time in history, the President's budget request to reflect the full cost of direct loans and loan guarantee programs, including the planned level of new loan obligations and loan guarantee commitments associated with each appropriation request. Congress, in the act, stated that the purposes of the act were to:

- Ensure a timely and accurate measure and presentation in the President's budget request of the full costs of direct loan and loan guarantee programs
- Place the cost of credit programs on a budgetary basis equivalent to other federal spending
- Encourage the delivery of benefits in the form most appropriate to the needs of beneficiaries
- Improve the allocation of resources among credit programs and between credit and other spending programs

This law concluded a 200-year history of accounting for less than the full cost of federal loans and loan guarantees. Federal departments and agencies now had to recognize, at the time of legislative action, the true cost that these programs were likely to incur, such as projected default costs, interest subsidy costs, and recognition, at the time of loaning, the current market rate of interest. To accomplish its objectives, the act's provisions required that:

- For each fiscal year in which the direct loans or the loan guarantees are to be obligated, committed, or disbursed, the President's budget request reflects the long-term costs to the government of subsidies associated with the direct loans and loan guarantees. Prior to the act, such costs were not reflected in any fiscal year's accounting.
- Before direct loans are obligated or loan guarantees committed, the annual appropriations be enacted to cover the full costs of projected defaults, interest subsidy costs, and recognition, at the time of loaning, of the current market rate of interest.
- Borrowing authority had to be formally provided and recognized by the Treasury Department to cover the nonsubsidy portion of direct federal loans.

Recording *interest subsidy* costs recognizes that federal loans provide for payment of interest rates that were well below the going market rates. This lower interest rate, in essence, gave borrowers and recipients of loan guarantees a break or subsidy. To finance this subsidy, the Treasury Department was borrowing money at higher market interest rates.

Historically, agency accounts recorded only a cash disbursement and made no formal accounting for the future repayment (i.e., as a loan receivable) or possible default of the loan. This type of accounting avoided the embarrassing need of the federal government to recognize loan defaults and to later account for uncollected loans. This underrecognition of costs had been further compounded by having no accounting until the loan defaulted or the federal government had to make payment under a defaulted loan guarantee program. For the most part, these events happened years later, were not anticipated, and, in the case of failures of hundreds of savings and loan associations and banks in the 1980s, resulted in billions of dollars of losses being passed along to later generations to finance.

CHIEF FINANCIAL OFFICERS ACT OF 1990

In the 1990s, congressional and executive branch interest in financial systems, controls, performance reporting, and other management improvement exceeded that of any decade in the preceding 200 years. The Chief Financial Officers Act (CFO Act) was typical of legislation enacted in the 1990s. In the act, Congress reaffirmed its intent to oversee and control the financial management process of the federal government and to centralize authority and responsibilities for better accounting, controls, and financial management. For the first time, department comptrollers were required to adhere to applicable accounting and reporting standards, annual financial statements by federal entities, and independent audits of those financial statements.

Concerns of Congress

The CFO Act was a significant, but partial, response to financial management issues known to Congress and the executive branch for decades. This was noted by the prefatory thoughts of Congress in the act, which described a deteriorated financial reporting and internal controls environment within the federal government. Highlights included:

- Billions of dollars are lost each year through fraud, waste, abuse, and mismanagement among hundreds of programs in the federal government.
- These losses could be significantly decreased by improved management, including improved central coordination of internal controls and financial accounting.
- The federal government is in great need of fundamental reform in financial management requirements and practices as financial management systems are obsolete and inefficient, and do not provide complete, consistent, reliable, and timely information.
- Current financial reporting practices of the federal government do not accurately disclose the current and probable future costs of operating and investment decisions, including the future need for cash or other resources, do not permit adequate comparison of actual costs among executive agencies, and do not provide the timely information required for efficient management of programs.

Among several objectives noted in the CFO Act was the improvement in each agency's systems of accounting, financial management, and internal controls to assure issuance of reliable financial information to deter fraud, waste, and abuse of government resources.

Financial Policy and OMB

By the CFO Act, Congress established separate Deputy Directors at OMB—one for budget and one for management. The Deputy Director of OMB for management, a senior executive position, was established by the CFO Act and the role of management in OMB for federal financial management was significantly expanded. OMB was required to perform rather specific financial management oversight and operational responsibilities, including:

- Settlement of differences arising among agencies regarding implementation of financial management policies
- Issuance of those policies and directives necessary to carry out the CFO Act
- Provision for complete, reliable, and timely information to the President, Congress, and the public regarding management activities of the executive branch
- Chairing of the new Chief Financial Officers Council, established by section 302 of the CFO Act

Additionally, OMB was required to directly communicate with financial officers of states and local governments and to foster exchanges of information concerning financial management standards, techniques, and processes.

To correct perceived and existing federal financial management deficiencies, Congress made OMB responsible for such things as:

- Giving direction, leadership for, and establishment of financial management policies and requirements and for monitoring establishment and operation of federal government financial systems
- Reviewing agency requests for financial management systems and operations and advising on required resources to develop, effectively operate, and maintain and correct federal financial management systems
- Establishing the general management policies for executive agencies and performing several general management functions relating to

  - Managerial systems
  - Systematic measurement of performance
  - Procurement policy
  - Grants, cooperative agreements, and assistance management
  - Information and statistical policy
  - Property management
  - Human resource management
  - Regulatory affairs

- Conducting organizational studies, long-range planning, program evaluation, productivity improvement, and experimentation and demonstration programs
- Reviewing and recommending changes to budget and legislative proposals of federal entities to ensure these organizations respond to program evaluations and are in accordance with general management plans

This guidance would be promulgated to federal agencies through OMB's circular and bulletin series.

New Financial Managers: Agency and Deputy Financial Officers

The CFO Act of 1990 is unique among federal law because it requires that the persons appointed to senior federal financial management positions be competent and possess relevant experience. The act gave OMB other important responsibilities in this area. These included development and maintenance of qualification standards for agency CFOs and agency deputy CFOs appointed under the act, and advising departments and agencies regarding selection of their CFOs and deputy CFOs.

The CFO Act (as amended) requires the appointment of a chief financial officer in operating departments and agencies and some independent offices. Each federal chief financial officer is, for cabinet and larger agencies, appointed by the President, and serves with the advice and consent of the Senate, or is designated by the President, in consultation with agency heads. (CFOs of smaller agencies and offices are appointed by the head of the agency.) Congress mandated that these executives be experienced and possess a certain level of competence; the chief financial officers for both large and small federal entities were to be appointed or designated

> *...from among individuals who possess demonstrated ability in general management of, knowledge of, and extensive practical experience in financial management practices in large governmental or business entities.*

Chief Financial Officer Responsibilities

The duties for department and agency CFOs included financial as well as nonfinancial roles, such as financial and nonfinancial systems, monitoring and accounting for budget execution, all aspects of all entity personnel having financial responsibilities, and certain department-wide reporting and budget-type responsibilities.

Prior to the enactment of the CFO Act, the financial management function was not, organizationally, at a uniform level across the federal government, and responsibilities for financial management were dispersed among several senior executives. The average tenure of these executives was about 18 months—a term of service that produced constant turnover and was too short to permit these executives to effectively preside over projects that span fiscal years. The CFO Act requires that department and agency CFOs report to the head of the agency. The CFO is charged with overseeing all financial management activities relating to the programs and operations. Before the act, the program and operational managers often had their own financial personnel reporting to them.

The responsibilities of agency CFOs and deputy CFOs were extended to include developing and maintaining integrated agency accounting, financial management systems, and personnel issues, including responsibilities to:

- Comply with applicable accounting principles, standards and requirements, and internal control standards
- Comply with policies and requirements prescribed by OMB
- Comply with other requirements applicable to systems
- Provide for:

- Complete, reliable, consistent, and timely information that is prepared on a uniform basis and that is responsive to the financial information needs of agency management
- The development and reporting of cost information
- The integration of accounting and budgeting information
- The systematic measurement of performance

- Develop and support agency financial management budgets
- Approve and manage agency financial management systems design and enhancement projects
- Implement agency asset management systems, including systems for cash management, credit management, debt collection, and property and inventory management and control
- Retain and financially support competent financial personnel to make recommendations to the agency head regarding the selection of the Deputy Chief Financial Officer.

Until the CFO Act, the financial management function in federal entities was typically split between the budgetary responsibilities and the fiscal accounting and reporting responsibilities, with the accounting officials having almost no role with respect to budget preparation or for budget execution. The act now requires that CFOs shall

- Provide for the integration of accounting and budgeting information
- Monitor the financial execution of the budget in relation to actual expenditures
- Prepare and submit timely performance reports
- Prepare and submit to the agency head and OMB an annual report that includes:
  - A description and analysis of the status of financial management of the agency
  - Annual agency financial statements
  - Annual audit report of the agency
  - Summary of reports required under the Federal Managers' Financial Integrity Act

The CFO Act: Financial Statements (Agency and Government-Wide)

The CFO Act dictated that annual financial statements be prepared for each agency and for the government as a whole. These financial statements to be submitted to OMB must reflect the overall financial position, result of operations, and cash flows or changes in financial position of each revolving fund, trust fund, and the accounts of each office, bureau, and activity of a federal entity performing substantial commercial functions during a preceding year. OMB was directed to prescribe the form and content of these agency financial statements. This guidance is promulgated through the OMB circulars and bulletins.

The CFO Act: Annual Independent Audits

Annual independent audits of an agency's financial statements are another new financial management requirement of the CFO Act. The other three areas are the (1) appointment of chief financial officers; (2) requirement to comply with applicable accounting standards and principles; and (3) publishing of financial statements by federal departments and agencies.

Section 304 of the CFO Act requires each financial statement to be prepared pursuant to criteria cited in the act and to be independently audited in accordance with *Government Auditing Standards*. Where an agency has an inspector general, this audit is performed by the Inspector General or an independent auditor, as determined by the inspector general. Where there is no Inspector General, the head of the federal entity determines the independent auditor to perform the audit.

The Comptroller General is authorized to review these audits or may perform the audit of the financial statements at the discretion of the Comptroller General or a committee of Congress. The director of OMB periodically publishes guidance on the scope and other details of these audits in the OMB circulars and bulletins.

The CFO ACT: "Applicable Accounting Principles"

Various sections of the CFO Act make reference to "applicable" accounting principles and standards. For example:

- Section 301 requires that the five-year plans of the director of OMB, Deputy Director of OMB, and agency heads be consistent with "applicable accounting principles, standards, and requirements."
- Section 303 states that the director of OMB shall prescribe the form and content of financial statements "consistent with applicable accounting principles, standards, and requirements."
- Section 902 requires that agency CFOs comply with "applicable accounting principles, standards, and requirements, and internal control standards."

In the CFO Act, Congress did not detail (1) what these "applicable" financial criteria would be, or (2) designate which agency or federal executive is responsible for determining the "applicable" financial criteria. But at the time the act was enacted, in 1990, the Comptroller General of the United States, the secretary of Treasury, and the director of OMB, by agreement, established the Federal Accounting Standards Advisory Board.

With the enactment of the CFO Act, the responsibility for setting accounting and financial reporting standards shifted from GAO, in the legislative branch, to OMB, in the executive branch. Then in a 1990 agreement between GAO, OMB, and the Treasury Department, the Federal Accounting Standards Advisory Board was established to recommend the *applicable accounting principles* required by the CFO Act.

Over the decade of the 1990s, FASAB recommended several *applicable accounting principles* now regarded as the *generally accepted accounting principles* for each federal agency and the federal government as a whole. In 1999, FASAB was formally recognized by the American Institute of Certified Public Accountants as the sole and official standard setter of generally accepted accounting principles for federal entities. In 1996, the Federal Financial Management Improvement Act (FFMIA) also compelled federal entities to implement and maintain financial management systems that comply substantially with the "applicable" accounting standards.

The CFO Act: Other Changes

The CFO Act required, among other mandates, that there be integrated agency accounting and financial management systems throughout the federal government. These integrated systems were to be designed to ensure compliance with internal control standards and the implementation of policies to provide consistency over data entry, transaction processing, and reporting and to also eliminate unnecessary duplication of transaction entries. *Integrated* agency accounting and financial management systems, including internal controls, were to be developed and maintained to ensure:

- Agency compliance with applicable accounting principles, standards and requirements, and internal control standards
- Agency compliance with policies and procedures of OMB relative to accounting, auditing, reporting, and several other areas of financial management
- Complete, reliable, consistent, and timely information is prepared on a uniform basis, responsive to the financial information needs of agency management
- The integration of accounting and budgeting information by each agency
- The systematic measurement of agency performance

System requirements of the federal government now defined an *integrated agency accounting and financial management system* as a system that coordinates a number of previously unconnected functions in order to improve the overall efficiency and control, which has four essential characteristics:

1. Standard data classifications for recording financial events
2. Common processing for similar transactions
3. Consistent control over data entry, transaction processing, and reporting
4. A system design that eliminates unnecessary duplication of transaction entry[4]

GOVERNMENT MANAGEMENT REFORM ACT OF 1994 AND ACCOUNTABILITY OF TAX DOLLARS ACT OF 2002

In 1994, the Government Management Reform Act (GMRA) mandated the requirement for annual financial audits, previously established by the CFO Act of 1990. In addition, GMRA required the compilation of consolidated governmentwide financial statements, increased the scope of agencies subject to annual audit, and instructed the director of OMB to identify components of cabinet level agencies that would be subject to separate financial statement audits (i.e., these agen-

---

[4] *See GAO-02-791T, "Effective Implementation of FFMIA Is Key to Providing Reliable, Useful, and Timely Data," June 2002.*

cies must be included in the consolidated financial statements of the cabinet level agency they are a component of and must issue separate stand-alone audited financial statements).

The Accountability of Tax Dollars Act, passed in 2002, required all but the smallest of executive agencies (generally executive agencies with $25 million or less in budget authority) to also issue annual audited financial statements.

GOVERNMENT PERFORMANCE AND RESULTS ACT OF 1993

Congress, in enacting the Government Performance and Results Act (GPRA) of 1993, noted that federal managers were seriously handicapped in their efforts to improve program efficiency and effectiveness because of an insufficient articulation of program goals and inadequate information on program performance. Also, congressional policy making, spending decisions, and program oversight were seriously handicapped by insufficient attention to agency program performance results.

The purposes detailed in the GPRA included:

- Initiation of program performance reform by requiring agencies to set program goals, measure program performance against those goals, and report publicly on progress
- Improvement in federal program effectiveness and public accountability by promoting a new focus on results, service quality, and customer satisfaction
- Helping federal managers improve service delivery by requiring that they plan to meet program objectives, and by providing them with information about program results and service quality
- Improvement in congressional decision making by providing more objective information on achieving statutory objectives and on the relative effectiveness and efficiency of federal programs and spending
- Improvement in the internal management of the federal government

To promote consistency and comparability in communicating program information and corresponding with Congress and the public, the GPRA provided these definitions that were to be used throughout the federal government:

- *Outcome measure:* An assessment of the results of a program activity compared to its intended purpose.
- *Output measure:* The tabulation, calculation, or recording of an activity or effort expressed in a quantitative or qualitative manner.
- *Performance goal:* A target level of performance expressed as a tangible measurable objective, against which factual achievement shall be compared, including a goal expressed as a quantitative standard, value, or rate.
- *Performance indicator:* A particular value or characteristics used to measure output or outcome.
- *Program evaluation:* An assessment, through objective measurement and systematic analysis, of the manner in and the extent to which an agency program achieves intended objectives.

FEDERAL FINANCIAL MANAGEMENT IMPROVEMENT ACT OF 1996

Among its findings when it enacted the Federal Financial Management Improvement Act of 1996 (FFMIA), Congress stated:

- Federal accounting standards have not been uniformly implemented.
- Federal financial management continues to be seriously deficient.
- Federal financial systems and fiscal practices have failed to identify costs fully, reflect total liabilities of congressional actions, and accurately report the financial condition of the federal government.
- Continued use of these practices undermines the government's ability to provide credible and reliable financial data.

The FFMIA emphasized that control standards and systems of control had not been uniformly implemented by agencies relative to their federal financial management systems[5] and that these federal financial management systems continued to be seriously deficient. FFMIA acknowledged that much effort had been devoted to federal internal controls in past years and that uniform control standards still had not been implemented as part of an agency's *integrated* financial management system. More specifically, Congress declared that:

- Federal financial management continues to be seriously deficient because federal financial management and fiscal practices have failed.
- Systems of controls have not been uniformly implemented and applied.
- Current accounting practices do not accurately report financial results of the federal government or full costs of programs and activities.

The intent of the FFMIA of 1996 was that federal agencies would:

- Implement the federal government's standard general ledger "at the transaction level"
- Eliminate past practices such as manual crosswalks of data between accounts and systems
- Cease reliance on workpaper adjustments that might never be formally posted to the records
- Discontinue the overreliance on cash accounting in lieu of the more complete accrual accounting recommended by the Federal Accounting Standards Advisory Board
- Have federal financial statements and reports routinely flow from the formal journal entries and ledger accounts that were a product of an effective system of internal controls

Systems growth over the years, with complexities resulting from increased automation and streamlining, continued decentralization and dispersion of program operations, and remote on-location, real-time accounting data inputted hundreds or thousands of miles from headquarters all compounded the internal controls problem. Changes to agency systems environments, particularly the move to increasingly

---

[5] *Federal financial management systems are defined to include internal financial controls, data, computer hardware, computer software, and competent and trained personnel.*

computerized databases, heightened the need to revamp existing federal agency controls where possible, but more than likely would require the design and implementation of entirely new controls.

FFMIA Noncompliance

Congress, in the FFMIA, required each annual financial statement audit called for by the CFO Act of 1990 to comply with Section 803 of the FFMIA (31 USC 3512). This section mandated each federal agency to implement and maintain financial management systems that:

- Comply substantially with federal financial management systems requirements
- Comply substantially with applicable federal accounting standards
- Comply substantially with the United States Government Standard General Ledger at the transaction level

And Congress required each of the required annual financial statement audits to specifically report on whether the agency financial management systems comply with the three requirements of the FFMIA. When an auditor finds that the agency's financial management systems do not comply with these three FFMIA requirements, Congress states the auditor shall identify in the audit report:

- The entity responsible for the financial management systems found to be in noncompliance
- All the facts pertaining to the failure to comply with these three conditions of the FFMIA, including

  - The nature and extent of noncompliance, including where there is substantial but not full compliance
  - The primary reason or cause of noncompliance
  - The entity or organization responsible for the noncompliance
  - Any relevant comments from any responsible officer or employee
  - A statement with respect to the recommended remedial actions and the time frames to implement such actions

SINGLE AUDIT ACT OF 1984 (AMENDED IN 1996)

In the 1950s, problems arose with the manner in which the federal government performed audits of state and local governmental entities and other organizations receiving federal financial assistance. These problems were cataloged by GAO and government-wide studies and were the subject of numerous congressional committee hearings into the 1980s. Examples of the federal government's problems and the ripple-type problems created at the state and local government levels were numerous, but fell into a few general categories:

- Excessive duplication of federal audit by many agencies with no coordination or cooperation
- Biased audits reports, since many audits were reported to senior executives under audit who had the authority to make changes and did change audit reports for the "better"

- Federal resistance to transferring audit responsibility to state and local government auditors despite laws, regulations, and policy statements directing that this be done
- Prohibiting, preventing, or resisting the sharing of federal audit findings with senior executives of other governments, or giving the public access to such reports

Initially passed in 1984 and amended in 1996, the Single Audit Act ordered federal organizations to implement an audit concept whereby recipients receiving $500,000 or more of federal assistance need undergo only one audit, each year, by one auditor. The results of this single audit would then be shared with all organizations having a financial interest in that recipient. Further, the act declared that audits made in accordance with the Single Audit Act "*shall be in lieu of any financial audit of federal awards which a non-federal entity is required to undergo under any other federal law or regulation.*" This act changed the historical focus of federal oversight, eliminating financial and human resource costs related to thousands of duplicative and uncoordinated federal audits and reviews.

Scope of a Single Audit, as Amended

Studies submitted to Congress and witnesses appearing before committees of Congress relative to the 1996 amendments were uniformly supportive of the Single Audit Act. While improvements could be made, and were, the consensus was that this law had instituted an efficient and effective audit concept contributing to an enormous reduction in overlap and duplication in comparison to earlier federal audit approaches.

The legally defined comprehensive single audit required that (1) an annual financial statement audit be made of the recipient of federal funds in its entirety; (2) this annual audit includes tests and reports made on an entity-wide basis, and for each major federal program relative to: (a) financial controls and controls to manage the federal assistance programs; and (b) compliance with laws and regulations for major federal award programs. These single audits were required to be made pursuant to GAO's *Government Auditing Standards,* plus the audit procedures and reporting requirements in the OMB regulation, OMB Circular A-133, *Audits of State and Local Governments and Non-Profit Organizations,* as amended.[6]

Working Papers

The Single Audit Act addressed the need for access to working papers by requiring that working papers be made available to a federal agency or the Comptroller General of the United States, upon request, to carry out audit and oversight responsibilities. Such access, by law, included the right of the federal gov-

---

[6] *When first enacted, the Single Audit Act of 1984 was implemented through two separate OMB Circulars: OMB Circular A-128, Audits of State and Local Governments, and OMB Circular A-133, Audits for Institutions of Higher Education and Nonprofit Entities. In 1997, the OMB Circulars A-128 and A-133 were replaced and superceded by a single circular, titled OMB Circular A-133,* **Audits of State and Local Governments and Non-Profit Organizations,** *last amended in June 2003.*

ernment to obtain copies. OMB Circular A-133 in turn required auditors to retain the working papers for a minimum of at least three years after date of issuance of the auditor's report, unless the auditor is notified in writing by a federal cognizant agency or oversight agency or a pass-through entity to extend the retention period beyond the three-year minimum. When the auditor becomes aware that an audit finding is being contested, the auditor must contact the contesting parties for guidance prior to destruction of the working papers and reports.[7]

Single Audit Act: Application

Congress in the Single Audit Act, and OMB in its Circular A-133, provided these definitions of *awards, financial assistance*, and *programs* that Congress wanted audited and opined on:

- *Federal awards:* Federal financial assistance and federal cost-reimbursement contracts that nonfederal entities receive directly from federal awarding agencies or indirectly from pass-through entities.
- *Federal financial assistance:* Assistance that nonfederal entities receive or administer in the form of grants, loans, loan guarantees, property, cooperative agreements, interest subsidies, insurance, food commodities, direct appropriations, or other assistance, but not amounts received as reimbursement for services rendered to individuals in accordance with guidance by the director of OMB.
- *Federal program:* Federal awards and financial assistance that have been assigned a number in the OMB Catalog of Federal Domestic Assistance or encompassed within a group of numbers.
- *Major program:* A federal program, identified by OMB, that must, by the act, be audited and opined on and reported on would generally be each individual federal program whose expenditures in a single year exceed the larger of $300,000 or 3% of the total federal expenditures for that nonfederal entity.

Additional "Standards" for Single Audits

The Single Audit Act, the *Government Auditing Standards,* and the OMB Circular A-133 in combination comprise the audit reporting "standards" or criteria that must be met if the Single Audit is to comply with the law. This combination of the Act, GAO's audit standards, and OMB regulations requires that an audit report for a Single Audit be a package of up to 12 and possibly more reports, some with audit opinions, some with audit assurances, and some transmitting information required by the federal overseers.

Unless specifically required by OMB, the scope of a Single Audit does not automatically encompass performance audits.

---

[7] *The Public Company Accounting Oversight Board, established by the Sarbanes-Oxley Act, proposed that for companies with publicly traded securities, auditors retain working papers for a period of seven years following the audit. At this time, the longer retention period has not been extended to audits performed pursuant to the Single Audit Act.*

SARBANES-OXLEY ACT OF 2002[8]

On July 30, 2002, with the passage of the Sarbanes-Oxley Act, Congress, for publicly listed companies, mandated that the effectiveness of internal controls must be assessed and audited. Until Sarbanes-Oxley, no law, federal regulation, or generally accepted auditing standard had required that internal controls over financial reporting be regularly assessed and reported on by management and, additionally, that the controls then be audited and opined on by an independent auditor.

Sarbanes-Oxley is directed toward public companies, but concerns addressed by this act parallel congressional concerns about the ineffectiveness of internal financial controls in the federal government. Sound and effective internal controls have proven to be a basic, essential prerequisite to competent financial management. Absent sound controls, minimal or no assurance exists that balances in financial statements of federal agencies are complete, reliable, accurate, consistent, and timely.

Release No. 2003-001 of the Public Company Accounting Oversight Board[9] states that to achieve reliable financial statements, internal controls must be in place to:

- Ensure that financial records accurately and fairly reflect transactions
- Provide assurance that records of transactions are sufficient to prepare financial statements
- Provide assurance that receipts and expenditures are made only as authorized by management

PCAOB's position is that users of financial statements can have more confidence in the reliability of a financial statement if management demonstrates that it exercises adequate internal control over the bookkeeping, sufficiency of books of accounts and records for the preparation of accurate financial statements, and adherence to rules about the use of assets and the possibility of misappropriation of an organization's assets. Similar words and intent about internal financial controls can be found in federal law, OMB regulations, and issuances of GAO for more than 30 years.

De Facto Federal Policy

It appears that the current minimal requirements relative to assessing, auditing, and reporting on the financial controls of federal agencies could soon change. Given that the stated purpose and governance goals of Sarbanes-Oxley are similar to congressional desires for federal agencies, the Sarbanes-Oxley Act might well be imposed on the federal financial management community. At this time, though, the essence of Sarbanes-Oxley may already be the de facto federal financial management policy. Some examples include:

---

[8] *This section relating to the Sarbanes-Oxley Act of 2002 is an adaptation of the Kearney & Company study, "Audit Federal Financial Controls: Sooner Rather than Later," published in "AGA's" Journal of Government Financial Management, Winter 2004-Volume 53 Number 4*

[9] *The Public Company Accounting Oversight Board was established by Congress to implement the Sarbanes-Oxley Act. Standards proposed by PCAOB must be subsequently approved by the Securities and Exchange Commission.*

- A de facto collective federal policy relative to internal controls that addresses the same issues as Sarbanes-Oxley already exists. In many ways this de facto controls policy may have arisen through actions over the years taken by: Congress in enacting laws; OMB in implementing policy circulars and bulletins; federal departments and agencies in adopting systems of accounting, controls, financial management, and auditing guidance; and corrective and follow-up actions taken by federal agencies pursuant to recommendations of federal Inspectors General and GAO.

- Section 404 of Sarbanes-Oxley requires public companies to make assessments and assertions on the effectiveness of their internal controls based on a "suitable, recognized control framework established by a body of experts that followed due process procedures to develop the framework," specifically citing the *Internal Control—Integrated Framework* developed by the Committee of Sponsoring Organizations (COSO) of the Treadway Commission in 1992.

  By 1994, the COSO *Internal Control—Integrated Framework* (its controls definition, structural components, specific control subelements, and other aspects) had been adopted and integrated into federal policies and guidance enunciated by Congress in laws, OMB in circulars and bulletins, and GAO in its federal internal control standards and *Government Auditing Standards.*

- Federal agencies generally do not earn income, but do have significant legal responsibilities for accurate and timely accounting, controlling, and reporting of the receipts, disbursements, and applications of public monies. The Sarbanes-Oxley Act requires that the internal controls report that must accompany a public company's report on its financial statements will:

  - Present the scope of the auditor's testing of the internal control structure and assessment procedures of management
  - Present the findings of the auditor as a result of such testing
  - Present an evaluation by the auditor of whether such internal control structure and procedures include maintenance of records that, in reasonable detail, accurately and fairly reflect the transactions and dispositions of the assets of the issuer
  - Provide reasonable assurance that transactions are recorded as necessary to permit preparation of financial statements in accordance with generally accepted accounting principles
  - Provide reasonable assurance that receipts and expenditures are being made only in accordance with authorizations of management and directors of the issuer
  - Provide a description of material weaknesses in such internal controls, and of any material noncompliance found on the basis of such testing

The essence of these requirements by Sarbanes-Oxley appears to be the same as, or quite similar to, sections of laws and federal policies of the 1990s for improving the accounting and controls within federal agencies.

Federal Agencies May Not Have to Comply Yet

Following 2005 committee hearings on the Department of Homeland Security's (DHS) Financial Accountability Act, Congress placed a requirement similar to those of the Sarbanes-Oxley Act on DHS. At that time, OMB had begun an initiative to require stricter financial reporting and documentation requirements at all federal agencies through the revision of OMB Circular A-123, *Management's Responsibility for Internal Control* (effective beginning fiscal year 2006).

On December 21, 2004, OMB issued revised Circular A-123. Draft implementation guidance applicable to cabinet level and other agencies identified by OMB ("the CFO Act agencies") was issued in May 2005. The revised guidance more closely parallels COSO requirements and significantly increases the documentation requirements and level of assurance by agency management that internal controls are sound. The revised guidance does not require independent audits of internal control; however, under the new OMB guidance, if an agency demonstrates consistently poor financial accountability, OMB may require an internal controls audit.

CONGRESSIONAL SUBCOMMITTEE ON GOVERNMENT MANAGEMENT, FINANCE, AND ACCOUNTABILITY

The Subcommittee on Government Management, Finance, and Accountability (a subcommittee within the Committee on Government Reform) is currently holding hearings on "the Evolution of Federal Financial Management: A Review of the Need to Consolidate, Simplify, and Streamline." The long-term goal of the committee is "legislation that would simplify, streamline, and enhance the laws governing agency financial management." More specific objectives include:

- The development of a consolidated law governing agency financial management
- The simplification and clarification of federal financial management guidance
- A review and possible redefinition of the roles of the chief financial officer, the chief information officer, the chief acquisition officer, and the chief human capital officer to promote the full and efficient integration of the positions.

Whether Congress imposes Sarbanes-Oxley-like requirements on the federal government or accepts the guidance provided by the revised OMB Circular A-123, could very well depend on the outcome of these ongoing hearings.

3 THE FEDERAL GOVERNMENT AND SARBANES-OXLEY

In 2002 Congress, by the Sarbanes-Oxley Act, gave a pre-eminence to internal controls in financial reporting. The act mandated the management of publicly traded corporations to assess and report on their controls, conduct a review of their controls assessment, and have an independent audit of the financial controls. As a result of the print and other news media accounts, supportive or antagonistic, Sarbanes-Oxley was the most publicized and most reported on financial legislation since the Securities and Exchange Laws of 1933 and 1934. Not reported at the time of Sarbanes-Oxley was the fact that similar internal controls assessment and reporting responsibilities required of federal agencies had been embedded in several laws concerned with federal financial management dating to the early 1980s. This chapter highlights the controls and governance provisions of Section 404 of Sarbanes-Oxley and describes similar or corollary practices within the federal government.

SARBANES-OXLEY: PURPOSE AND MANDATES

On July 30, 2002, with the passage of the Sarbanes-Oxley Act, Congress gave a preeminence to internal controls in financial reporting by mandating reporting, disclosures, and independent auditing requirements that, until this Act, were not much discussed. By Section 404(a) and (b) of this Act, Congress required

Each annual report submitted to the Securities and Exchange Commission by a publicly listed corporation is to contain an internal control report, which shall

1. *State the responsibility of management for establishing and maintaining an adequate internal control structure and procedures for financial reporting; and*
2. *Contain an assessment by management of the effectiveness of the internal control structure and procedures of the issuer for financial reporting.*

and

With respect to the internal control assessment made by management, the public accounting firm that prepares or issues the audit report shall attest to, and report on, the assessment made by the management of the effectiveness of internal control.

The Sarbanes-Oxley Act changed corporate governance and financial reporting and permanently altered the regulatory environment for publicly listed companies that had prevailed since the 1930s. This act created a broad new oversight regime by prescribing specific procedures, steps, and practices to address governance failures. It also codified several new responsibilities of corporate executives, corporate directors, and their lawyers, accountants, and regulators.

Section 404 of the act underscored the importance Congress placed on having effective internal controls over financial reporting and gave these controls a prominence equal to that of financial statements in all future financial reportings by these companies. The Sarbanes-Oxley Act requires all publicly listed companies to include in their annual report to the Securities and Exchange Commission a separate auditor's report attesting to management's assessment of the company's internal control. The auditors must independently attest or audit and independently opine on the operational effectiveness of a public company's internal controls.

Public Company Accounting Oversight Board

A new player. The new priority given to internal controls over financial reporting was clear in the Public Company Accounting Oversight Board Release No. 2004-001, wherein PCAOB stated that, in order to achieve reliable financial statements, internal controls must be in place to:

- See that records accurately and fairly reflect transactions in, and dispositions of, a company's assets
- Provide assurance that the records of transactions are sufficient to prepare financial statements in accordance with generally accepted accounting principles
- Provide assurance that receipts and expenditures are made only as authorized by management and directors
- Ensure that steps are in place to prevent or detect theft or unauthorized use or disposition of the company's assets of value that could have a material effect on the financial statements

PCAOB's stated position is that users can have more confidence in the reliability of a financial statement if management demonstrates that it has exercised adequate internal control over the bookkeeping, the sufficiency and accuracy of books of accounts and records, adherence to rules about the use of the company's assets, and the possibility of a misappropriation of company assets.

MANAGEMENT: ASSESS CONTROLS

Compliance with the Sarbanes-Oxley Act requires an entity's management to do three things:

1. Establish and maintain adequate internal control structure
2. Have and implement policies and procedures for governing financial reporting
3. Annually assess and report to the government on the effectiveness of their internal controls and procedures

The Sarbanes-Oxley Act requires the independent auditor's report for the financial statements of a publicly listed corporation to be accompanied by a separate auditor's report on controls. The Securities and Exchange Commission, in May 2003, clarified and amplified the provisions of the act by stating that management's assessment of the internal controls over financial reporting must include:

- A statement of management's responsibilities for establishing and maintaining adequate internal control
- A statement identifying the framework used by management to evaluate the effectiveness of the entity's internal control

- Management's assessment of the effectiveness of the internal control as of the end of the most recent year, including a statement as to whether the internal control over financial reporting is effective or not
- A statement confirming that the accounting firm that audited the financial statements included in the annual report an attestation report on management's assessment of the entity's internal control
- Any changes in internal control that materially affect or are reasonably likely to affect the entity's internal control
- An attestation report by the registered public accounting firm on management's assessment of the entity's internal control

AUDITOR: AUDIT CONTROLS

With respect to a publicly listed company's internal controls, standards proposed by PCAOB require independent auditors to:

- Review management's assessment of the company's internal control
- Form an opinion about management's assessment of the effectiveness of internal control
- Form an audit opinion relative to management's assessment of controls after having:
  - Evaluated the reliability of the process used by management to assess the company's internal control
  - Reviewed the results of tests performed by management, internal auditors, and others during their assessment process
  - Performed their own audit tests, and attested to and reported on the assessment made by management

Thus, compliance with the Sarbanes-Oxley Act requires an independent auditor to separately audit the operational effectiveness of internal controls over financial reporting to be satisfied that management's assessment conclusion is correct and fairly stated.

This requirement dictates that the auditor separately test and report on the effectiveness of controls over financial reporting. To comply, the auditor is to provide an audit and report of findings resulting from audit tests that include:

- An evaluation of whether the control structure and procedures are reasonably detailed to accurately and fairly reflect the transactions and dispositions of the assets
- Reasonable assurance that transactions are recorded, as necessary, to prepare financial statements in accordance with generally accepted accounting principles
- Reasonable assurance that receipts and expenditures are made only in accordance with authorizations of management and directors of the entity
- Descriptions of material weaknesses and any material noncompliance found on the basis of testing
- An audit opinion on whether management's assessment of effectiveness of controls is "fairly stated "

One Audit, Two Audit Opinions

The Sarbanes-Oxley Act and its related implementation standards are clear that the required audit of the internal controls over financial reporting is to be integrated, not separate from the audit of an entity's financial statements. PCAOB *Auditing Standard* No. 2 explains that Congress desires that an *integrated* audit be made of the financial statements and internal controls over financial reporting, further noting that

> *Notwithstanding the fact that the two audits are interrelated, the integrated audit results in two separate objectives: (1) to express an opinion on management's assessment of the effectiveness of the company's internal control over financial reporting, and (2) to express an opinion on whether the financial statements are fairly stated.*

Thus, *Auditing Standard* No. 2 is a standard that both

1. Addresses both the work required to audit internal controls over financial reporting and the relationship of that audit to the audit of the financial statements; and
2. Refers to the attestation of management's assessment of the effectiveness of the internal control as the audit of internal control over financial reporting.

PCAOB decided that the audits of controls and financial statements should be integrated because the objectives and work involved in performing an audit of internal controls over financial reporting and an audit of an entity's annual financial statements are so closely related.

THE STANDARD: *"SUITABLE, RECOGNIZED CONTROL FRAMEWORK"*

The Sarbanes-Oxley Act requires management of a publicly traded company to base its assessment of the effectiveness of internal controls over financial reporting on a "suitable, recognized control framework established by a body of experts that followed due-process procedures to develop the framework." The guidance in *PCAOB Standard* No. 2 is based on the *Internal Control-Integrated Framework* developed by (COSO) in 1992. The act recognizes that other suitable, possibly different, frameworks not containing exactly the same elements as COSO may be used, but PCAOB cautions that these other frameworks should have elements that encompass all of the COSO general themes.

COSO Definition

Since its release in 1992, COSO's *Internal Control—Integrated Framework* (hereafter referred to as the *Framework*) has become the controls standard for much of the business world. The COSO control concepts have been tested by many, have been applied in thousands of audits, and have been adopted by numerous private and public sector organizations as their own controls framework.

In the COSO *Framework,*[1] *internal controls* are broadly defined as

A process, effected by the governing board, management, and other personnel of an audited entity, that is designed to provide reasonable assurance regarding the achievement of objectives in the following categories:

- *Effectiveness and efficiency of controls in operations—relates to the entity's performance and financial goals and safeguarding of entity resources.*
- *Reliability of financial reporting—relates to the preparation of reliable published financial statements, including interim and condensed financial statements, and selected financial data extracted from such statements.*
- *Compliance with applicable laws and regulations—that relate to or apply to the audited entity.*

COSO Structural Components

Under the COSO definition, **internal controls** encompass or consist of five interrelated structural components.

1. **Control environment.** The environment "sets the tone" of an organization, provides the discipline and structure, and is the foundation for all other components of internal control.
2. **Risk assessments.** Identification, analysis, and assessment of the relative risks to achievement of entity objectives.
3. **Control activities.** The policies, procedures, and practices that help ensure management directives are carried out, including a range of activities such as: approvals, authorizations, verifications, reconciliations, reviews of operating performance, security of assets, and segregation of duties.
4. **Information and communication.** The information systems that produce reports containing operational, financial, and compliance-related information that make it possible to administer, control, and manage an organization's performance.
5. **Monitoring.** The periodic, regular monitoring of systems of internal controls to assess the controls systems performance over a period of time that includes regular management and supervisory activities and other actions personnel take in performing their duties.

With respect to information technology–related controls, COSO identified two types.

1. General controls—Controls over:
   a. Data center operations (scheduling, backup, recovery procedures)
   b. Systems software controls (acquisition and implementation of operating systems)
   c. Access security

---

[1] *The **Framework** is documented in a 1992 report by the Committee of Sponsoring Organizations (COSO), a consortium of cooperating organizations that includes the Financial Executives Institute, American Institute of Certified Public Accountants, American Accounting Association, Institute of Internal Auditors, and the Institute of Management Accountants.*

    d. Application system development and maintenance controls (acquisition and implementation of individual computer software applications)

2. Application controls—Controls designed to

    a. Control information processing

    b. Help ensure the completeness and accuracy of transaction processing, authorization, validity, and effectiveness of interface of applications

CONTROLS: REPORTING BY AGENCIES

From the time of the Constitution, Congress has desired that sounder, more effective internal controls be designed, implemented, and used by federal agencies. Congress has held hearings, commissioned studies, and heard speeches and presentations before its committees about the importance of internal controls over financial reporting. Congress's attempts to address the historically weak and deteriorated controls of the federal government are unmistakable, based on the trail of laws addressing the installation and strengthening of controls.

In the single decade of the 1990s, a number of laws were enacted with respect to federal financial management systems. With few exceptions, parts of each law emphasized the need for strengthened controls. But until 2002 and the Sarbanes-Oxley Act, no law required that any entity, in either the private or the public sector, have an independent management assessment and public reporting of internal controls over financial reporting and also have an independent audit of those controls simultaneously with the audit of the entity's financial statement. In July of 2002, Congress sent a clear, simple message to public corporations: "assess internal controls over financial reporting; audit internal controls over financial reporting." But at that time, Congress did not send the same message to federal agencies.

Today, federal agencies, pursuant to OMB Circular A-123, *Management's Responsibility for Internal Control,* make a reporting to the President, Congress, and the interested public in two principal formats:

1. The annual Performance and Accountability Report by heads of federal agencies that consolidates controls information required by the 1982 Federal Managers' Financial Integrity Act with performance-related reporting mandated by laws passed in the 1990s into a broader Performance and Accountability Report issued annually by the agency head

2. The annual reporting of tests of an agency's controls over financial reporting by independent auditors as part of an audit of that agency's annual financial statements pursuant to *Government Auditing Standards*

Beginning in 1982, Congress displayed its continuing concern over the financial management practices of the federal government by requiring, under a composite of laws, each executive agency to establish systems of accounting and administrative controls, to assess those controls, and to issue an annual report. But none of these laws required a federal agency to have its internal controls over financial reporting independently audited in the manner of all publicly listed corporations required by Sarbanes-Oxley.

OMB, in its internal controls guidance in Circular A-123 of 2005, highlighted specific legislation of the 1980s, 1990s, through 2002 that approximates the public sector governance rules for internal controls imposed by the Sarbanes-Oxley Act.

CONTROLS: TWO GROUPS

Typically, laws of Congress identified overall government-wide financial management policies, but by the same legislation, Congress would delegate the implementing responsibility for controls to the head of each federal agency. This legislative approach generally had an adverse effect on uniformity of data across the government and consistency of financial reporting between agencies. Generally, out-of-balance conditions resulted and created a need for costly and time-consuming data reconciliations.

Delegating implementation to the discretion of agency heads was noted by OMB in a revised circular, A-123, *Management's Responsibility for Internal Control,* wherein OMB stated that a defined assessment process for controls was needed, described such a controls assessment process, and identified, for policy purposes, two groupings of controls:

1. For purposes of the Performance and Accountability Report, internal controls encompass program, operational, and administrative areas as well as accounting and financial management, and should be an integral part of an agency's entire cycle of planning, budgeting, management, accounting, and auditing. From this view, internal control "is an integral component of an organization's management that provides reasonable assurance that the following objectives are being achieved: effectiveness and efficiency of operations, reliability of financial reporting, and compliance with applicable laws and regulations."

2. For purposes of assessing, documenting, and reporting on internal controls over financial reporting (a subset of internal controls), *effective internal control over financial reporting* provides reasonable assurance that financial reporting misstatements, asset losses, or noncompliance with applicable laws and regulations, material in relation to financial reports, would be prevented or detected. Financial reporting for this purpose encompasses the annual financial statements of an agency as well as other significant internal and external financial reporting.

"Other significant internal and external financial reporting" would be any financial reporting that could have a material effect on significant spending, budgeting, or other financial decisions of an agency, or that is used to determine compliance with laws and regulations by an agency.

These and other financial management issues are addressed by OMB in its revised, renamed, and reissued Circular A-123, *Management's Responsibility for Internal Control.*[2] This circular describes internal controls of federal entities as

---

[2] *Citations of OMB Circular A-123 in this and other chapters refer to a working draft revision of November 2004 or later drafts that preceded publication of this book. The earlier version of OMB Circular A-123, in 1995, was titled **Management Accountability and Control**.*

broader than just controls over accounting and financial management, but also encompassing program, operations, and administrative areas. By this newer policy statement, internal controls over financial reporting are described and considered to be a subset of the overall controls of a federal agency.

THE LAW: *"SUITABLE RECOGNIZED CONTROLS FRAMEWORK"*

The Sarbanes-Oxley Act requires publicly listed companies to base their annual assessment of controls on a "suitable, recognized control framework," particularly that of the Committee of Sponsoring Organizations. Prior to the Sarbanes-Oxley Act, other laws resulted in the COSO *Framework* being adopted and applied to operations of federal agencies. Government-wide policy, regulations, guidance, and auditing standards had essentially adopted a significant portion of the COSO *Framework* as the financial management standard of internal controls for the federal government as early as 1995.

The extensiveness of COSO adaptation by federal agencies is evident by a partial listing of the laws, regulations, accounting, and auditing standards, dating back to 1995, that reference, and in some instances require adoption of, COSO's *Internal Control—Integrated Framework,* for example

- AICPA: *Generally Accepted Auditing Standards.* As early as 1995, the COSO definition of internal controls, structural components, and specific control elements of an effective controls system were incorporated by the AICPA into its *generally accepted auditing standards* (GAAS).[3]
- OMB: *Federal Policy – Management Accountability and Control.* In 1995, OMB Circular A-123, *Federal Management Accountability and Control,* issued under the authority of the Federal Managers' Financial Integrity Act of 1982, places reliance on the COSO *Framework.*
- Congress: *Federal Financial Management Improvement Act.* The Federal Financial Management Improvement Act of 1996 incorporated the substance and specifically referenced the control elements highlighted in the COSO *Framework.*
- GAO: *Government Auditing Standards.* The GAO's *Government Auditing Standards* give prominence to the COSO *Framework,* specifically identifying the five COSO structural control components as necessary to an effective system of internal controls over financial reporting.
- GAO: *Standards for Internal Control in the Federal Government.* GAO prescribes for federal departments and agencies essentially the same definition of controls, structural components, and control elements as delineated in the COSO *Framework.*
- OMB: *Audit Requirements for Federal Financial Statements.* OMB Bulletin 01-02, of October 2000 (which implements audit provisions of the Chief Financial Officers Act, the Government Management Reform Act, and the

---

[3] *The AICPA's GAAS was the governing audit guidance through 2004 for audits of private sector entities and became the audit standards for public entities after incorporation by reference in the Government Auditing Standards as early as 1972.*

Federal Financial Management Improvement Act), closely parallels the substance of the COSO *Framework,* adopts the COSO definition of controls as federal policy, and references the AICPA's GAAS that adopted the COSO *Framework* in total.

However, none of the above controls criteria require federal agencies to have an independent audit of their controls or that the independent auditor render an audit opinion on the effectiveness of that agency's internal controls over financial reporting, as the Sarbanes-Oxley Act requires of publicly listed corporations.

THE GOVERNMENT'S PERFORMANCE AND ACCOUNTABILITY REPORT: CONSOLIDATION OF REPORTS CRITERIA

The genesis of the federal government's Performance and Accountability Report is Section 4 of the FMFIA of 1982, which requires an annual statement on whether the agency's financial management systems conform with government-wide requirements presented in OMB Circular A-127, *Financial Management Systems.* OMB Circular A-123, *Management's Responsibility for Internal Control,* is a consolidating policy statement blending financial management requirements of laws, earlier OMB regulations, positions of federal Inspectors General, and guidance promulgated over the years by the Government Accountability Office.

Exhibit 3.1 highlights several tasks required to assess and render an annual statement regarding the effectiveness of an agency's internal controls to comply with OMB Circular A-123.

For *Performance and Accountability* reporting, the circular states that an agency's entity-wide internal controls include the agency's processes for planning, organizing, directing, controlling, and reporting on agency operations. The overall objectives include the effectiveness and efficiency of operations, reliability of financial reporting, and compliance with applicable laws and regulations. The specific statutory guidance considered by OMB in its deliberations on Circular A-123 emanates from:

- *Federal Managers' Financial Integrity Act of 1982 (FMFIA):* OMB, in consultation with the Comptroller General, established guidelines for evaluation by individual agencies of their own systems of accounting and administrative controls. The head of each agency was required to annually assess the agency's systems for compliance with this guidance, make an annual determination concerning the controls, and report on this compliance with the FMFIA to the President and Congress. FMFIA stated that controls systems were to provide reasonable assurance that: (1) obligations and cost incurred and reported by federal agencies are in compliance with applicable law; (2) federal funds, property, and other assets are safeguarded against waste, loss, unauthorized use, or misappropriation; and (3) revenues and expenditures applica-

Exhibit 3.1: Management assessment of internal controls

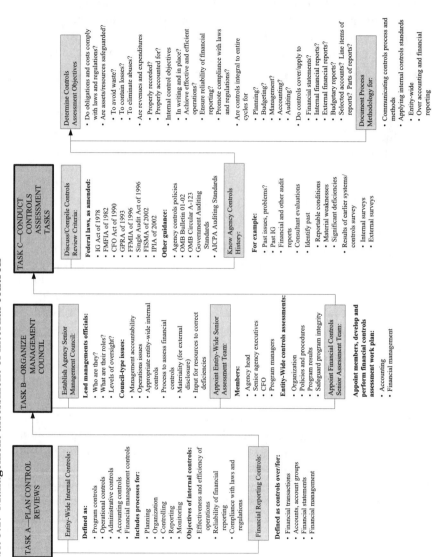

TASK A—PLAN CONTROL REVIEWS

Entity-Wide Internal Controls:

Defined as:
- Program controls
- Operational controls
- Administrative controls
- Accounting controls
- Financial management controls

Includes processes for:
- Planning
- Organization
- Controlling
- Reporting
- Monitoring

Objectives of internal controls:
- Effectiveness and efficiency of operations
- Reliability of financial reporting
- Compliance with laws and regulations

Financial Reporting Controls:

Defined as controls over/for:
- Financial transactions
- Accounts, account groups
- Financial statements
- Financial management

TASK B—ORGANIZE MANAGEMENT COUNCIL

Establish Agency Senior Management Council:

Lead managements officials:
- Who are they?
- What are their roles?
- Levels of oversight?

Council-type issues:
- Management accountability
- Operations issues
- Appropriate entity-wide internal controls
- Process to assess financial controls
- Materiality (for external disclosure)
- Input for resources to correct deficiencies

Appoint Entity-Wide Senior Assessment Team:

Members:
- Agency head
- Senior agency executives
- Program managers

Entity-Wide controls assessments:
- Organization
- Policies and procedures
- Program results
- Safeguard program integrity

Appoint Financial Controls Senior Assessment Team:

Appoint members, develop and perform financial controls assessment work plan:
- Accounting
- Financial management

TASK C—CONDUCT CONTROLS ASSESSMENT TASKS

Discuss/Compile Controls Review Criteria:

Federal laws, as amended:
- IG Act of 1978
- FMFIA of 1982
- CFO Act of 1990
- GPRA of 1993
- FFMIA of 1996
- Single Audit Act of 1996
- FISMA of 2002
- IPIA of 2002

Other guidance:
- Agency controls policies
- OMB Bulletin 01-02
- OMB Circular A-123
- Government Auditing Standards
- AICPA Auditing Standards

Know Agency Controls History:

For example:
- Past issues, problems?
- Past IG
- Financial and other audit reports
- Consultant evaluations
- Identify past
  - Reportable conditions
  - Material weaknesses
  - Significant deficiencies
- Results of earlier systems/controls survey
  - Internal surveys
  - External surveys

Determine Controls Assessment Objectives

- Do obligations and costs comply with laws and regulations?
- Are assets/resources safeguarded?
  - To avoid waste?
  - To contain losses?
  - To eliminate abuses?
- Are revenues and expenditures
  - Properly recorded?
  - Properly accounted for?
- Internal control objectives
  - In writing and in place?
  - Achieve effective and efficient operations?
  - Ensure reliability of financial reporting?
  - Promote compliance with laws and regulations?
- Are controls integral to entire cycles for
  - Planning?
  - Budgeting?
  - Management?
  - Accounting?
  - Auditing?
- Do controls cover/apply to
  - Financial statements?
  - Internal financial reports?
  - External financial reports?
  - Budgetary reports?
  - Selected accounts? Line items of reports? Parts of reports?

Document Process Methodology for:

- Communicating controls process and methods
- Applying internal controls standards
  - Entity-wide
  - Over accounting and financial reporting

Exhibit 3.1: Management assessment of internal controls (continued)

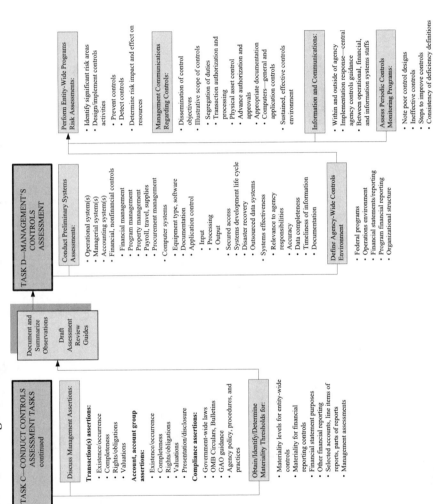

Exhibit 3.1: Management assessment of internal controls (continued)

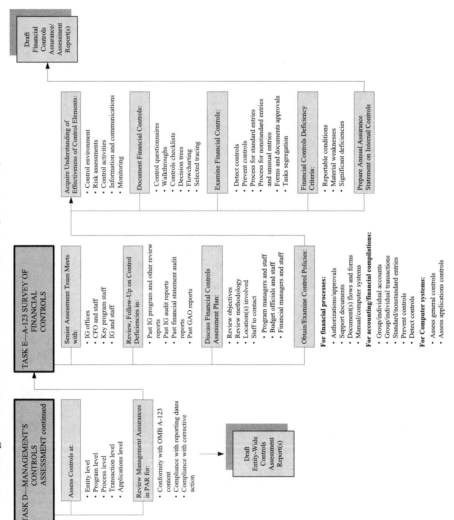

ble to a federal agency's operations are properly recorded and accounted for, to permit the preparation of accounts and reliable financial and statistical reports, and to maintain accountability over the assets.

- *Inspector General Act (IG Act) of 1978:* Inspectors General and/or external auditors are required by the *Government Auditing Standards* and OMB Bulletin 01-02, *Audit Requirements of Federal Financial Statements* to report material weaknesses in the internal control and noncompliance with laws and regulations as part of the annual financial statement audit.

- *Single Audit Act of 1984:* This act requires financial statement audits of nonfederal entities that receive or administer grant awards of federal monies that include testing the effectiveness of *the* internal control and determining whether the award monies have been spent in compliance with laws and regulations.

- *Chief Financial Officers Act (CFO Act) of 1990:* Agencies are required to prepare *annual* financial statements and have those statements independently audited, at which time the auditors must, in compliance with *Government Auditing Standards*, report on the agency's internal controls and its compliance with laws and regulations. As noted earlier, the scope of this legislation was expanded by the Government Management Reform Act of 1994 and the Accountability of Tax Dollars Act of 2002.

- *Government Performance and Results Act (GPRA) of 1993:* This act requires agencies to develop *strategic* plans, set performance goals, and report annually on actual performance compared to goals. These plans and goals must be integrated into (1) the budget process, (2) the operational management of agencies and programs, and (3) accountability reporting to the public on performance results and on the integrity, efficiency, and effectiveness with which they are achieved.

- *Federal Financial Management Improvement Act (FFMIA) of 1996*: This act requires agencies to have financial management systems that substantially comply with (1) federal financial management systems requirements, (2) accounting and financial reporting standards promulgated by FASAB, and (3) the Standard General Ledger "at the transaction level." Agency heads shall make an annual determination about whether their financial management systems substantially comply with FFMIA.

- *Federal Information Security Management Act (FISMA) of 2002:* This act requires agencies to *provide* a comprehensive framework for ensuring the effectiveness of information security controls over information resources that support federal operations and assets and annually report on the effectiveness of the agencies' security programs. Weaknesses found under FISMA, categorized as "significant deficiencies," must also be reported as material weaknesses under FMFIA.

- *Improper Payments Improvement Act (IPIA) of 2002:* Agencies are to review and "identify programs and activities that may be susceptible to significant improper payments" and annually submit estimates of improper payments, corrective actions to reduce the improper payments, and statements as to whether the agencies' current information systems and infrastructure can support the effort to reduce improper payments. The incidence of improper payments should be considered when assessing the effectiveness of the internal control.

- *Reports Consolidation Act of 2000:* This act required consolidation of numerous performance, management, and accountability reports, mandated by many earlier laws, into one annual report, the Performance and Accountability Report, to be annually submitted by the head of a federal agency to the President, Congress, and the general public.

By these laws, implementing regulations, and practices, federal agencies are responsible for developing, maintaining, and reporting on internal controls that address each of the five components of internal control:

1. *Control environment:* The organization structure, including the culture, tone of integrity, and ethical behavior defined by agency management
2. *Risk assessment:* Identification and assessment of internal and external risks that might prevent the agency from meeting its objectives
3. *Control activities:* Such as properly segregating employee and management duties; physical control over assets; appropriate transaction approval, authorizing, and executing procedures; prompt recording and appropriate documentation of all transactions; and inclusion of effective general and application controls relative to computer-based systems
4. *Information and communications:* The timely communications to relevant personnel within the agency
5. *Monitoring:* Periodic reviews, reconciliations, and comparisons of data as part of the regular assigned duties of designated personnel

These are the same structural components of an effective system of internal controls that appear in the COSO *Framework* recommended by the Treadway Commission in 1992 and mandated by Sarbanes-Oxley.

REPORTABLE DEFICIENCIES

To comply with the above statutes and OMB's consolidating Circular A-123, agency managers must identify and report deficiencies in internal control that are or should be of interest to the next level of management. Some working definitions of reportable deficiencies, in the OMB circular are:

- *Reportable condition:* A deficiency reported to the next supervisory level that represents significant deficiencies in the design or operation of the internal control that could adversely affect the organization's ability to meet its internal control objectives.
- *Material weakness:* A reportable condition that the agency head determines to be significant enough to be reported outside of the agency and included in the FMFIA report to the President and Congress.

- *Significant deficiency:* A control weakness, as defined in the Federal Information Security Management Act of 2002, is a material weakness for Performance and Accountability Report purposes.[4]

The above definitions of *reportable condition* and *material weakness* are different from, and should not be confused with, identically worded terms used by auditors in financial statement audit reports. As applied, under *Government Auditing Standards*, reportable conditions and material weaknesses must be identified and reported in the audit report regardless of whether agency management elects not to report the weaknesses outside of the agency. *"Significant deficiencies"* are not cited or noted by GAO in its *Government Auditing Standards*.

PERFORMANCE AND ACCOUNTABILITY REPORTS

The specific content of an agency's *Performance and Accountability Report* may vary from one year to the next, and between one agency and another, depending on program operations, circumstances and conditions encountered during a fiscal year, and the goals and objectives of the reporting agency. Generally, though, the Performance and Accountability Report is comprised of several sections.

- *Management Discussion and Analysis (MD&A):* A high-level overview and description of an agency's mission and structure; performance goals and results against the goals; financial highlights of the past year; systems and controls issues; future or possible demands, risks, uncertainties, events, conditions, and trends that could affect agency performance
- *Annual Performance Report:* A narrative description of the operational achievements, setbacks, attained outputs and outcomes, and changes among the constituencies served during the reporting year
- *Annual Accountability Report:* Highlights an agency's key financial outputs and outcomes for the reported year, plus the audited financial statements of the agency, along with the footnotes and other supplementary information to conform to the generally accepted accounting principles of federal entities, as prescribed by FASAB
- *Annual, Audited Financial Statements:* Prepared in conformance with the accounting principles prescribed by FASAB and independently audited in conformance with the *Government Auditing Standards*
- *Management and Performance Challenges Report:* A report by the Inspector General regarding the 10 areas considered by the Inspector General to be the most serious management challenges facing the agency

CONTROLS: NOT AUDITED

OMB, in Circular A-123, describes internal controls over financial reporting to be a subset of a federal entity's overall system of internal controls. OMB requires

---

[4] *The Federal Information Security Management Act is specifically concerned with national security systems, whether such a system is used by or operated on behalf of the agency, but would not include systems of routine administrative and business applications (e.g., payroll, finance, logistics, and personnel management applications).*

that these controls to be "assessed" by agency management. But this assessment is separate from the tests of controls that require the auditor to "understand the internal controls," assess internal controls for purposes of reliance thereon during the audit, and test the internal controls in conducting the audit and opining on financial statements. At time of publication, no agency is required to make an audit of its internal controls over financial reporting.

GOVERNMENT AUDITING STANDARDS: NO AUDIT OF CONTROLS

For years, numerous laws and several OMB circulars and bulletins have required audits involving federal monies to be conducted in accordance with the *Government Auditing Standards*. However, these auditing standards, issued by GAO, do not require that a federal agency's internal controls be audited. Instead, *Government Auditing Standards* conform to the AICPA's generally accepted auditing standards and require only that the internal controls be tested by auditors of federal financial statements and that the results of those tests be reported. Specifically, the second standard of fieldwork requires

> *A sufficient understanding of internal control is to be obtained to plan the audit and to determine the nature, timing, and extent of tests to be performed.*

This fieldwork standard has been further refined by the AICPA's Statements on Auditing Standards (SASs), which direct CPAs to obtain an *understanding* of (1) the design of a client's internal control policies and procedures, and (2) whether the control policies and procedures have been placed in operation. This *understanding* of the controls structure must be documented (e.g., internal control questionnaires, checklists, flowcharts, decision tables, memorandum) by the auditor.

Government Auditing Standards adopt the four AICPA standards of reporting, but also prescribe additional reporting standards, in particular:

- *When providing an opinion or a disclaimer on financial statements, auditors should include in their report on the financial statements either a*
  1. *Description of the scope of the auditors' testing of internal control over financial reporting and compliance with laws, regulations, and provisions of contracts or grant agreements, and the results of those tests or an opinion, if sufficient work was performed, or*
  2. *Reference to the separate report(s) containing that information. If auditors report separately, the opinion or disclaimer should contain a reference to the separate report containing this information and state that the separate report is an integral part of the audit and should be considered in assessing the results of the audit.*

- *For financial audits, including audits of financial statements in which the auditor provides an opinion or disclaimer, auditors should report, as applicable to the objectives of the audit*
  1. *Deficiencies in internal control considered to be reportable conditions, as defined in AICPA standards*
  2. *All instances of fraud and illegal acts unless clearly inconsequential*
  3. *Significant violations of provisions of contracts or grant agreements and abuse.*

For these financial audits, the AICPA's auditing standards define *reportable conditions* as significant deficiencies in the design or operation of internal controls that could adversely affect the entity's ability to record, process, summarize, and report financial data consistent with the assertions of management in financial statements.

OMB CIRCULARS AND BULLETINS: NO AUDIT OF CONTROLS

OMB Bulletin 01-02, *Audit Requirements for Federal Financial Statements* (issued in October 2000), states that an auditor of a federal agency's financial statements must issue an audit disclaimer stating that "the objective of the financial statement audit was not to provide assurance on internal control. Consequently, we do not provide an opinion on internal control." With respect to internal controls, Bulletin 01-02 requires an auditor to conduct tests sufficient to obtain an understanding of the components of internal control and to assess the level of control risk relevant to the management assertions embodied in the classes of transactions, account balances, and disclosure components of the financial statements. These controls include relevant data processing general and application controls and controls relating to intra-entity and intragovernmental transactions and balances.

For decades, laws have held the heads of federal agencies responsible for developing and maintaining effective internal controls over their agencies' programs, operations, and activities. By its Circular A-123 (issued in 2005), OMB directed agencies to study, analyze, continuously monitor, annually assess, and provide Congress and the President with both:

1. An annual statement of assurance as to the overall adequacy and effectiveness of the internal controls within the agency; and
2. An annual statement of assurance over the effectiveness of internal control over financial reporting.

That annual assurance statement by the head of a federal agency, relative to internal controls over financial reporting suggested by OMB, provided it was warranted by observed conditions and circumstances might be:

> *The department's management is responsible for establishing and maintaining adequate internal control over financial reporting. As required by the Federal Managers' Financial Integrity Act, the agency conducted its evaluation of the effectiveness of the department's internal control over financial reporting in accordance with OMB Circular A-123, **Management's Responsibility for Internal Control**. Based on the results of this evaluation, the department can provide reasonable assurance that internal control over financial reporting as of June 30, 2XXX, is operating effectively, and no material weaknesses were found in the design or operation of the internal control over financial reporting.*

Circular A-123 does not require a separate audit opinion on internal controls, but allows agencies to elect to receive such an opinion.

CONGRESS: NO AUDIT OF CONTROLS, BUT STUDIES

By Section 4 of the Homeland Security Financial Accountability Act (October 16, 2004), Congress required that for each fiscal year, the Department of Homeland Security must submit a Performance and Accountability Report that includes an audit opinion of the department's internal controls over its financial reporting. However, with respect to the implementation of this audit opinion requirement, the department shall include audit opinions in its Performance and Accountability Reports only for fiscal years *after* fiscal year 2005. For fiscal year 2005, Homeland Security shall include in the Performance and Accountability Report an assertion on the internal controls that apply to financial reporting by the department.

With respect to the requirement for an audit opinion related to internal controls over financial reporting by each of the federal government's Chief Financial Officer Act agencies, Congress opted to study this requirement further, to wit

1. In general—Not later than 180 days after the date of the enactment of this Act, the Chief Financial Officer's Council and the President's Council on Integrity and Efficiency shall jointly conduct a study of the potential costs and benefits of requiring the agencies to obtain audit opinions of their internal controls over their financial reporting.
2. Report—Upon completion of the study under paragraph 1, the Chief Financial Officer's Council and the President's Council on Integrity and Efficiency shall promptly submit a report on the results of the study to the Committee on Government Reform of the House of Representatives, the Committee on Governmental Affairs of the Senate, and the Comptroller General of the United States.
3. Not later than 90 days after receiving the report, the Comptroller General shall perform an analysis of the information provided in the report, and report the findings of the analysis to the Committee on Government Reform of the House of Representatives and the Committee on Governmental Affairs of the Senate.

4 AUDITORS OF FEDERAL AGENCIES AND PROGRAMS: FEDERAL AUDITORS, STATE AUDITORS, INDEPENDENT AUDITORS

By law, a significant number of activities supported by federal monies must be audited, or are subject to audit. In general, this scope includes federal departments and agencies, state and local governments, contractors and subcontractors, grantees and subgrantees, and various other recipients of federal assistance (i.e., borrowers and beneficiaries of loan guarantee programs).

Over the years, the organizations making audits of federal activities have changed. During the 1950s and 1960s, auditors employed by federal agencies conducted internal audits of their agency and external audits of organizations receiving financial assistance from their agency. Throughout the 1970s, federal agencies placed increasing reliance on audits by independent accounting firms under contract to federal agencies. In the 1980s and since, with the passage of the Single Audit Act, tens of thousands of federal programs, contracts, grants, and other financially assisted programs' activities are annually audited by auditors who are employed by state and local governments, by accounting firms under contract to these governments, and by firms that may audit nonprofit and other nongovernmental organizations receiving federal financial assistance.

During these pivotal decades, the types of audits and examinations made by audit organizations changed. Until the 1970s, internal audits of a federal agency's finances, activities, and programs were primarily the province of the agency's internal auditors. Federal internal auditors were also charged with auditing the agency's contractors, grantees, and other recipients of agency assistance. Independent accounting firms may have made audits of federal contracts and grants, but only under contract with federal agencies.

The 1980s were witness to tens of thousands of recipients of federal assistance having to annually undergo a comprehensive audit that included a financial statement audit, tests of compliance with laws and regulations, and tests of internal controls for the audited entity as a whole and for each major federal program. Federal law and policy provided that these expanded comprehensive audits would be performed by auditors of state and local governments and by independent accounting firms that could be employed by those governments. Audits of these entities were also changing to include increased audits of compliance with laws and regulations, operations, and program performance. Then in 1990, the passage of the Chief Financial Officers Act imposed on the federal government a requirement that, for the first time in the history of the country, annual department or agency-wide financial statements must be prepared and that these statements must be independently audited.

In 2002, Congress passed the Sarbanes-Oxley Act requiring management of publicly listed companies to annually assess and report on their internal controls over financial reporting. This management reporting had to be evaluated and opined on by the company's independent auditor in conjunction with the annual audit of the company's financial statements.

AUDIT STANDARDS FOR AUDIT ORGANIZATIONS

The beginnings of *Government Auditing Standards* can be traced back to several 1968 meetings between state auditors and the Comptroller General, at which time the case was brought to GAO that state and federal auditing practices left much to be desired. In 1972, GAO issued the first edition of *Government Auditing Standards,* which, over the years, has popularly become known as the yellow book, a reference to the color of the book's cover.

Government Auditing Standards are audit criteria applied by any auditor, regardless of employer, when required by law, regulation, agreement, contract, grant, or governmental policy. If required, the *Government Auditing Standards* are to be applied by all types of auditors, not just governmental auditors. This includes:

- Federal, state, and local governmental internal auditors
- Staffs of federal Inspectors General
- Accounting firms under contract to the federal and other governments
- Certified public accountants and non-CPA auditors
- Nonaudit personnel who are members of the audit teams

It is important to underscore that the *Government Auditing Standards* are not standards imposed solely on nonfederal governmental entities. Rather, *Government Auditing Standards* are the audit criteria applied to audits of all federal agencies and nonfederal organizations receiving or benefiting from any form of federal financial assistance. It does not matter whether the audited federal assistance was obtained under a federal contract or grant, federal loans and federal loan guarantees, federal insurance programs, or government food commodity initiatives. Nonfederal entities are comprised of organizations such as: state and local governments, federal contractors and grantees, nonprofit organizations, colleges and universities, Indian tribal nations, public utilities and authorities, financial institutions, hospitals, and more.

Government Standards: Not Stand-Alone Standards

The *Government Auditing Standards* are not a stand-alone set of audit criteria, but are a combination of various audit criteria. The June 2003 edition of the yellow book, as well as all earlier editions, does not contain sufficient audit guidance to ensure the performance of an acceptable financial audit. *Government Auditing Standards* and the generally accepted auditing standards promulgated by the AICPA must be blended and applied by the auditor in order for an audit to fully meet all of the federal audit criteria. Each revision of the *Government Auditing Standards* contains references to the fact that the *Government Auditing Standards* incorporate all of the AICPA's generally accepted auditing fieldwork and reporting standards and all of the AICPA's SASs, unless specifically exempted by GAO. Since the initial edition in 1972, GAO has never exempted an AICPA auditing standard.

Government Auditing Standards describe criteria for the conduct of financial statement audits, attestation engagements, and performance audits that are in addition to any issued by the AICPA. For example, the *Government Auditing Standards* relating to financial statement audits include 14 standards in addition to the AICPA's 4 general auditing standards, 4 fieldwork auditing standards, and 6 reporting standards. The *Government Auditing Standards* also include audit criteria for attestation engagements that involve examining, reviewing, or performing agreed-upon procedures on a subject matter, or an assertion about a subject matter, and reporting on the results of the examination. These standards, like those relating to financial audits, build on the AICPA's standards for attestation engagements. *Government Auditing Standards,* in June 2003, include an additional 11 attestation engagement standards: 6 fieldwork standards for attestation engagements and 5 reporting standards for attestation engagements.

AUDIT RESPONSIBILITIES FOR AUDITORS

Independence: Organizational and Personal

Under *Government Auditing Standards,* all audit organizations undertaking audits, examinations, and attestation agreements agree to accept and implement several safeguards to ensure that:

- Independence and objectivity are maintained in all phases of the assignment.
- Professional judgment is used in planning and performing the work and reporting the results.
- Work is performed by personnel who are professionally competent and collectively have the necessary skills and knowledge.
- An independent peer review is periodically performed, and an opinion issued, as to whether an audit organization's system of quality control is designed and being complied with to provide reasonable assurance of conformance with professional standards.
- Policies and procedures exist for follow-up of findings of earlier audits and attestation engagements and reporting on the status of earlier audit recommendations.
- Previous significant audit and attestation engagement findings are addressed and considered in planning future engagements.

Government Auditing Standards place considerable emphasis on the independence of both audit organizations and individual auditors and require that both be free, in fact and appearance, from all personal, external, and organizational impairments. Audit organizations and governmental and independent accounting firms must consult the provisions and illustrations within *Government Auditing Standards* for an understanding of factors that might affect governmental audit organizations differently from an independent accounting firm.

When impairments to independence cannot be mitigated or eliminated altogether, audit organizations are instructed by the *Government Auditing Standards* to withdraw from the engagement. *Government Auditing Standards* recognize that government auditors may have independence impairments resulting from their position within the government and offer specific guidance for such circumstances.

Continuing Professional Education: Mandatory and Different

Government Auditing Standards require auditors planning, directing, performing fieldwork, or reporting on an audit or attestation engagement subject to *Government Auditing Standards* to maintain professional competence through continuing *professional* education (CPE). Note that this education is different from and in addition to that imposed by the AICPA on those subject to its rulings. The CPE requirements of the *Government Auditing Standards* apply to all auditors subject to these audit criteria, whether employed by governments or by independent accounting firms.

Compliance with *Government Auditing Standards* requires all auditors planning, directing, performing fieldwork, or reporting on an audit or attestation engagement to maintain their professional competence through continuing professional education:

- Each auditor performing work under *Government Auditing Standards* should complete, every two years, at least 80 hours of CPE that directly enhances the auditor's professional proficiency to perform audits and/or attestation engagements.
- Team members must collectively possess the technical knowledge, skills, and experience necessary to be competent for the type of work being performed before beginning work on a *Government Auditing Standards* assignment. (Under an exception by GAO, individual auditors have two years, from the date they start an audit or attestation engagement conducted under generally accepted government auditing standards, to comply with CPE requirements.)
- At least 24 of the 80 hours of CPE should be in subjects directly related to government auditing, the government environment, or the specific or unique environment in which the audited entity operates.
- At least 20 of the 80 hours should be completed in any one year of the two-year period. (As an exception, GAO provides that staff members not involved in planning, directing, or reporting on the audit or attestation engagement, and who annually charge less than 20% of their time to audits and attestation engagements following *Government Auditing Standards*, do not have to comply with the 24-hour CPE requirement.)

Each audit organization is responsible, under the *Government Auditing Standards*, for ensuring that auditors meet CPE requirements and for maintaining documentation of the CPE completed by each staff member.

GAO offers additional guidance under *Guidance on GAGAS Requirements for Continuing Professional Education.*

Professional Qualifications: Licensing of Independent Accountants

Auditors engaged to perform financial audits or attestation engagements should be licensed Certified Public Accountants or persons working for a licensed CPA firm or government auditing organization. Public accountants licensed on or before December 31, 1970, or persons working for a public accounting firm licensed on or before December 31, 1970, are also considered qualified under this standard.

Public accountants and accounting firms meeting licensing requirements must also comply with applicable provisions of the public accountancy laws and rules of the jurisdiction(s) where the audit is being performed and the jurisdiction(s) in which the public accountants and their firms are licensed.

FEDERAL AUDITORS AND INDEPENDENT ACCOUNTANTS

Federal government auditing settles within the scope of a variety of different organizations and entities. Examples include GAO, federal Inspectors General, Congress, and the Defense Contract Audit Agency. These and others are discussed in detail in the next sections.

US Government Accountability Office

GAO is a federal agency in the legislative branch, established by Congress in 1921 to be its audit, evaluation, and investigative arm. GAO, completely independent of the executive branch and answerable only to Congress, is headed by the Comptroller General. The Comptroller General is appointed by the President and serves with the guidance and consent of Congress for a 15-year term of office. The Comptroller General cannot be reappointed and can be removed only through formal impeachment proceedings by Congress. GAO is staffed by career professionals appointed under a meritorious process that requires each appointee to meet certain academic and experience qualifications.

GAO's audit responsibilities have roots in its founding legislation, the Budget and Accounting Act of 1921. The Act determined that a core responsibility of GAO's would be to investigate, *at the seat of government or elsewhere*, the *receipt*, *disbursement*, and *application of public funds*, and to report annually to Congress on its work and recommendations for needed legislation. Later legislation extended the scope of GAO's investigatory and auditing authority to all nonfederal organizations receiving various types of federal financial and other assistance. This gave GAO right of access to records of state and local governmental organizations, educational institutions, private companies awarded federal contracts, and tens of thousands of nonprofit organizations that receive federal grants and other federal financial monies and subsidies.

Within and external to the auditing profession, GAO is highly regarded for its history of professionalism, independence, and objectivity. Some academics have referred to GAO as the world's premier audit organization for the quality of its financial audits and for being at the forefront of *performance auditing* (special-focus audits designed to assess the relative efficiency, economy, and effectiveness of an entity's operations).

Government Auditing Standards, initiated in 1972 by GAO, were viewed as criteria for scopes of audits that better addressed the needs and uniqueness of audits of governmental financing, accounting, operating, and reporting practices. GAO's activities in the 1980s and 1990s are typical examples of the work performed by GAO professionals. Many GAO recommendations have become laws and federal regulations affecting the country's entire citizenry. In a typical year, GAO auditors could audit and report on an agriculture crisis, weapons development problems, or examine the financing, management, and operations of such unique government undertakings as the nuclear breeder reactor, the Social Security Trust Fund, the Internal Revenue Service, and the state of America's environment and defense programs. During the decade of the 1990s, at GAO's urging, laws were passed requiring executive branch departments and agencies to: revamp and strengthen federal financial management practices; modernize outdated financial systems; implement a government-wide, uniform accounting system; and prepare, for the first time in 200 years, annual agency financial statements that had to be independently audited.

Federal Inspectors General

The Inspector General Act of 1978, and as amended, created Inspector General offices in federal departments and agencies. By 2003, there existed over 50 statutory Inspectors General. Inspectors General of larger federal establishments serve by appointment of the President and with the advice and consent of the Senate. They may be removed by the President, who must communicate the reason for the removal to Congress. Inspectors General of smaller federal establishments are appointed to their positions by the head of their respective agencies or offices.

The intent of Congress with respect to the Inspector General Act was to create within federal departments, agencies, and offices independent and objective audit and investigative functions. Under the Act, offices of Inspectors General were charged with:

- Conducting, supervising, and coordinating audits and investigations relating to programs and operations of their respective agencies
- Providing leadership and coordinating and recommending policies for activities designed to promote economy, efficiency, and effectiveness in the administration and prevention and detection of fraud and abuses in such federal programs and operations
- Keeping the head of the agency and Congress informed of problems, deficiencies, and progress of corrective actions taken

In carrying out their responsibilities, each Inspector General shall (1) comply with standards of the Comptroller General for audits of federal establishments, organizations, programs, activities, and functions; (2) establish guidelines for determining when it shall be appropriate to use nonfederal auditors; and (3) take appropriate steps to assure that any work performed by nonfederal auditors complies with the Comptroller General's *Government Auditing Standards*.

The Chief Financial Officers Act of 1990 required an agency's annual financial statements to be audited in accordance with the *Government Auditing Standards* by

(1) the Inspector General, (2) by an independent external auditor, as determined by the Inspector General of the federal agency, or (3), if there is no Inspector General, by the head of the agency.

Direct Reporting to Congress and Other Authority

Congress was particularly concerned with ensuring that Inspectors General had the independence and authority to perform their intended functions. To this end, the Inspector General Act:

- Requires that each Inspector General, annually and semiannually, prepare and transmit a report to the head of his or her establishment. The head of the establishment, in turn, must transmit these reports to committees and subcommittees of Congress within 30 days after receipt of the reports from the Inspector General.
- Empowers federal Inspectors General to report immediately to the head of their establishment when the Inspector General became aware of serious or flagrant problems, abuses, or deficiencies. The head of the federal establishment then has seven days to transmit the report to Congress. When heads of federal establishments fail to act within 12 months, such inaction must be reported by the Inspector General to Congress in all subsequent semiannual or annual reports until management action is completed.
- Gives federal Inspectors General necessary access to all information, records, reports, audits, reviews, documents, papers, recommendations, and other materials available to the establishment under investigation or audit.
- Provides Inspectors General with legal authority to assist in investigatory and audit roles to require, by subpoena, all information, records, reports, audits, reviews, documents, papers, recommendations, and other materials necessary to perform the functions of the office. Neither the head of the agency nor the next in rank shall prevent or prohibit the Inspector General from carrying out or completing any audit or investigation, or from issuing any subpoena during the course of any audit or investigation.
- Empowers Inspectors General to administer or take oaths, affirmations, and affidavits.

Nonfederal Auditors

Of particular concern to nonfederal auditors—employees of independent accounting firms and employees of state and local governments—is the quality control monitoring program established by federal Inspectors General. This program is comprised of two phases:

1. Centralized desk reviews of thousands of audit reports each year by Inspectors General staffs or staffs under contract to the Inspectors General
2. On-site quality control reviews by Inspectors General staffs or staffs under contract to Inspectors General of audit documentation

Inspector General desk reviews. If the Inspector General's desk review of an audit report or audit documentation by a nonfederal auditor discloses inadequacies or deficiencies that are remediable, the nonfederal audit organization is contacted and afforded the opportunity to take corrective action. If an Inspector General concludes from the desk review that the audit report and audit documentation is substandard, the matter can be submitted directly to state boards of accountancy with no prior notification to the involved auditor.[1] At the same time, the federal Inspector General would typically commence an on-site quality control review of the nonfederal audit organization to further determine the nature, extent, and cause of audit deficiencies and possibly mandate that remedial actions, or even sanctions, be instituted.

A desk review is limited to a centralized off-site examination, conducted pursuant to a checklist, of the form and content of audit reports. During the review, communication between the Inspector General representative and the nonfederal audit organization (which could be an independent accounting firm or a nonfederal governmental audit organization) is common. Since only the audit report is examined in this phase, no assessments can be made of the underlying quality of a questionable audit report at the time of the desk review. At this time, the Inspector General or representatives would not have access to the audit working papers.

Since 1984, tens of thousands of desk reviews have been made of audits conducted pursuant to the Single Audit Act. When well done, the single audit report can contribute to improved management of assistance programs and elimination of the need and costs for additional or further federal field inspections and evaluations. Ideally, the single audit report should "stand on its own," containing sufficient information to permit the auditee to facilitate resolution of audit findings and implement any recommended corrective actions. Over the years, reviews by Inspectors General and GAO have disclosed a commonality of noted deficiencies and problems with submitted audit reports,[2] some of which have included:

- *Failure of auditors to report compliance with laws and regulations*: These audit deficiencies included a failure by the auditor to address the extent of compliance (or noncompliance) with laws and regulations; omitted statements of the audit assurances of compliance with laws and regulations required by the act and the related OMB Circular A-133 governing the performance and reporting of single audits; and the failure to report (or the inadequate reporting of) noted noncompliance issues.
- *Failure of auditors to report internal control problems or issues*: The reviewed audit reports did not contain the required statements of tests of controls; and omitted identification of significant controls and identification of those controls that were tested.

---

[1] *Over the years, federal Inspectors General have applied desk reviews and audit checklists. Two checklists currently used are titled:* **Uniform Guide for Initial Review of A-133 Audit Reports** *and* **Uniform Guide for Initial Review of A-133 Audits**. *Both of these are prepared and periodically updated by the President's Council on Integrity and Efficiency (more commonly referred to as the PCIE).*

[2] *The periodic, generally annual, AICPA publication titled* **Audit Risk Alerts: State and Local Governmental Developments** *is an excellent source of deficiencies and problems noted in these audit reports by federal examiners.*

- *Failure of auditors to use due professional care*: Audit reports containing unqualified audit opinions and the accompanying financial statements were deficient in several instances. Audit reports of nonfederal audits contained: inaccuracies in reported account balances; had accounts with inaccurate amounts; displayed improper statement formats; failed to include necessary schedules and other required information; had no, or inadequate, descriptions of the audit work performed; and were missing dates, auditor signatures, and citations of audit guidance used in conducting the audit.
- *Citation of wrong auditing standards*: Audit reports of nonfederal auditors failed to comply with a prescribed auditing standard, or failed to cite that the audits were conducted pursuant to *Government Auditing Standards*. An audit made pursuant only to the AICPA's generally accepted auditing standards would be deemed unacceptable and substandard since several additional audit criteria of the *Government Auditing Standards* would not have been met. Still other nonfederal auditor reports were found to contain references to auditing standards that have been superseded.

Inspector General on-site quality control reviews. The Single Audit Act and OMB Circular A-133, as of 2003, continued to require federal agencies to:

- Obtain or conduct quality control reviews of selected audits made by nonfederal audit organizations, and provide the results, when appropriate, to other interested organizations.
- Advise the nonfederal auditor and, where appropriate, the auditee of any deficiencies found in the audits when the deficiencies require corrective action by the nonfederal auditor.
- If corrective action is not taken, the cognizant agency shall notify the nonfederal auditor, the auditee, federal awarding agencies, and pass-through entities of the facts and make recommendations for follow-up action.
- Any major inadequacies or repetitive substandard performance by nonfederal auditors shall be referred to appropriate state licensing agencies and professional bodies for disciplinary actions.

An *on-site quality control review* by a federal Inspector General is an "audit" of both the nonfederal auditor and the nonfederal audit organization. With a notable exception, an on-site quality control review is instituted when the audit report has failed federal desk reviews and was deemed almost uncorrectable. An on-site federal quality control review is intended to obtain several objectives:

- Be an exhaustive review of the nonfederal audit team and audit procedures employed by that team and its audit organization
- Be a validation of the control system in place to plan, supervise, monitor, and train the professional staff of the nonfederal audit organization
- Be a reaudit of the auditee's records to assess the adequacy of the audit planning and execution by the nonfederal auditor
- More often than not, be a survey of auditee management and their accounting and control practices

The exception to being selected for an on-site quality control review as a result of failing a desk review relates to the Big 4 accounting firms; periodic random quality control reviews are made of a sampling of their offices nationally. For the most part, the Inspectors General, by agreement, have one federal agency conduct the quality control review of the larger audit firm after coordinating with other federal entities that may have provided federal assistance to the auditee.

Like the desk review examiner, the quality control review examiner generally conforms to a checklist developed by the President's Council on Integrity and Efficiency (PCIE) that requires adherence to a four-step process:

1. Schedule an entrance conference with the nonfederal audit organization's senior management to explain the quality control review process, the condition precipitating the quality control review, and respond to questions.
2. Assess the adequacy and sufficiency of audit evidence to support the nonfederal audit opinion or report submitted.
3. Review the auditee's financial statements and audit working papers showing audit procedures performed.
4. On a selective basis, trace working paper evidence to the financial statements, specific audit findings, and the auditee's books of accounts and original documentation.

A major objective of the quality control review is the evaluation of the quality of the nonfederal audit performed, which requires the quality control review examiner to:

- Ascertain whether the financial statements, the nonfederal audit program, the audit procedures, the reported findings, and the audit opinion or assurances are consistent with the audit evidence appearing in the audit working papers
- Evaluate the appropriateness of the nonfederal audit plan, the supporting audit programs, and the audit procedures applied for consistency with *Government Auditing Standards*
- Examine the applied nonfederal audit procedures, as evidenced by the audit working papers, to test compliance with the fieldwork audit standards for government audits, particularly the standard relating to sufficiency of audit evidence
- Assess the audit organization's system of quality control over governmental audits to ensure compliance with applicable laws, regulations, contracts, and grant agreements
- Determine the manner in which significant audit findings were disclosed, subsequently followed up with the auditee, and ultimately reported in the nonfederal audit report
- Critique the nonfederal auditor's conclusions relative to significant aspects of the audit and its execution
- Confirm the technical competence of all staff on the nonfederal audit team and the currency of the team's compliance with continuing professional education mandated by *Government Auditing Standards*

- Conclude the quality control review with an exit conference, prior to which a written draft of the quality control review report should be provided to the audit organization, including any noted deficiencies, recommendation for corrective actions, and suggestions for the nonfederal auditor to correct the deficiencies

Hundreds of on-site quality control reviews have been performed of nonfederal audit organizations by the federal government. The findings, reported by OMB, GAO, federal Inspectors General, and state audit organizations that also may conduct quality control review, noted audit deficiencies and problems such as:

- Little evidence that the nonfederal audit was properly planned, supervised, executed, or reviewed
- Minimal or no evidence of tests being made for compliance with applicable laws and regulations
- Insufficient evidence to document that the auditor made a study and evaluation of the controls or that controls work was or was not performed
- No evidence to demonstrate that tests were made of financial operations, transactions, account balances, and categories of accounts in the financial statements
- Material errors existed with respect to federal financial programs (i.e., significant federal financing programs were omitted from reports, numerous and at times large mathematical errors existed, editorial mistakes were present)
- Citation of inappropriate audit scopes assuming, according to examiners, that the nonfederal auditor did not misrepresent the scope of the audit altogether
- Unreported, but detected, instances of fraud, irregularities, significant findings of noncompliance, and internal control deficiencies
- Use of unqualified staff on the nonfederal audit team due to inappropriate or no licensing, conflicts affecting the nonfederal auditors' or the nonfederal audit organization's independence, and failure to meet the continuing professional education requirements, as required by *Government Auditing Standards*
- Failure of the nonfederal auditor or the nonfederal audit organization to satisfactorily correct earlier instances of substandard audit work[3]

Federal entity actions related to quality control reviews. A number of actions may be taken as a result of quality control reviews. Some of the more common reactions are detailed in the next sections.

Communication: Of on-site quality control review reports. With few exceptions, the result of an on-site quality control review of nonfederal audits will be communicated directly by the reviewing federal agency to the involved auditee and to all federal departments and agencies providing financial assistance to that auditee. In many instances, federal Inspectors General and their counterparts at state levels will simultaneously send the quality control review report directly to the AICPA and state boards of accountancy. There may be no "courtesy" or other direct

---

[3] *See the AICPA's **Audit Risk Alerts: State and Local Governmental Developments**.*

transmittal of the quality control review report to the nonfederal audit organization examined.

The practice of communicating to all but the auditor is of considerable concern to nonfederal audit organizations that undergo a quality control review. One concern is that federal quality control review examiners have erred in their review or in the reporting of the quality control review results. Additionally, once a report on a nonfederal audit organization is entered into a federal database, considerable effort must be expended by the nonfederal audit organization to correct any misinformation or have an erroneous file deleted.

The audit organization, having undergone an on-site quality control review, must accept the fact that any reported deficiencies, issues, or problems will be adjudicated by the involved federal agencies only through a formal, written appellate process. Extensive phone calls and face-to-face conferences are seldom worth the time. Any nonfederal audit organizations regularly involved with audits of government should periodically confirm or authenticate the nature of data residing in a government's file concerning the firm. Since the federal quality control review examiner will have communicated the report to many parties, this is no longer an issue between just the quality control review examiner and the audit organization. The aggrieved nonfederal audit organization must take the initiative to set the record straight. Rarely will the federal examiner monitor, correct, or delete quality control review files on his or her own volition.

Sanctions for substandard audits: serious. When a nonfederal audit organization fails to provide a timely, comprehensive, and responsive written rebuttal to an alleged substandard quality control review report, there exists the risk that the response will be deemed inadequate and sanctions could be imposed on the nonfederal audit organization immediately, even before the AICPA or a state board of accountancy is notified. Nonfederal audit organizations should be aware of the possibility that the federal quality control review examiner may disagree with the nonfederal audit organization's reply, but that the nonfederal auditor is not informed of the disagreement or a perceived inadequacy of the rebuttal. The nonfederal audit organization should also be concerned with the possibility that a federal examiner may begin proceedings to suspend or disbar the nonfederal audit organization from doing future audits without advance notice.

In addition to the harm to the professional reputation of a nonfederal audit organization, sanctions may be imposed on an individual nonfederal auditor and his or her nonfederal audit organization, or both. Examples of past sanctions include:

- *Training and practice sanctions*: Individual nonfederal auditors involved with substandard audits have been required, within a specified time period, to complete significant additional training directly relevant to government audits. A similar sanction might be imposed on the entire nonfederal audit organization or particular offending offices of the nonfederal audit organization. Similarly, federal agencies have been known to prohibit individual nonfederal auditors, specific offices, or entire firms from doing federal audits for significant periods of time, even years.

- *Direct financial sanctions*: If convinced that an audit is substandard, a federal examiner may proceed immediately to impose direct financial sanctions, such as dollar fines or cash penalties, on an individual auditor, the audit organization, or both. Also, convinced that a substandard audit has occurred, federal agencies have refused to pay the requested audit fee or have demanded that the nonfederal auditor or nonfederal audit organization refund the audit fee, if paid earlier.

    OMB Circular A-133 states that no audit costs may be charged to a federal award when the audit required by the circular has not been made or the audit is not in full compliance with the circular.

- *Suspension of a nonfederal auditor or nonfederal audit organization:* By Presidential executive order and departmental regulations,[4] the term *suspended* means

    > *The exclusion of a person, an audit organization, or an office of an audit organization, from receiving payments from any recipient or subrecipient of federal assistance for a temporary period, generally pending the completion of a further review, appeal, or reinstating provisos.*

Alternatively worded, no one doing business with the federal government is allowed to do business with a suspended party during the suspension period. A suspension is a government-wide exclusion of a party from assisting any recipient of federal assistance for a determined time period. Should the auditee or others receiving federal assistance continue to do business with a suspended party, the auditee or other federal recipient could itself have certain costs disallowed for payment, have its federal awards annulled or terminated, be served with stop-work orders, or be suspended or disbarred.

An action to suspend a party for a substandard audit can be instituted by any federal department or agency independent of, or in advance of, referring the accused party to appropriate professional organizations or a state board of accountancy for disciplinary or other remedial actions.

- *Debarment of an auditor or audit organization*: A *debarment* action refers to a government-wide prohibition on a party from providing services or doing business with any recipient or subrecipient of federal assistance over the debarred period. Whereas the period of suspension could be months or end upon completion of certain training, the debarment period could be significant, for example, for 10 years or more or forever. A debarment action could exclude debarred persons and nonfederal audit organizations from doing business directly with the federal government, or prohibit other entities that do business with the government from doing business with a disbarred party or organization.

    An action to debar a party or organization for a substandard audit can be instituted by any federal department or agency independent of, or in advance of, referring the accused party to appropriate professional organizations or a

---

[4] *See Presidential Executive Order No. 12549 and related implementing regulations published in the* **Federal Register** *of October 20, 1987, and the March 3, 1988, revision to OMB Circular A-102.*

state board of accountancy for disciplinary or other remedial actions. Should the auditee or others receiving federal assistance continue to do business with a debarred party, the auditee or other federal recipient could itself have certain costs disallowed for payment, have its federal awards annulled or terminated, be served with stop-work orders, or be suspended or disbarred.

- *Professional sanctions*: Certified public accountants, suspended or disbarred, or who are the subjects of an on-site quality control review report or other report alleging performance of substandard audits, will likely experience repercussions from the state boards of accountancy and the AICPA. Typically, state boards of accountancy, when notified of a suspension or debarment action, will institute a formal inquiry into the allegation. If the allegation of substandard performance is sustained, the practitioner's license to practice in that jurisdiction(s) will be revoked. The AICPA could separately review the facts, sustain the allegation that a substandard audit has indeed been done, and conclude that the deficient audit constitutes an "act discreditable to the profession," in violation of the profession's Code of Ethics Rule 501.

DEFENSE CONTRACT AUDIT AGENCY

The Defense Contract Audit Agency (DCAA) is an external audit function, within the Office of the Secretary of DoD, responsible for performing all contract audits for the department. This includes contracts issued by the DoD, as well as DoD constituent agencies of the Departments of Army, Navy, and Air Force. The director of DCAA is a senior executive of the federal service, appointed by the secretary of DoD. DCAA itself is staffed by career professionals appointed under a meritorious process that requires each appointee to meet certain academic and experience qualifications.

DCAA: Background

Because of the business acumen and accounting and financial management expertise acquired by auditing cost-type, fixed price, and other forms of contracts awarded by the DoD to thousands of corporate organizations and educational institutions, DCAA also provides expert advice and accounting and financial advisory services to those DoD components responsible for procurement and contract administration, most frequently in connection with the negotiation, administration, and settlement of any significant DoD contract or subcontract. Other federal departments and agencies, through cost-reimbursable interagency agreements, retain DCAA professionals to provide expert consultation, audits, and other assistance with respect to the contracts and grants awarded by these agencies to private companies, educational institutions, and nonprofit organizations.

The need for and origin of DCAA dates to the era of World War II, and perhaps earlier, when each of the military services desired its own contract audit function, with its own attendant instructions, regulations, and cost accounting rulings. Uniformity of defense contract policy, project management, contract evaluations, pricing reviews, and audits was nonexistent. A consistency of guidance was needed, particularly for contract administration and audit. In 1962, the DoD secretary examined the feasibility of centrally managing the field activities concerned with contract administration and audit. The outcome of this initiative was the establishment of a single contract audit function, the Defense Contract Audit Agency, in January 1965.

DCAA: Organizational Structure

DCAA consists of several organizational components, some managing hundreds of the 300 subordinate field audit offices, branches, suboffices, or resident offices located throughout the United States and overseas. Where the amount of audit workload justifies, DCAA's practice is to physically locate a permanent team of auditors and support staff on-site, in contractors' offices, facilities, and plants.

To the individual service departments, Army, Navy (the Marines being part of the Navy Department), and Air Force, DCAA is an external audit function focusing on the accounting, reporting, billing, and payment of *allowable costs* (i.e., those costs defined by federal law and regulation as permissible charges) charged to and claimed by the contractors and subcontractors of DoD.

Within each service department— Army, Navy, and Air Force—there exists an internal audit organization, also professionally staffed, performing the full range of examinations and reviews of the department's own management, administrative, and operational activities.

STATE AND LOCAL GOVERNMENT AUDITORS

Because laws affecting the lead auditor position for states and local governments vary, generalization is almost precluded, and difficulty arises in describing the specifics of each lead governmental audit position. In most instances, though, the governments have passed enabling legislation for the lead audit position that specifically delineates several aspects of the position, such as: nature of appointment, term of office, organizational stature, scope of investigative and audit authority, organizational and reporting independence, and size and salaries of employed auditors. While the lead governmental auditor could be appointed or elected, the staffs of the lead auditor are most often career civil servant appointments.

State Auditors: Elected or Appointed

The chief or lead auditor position of a state could retain one of a variety of titles. Some titles include: State Auditor, Auditor General, Legislative Auditor, Comptroller, Examiner Of Public Accounts, and, in one state, Comptroller General. Most of the laws governing appointment or election to a state's lead audit position include prerequisite conditions, such as minimal age, citizenship and minimal years as a citizen, minimal years of residency in that state, and, at times, minimal years of specified experience. Laws of a few states, but by no means a significant number, require incumbents to be a Certified Public Accountant or possess a certain competency in accounting.

In some states, the lead auditor is elected in a general state-wide election. Whether elected or appointed, the staffs of the state auditor are most often career civil servants who hold appointed positions. The state auditor, if elected, is viewed, under generally accepted auditing standards and *Government Auditing Standards*, as independent of the respective executive and legislative branches, answerable primarily to the state's electorate, and often removable from office only by recall or impeachment-type proceedings.

The state's lead auditor may hold the title "legislative auditor," an appointed position where the incumbent would be independent with respect to audits and reviews of the executive branch, but not independent for matters involving the legislative branch. If the government's lead auditor is appointed, law would describe whether the executive or legislative branch has appointive authority for the position. The appointee could serve for a fixed term specified in law or serve "at the pleasure" of the appointing body or governmental executive for an unspecified or indefinite term.

Audit authority and responsibilities of state auditors can be extensive and include the responsibility to conduct: examinations; financial and operational audits; financial statement audits; and special reviews and examinations of state departments, agencies, and offices, and possibly state authorities, commissions, various governing boards, educational institutions, and government contractors and grantees that receive or expend the government monies. In connection with the federal government's Single Audit Act, state auditors exercise considerable oversight and review authority of the single audits made within their jurisdictions, and in conjunction or coordination with the federal government's Inspectors General.

Local Government Auditors

Auditors at the county, city, and municipal levels are generally appointed to their positions by the local government's chief elected executive or the legislative council or governing body. Almost no lead local government auditor is elected to the auditor's office. If appointed, the lead local government audit position may be a civil service or meritorious position. The vast majority of audits performed by these auditors are referred to as financial-related audits, as defined in the *Government Auditing Standards*. These auditors, being primarily appointed, must make a careful review of the independence provisions of the *Government Auditing Standards*, particularly provisions relating to circumstances common to these types of audit positions.

INDEPENDENT PUBLIC ACCOUNTANTS

To comply with *Government Auditing Standards*, independent accounting firms auditing governmental financial statements, and those performing attestation engagements of governments, must be licensed certified public accountants or persons working for certified public accounting firms or a government auditing organization. A provision in *Government Auditing Standards* also permits public accountants (who are not certified public accountants) licensed on or before December 31, 1970, or persons working for a public accounting firm (not a certified public accounting firm) licensed on or before December 31, 1970, to perform government audits. Individual public accountants and their accounting firms must meet the licensing requirements and be in conformance with public accountancy laws and regulations of the jurisdiction (1) where the audit or attestation work is performed, *and* (2) the state in which the public accountant and their firms are licensed.

The vast preponderance of financial statement audits of state and local governments are performed by independent CPA firms. Similarly, independent accounting firms conduct or have major roles in the financial statement audits of almost all federal departments and agencies. Accounting firms typically are retained by federal, state, and local governments under competitively awarded multiyear contracts. If retained solely for the audit of a government's financial statements, the governmental auditee is concurrently the audit client.

However, if the accounting firm is also retained to perform an audit pursuant to the federal government's Single Audit Act, the relationship is slightly more complicated. Under the Single Audit Act, a state or local government may be the auditee. But while the government is the auditee, the audited government is not the full or sole audit client. By the Single Audit Act and federal regulations, the independent auditor has reporting responsibilities to a range of "clients" in addition to the contracting government. For example, the Single Audit Act imposes, as a condition of federal assistance, the requirement that the auditee's annual comprehensive audit report be distributed, within 30 days after completion, to every federal organization that provided funds to the governmental auditee.

OTHER AUDITORS OF GOVERNMENT

Nomenclature other than the above classifications can be used to identify or describe auditors who might participate in the audit of a governmental entity. Terminology discussed in the following paragraphs could apply equally to independent CPA firms retained under contract to audit the government or auditors who are employees of a governmental auditee.

Principal Auditor

To be a *principal auditor* of a general or primary local government, the auditor, at a minimum, (1) must be engaged by the general or primary local government as the principal auditor for the financial reporting entity, *and* (2) must be responsible for auditing the primary government's general fund. The principal auditor, of course, must be independent of the financial reporting entity and its component units, and must decide whether to assume responsibility for the work of participating auditors or make a separate reference to the work of these auditors at the time of reporting on the audit.

Component Unit Auditor

A *component unit auditor* must be independent of general primary government and the component unit's government of which the component unit auditor is to conduct an audit. The component unit auditor may not necessarily be the same as the primary government's auditor (i.e., the principal auditor). For that reason, the component unit auditor must be prepared to, and is required to, facilitate the principal auditor's audit of the primary government through:

- Providing a representation of the component unit auditor's independence to the principal auditor
- Communicating an awareness to management of the component unit that the component unit's financial statements are required to be incorporated into those of the primary government
- Permitting the principal auditor to review audit documentation relating to the component unit's audit
- Undertaking to restate the component unit's financial statements to a basis of accounting or a fiscal year that parallels the fiscal period used for the primary government's financial statements, although that basis of accounting or fiscal year may not be used by the component unit for its separate financial reporting

Joint Audits

Governmental statutes or regulations may require or provide for the retention or use of another audit organization by the principal auditor, that is, a *joint audit*. In such circumstances, the audit could be performed either (1) in the role of a joint auditor, or (2) in a contractor/subcontractor relationship. This other auditor could be a state or other governmental audit organization, or a minority or small accounting firm. Each governmental auditor who cosigns a joint-audit audit report must meet the independence standards of the *Government Auditing Standards*, plus each audit organization must meet the required continuing professional education conditions and organizational quality control requirements, and apply the government field-work and audit reporting standards.

The AICPA's generally accepted auditing standards do not provide for two or more auditors to divide the responsibility for an audit of basic financial statements. That is, each audit firm or individual auditor who signs the audit report is separately and collectively liable for the entire audit. A cosigned audit report is viewed by the AICPA as if *each* audit firm or individual auditor is separately expressing an audit opinion on the financial statements and as if *each* is attesting that they have fully complied with the *Government Auditing Standards*.

Joint Ventures

The AICPA views a *joint venture* of two or more auditors as a separate legal entity. In this instance, the audit report must be signed with the joint venture name. However, the AICPA warns audit firms in a joint venture relationship to closely examine the ethics and rules relating to the use of fictitious names and the fact that state accountancy licensing statutes may not recognize a joint venture audit firm.

PART II

FEDERAL BUDGETING, ACCOUNTING, AND FINANCIAL STATEMENTS

5 THE FEDERAL BUDGET

Work on the federal budget never ceases. In practice, on any given year, a department or agency is addressing the accounting and budgeting of multiple years. For example, at the same time a current year's budget (e.g., fiscal year 2005) is being executed and accounted for, budget proposals for fiscal year 2006 are being vigorously defended before congressional committees. In addition, during the same year, agency executives are discussing with OMB the proposed budgets for fiscal years 2007 and 2008. Finally, also in the same year, financial personnel are concerned with applying the appropriate accounting and reporting to expired or "old" appropriations (e.g., for the years 2003 and 2004).

MULTIYEAR BUDGETS

The focus of the news media, committees of Congress, the President, and the public is most often concentrated on a single federal fiscal year: the next one. However, the compilation of federal budget estimates requires a multiyear perspective. The number of years that must be considered when structuring the budget estimates could include as many as eight, possibly more, years.

Budget indicator	*Period or year referred to*
PY (Past year)	The fiscal year immediately preceding the current year; the last completed fiscal year
PY- 1 (Past year-1)	The fiscal year immediately preceding the past year
CY (Current year)	The fiscal year immediately preceding the budget year
BY (Budget year)	The next fiscal year for which estimates are submitted to Congress
BY+1 (Budget year + 1)	The fiscal year following the budget year
BY+2 (Budget year + 2)	The second fiscal year following the budget year
BY+3 (Budget year + 3)	The third fiscal year following the budget year
BY+4 (Budget year + 4)	The fourth fiscal year following the budget year

For a federal agency, congressional enactment of the agency's appropriation legislation is the defining event from an accounting viewpoint—formally recording the appropriation is the first entry of a fiscal year, in federal accounting. The accounting for budget execution, as noted in an earlier chapter, must, by law, cover the current fiscal year and the two fiscal years after the expiration of the appropriation. Then, any remaining obligated balances of an appropriation are transferred to the expired or merged (or "M") accounts in the Treasury Department, where such balances remain available for several years to meet claims that might be submitted against earlier valid obligations.

BUDGET CYCLE

The federal budget cycle might better be viewed as a never-ending process rather than a cycle, which implies an event with a distinct beginning and end. In practice, the cycle consists of several phases, not always clearly distinguishable, but always present.

Phase I: Budget Preparation
Phase II: Congressional Action
Phase III: Budget Execution
Phase IV: Review and Audit

Phase I: Budget Preparation Phase

The *budget preparation phase* begins some 15 to 18 months (or more) before the start of the fiscal year to which it will apply. During this phase there is a continuous exchange of information and decision making by the President, assisted by OMB, and heads of individual departments, agencies, and special advisors.

Partial budgeting prohibited. Federal departments and agencies are prohibited by law and OMB regulations from deliberately minimizing budget requests by a ploy of submitting estimates for partial or less than full funding of anticipated programs. For example, requests for major procurement programs must provide, by the years involved, for the entire cost of the program (with certain legally permitted exceptions, such as reclamation, rivers and harbors, and flood control projects).

There is an exception to this partial funding prohibition. Although OMB budget guidance requires that departmental and agency budget requests include the effect of inflation, the budget estimates will *not* necessarily include an allowance for the *full* rate of anticipated inflation. As an example, for discretionary programs, approved departmental totals may include an allowance for less than the full rate of anticipated inflation or even no allowance for inflation, as determined by OMB. Often these deliberate underestimates for inflation are extensively and heatedly discussed in Congress and are the subject of much coverage by the news media. Approved agency totals must reflect the full inflation rate where such an allowance is required by law and a decision is made by OMB not to propose an inflation rate less than is required.

Confidential information. Budget information compiled or considered by the executive branch has historically been viewed as privileged information of the executive branch of government. A specific regulation (OMB Circular A-11) sets executive branch policy with respect to disclosure of budget preparation data. By the Budget and Accounting Act of 1921, the President is required to submit an annual budget request to Congress. This same law prohibits an agency submission to Congress in any other manner, unless at the formal request of either House of Congress.

OMB Circular A-11 emphasizes that the executive branch communications that led to the preparation of the executive branch budget request are not to be disclosed by agencies or by those who prepared the budget request. Maintaining the confidential nature of agency submissions, requests, recommendations, support materials, and similar communications is important because these documents are an integral part of the decision-making process by which the President resolves budget issues and develops recommendations for Congress. Budget decisions are not final until the President submits the budget request to Congress. Thus, until released by the President, information relating to the executive branch's proposed budget is considered "*executive privileged.*"

Office of Management and Budget and Congressional Budget Office. In budget preparation phase, iterations of views and exchanges of financial and operational information transpire between various departments and agencies and OMB, beginning with the submission of an agency's initial budget requests. Once more definite, and after the initial "*pass-backs*" of the early OMB budget decisions, agencies provide revised budget data, consistent with Presidential guidelines. These budget data are collected and processed by OMB in a computer system, and ultimately compiled into the final budget request submitted by the President to Congress.

The Congressional Budget Office (CBO) is an agency in the legislative branch, responsible to Congress, that has no role in preparing the proposed budget and issues no regulations or guidance concerning the executive branch's budget process. CBO and OMB, though, must cooperatively calculate federal deficit estimates and measure compliance with congressional budget targets as congressional committees proceed through the budget deliberation process. CBO calculations must use the "scorekeeping" conventions of House and Senate budget committees. Monitoring by CBO, on behalf of the Congress, is necessary to assess compliance with congressional budget targets and budget agreements between the executive and legislative branches. In contrast, OMB, an entity in the Executive Office of the President, has extensive control and monitoring responsibilities for preparing and executing federal budgets. Exhibit 5.1 illustrates the executive branch's budget process.

Exhibit 5.1: Overview of the budget process

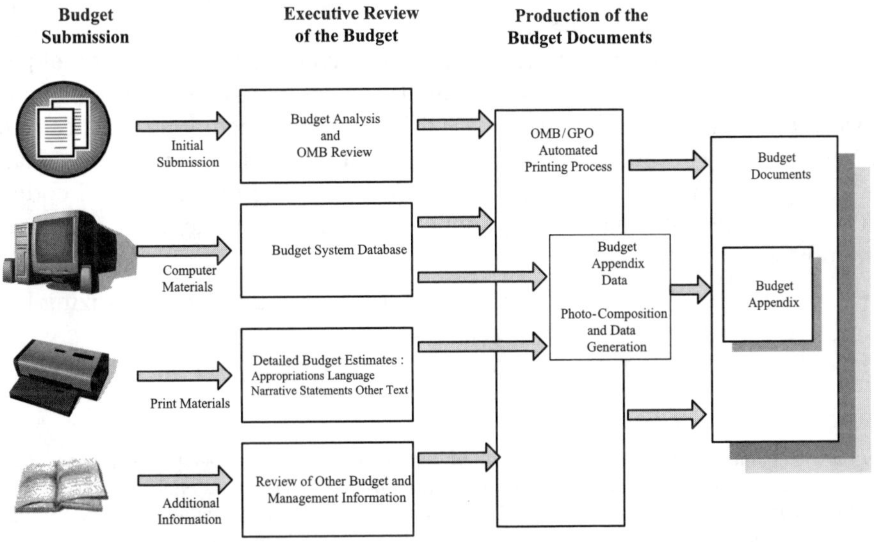

OMB annually issues guidance to executive branch departments and agencies relating to preparation and submission of budget estimates.[1] OMB guidance is both government-wide and agency-specific, including details such as formats, tables, schedule contents, definitions, and codes that must be used in submitting the department and agency final budget estimates to OMB. The guidance for individual departments and agencies generally relates to subjects such as ceilings and limitations (dollars, personnel, other resources, geographic operations, program levels, etc.), restrictions, new or revised policy direction, and so on. The issuance of this guidance is followed by innumerable meetings between OMB and department and agency executive management. On occasion, heads of federal organizations who disagree with the impositions of OMB make direct appeals to the President. It is rare, though, that OMB guidance is at odds with Presidential intent.

Support for department proposals. Agency budget requests are the output of a comprehensive financial system that integrates analyses, planning, evaluation, budgeting, accounting, and reporting. Budget estimates ultimately sent to Congress reflect OMB and Presidential views on the scope, content, and quality of federal agencies and all programs and activities for which the agency is responsible. For example, the budget request of a single agency must consider the roles, support responsibilities, and costs to state and local governments, academic institutions, nonprofit organizations, and even foreign governments. These budget requests will be compiled in a variety of funding formats. Congress could provide financing for a federal agency's operations through any or a combination of: direct appropriations, contract authority, reimbursable authority, loans, loan guarantees, grants, contracts, formula entitlement-type financing, and the like.

Budget preparation requires federal entities to develop considerable demographic and economic data that, depending on the nature of the program, could also entail the aggregation of information for over 500 congressional districts, 3,000 counties, and over 50,000 cities, municipalities, towns, townships, other special units of government, and hundreds of thousands of nonprofit, academic, and corporate organizations. All of this information must be compiled in a manner that permits its examination and evaluation by OMB and Congress in an expeditious manner.

Nature of agency budget requests. OMB budget preparation guidance requires agencies to segregate budget requests by the nature of the estimate, for example, regular, supplemental, or multiyear funding requests. The regular annual budget estimates must reflect all financial requirements anticipated at the time of budget submission by several categories.

- *Continuing activities*, including those for which additional authorizing legislation is required for the budget year
- Authorized activities that are to be *proposed activities* for the budget year

---

[1] *For decades, the primary source of detailed budget guidance has been promulgated by OMB through two of its circulars, A-11 and A-34, updated and redistributed annually (OMB Circular A-11, **Preparation and Submission of Budget Estimates,** and OMB Circular A-34, **Instructions on Budget Execution**). Definitions in this chapter relating to budget preparation and execution appear in these circulars.*

- Amounts necessary to meet *other specific financial liabilities* of activities imposed by law

No supplemental estimates or upward adjustments of past years' funding levels can be submitted by departments unless these adjustments are for circumstances that were unforeseen or due to subsequent action by Congress.

Phase II: Congressional Action Phase

Congress can approve, change, disapprove, or ignore the President's proposed budget. The congressional action phase generally consists of two sets of hearings:

1. Hearings for authorization or continuation of a federal program or activity
2. Hearings for funding or approval of an appropriation, or other funding of a program or activity

These phases are often comprised of several activities involving interested parties and, at times, even foreign countries:

- The President could, but generally does not appear before committees of Congress to defend, explain, and justify the need for the proposed programs and the level of dollars requested; OMB and agency representatives generally will.
- Congress may hold hearings attended by citizens, state and local governments, companies, nonprofit organizations, the general public, and even foreign governments to support or oppose particular programs or levels of requested financing.
- Special reviews and studies could be made and submitted to Congress, and Congress itself will authorize independent reviews to provide data that are valuable in reaching conclusions on various budget requests. CBO is a valuable contributor to these efforts.
- Executive sessions and private meetings are held among members and committees of Congress and persons and organizations involved or interested in particular programs.
- Continual release of budget information is made to the public media relating to suggested alternatives, program options, possible tax consequences, and the effect on projected debt ceilings of various programs. The purpose of such publicity is generation of interest, support, or opposition to competing positions on these programs. Sooner or later Congress, through its committees, must develop legislated financial plans for the authorization and appropriation bills proposed, debated, changed, and then voted upon by Congress.

Once congressional consensus is reached, the various appropriations are submitted to the President for review and approval or veto. Note that the submissions are not made to the President as a single package, but rather in the form of several appropriation laws.

Congressional approval of a program, with permission to obligate the federal government and spend federal monies, is referred to as an *appropriation* (i.e., the legal or budget authority that makes funds available to individual departments and agencies for spending). The appropriation may be a *single-year* or *multiyear appro-*

priation. In some cases, the congressional *budget authority* may be *permanent budget authority*, in which case funds become annually available to an agency without further congressional action.

On occasion, Congress will not complete action on all budget requests before the beginning of a fiscal year. In such circumstances, Congress may enact a *continuing resolution*, temporary financing authority for an agency to continue operations usually, but not always, until an appropriation is approved. While under a continuing resolution, the federal agency must conform to certain fiscal restraints, including these three:

1. Generally, the federal agency may not undertake any new initiatives.
2. The federal agency must maintain its rate of expenditure at the same level of the preceding program year.
3. If one House of Congress has acted on an agency's budget request, then the federal agency may not exceed the expenditure rate of that action or the expenditure rate of the last year's appropriation, whichever is less.

Phase III: Budget Execution Phase

An agency's accounting during the budget execution phase is directly related to the status of appropriations for which it is responsible. Examples of status include whether the appropriation is unexpired and still active or whether the appropriation is expired and inactive.

Active, unexpired appropriations. Once passed by Congress and approved by the President, appropriations and other approved budget authority, in combination, become the financial operating plan for the federal government for a fiscal year. Within each department and agency, several activities must occur:

- At each department and agency, there must exist a system of accounting and financial controls for recording apportioned appropriated funds throughout the year to ensure that legislated goals and objectives are achieved and that budget deficiencies do not occur.
- The specific appropriation(s) (i.e., there may be more than one appropriation for which an agency is responsible) or other budget authority approved by Congress becomes the financial budget and operating plan for an agency. Activities financed by these appropriations must be monitored, controlled, and tracked to ensure full compliance with the intent of Congress.
- Accounting for the execution of a federal entity's budget will span several fiscal years.
  - The initial accounting entry to formally record appropriation(s) is prepared by each responsible federal entity after the Treasury Department and OMB establish an account number for that appropriation or other budget authority. This will be done at the outset of a fiscal year.
  - A current accounting is maintained by all federal entities responsible for an appropriation(s) throughout the active or unexpired years of an appropriation(s) or budget authority.

- Once an appropriation has expired, a detailed accounting and reporting is required for legally incurred obligations and expenditures for two fiscal years after the fiscal year in which the appropriation expired.

Expired, inactive appropriations. Two years following the expiration of an appropriation, there is another accounting and reporting phase. In all instances where there remain outstanding obligated amounts from earlier expired appropriations, the amounts or balances are transferred to the *merged* or *"M" accounts* of the Treasury Department. In recent years, Congress has limited the spending viability of "M" account balances to five years. Historically, balances of expired appropriations that related to valid outstanding obligations at the time of expiration would remain available in the "M" accounts forever for payment of these obligations.

In comparison to the typical one-year accounting for a corporate entity, federal agencies are legally required to maintain formal accounts and make reports for each appropriation or budget authority for a period that could span 10 years (e.g., the current year of the appropriation, the two additional years following expiration of the appropriation, and the five-year "M" period).

This accountable time span is illustrated in Exhibit 5.2.

Exhibit 5.2: Illustration of appropriation account closing for fixed period appropriations

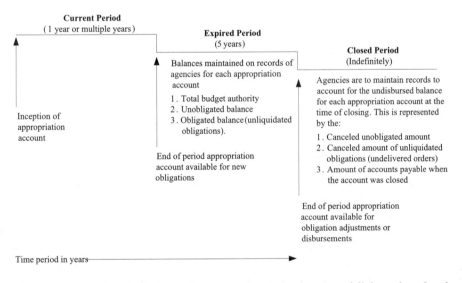

Entity controls. Each federal agency must, by law, establish and maintain systems of accounting and internal controls to provide reliable accounting for the activities of that federal establishment. These systems are the basis for preparing and supporting the budget request of the federal establishment. Additionally, the agency systems must provide accurate financial information for reporting externally to Congress, the President, OMB, and the Department of Treasury, and for internal agency needs related to managing, controlling, and reporting on current operations. Agency systems of accounting and controls must provide accurate and timely information on actual obligations, outlays, unexpended and expended budgetary fund balances, and other resources. Agency internal controls must be established to ensure that conditions, restrictions, limitations, and other provisions of the appropriation or other laws are continually and consistently met and that the assets, investments, and other resources of the federal government are constantly safeguarded.

Section 3679 of the Revised Statutes. Section 3679 of the Revised Statutes mandates the head of each agency, subject to approval by OMB, prescribe a system for the administrative control of funds. This system of control, which cannot be inconsistent with any budgeting requirements or prescribed accounting procedures, must be designed to:

- Restrict obligations and expenditures against each appropriation or fund to the amount of OMB apportionments or reapportionments.
- Enable the agency head to fix responsibility for the obligation or expenditure in excess of an OMB apportionment or reapportionment.
- Comply with OMB requirements, which are but one of many external (to an individual federal establishment) fiscal and financial criteria that federal systems of accounting and controls must achieve. Congress outlined numerous additional accounting, controls, and financial reporting criteria standards in financial management legislation of the 1990s, in particular the Chief Financial Officers Act.

Budgeting concepts. The federal government has made various attempts to achieve more precision in estimating required resources, in monitoring the expenditure rate of budgeted funds, and in determining the cumulative costs of agency programs. These efforts are dictated by concerns over the efficiency and effectiveness with which budgeted funds are being utilized and whether the objectives that Congress noted in laws are being attained, and in an economical manner. Not to be overlooked, though, is the fact that the budget is a statutory directive, violations of which must be reported to OMB, the President, and Congress.

PPBS, ZBB, AND MBO CONCEPTS

Three budgeting or planning concepts have been applied at various times by the federal government in an attempt to better manage federal monies. Still in use, but more popular in the 1960s, is PPBS (planning, programming, budgeting systems). At times, some federal organizations have found merit in attempting to apply ZBB (zero-based budgeting) and MBO (management by objectives) to federal activities. Departments and agencies, however, were formally relieved of compiling budget requests in the ZBB format in 1981 when OMB rescinded Circular A-115, ending the use of ZBB in the federal government.

In the 1980s, some federal agencies took advantage of an option and were relieved of the responsibility to compile, defend, execute, account, and report their financial requests and activities under the PPBS concept. Almost 50 years after its adoption, PPBS continues to be the principal financial management and control process of the Department of Defense.

PLANNING, PROGRAMMING, BUDGETING SYSTEM

PPBS, implemented by Presidential directive in the 1960s, was intended to be the integrated process by which federal organizations planned, managed, and made decisions about the types, nature, and funding of programs. Where PPBS was successfully integrated into the decision-making process of a department or agency, the concept provided a sound basis for determining, monitoring, and accounting for federal programs and activities. There are several phases involved in a PPBS:

- *Planning:* Study agency objectives; construct alternative approaches to achieve objectives; identify and assess contingencies.
- *Programming:* The structure of activities consistent with an agency's objectives and expected outputs in relation to the estimated cost of resources needed to attain those objectives and outputs.
- *Budgeting:* Request and defense of funds to the President and Congress in support of the agency's programmed activities as approved, the budget request became the operating plan for the agency.
- *Execution:* Subsequently, the Department of Defense formalized a fourth phase: the execution phase. Thus, in the 1990s, one will encounter the term PPB*E*S.

PPBS included several processes or stages. Its activities could span several fiscal years and required the participation and active involvement of several federal entities including the President, OMB, Congress, and the Department of Treasury. Exhibit 5.3 highlights the several concurrent activities of PPBS.

FEDERAL ACCOUNTING

The government-wide uniform accounting and reporting standards are developed by FASAB, after being jointly agreed on by the Secretary of the Treasury, director of the Office of Management and Budget, and the Comptroller General. FASAB's standards are then incorporated into the federal government's standard general ledger account and transaction structure by the Treasury Department. The Federal Financial Management Improvement Act of 1996 (P.L. 104-208) sets forth a mandate that agencies comply with *"applicable federal accounting standards, and the United States Government Standard General Ledger at the transaction level."*

Federal accounting, like other accountancy specialties, adopted or requires the use of phrases, terms, concepts, and conventions having specialized meaning. These words have significance to practitioners involved directly with a federal department or agency or indirectly through audits, federal contracts, grants, loans or loan guarantee programs, or other types of federal financial assistance.

A federal entity's systems of accounting, controls, and financial reporting must be sufficiently integrated to provide complete financial disclosure of each appropriation, budgetary authority, and all other resources received under some law of Congress. That same system must also be capable of providing data on several accounting bases: types of funds, specific obligations, accruals, costs and accrued expenditures, and cash disbursement, to cite a few. Additionally, this financial system must provide financial information by the entity's component organizations and programs. The system may have to report by states and tens of thousands of counties, cities, academic institutions, and over 100,000 nonprofit organizations.

Exhibit 5.3: Responsibilities for planning, programming, budgeting, and execution in the Federal Government

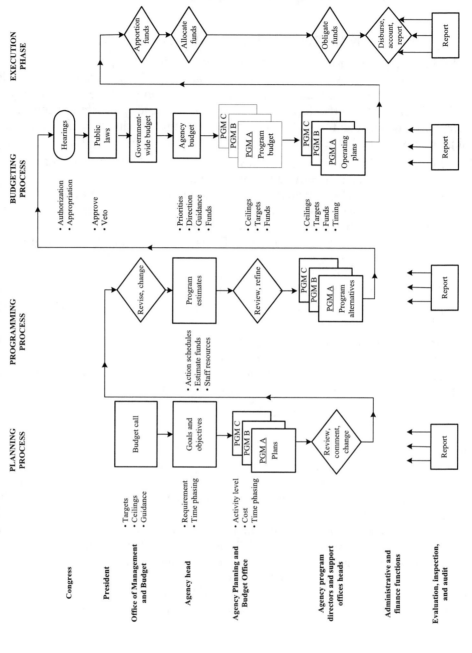

Basis for Federal Accounting

For the better part of 200 years, federal accounting was equated almost exclusively with *budgetary accounting* or cash accounting and dealt with monitoring compliance with the legal restraints and controls over congressionally appropriated funds. Of itself, however, the budgetary accounting basis did not provide a full accounting, was not an accurate and timely reporting of program costs, and did not provide for reporting of long-term investments, capital versus operating expenses, or outputs and outcomes. Other accounting bases requires an agency's system to accumulate total costs, true costs, full costs, accrued costs, whatever the source of financial support or however many appropriations were assigned to an entity. This latter accounting need requires the agency to also perform *proprietary accounting*.

Budgetary accounting is construed by some to be a separate accounting requirement or even a separate system. Budgetary accounting can be viewed as a bookkeeping refinement supporting fund accounting, operational accounting, and cost accounting requirements of a federal agency. In practice, concurrent accounting entries are made to both budgetary accounts and proprietary accounts. The proprietary accounts are not separate, but part of an accounting and reporting continuum for each congressional appropriation.

Two financial systems are not operating in parallel within a federal agency. A federal agency's single integrated financial system must record all financial activity for the agency at the elemental transaction level and provide both budgetary and proprietary data from this single system. Exhibit 5.4 highlights the economic or fiscal activities for which there must be an accounting, budgetary or proprietary. In total, there are some 15 specific events in the life cycle of a federal transaction for which an accounting entry must be made.

Exhibit 5.4: Financing federal programs and activities

Responsible Body

	Congress	*Treasury*	*OMB*	*Individual entities*
A	1. Appropriation of $			
C	2. Allocation of the $			
C	3. Other budget authority			
O		4. Appropriation warrant		
U				
N			5. Apportionment	
T				6. Allotment
A				7. Allowances
B				8. Commitments
L				9. Obligations
E				10. Accrued expenditures
E				11. Costs
V				12. Accruals
E		13. Disbursements		
N				14. Expired accounts
T				
		15. Merged accounts		

Budgetary Accounting

The term *budgetary accounting* encompasses a breadth of accounting transactions, each with legal or economic implications. In Exhibit 5.4, the events beginning with the congressional appropriation (event 1) through the outlay (e.g., disbursements) (event 13) are generally viewed as the scope of federal *budgetary accounting*.

Exhibit 5.5: Transaction life cycle for purchase of materials

		Recorded in period which		
Economic event/activity	*Order is placed*	*Materials are delivered*	*Materials are used*	*Vendor is paid*
Order placed for material	As an obligation			
Materials received		Liquidate earlier obligation		
Add to inventory		Increase inventory account		
Billed by vendor		Increase payable account		
Used/consumed inventory			As an applied cost or expense	
Pay vendor				As a cash disbursement
Fiscal period	**1**	**2**	**3**	**4**

Fund Accounting

In federal accounting, the term *fund* is synonymous with a congressional appropriation or legal budget authority directing an agency to incur obligations and make expenditures on behalf of the federal government. In some instances, an agency is responsible for a single appropriation (i.e., fund), which simplifies the accounting considerably. More common is the circumstance where an agency is responsible for more than one appropriation or source of budget authority.

Funding federal operations. Funding of federal operations by Congress is a two-step process:

1. The congressional "authorization" to operate and spend for a program or activity
2. The subsequent congressional "appropriation" of monies providing specific expenditure authority

Both steps are necessary; mere authorization of a program by Congress does not grant permission to a federal agency to spend federal money.

Before obligations or expenditures can be incurred or cash disbursed by a federal agency, an *appropriation* must be made available by Congress. "Availability" means (1) that an appropriation law exists granting an agency permission to enter into obligations or make expenditures, and (2) this appropriation must be current or unexpired for the period during which the obligation or expenditure occurs. The use or availability of appropriations, once enacted by Congress and then apportioned by OMB, is governed by:

- The terms of the appropriation act
- Legislation, if any, authorizing the activity or program
- General statutory provisions that allow or prohibit certain uses of appropriated funds
- Numerous Treasury Department and OMB regulations
- General rules that have been developed through decisions of the Comptroller General (who heads GAO) and the courts[2]

GAO decisions: like law to agencies. Congressional authorizations and appropriations, together with the Constitution and GAO decisions, form the basis of the legal precedence governing federal expenditures. Based on other laws, the Comptroller General has the authority to render GAO decisions concerning the availability of appropriated funds, often relating to transactions made by federal disbursing, certifying, and other accountable officers. Individual claimants may also request review or reconsideration of earlier settlements by the Comptroller General that disallowed claims in whole or part. GAO decisions are binding on executive branch agencies, but not on a private party who, if dissatisfied, retains the right to pursue the issue in the courts.

"Laundering funds" not permitted. Federal entities cannot thwart the intent of Congress by transferring part of their appropriation to another entity. GAO has maintained that funds appropriated under one law are not available by means of a transfer to a working fund or another appropriation to be spent for purposes not permitted under the original appropriation from which the transfer was made. That is, the original terms and conditions of an appropriation cannot be "laundered," or another appropriation or fund cannot be used to "change the color" (i.e., no party can change the terms, conditions, limits, period of availability, or other prohibitions imposed by Congress) of an appropriation or fund. The use of a specific appropriation to pay obligations under another appropriation during a temporary exhaustion of funds is also in violation of 31 United States Code 628, even though repayment may be contemplated after the supplemental appropriation is made.[3]

Other spending authority. An appropriation law is the most common means by which Congress provides spending authority to a federal agency. In some cases, though, the authorizing legislation may provide *authority to borrow* or *contract authority*.

- *Authority to borrow:* The statutory authority that permits a federal agency to incur obligations and make payments for specified purposes out of borrowed monies.
- *Contract authority:* The statutory authority under which contracts or other obligations may be entered into prior to a congressional appropriation for the payment of such obligations. A later-enacted appropriation would provide the cash to liquidate such obligations.

---

[2] *U.S. GAO, **Principles of Federal Appropriation Law,** Washington, DC, 1982, pp.1–2.*
[3] *See also 36 Comp. Gen. 386.*

It is important to note that budget authority does not provide authorization to a federal entity to incur new or additional obligations, but merely to meet earlier obligations and liabilities of the government.

NATURE OF CONGRESSIONAL ALLOCATIONS

An *allocation* of an appropriation is a transfer by Congress of obligational authority from one federal entity to another to carry out the purpose of the parent appropriation. It is an amount of obligational authority set aside by Congress in a transfer appropriation account (i.e., an allocation account) to carry out the purposes of the parent appropriation or fund. A "transfer appropriation account" is a separate account established to receive (and later obligate and expend) appropriations allocated from a parent appropriation that is under the control of another department or agency.

OMB APPORTIONMENT

An *apportionment* is a formal distribution made by OMB to federal entities of amounts available to an agency for obligation from an appropriation or other budget authority. OMB apportions appropriated monies to agencies by (1) making specific amounts available for specified time periods, generally the fiscal quarters of the year (referred to as a *"Category A" apportionment*), or (2) making specific amounts available for particular activities, projects, objects, and so on (referred to as a *"Category B" apportionment*). The apportionment of funds is supported by a formal written notice from OMB (SF 132) to the federal agency describing the specifics of any apportionments of a congressional appropriation.

AGENCY ALLOTMENTS

For control purposes, heads of departments and agencies must limit or restrict the rate of spending of apportioned appropriations or other budget authority or funds within their organizations. The term used for this action is allotment. An *allotment* is a formal delegation of authority by the head of a federal entity to departments, programs, and/or employees to incur obligations within the amount allotted. An *advice of allotment* is the formal notification to agency allottees of their responsibility for funds.

AGENCY ALLOWANCES

In some agencies, allotted funds are further subdivided through issuance of *advices of allowances* to agency personnel. Unlike allotments, though, agencies may not record journal entries to formalize this subaccounting for agency funds. The detailed accounting and fund tracking generally occurs at program or allottee levels in an agency, although there may be instances in which certain funds are recorded and accounted for above allottee levels.

AGENCY OBLIGATIONS

An obligation is a legal event, meaning two or more parties have rights, liabilities, and obligations. From an accounting perspective, the incurrence of an obligation is an economic event that must be entered in the official records of the government. Thus, the term *obligation* has accounting and legal connotations. *Obligations* are the amounts of orders placed, contracts awarded, services received, grants issued, and similar transactions during a fiscal period that will require payments in the same or a future period. Once an obligation is incurred with respect to a specific appropriation or budget authority, the same amount cannot be used for another obligation.

Legal Obligations

At times, references are made to "commitments." *Commitments* cannot legally encumber an appropriation, as do obligations. Commitments are not legal reservations or obligations of appropriated funds (i.e., a commitment is not one of the eight legal forms that an obligation must take to be legally binding on the federal government). The Supplemental Appropriation Act of 1955 (Section 1311 of the Revised Statutes) requires that an obligation of the federal government be supported by specific documentary evidence. Eight forms for valid obligations include:

1. A binding agreement, in writing, between parties in a manner and form, and for a purpose authorized by law, executed before the expiration of the appropriation period of availability for obligation of the appropriation or fund for specific goods to be delivered, real property to be purchased or leased, or work or services to be performed
2. A valid loan agreement showing the amount of the loan to be made and the terms of repayment
3. An order required by law to be placed with a government agency
4. An order issued pursuant to a law authorizing purchases without advertising, when necessitated by public exigency or for perishable subsistence supplied or within specific monetary limitation
5. A grant or subsidy payable from appropriations made for payment of, or contributions toward, sums required to be paid in specific amounts fixed by law or in accordance with formulas prescribed by law; or payable pursuant to agreement authorized by, or plans approved in accordance with, an authorized law
6. A liability that may result from pending litigation brought under authority of law
7. Employment or services of persons, or expenses of travel in accordance with law, and services performed by public utilities
8. Any other legal liability of the government against an appropriation or funds legally available

All paid obligations must meet one of the above legal criteria and be supported by relevant documentation. Upon failing to meet one of these criteria, the agency has no authority to make payment since there is no legally binding obligation. In dealings with the federal government, there is no implied or apparent legal authority with respect to federal obligations or liabilities.

Other Conditions for Obligations

In addition to meeting one of the eight legally required forms, an obligation may be incurred only if there is a current or unexpired appropriation in existence at the time the obligation is incurred. General rules have arisen and GAO decisions have been rendered that define conditions under which obligations may be incurred. Some of these relate to:

- The general rule regarding obligation of a fiscal year appropriation for payments to be made in a succeeding year is that the contract or other instrument imposing the obligation must be made within the fiscal year sought to be charged and the contract must be to meet a bona fide need of that fiscal year (33 Comp. Gen. 57, 61).
- The bona fide need of the service of a particular year depends on the facts and circumstances of the specific case; no general rule for application to all situations exists (73 Comp. Gen. 155, 159).
- The obligated balance of an appropriation available for a definite time period must be transferred at the end of the second [now fifth] full fiscal year following the close of the period of availability of the appropriation. (The transfer will be to the successor "M" or merged accounts of the Treasury Department.) (7 Comp. Gen. 19.6; P. L. 101-510).
- Working capital or revolving-type funds cannot operate to divest appropriated funds of their identity or change the requirement that appropriated funds must be expended solely for the purpose for which the appropriation was made available (26 Comp. Gen. 545, 548).
- The use of a specific appropriation to pay obligations under another appropriation, even during a temporary exhaustion of funds, is in contravention of 31 U.S.C. 628, even though repayment may be contemplated after a supplemental appropriation might be made (36 Comp Gen. 368).

In practice, confusion regularly arises over whether appropriated funds may be obligated in one fiscal year and liquidated in a succeeding fiscal year. Some common areas of uncertainty include:

- The Comptroller General has stated that, unless prohibited by the terms of the authorizing or appropriating legislation, this practice is acceptable and legal.
- Unless specifically prohibited or precluded by law, it is not necessary for the obligation and its liquidation or settlement to occur in the same fiscal year.
- Legally, valid obligations remain available to meet expenditures for years after the fiscal year in which the appropriation expired.
- No new obligations may be entered into after an appropriation has expired, but funds from the expired appropriation may be used to pay legally incurred obligations of the appropriation.
- Amounts from one appropriation or working capital or revolving fund cannot be used to incur obligations or make expenditures for a "customer," or other appropriation, that would have been prohibited by the conditions of the first appropriation.

Recording Obligations

Once funds are obligated by federal executives, a formal accounting entry and a budgetary accounting entry must be made in the entity's system to record the obligation of allotted funds. Federal accounting standards require that an agency match every obligation to an appropriation or other budgetary authority and then create an accounts payable or make a payment for previously obligated amounts when due.

Agency Expenditures

An *expenditure* is defined by OMB and the Department of Treasury as disbursements or outlays, or the amount of checks issued, interest accrued on public debt, or other payments made by a federal entity (including advances to others), net of any related refunds and reimbursements. However, an *appropriation expenditure* is a reduction in an appropriation or other budget authority through the receipt of goods and services ordered. The *expended appropriation* status is not dependent on whether the related obligations have been paid or an invoice received. The *expending* of an appropriation reverses the earlier entry made to record the formal obligation (i.e., also referred to as "undelivered orders") of appropriated funds.

Each time an expenditure is accrued, an earlier obligation must be reduced by a formal accounting entry—a budgetary accounting entry. In recent years, OMB adopted a definition of expenditures that is the same as "outlays." The latter term is defined in OMB Circular A-34 as *"the amount of checks issued, interest accrued on the public debt, or other payments made (including advances to others)."* OMB uses *expenditure* and *net disbursement* interchangeably with the term *outlay*. Thus, after many years of support by GAO, the term *accrued expenditures* seems to be passing from the lexicon of governmental accounting.

PROPRIETARY ACCOUNTING

As noted earlier, the term *proprietary accounting* refers to that accounting performed by federal entities within the nonbudgetary accounts. Generally, *proprietary accounting* is concerned with accounting for a federal entity's assets, liabilities, net residual federal position or cumulative federal investment, any revenues or receipts, and expenses and costs. In Exhibit 5.4, events beginning with accrued expenditures (event 10) through the final accounting performed in the merged accounts (event 15) are generally viewed as the scope of federal proprietary accounting.

Accrual Accounting

The proprietary basis of accounting requires costs incurred for goods and services benefiting more than one fiscal year to be recorded as assets and reported as costs when consumed or used, irrespective of when payment is made for the goods or services. Increasingly, accrual or proprietary accounting is the basis for recording and reporting of financial information by federal agencies. The nature of federal proprietary accounting closely parallels that of a corporation complying with generally accepted accounting principles for the private sector. Exhibit 5.5 illustrates an example of a purchase order placed in one fiscal period, the goods received in another period, with the goods used or consumed in a third and paid for in a fourth fiscal period. The nature of this particular illustration requires that the accounting be performed in four fiscal periods.

1. A budgetary entry is made in the first period to record the obligation incurred (a budgetary entry).
2. An entry is required for goods received (a proprietary entry) and another for the reduction of the earlier outstanding obligation (a budgetary entry).
3. When the goods are consumed, an entry must be made to record the cost of the current period (a proprietary entry).
4. When payment is made, an entry is required for the cash disbursed (a proprietary entry).

Asset Accounting

Assets are defined as tangible or intangible items owned by the federal agency government that would have probable economic benefits that can be obtained or controlled by the federal agency.[4] These assets include cash, investments, real and personal properties, and also claims of the federal entity against nonfederal agency or parties (e.g., accounts receivable, interest receivable, amounts due from federal advances, and advances or prepayments to these nonfederal entities or parties). With some exceptions, assets are initially recorded by a proprietary accounting entry when received at purchased costs or donated values, regardless of when payment is made or the asset is used or consumed.

Liability Accounting

FASAB and OMB define a federal *liability* as a "probable and measurable future outflow of resources arising from past transactions or events." The liabilities grouping of accounts include an enormity of transactions and events such as accounts payables, end-of-period accrual liabilities, federal commitments and guarantees legally assumed or entered into, contingencies, damages from litigious proceedings, and the like. Liabilities are recorded as proprietary entries in a federal agency's accounts in the period incurred and removed from these accounts in the period paid or liquidated. Liabilities represent amounts owed and are not dependent on receipt of an invoice or request for payment. Also, liabilities must be reported regardless of whether federal funds are available or authorized for their payment.

Revenues or Receipts Accounting

No agency may collect receipts and earn revenues unless specific authorization is provided by Congress. Additionally, an agency may have the authority to collect receipts, but such receipts are unavailable for expenditure by that collecting agency. Inflows from revenue and other financing sources would be those resources that the government demands, earns, or receives by donation.

---

[4] *Federal Accounting Standards Advisory Board, **FASAB Original Statements**, Vol. I, Consolidated Glossary, March 1997.*

From an accounting perspective, exchange-type revenues are to be recognized when goods or services are provided to the public or to another government entity at the actual price received or receivable under established pricing arrangements. The accounting for nonexchange revenues or inflows of resources is recognized when:

1. A specifically identifiable, legally enforceable claim arises, and
2. To the extent that collection is probable (more likely than not) and the amount is reasonably estimable. The accounting for exchange and nonexchange revenues is reflected in proprietary-type accounts.

Expenses Accounting

Federal expenses are defined as outflows or other expending of assets or incurring liabilities (or both) from providing goods, rendering services, or carrying out other activities related to an entity's programs and missions, the benefits from which do not extend beyond the present operating period. Expenses are charged to proprietary-type expense accounts.

Costs Accounting

Costs, depending on the nature of the transaction, may be charged to operations immediately and recognized as an expense of the period. Costs might also be charged initially to an asset account (i.e., "capitalized") and then transferred to an expense account by depreciation or amortization entries in a subsequent period, upon being used or consumed. Most often, in federal entity accounting, costs are synonymous with expense. Formal, proprietary-type accounting entries must be made for each cost incurred, regardless of when payments are made or whether invoices have been received.[5]

Disbursements Accounting

Disbursements in the federal government are payments of cash that take a variety of forms, including checks issued, direct cash payments made, letters of credit drawn down, and electronic fund transfers. In recent years, OMB has adopted a definition of disbursements that includes expenditures and outlays. Expenditures and outlays are proprietary-type accounting transactions that are recorded for the amounts of checks issued, interest accrued on public debt, and other payments, such as advances and federal loans.

---

[5] *These definitions are set forth by OMB in its Circular A-34 and GAO in its **Accounting Guide** (GAO/AFMD-PPM-2.1).*

6 FEDERAL FINANCIAL STATEMENTS

The financial statements issued by component entities of the federal government differ significantly from the statements issued by commercial entities, not-for-profit organizations, and state and local government entities. In addition, the requirements for financial statements and their requisite form and content also differ among the three branches of the federal government.

FEDERAL FINANCIAL REPORTING

Historically, within the federal government, considerable effort was expended to meet only legally required reporting mandates of Congress. Although such reports were important, these requirements were not the reporting information most needed by federal entity executives to manage activities and operations properly. As a result, significant changes and improved financial reporting requirements were implemented by the federal government in the 1990s.

Since the 1700s Congress and executives of federal agencies were almost exclusively concerned with appropriated amounts, the status of apportioned budget authority, and the rate of obligation and expenditure. So long as the obligated and expended amounts remained below the amounts appropriated by Congress, few expressed any concern about the absence of other types of data. Information presented by federal entities for both external and internal uses were essentially the dollar values of obligated balances and cash-expenditures amounts.

In the 1940s and 1950s, Congress, GAO, OMB, federal executives, and two Hoover Commissions all recognized the limitations of obligation and expenditure accounting and reporting. This type of stewardship reporting was not sufficient to meet the scope of the financial management needs of the government. In the 1960s and 1970s, Congress became concerned that federal entities were not managing programs to ensure that the rates of expenditures were consistent with program plans and desired economic thrusts, and were not reflective of promised accomplishments or results. As a result, laws imposed fiscal and performance restrictions on programs. Time limitations were placed on the period for obligation of appropriated funds and on the time periods by which the federal monies had to be fully expended. If both time limitations were not met, the entity's funding authority might lapse.

FEDERAL ACCOUNTING PRINCIPLES

For the 200 years preceding passage of the CFO Act, Congress did not require, nor did federal entities apply, consistent and uniform accounting and reporting standards, prepare annual agency financial statements, or have independent audits made of financial statements. This changed with the CFO Act. Also in 1990, the newly established FASAB set forth that federal accounting and financial reporting should assist in fulfilling the government's objective of public accountability for monies raised through taxes.

FASAB suggested that there could be several levels of accountability: policy, program, performance, processes and procedural, and legal. In its statement of objectives, FASAB noted that this accountability must have utility to a variety of users, which FASAB categorized into four groups:

1. Individual citizens (e.g., taxpayers, voters, or service recipients of federal assistance)
2. Congress (individual members, committees, plus legislative agencies with budget and other federal financial responsibilities, such as CBO and GAO)
3. Federal executives and those with oversight responsibilities (including the President and those acting as the President's agents)
4. Program managers (i.e., those federal entity executives responsible for operating plans, program operations, and budget execution)[1]

To meet the needs of this myriad of users, FASAB recommended that financial statements and reports be issued for individual federal entities and for all entities, in total, government-wide.

FEDERAL ACCOUNTING HIERARCHY

The hierarchy of accounting for federal entities was established by the AICPA through the issuance of SAS 69, *The Meaning of Present Fairly in Conformity with Generally Accepted Accounting Principles [GAAP] in the Independent Auditor's Report*,[2] and as amended by SAS 91, *Federal GAAP Hierarchy*. The established hierarchy, from the more authoritative to the less authoritative, is:

- FASAB statements and interpretations
- AICPA and FASB pronouncements, if made applicable to federal government entities by a FASAB statement or interpretation
- FASAB technical bulletins
- AICPA industry audit and accounting guides (if specifically made applicable to federal government entities by the AICPA and cleared by FASAB)
- AICPA Accounting Standards Executive Committee (AcSEC) and technical releases of the Accounting and Auditing Policy Committee of FASAB (if specifically made applicable to federal government entities by the AICPA and cleared by FASAB)
- Implementation guides published by FASAB and practices that are widely recognized and prevalent in the federal government

In the absence of guidance provided by the above hierarchy, the auditor of a federal government entity may consider other accounting literature, including:

---

[1] *Financial Accounting Standards Advisory Board, **Objectives of Federal Financial Reporting-- Statement of Recommended Accounting and Reporting Concepts**, Washington, DC, July 1993.*
[2] *Issued April 2000.*

- FASAB concept statements
- AICPA standards listed above, but *not* specifically made applicable to federal government entities and cleared by FASAB
- GASB statements

THE FEDERAL REPORTING ENTITY

There is only one overall economic entity: the federal government as a whole. But, on a daily basis, the federal government operates as a network of somewhat autonomous entities: departments, agencies, subdepartments and subagencies, commissions, and other federally funded or federally assisted organizations. Each entity manages activities, can legally obligate the government, and is authorized by Congress to spend federal monies.

Until the 1990s, there had been no uniform resolution of what constituted a federal accounting and reporting entity. The individual congressional appropriations were viewed by most as the "accountable" entity, while the departments and operating agencies were viewed as the "reporting" entities. This distinction was an impediment to implementing consistent, uniform cost-based, accrual financial reporting within federal departments and agencies, between these and other entities of the government, and for the government as a whole. Others within the federal government, with different responsibilities, believed that congressional budget accounts or Treasury accounts (and these accounts do not provide for the same accounting) provided more accurate and revealing financial disclosures. Still others in Congress and agencies thought the primary reporting entity should be special funds and trusts established by various laws. Further complicating federal accountability was the fact that congressional appropriations and other forms of spending authority were not clearly or neatly aligned by federal departments and agencies. A final void in the federal reporting was the fact that no financial statements were prepared to report on the operations of the federal government as a whole.

APPROPRIATION ACCOUNTING

Historically, federal accounting and reporting for some departments and agencies was based on congressional legislation that provided a single appropriation to a single federal agency as the primary financing resource for operations, which considerably simplified accounting and reporting. However, this was not the norm, particularly for the larger federal departments, which frequently had responsibility for two or more congressional appropriations. When a single department or agency is responsible for multiple appropriations, these appropriations supported a variety of operations and usually a combination of programs; each appropriation was separately reported. Then, at its discretion, Congress might opt to provide funding not through an appropriation at all, but rather through another form of spending authority whereby the agency is authorized to first spend federal money and then report to Congress for "reimbursement." In other instances, an agency's operations are supported by none of these funding devices, but rather through a congressionally mandated "allocation" of money from another agency's appropriation; in such cases, it is unclear as to which agency should report what amounts and how. Financial information on individual federal entities and programs arrayed only by appropriation or budget authority was of limited value to federal executives and managers in operating the day-to-day activities. These were macrolevel reports and statements of appropriation balances, essentially a cash-basis reporting, that provided few clues as to the economy, efficiency, or relative effectiveness of federal operations.

Resolution of this 200-year accountability and reporting conundrum began in earnest with passage of the CFO Act, which mandated federal agencies to annually prepare entity-wide financial statements for all resources for which they were responsible, using the uniformly applicable accounting standards for federal agencies, and that these financial statements be independently audited. By 1994, FASAB recommended federal departments and agencies to report on all of their stewardship responsibilities in a single set of financial statements and not separately, by individual appropriations and funding sources. FASAB, in its accounting concepts, stated that a basic postulate of accounting is that accounting information pertains to entities (meaning a federal agency or organization) and that reporting should be performed by the agency regardless of the numerous and distinct appropriations or other funding devices used to finance an agency's operations.

AGENCY ACCOUNTABILITY

Federal entities must provide financial data on a variety of reporting bases, often for differing time periods, and by many organizational structures (e.g., individual departments and agencies, subordinate offices, bureaus, branches). Reporting details must include an accounting by appropriations of related financial positions, obligations, expenditures, cash disbursements, and costs of authorized programs, products, activities, and services managed. Also, systems of federal entities are expected to provide a ready and accurate reporting by every congressional district in America for an entity's programs that could impact tens of thousands of states, counties, cities, towns, and other governmental units receiving federal financial assistance. Not to be overlooked, several agencies make payments directly to tens of millions of individual citizens, each requiring an individual "account" and requiring some type of reporting. Such an accounting and financial reporting has no counterpart in or out of government.

AGENCIES AND GOVERNMENT-WIDE STATEMENTS

Executive branch agencies subject to the requirements of the CFO Act, GMRA of 1994, the FFMIA, and the Accountability for Tax Dollars Act of 2002 must prepare their financial statements in accordance with policies and guidance prescribed by OMB. The latest guidance issued by OMB is Bulletin 01-09, *Form and Content of Agency Financial Statements.*[3] Several agencies in the legislative branch of government have elected to prepare financial statements based on the guidance contained in this bulletin, but are not required to comply with all of its provisions. To date, the judicial branch of government has elected not to issue financial statements.

---

[3] *Issued under the authority of 31 U.S.C. 3515 (d).*

The majority of this discussion focuses on financial statements prepared in accordance with OMB Bulletin 01-09.

Performance and Accountability Reports

Each agency subject to the CFO Act or Accountability for Tax Dollars Act is required to annually submit its audited financial statements in a *Performance and Accountability Report* (PAR), which combines performance and financial reporting into a single document. In addition to the base financial statements, the PAR will include a management's discussion and analysis (MD&A), a performance section (where the agency will discuss its strategic goals), the independent auditor's reports, the required supplementary stewardship information (RSSI), and other information, such as Improper Payments Information Act reporting details. In conducting an audit of a federal agency, the auditor is responsible for forming an opinion on the basic financial statements taken as a whole. The MD&A and other information that is not part of the basic financial statements, but required by OMB Bulletin 01-09, are subjected only to certain limited audit procedures. The auditor does not opine on the information, including financial, presented outside of the basic statements. The rest of this chapter focuses on the six financial statements on which the auditor does opine.

FEDERAL FINANCIAL STATEMENTS

The financial statements of federal departments, agencies, and other entities must comply with 31 U.S.C. 3515 and other legal criteria for presenting the financial position and results of operations of federal entities. The OMB circulars and bulletins prescribing the form and content of six federal financial statements essentially incorporate the federal financial accounting concepts and standards researched and recommended by FASAB. The six principal financial statements required of federal entities discussed in this chapter include:

1. Statement of financial position or balance sheet (see Exhibit 6.1)
2. Statement of net cost (see Exhibit 6.2)
3. Statement of changes in net position (see Exhibit 6.3)
4. Statement of budgetary resources (see Exhibit 6.4)
5. Statement of financing (see Exhibit 6.5)
6. Statement of custodial activity (see Exhibit 6.6)

To be complete, an agency's financial statement must also include several required footnotes, plus other notes necessary to describe the financial and other activity of the agency. Additionally, the prescribed federal financial statements must contain:

- *Supplementary stewardship information* relating to property, plant, and equipment, entity investments, and program-related risks
- *Supplementary information*, including a statement on budgetary resources, custodial activity, and segment-related information, where appropriate

- *Other accompanying information*, which would include data on performance measures and forgone federal revenues, on subjects such as tax burden and tax gaps, as appropriate for specific entities

The OMB-prescribed financial statements reflect summarized financial information contained in the 2,000 supporting ledger, subledger, and subsidiary accounts of the federal government's standard general ledger. In addition to providing meaningful reporting to citizens, the data in the entity-level financial statements form the basis for the consolidated financial statements of the US government, which are also required by the CFO Act. Agency financial statements are "rolled-up" by the Treasury Department when compiling the government-wide consolidated statements.

Currently, federal entities are required to submit a quarterly financial statement package to OMB that consists of their balance sheet, statement of net cost, and statement of budgetary resources. A complete audited set of financials statements, including all required statements and note disclosures, are required at year-end. The complete set of financial statements, for each entity and for the government as a whole, must annually undergo an independent audit.

Balance Sheet (Statement of Financial Position)

The balance sheet is the federal financial statement that most closely resembles the balance sheet of a commercial enterprise. The balance sheet presents the assets, liabilities, and net position of a federal agency as of a specific time. The example presented in Exhibit 6.1 illustrates the prescribed format reflected in OMB Bulletin 01-09. The key elements of a federal agency's balance sheet include and accounting for the:

- *Intragovernmental assets and liabilities* (i.e., assets and liabilities arising from transactions among federal entities) being shown separately from assets and liabilities arising from transactions with nonfederal entities.
- *Net position* broken down between unexpended appropriation (the portion of an entity's appropriation represented by undelivered orders and unobligated balances) and cumulative results of operation[4] (the net results of operations since inception plus the cumulative amount of prior period adjustments. This includes the cumulative amount of donations and transfers of assets in and out without reimbursement).

---

[4] *Effective for fiscal year 2006, a new FASAB pronouncement,* **Earmarked Funds**, *will require a third classification in net position.*

Exhibit 6.1: Consolidated balance sheet

Department/Agency/Reporting entity
Consolidated Balance Sheet
As of September 30, 20X2 and 20X1
(in dollars/thousands/millions)

		20X5	*20X4*
Assets (Note 2):			
Intragovernmental:		$ xxx	$ xxx
1.	Fund balance with Treasury (Note 3)	xxx	xxx
2.	Investments (Note 5)	xxx	xxx
3.	Accounts receivable (Note 6)	xxx	xxx
4.	Loans receivable	xxx	xxx
5.	Other (Note 11)	xxx	xxx
6.	Total intragovernmental	xxx	xxx
7.	Cash and other monetary assets (Note 4)	xxx	xxx
8.	Investments (Note 5)	xxx	xxx
9.	Accounts receivable, net (Note 6)	xxx	xxx
10.	Taxes receivable, net (Note 7)	xxx	xxx
11.	Loans receivable and related foreclosed property, net (Note 8)	xxx	xxx
12.	Inventory and related property, net (Note 9)	xxx	xxx
13.	General property, plant, and equipment, net (Note 10)	xxx	xxx
14.	Other (Note 11)	xxx	xxx
15.	Total assets	$ x,xxx	x,xxx
Liabilities (Note 12):		$ xxx	$ xxx
Intragovernmental:		xxx	xxx
16.	Accounts payable	xxx	xxx
17.	Debt (Note 13)	xxx	xxx
18.	Other (Notes 16, 17, and 18)	xxx	xxx
19.	Total intragovernmental	xxx	xxx
20.	Accounts payable	xxx	xxx
21.	Loan guarantee liability (Note 8)	xxx	xxx
22.	Debt held by the public (Note 13)	xxx	xxx
23.	Federal employee and veterans' benefits (Note 14)	xxx	xxx
24.	Environmental and disposal liabilities (Note 15)	xxx	xxx
25.	Benefits due and payable	xxx	xxx
26.	Other (Notes 16, 17, and 18)	xxx	xxx
27.	Total liabilities	x,xxx	x,xxx
28.	Commitments and contingencies (Note 19)		
Net position:			
29.	Unexpended appropriations	xxx	xxx
30.	Cumulative results of operations	xxx	xxx
31.	Total net position	$ x,xxx	$ x,xxx
32.	Total liabilities and net position	$ x,xxx	$ x,xxx

Classifications in a federal balance sheet. An entity's *balance sheet* presents data as of a specific moment in time; a federal balance sheet could present the financial position of a federal entity as of the end of a month, quarter, or fiscal year.

Exhibit 6.1 is a generic example of the classified balance sheet required of federal entities by OMB. OMB's form and content guidelines prescribe a classified balance sheet for federal entities. Not all federal entities will necessarily issue a balance sheet with this illustrated content or format due to differing missions and programs.[5]

Congress is the ultimate determinant of what a federal entity must report on and how. It is Congress that authorizes certain federal entities to operate certain programs and not others. Congress designates which constituencies a federal entity must serve and how (e.g., large corporations with big contracts; small businesses by subsidized loans and set-aside programs; nonprofit and educational institutions by grants; the young, old, hungry, and homeless by grants and direct subsidies; or others by loan and loan guarantees programs for education, health, economic development, natural disasters, etc.).

Accounting for assets. *Assets* are defined as tangible or intangible items owned by the federal government that could have probable economic benefits that can be obtained or controlled by the federal entity.[6] These assets include cash, investments, real and personal properties, and also claims of the federal entity against nonfederal entities or parties (e.g., accounts receivable, interest receivable, and amounts due from federal advances and advances or prepayments to these nonfederal entities or parties). With some exceptions, assets are initially recorded as purchased costs or donated values.

Accounting for liabilities. FASAB and OMB define a federal *liability* as a "probable and measurable future outflow of resources arising from past transactions or events." The liabilities grouping of accounts include an enormity of transactions and events, such as accounts payables, end-of-period accrued liabilities, federal commitments and guarantees legally assumed or entered into, contingencies, damages from litigious proceedings, and so on. Liabilities are measured and recorded in a federal entity's accounts in the period incurred and removed from the accounts in the period liquidated or paid. Also, liabilities represent amounts owed and are not dependent on receipt of an invoice or request for payment. Liabilities must be reported irrespective of whether federal funds are available or authorized for their payment.

Federal liabilities arise from

1. Exchange transactions (i.e., generally for services rendered)
2. Government-related events
3. Government-acknowledged events (i.e., voluntary assumption of debts, risks, or costs of others)
4. Nonexchange transactions (i.e., debts and amounts due the sovereign government, as taxes)

Any advance payments and prepayments from other entities for goods or services yet to be delivered by a federal entity must also be recorded as other current liabilities.

---

[5] *Office of Management and Budget, **Form and Content of Agency Financial Statements,** Bulletin 97-01, effective for the fiscal year ending September 30, 1998, Washington, DC, October 1996.*

[6] *Federal Accounting Standards Advisory Board, **FASAB Original Statements,** Vol. I, Consolidated Glossary, March 1997.*

Accounting for the net position of a federal entity. *Net federal* or *entity position* is defined by FASAB as the *"unexpended appropriations* and the *cumulative result* or *residual balance"* resulting from (1) the initial investment to commence a federal operation; (2) the cumulative results of the operation's revenues or resources and expenses; and (3) donations, collections, or transfers of funds or other property by or to a federal entity, as permitted by Congress.

- *Unexpended appropriations* are appropriations not yet obligated or expended, and undelivered orders.
- *Cumulative results of operations* include amounts accumulated over the years by an entity from its financing sources less expenses and losses, including donated capital and transfers in the net investment of the government account and the entity's liabilities (for accrued leave, credit reform, actuarial liabilities not covered by available budgetary resources).
- *Residual balance* is comprised of appropriated capital provided by Congress; invested capitalized assets or expended appropriations for purchased goods and property; or receivables due for loaned or advanced federal monies. The net position investment could relate to a single appropriation, several appropriations, or other congressional budgetary authority accounts.

In addition to the information presented on the face of the balance sheet, certain information related to the assets and liabilities of a federal entity is required to be disclosed in the notes to the financial statements, per the provisions of OMB Bulletin 01-09. Some disclosure requirements unique to the federal environment include:

- *Nonentity assets.* Nonentity assets are those assets that are held by the entity but are not available to the entity. Examples of nonentity assets include customs duty receivables that the Customs Service may ultimately collect, the federal income tax receivables that the Internal Revenue Service (IRS) collects, and the regulatory fees collected by the Federal Communications Commission (FCC). In each case, the federal entity holding or reporting the asset does not possess the congressional authority to spend these funds. Further disclosure is required to show the ultimate disposition of intragovernmental nonentity assets. Often the agency must provide other information needed to understand the nature of nonentity assets.
- *Fund Balance with Treasury.* The composition of Fund Balance with Treasury (i.e., amounts representing trust, revolving, appropriated, and other fund types) is required to be disclosed along with the Status of the Fund Balance (i.e., amounts unobligated—available, unobligated—unavailable, and obligated—not yet disbursed).
- *Cash and other monetary assets.* The balance is required to be broken into cash, foreign currency, and other monetary assets (i.e., gold, special drawing rights, US reserves in the international monetary fund). In addition, the entity is required to disclose any restrictions on cash.
- *Investments.* The cost, unamortized premium, or discount, amortization method, net investment, other adjustments, and market value of all material investments of a federal entity are required to be disclosed. In addition, any in-

formation relative to understanding the nature of reported investments, such as permanent impairments, should be disclosed.

- *Direct loans and loan guarantees.* Considerable additional disclosure is required for federal agencies subject to the provisions of the Federal Credit Reform Act. OMB SFFAS 2, 18, and 19 and OMB Bulletin 01-09 provide guidance for disclosure and formatting.
- *Liabilities not covered by budgetary resources.* These are liabilities for which congressional action is needed before budgetary resources can be provided. These disclosures should report intragovernmental and other liabilities separately. The distinction between funded and unfunded liabilities is

  - Federally funded liabilities would be *liabilities covered by budgetary resources.* That is, the federal entity has available to it congressionally approved expenditure authority, through an appropriation law or other budgetary or contract authority, that permits the entity to recognize and pay these liabilities.
  - Federal unfunded liabilities would be those liabilities recognized by a federal entity that are considered to be *liabilities not covered by budgetary resources,* as defined in the above paragraph. Payables and liabilities not covered by budgetary resources are unfunded and should be separately disclosed and segregated from payables or liabilities that are covered by budgetary resources.

- *Federal employee and veterans benefits.* Entities that are responsible for administering pensions, retirement benefits, and other postemployment benefits should calculate and report these liabilities and related expenses in accordance with SFFAS 5.

In addition, the normal required disclosures under GAAP for areas such as accounts receivable, inventory, property, plant, and equipment, debt, leases, and commitments and contingencies are also required for federal entities.

Statement of Net Cost

The statement of net cost is designed to show separately the components of the net cost of the reporting entity's operations for the period. The net cost of operations is the gross cost incurred less any exchange revenue earned from its activities. The gross cost of a program consists of the full costs of the outputs produced by the program, plus any nonproduction costs that can be identified and assigned to the program. Exchange revenue arises when a government entity provides goods or services to the public or another government entity for a price. Exchange revenue is synonymous with earned revenue. This statement should be presented in responsibility segments that align directly with the major goals and outputs described in the entity's strategic and performance plans, as required by GPRA.

In 1995, FASAB, in its recommended accounting standard related to entity and display, viewed the statement of net cost as specifically meeting the federal reporting objective to "provide information that helps the reader determine the costs of providing specific programs and activities and the composition of, and changes in, these costs."

The primary purpose of the statement of net cost is to display, in clear terms, the net cost (i.e., total costs less all revenues attributed to a program and permitted to be offset against program costs) of an entity's suborganizations and of its programs and other costs (i.e., administrative and other costs not allocated to specific programs). Exhibit 6.2 is an illustration of the statement of net cost.

Exhibit 6.2: Consolidated statement of net cost

Department/Agency/Reporting entity
Consolidated Statement of Net Cost
For the years ended September 30, 20X2 and 20X1
(in dollars/thousands/millions)

		_20X5_	_20X4_
Program costs:		$ xxx	$ xxx
Program A:		−xxx	−xxx
1.	Intragovernmental gross costs	xxx	xxx
2.	Less: Intragovernmental earned revenue		
3.	Intragovernmental net costs		
4.	Gross costs with the public	xxx	xxx
5.	Less: Earned revenues from the public	−xxx	−xxx
6.	Net costs with the public	xxx	xxx
7.	Total net cost	x,xxx	x,xxx
Other programs			
Program B:		xxx	xxx
Program C:		xxx	xxx
Program D:		xxx	xxx
Program E:		xxx	xxx
Program F:		xxx	xxx
Other programs:		xxx	xxx
Total other program costs:		x,xxx	x,xxx
8.	Cost not assigned to programs	x,xxx	x,xxx
9.	Less: Earned revenues not attributed to programs	−xxx	−xxx
10.	Net cost of operations	$ x,xxx	$ x,xxx

Occasionally, the structure and operations of an entity are so complex that, in order to fully display the major programs and activities of all of their suborganizations, additional supporting schedules are required. These schedules should be presented in the notes to the financial statements. Other note disclosures required for the statement of net cost include:

- Intragovernmental cost
- Cost of stewardship property, plant and equipment
- Stewardship assets acquired through transfer or donation
- Exchange revenue
- Gross cost and earned revenue by budget functional classification

Statement of Changes in Net Position

The Statement of Changes in Net Position reports changes in the two components of a federal entity's net position (cumulative results of operations and unexpended appropriations). As illustrated in Exhibit 6.3, the statement format was designed to show each component separately.

Exhibit 6.3: Consolidated statement of changes in net position

Department/Agency/Reporting entity
Consolidated Statement of Changes in Net Position
For the years ended September 30, 20X2 and 20X1
(in dollars/thousands/millions)

		20X2 Cumulative Results of Operations	20X2 Unexpended Appropriations	20X1 Cumulative Results of Operations	20X1 Unexpended Appropriations
1.	Beginning balances	$ xxx	$ xxx	$ xxx	$ xxx
2.	Prior period adjustments (+/–)	xxx	xxx	xxx	xxx
3.	Beginning balances, as adjusted	xxx	xxx	xxx	xxx
	Budgetary financing sources:				
4.	Appropriations received		xxx		xxx
5.	Appropriations transferred – in/out (+/–)		xxx		xxx
6.	Other adjustments (rescissions, etc) (+/–)	xxx	xxx	xxx	xxx
7.	Appropriations used	xxx	–xxx	xxx	–xxx
8.	Nonexchange revenue	xxx		xxx	
9.	Donations and forfeitures of cash and cash equivalents	xxx		xxx	
10.	Transfers – in/out without reimbursement (+/–)	xxx		xxx	
11.	Other budgetary financing sources (+/–)	xxx		xxx	
	Other financing sources				
12.	Donations and forfeitures of property	xxx		xxx	
13.	Transfers – in/out without reimbursement (+/–)	xxx		xxx	
14.	Imputed financing from costs absorbed by others	xxx		xxx	
15.	Other (+/–)	xxx		xxx	
16.	Total financing sources	xxx	xxx	xxx	xxx
17.	Net cost of operations (+/–)	xxx		xxx	
18.	Ending balances	$ x,xxx	$ x,xxx	$ x,xxx	$ x,xxx

The Statement of Changes in Net Position ties together several amounts from the other statements of an entity. Both components of net position are reflected as line items on the balance sheet. Budgetary appropriations received on the statement of changes in net position must agree with line 1 of the Statement of Budgetary Resources. The other financing sources section of the statement must agree to the statement of financing. The Net Cost of Operations on the Statement of Changes in Net Position must agree to the Statement of Net Cost.

The purpose of a federal entity's Statement of Changes in Net Position is to identify all financing sources available or used by a federal entity to support its net cost of operations and the net effect or change in the entity's financial position. As illustrated in Exhibit 6.3, these financial data are arrayed by the same organizational components and responsibility segments as appeared in the Statement of Net Costs.

Classifications of financing sources. Since the purpose of this statement is to identify changes in the net position, or how an entity's costs were financed, OMB has prescribed specific data classifications to be used. These classifications must be identified, whether shown in a Statement of Changes in Net Position or combined with the Statement of Net Cost.

- *Appropriation used* represents amounts of congressional budget authority, including all transfers of budget authority from other entities, that were used by federal entities to finance mandated operations.
- *Nonexchange revenues* include all receipts of taxes and nonexchange revenues, such as dedicated taxes, fines, and other revenues the federal government demands in its role as a sovereign power.

Once collected, these major funds then become monies to be appropriated by Congress. The collection function involves only a few federal entities (e.g., the Internal Revenue Service for personal and business taxes; Customs Service for import fees, and duties). These entities are not authorized to use all collections for their operations, but rather serve as the collecting agency and custodian of cash received and turned over to the Treasury Department. (For these entities, a statement of custodial activities, discussed later, would be appropriate.) For all other federal entities, nonexchange revenues collected would be shown on this statement.

- *Donations* are monies and materials given by private persons and organizations to the federal government without receiving anything in exchange. Not all federal entities are authorized to accept donations or contributions; specific authority must be provided by Congress.
- *Imputed financing sources* are costs incurred by a federal entity that are financed by another federal entity. This classification must include costs attributable to the reporting federal entity's activities but that do not require a direct cash payment in the reporting period (e.g., interest cost associated with carrying inventory or investing in physical assets). For example, Congress provides a direct appropriation of funds to the central Office of Personnel Management to pay retirement and other postretirement costs to former federal employees, most of whom were employed by federal entities other than OPM.
- *Transfers in* are amounts of cash or other capitalized assets received by one federal entity from another federal entity without reimbursement. *Transfers out* are amounts of cash or other capitalized assets provided by one federal entity to another federal entity without reimbursement. If exchange revenue, included in calculating an entity's net cost of operations, is transferred to the Treasury Department or another federal entity, the amount transferred is recognized as a transfer out and not netted against the entity's cost of operations. If the cash or book value is not known for these transferred amounts, the recorded value is the estimated fair value of the asset at transfer date.
- *Cost of Operations* must be the same amount as reported on the statement of net cost and on the entity's statement of financing for the same fiscal period.
- *Prior Period Adjustments* are corrections or adjustments to data reported for operations in a prior fiscal period. These adjustments are limited to the correc-

tion of errors and accounting changes having a retroactive effect that impacts the reported net position of the federal entity. OMB does not require that Statement of Changes in Net Position of prior periods be restated for prior period adjustments.

- *Unexpended Appropriations and Budgetary Authority* will exist at the end of any fiscal period. The increase or decrease in this amount affects the net position of a federal entity, but does not affect the reported net cost for that period. These unexpended appropriation amounts may become the costs reported for some future period.
- *Ending Balance (Net Position at the End of the Period)* is equal to the total unexpended appropriations and the cumulative results of operations of the federal entity and would also be reported in the entity's Statement of Financial Condition (i.e., the entity's balance sheet). The end-of-period balance becomes the beginning balance of unexpended appropriations for the next fiscal period.

The beginning balances section of the Statement of Changes in Net Position must agree to the amounts reported as net position on the prior years' balance sheets. The prior period adjustment amounts would be limited to the items defined as prior period adjustments in SFFAS 21, *Reporting Corrections of Errors and Changes in Accounting Principles*.

The Budgetary Financing Sources section reflects financing sources and nonexchange revenue that is also budgetary resources, or adjustments to those resources as reported on the Statement of Budgetary Resources and defined as such by OMB Circular A-11. The Other Financing Sources section reflects financing sources and nonexchange revenues that do not represent budgetary resources as reported on the Statement of Budgetary Resources, and as defined by OMB Circular A-11.

Effective for fiscal year 2006, SFFAS 27, *Identifying and Reporting Earmarked Funds*, will require federal component entities to show earmarked nonexchange revenue and other financing sources, including appropriations and net costs of operations, separately on the Statement of Changes in Net Position.

Statement of Budgetary Resources

The Statement of Budgetary Resources and related disclosures provide information regarding how budgetary resources were made available and the status of those resources at the end of the reporting period. Arguably, the Statement of Budgetary Resources is the statement most unique to the federal entity. It is the only statement prepared exclusively from the entity's budgetary general ledger and in accordance with budgetary accounting rules which have been incorporated into GAAP for federal entities.

The *Statement of Budgetary Resources* is particularly meaningful since data are provided on how a federal entity obtained its budgetary resources and the status or remaining balances of these resources at the end of the reporting period. This statement, illustrated as Exhibit 6.4, is prepared by federal entities whose financing comes wholly or partially from Congressional appropriations, budgetary or contract authority.

Exhibit 6.4: Combined statement of budgetary resources

Department/Agency/Reporting entity
Combined Statement of Budgetary Resources
For the Years Ended September 30, 20X2 and 20X1
(in dollars/thousands/millions)

	20X2 Budgetary	20X2 Nonbudgetary credit program financing accounts	20X1 Budgetary	20X1 Nonbudgetary credit program financing accounts
Budgetary resources:				
1. Budget authority:				
1a. Appropriations received	xxx	xxx	xxx	xxx
1b. Borrowing authority	xxx	xxx	xxx	xxx
1c. Contract authority	xxx	xxx	xxx	xxx
1d. Net transfers (+/–)	xxx	xxx	xxx	xxx
1e. Other	xxx	xxx	xxx	xxx
2. Unobligated balance				
2a. Beginning of period	xxx	xxx	xxx	xxx
2b. Net transfers, actual (+/–)	xxx	xxx	xxx	xxx
2c. Anticipated transfers balances	xxx	xxx	xxx	xxx
3. Spending authority from offsetting collections				
3a. Earned				
1. Collected	xxx	xxx	xxx	xxx
2. Receivable from federal sources	xxx	xxx	xxx	xxx
3b. Change in unfilled customer orders				
1. Advance received	xxx	xxx	xxx	xxx
2. Without advance from federal sources	xxx	xxx	xxx	xxx
3c. Anticipated for rest of year, without advances	xxx	xxx	xxx	xxx
3d. Transfers from trust funds	xxx	xxx	xxx	xxx
3e. Subtotal	xxx	xxx	xxx	xxx
4. Recoveries of prior year obligations	xxx	xxx	xxx	xxx
5. Temporarily not available pursuant to public law	xxx	xxx	xxx	xxx
6. Permanently not available	xxx	xxx	xxx	xxx
7. Total budgetary resources	$x,xxx	$x,xxx	$x,xxx	$x,xxx
Status of budgetary resources:				
8. Obligations incurred:				
8a. Direct	$ xxx	$ xxx	$ xxx	$ xxx
8b. Reimbursable	<u>xxx</u>	<u>xxx</u>	<u>xxx</u>	<u>xxx</u>
8c. Subtotal	xxx	xxx	xxx	xxx
9. Unobligated balance:				
9a. Apportioned	xxx	xxx	xxx	xxx
9b. Exempt from apportionment	xxx	xxx	xxx	xxx
9c. Other available	xxx	xxx	xxx	xxx
10. Unobligated balance not available	<u>xxx</u>	<u>xxx</u>	<u>xxx</u>	<u>xxx</u>
11. Total status of budgetary resources	<u>x,xxx</u>	<u>x,xxx</u>	<u>x,xxx</u>	<u>x,xxx</u>
Relationship of obligations to outlays:				
12. Obligated balance, net, beginning of period				
13. Obligated balance transferred, net (+/–)	xxx	xxx	xxx	xxx
14. Obligated balance, net, end of period:				
14a. Accounts receivable	xxx	xxx	xxx	xxx

Exhibit 6.4: Combined statement of budgetary resources (continued)

		20X2 Budgetary	20X2 Nonbudgetary credit program financing accounts	20X1 Budgetary	20X1 Nonbudgetary credit program financing accounts
14b.	Filled customer orders from Federal sources	xxx	xxx	xxx	xxx
14c.	Undelivered orders	xxx	xxx	xxx	xxx
14d.	Accounts payable	xxx	xxx	xxx	xxx
15.	Outlays:				
15a.	Disbursements	xxx	xxx	xxx	xxx
15b.	Collections	xxx	xxx	xxx	xxx
15c.	Subtotal	xxx	xxx	xxx	xxx
16.	Less: Offsetting reciepts	xxx	xxx	xxx	xxx
17.	Net outlays	$x,xxx	$x,xxx	$x,xxx	$x,xxx

The basis for accounting and reporting on this statement is prescribed by OMB in its long-standing and regularly updated Circular A-11, *Preparation, Submission, and Execution of the Budget*. The Statement of Budgetary Resources is required to be classified into three major sections or groupings.

1. *The Budgetary Resources* section presents the total obligational and nonbudgetary resources (generally from congressional appropriations, budgetary and contract authority) under the stewardship of a federal entity. These accountable resources could include new budget authority, various obligation limitations and spending authority, unobligated balances at the beginning of a period and those transferred in during the period, spending authority that could arise from offsetting collections, and any adjustments made to an entity's budgetary resources. The calculated total for budgetary resources is the total amount made available to the federal entity for the fiscal period.

2. *The Status of Budgetary Resources* section of the statement provides an analysis of the status of budgetary resources by such specific components as obligations incurred, unobligated balances of available budget authority, and unobligated balances that are unavailable except to adjust or liquidate obligations charged to a prior year's appropriations. The total of this section, *Total Status of Budgetary Resources*, is equal to the budgetary resources still available to the federal entity as of the reporting date.

3. *The Outlays* section shows the net outlays or cash disbursements by a federal entity for the fiscal period. This section reconciles the amount of obligations incurred, offsetting collections and adjustments, obligations transferred, and the end-of-period obligated amount to arrive at the total outlays for the period. Outlays would be the total of disbursement requests made to the Treasury Department for the period.

Data appearing on the Statement of Budgetary Resources are, in condensed form, the same data reported by federal entities to OMB on their report of budget execution (i.e., government's SF-133) pursuant to OMB Circular A-11, *Preparation, Submission, and Execution of the Budget*. Also, these data are reported government-wide in the Treasury Department's monthly Treasury statement and its annual report, as well as in the President's budget request annually submitted to Congress.

An important consideration for preparers and auditors of the Statement of Budgetary Resources is that the statement should be consistent with the budget execution information reported in the *Report on Budget Execution and Budgetary Resources* (SF-133) and with information reported in the *Budget of the United States Government* for the entity. The Statement of Budgetary Resources is an agency-wide report, which aggregates account-level information reported in the SF-133. Any material differences between the information reported must be disclosed in the Notes to the Financial Statements.

Consistent with the SF-133 and the general ledger for budgetary accounting, the Statement of Budgetary Resources tracks budgetary resources and their status independently. The total of Budgetary Resources and the Status of Budgetary Resources must always be in balance similarly to how total assets must always equal total liabilities plus net position. The Budgetary Resources section presents the total budgetary resources available to the reporting entity. Budgetary Resources include new budget authority, unobligated balances at the beginning of the period, spending authority from offsetting collections, recoveries of prior year obligations, and any adjustments to these resources. The Status of Budgetary Resources section is an accounting on entity resources that consists of a reporting on the:

- Obligations incurred
- Unobligated balances at the end of the period that remain available
- Unobligated balances at the end of the period that are unavailable
- Unobligated balance at the end of the period that is not available, except to adjust or liquidate prior year obligations

The final section of the Statement of Budgetary Resources displays the relationship between obligations incurred and outlays during the reporting period. Outlays consist of disbursements net of offsetting collections. The net outlays reported on the Statement of Budgetary Resources must agree to the total outlays reported in the budget of the United States, the aggregate outlays reported on the year-end SF-133 for all budget accounts, and the net total of all disbursements and collections reported to the United States Treasury on a monthly basis on the statement of transactions (SF-224) for the reporting period.

Additional financial statement disclosure related to the statement of budgetary resources includes:

- *Apportionment categories of obligations incurred:* The reporting entity is required to disclose the amount of direct and reimbursable obligations incurred against amounts apportioned under Category A, B, and Exempt from Apportionment. The disclosure must agree with the aggregate information on the entity's year-end SF-133s and lines 8a and 8b of the statement of budgetary resources. The apportionment categories are determined in accordance with the provisions of OMB Circular A-11, *Preparation, Submission, and Execution of the Budget.*
- *Adjustments to beginning balances of budgetary resources*

- *Legal arrangements affecting use of unobligated balances.*
- *Explanation of differences between the statement of budgetary resources and the budget of the United States government*: Differences between the statement of budgetary resources and the amounts reported in the budget do not always indicate a reporting error. Legitimate reasons for such differences can exist. The note disclosure should list and explain the reasons for all differences.

Statement of Financing

The statement of financing (see Exhibit 6.5) is a reconciling statement that ensures there exists a proper relationship between the proprietary accounts (accrual based) and the budgetary accounts (budget based) in an entity's accounting and reporting systems. Neither basis, cost nor budgetary, is superior to the other. Use of both bases is essential to the decisions that must be made by federal entities, and those entities' accounting and reporting systems must provide these data in parallel. The Statement of Financing provides data on the total resources provided by Congress to a federal entity for the fiscal period and on how those resources were used.

Exhibit 6.5: Consolidated statement of financing

Department/Agency/Reporting entity
Consolidated Statement of Financing
For the Years Ended September 30, 20X2 and 20X1

		20X2	20X1
Resources used to finance activities:			
Budgetary resources obligated			
1.	Obligations incurred	$ xxx	$ xxx
2.	Less: Spending authority from offsetting collections and recoveries	xxx	xxx
3.	Obligations net of offsetting collections and recoveries	xxx	xxx
4.	Less: Offsetting receipts	xxx	xxx
5.	Net obligations	xxx	xxx
Other Resources			
6.	Donations and forfeitures of property	xxx	xxx
7.	Transfers in/out without reimbursement (+/–)	xxx	xxx
8.	Imputed financing from costs absorbed by others	xxx	xxx
9.	Other (+/–)	xxx	xxx
10.	Net other resources used to finance activities	xxx	xxx
11.	*Total resources used to finance activities*	x,xxx	x,xxx
Resources used to finance items not part of the net cost of operations			
12.	Change in budgetary resources obligated for goods, services, and benefits ordered but not yet provided (+/–)	xxx	xxx
13.	Resources that fund expenses recognized in prior periods	xxx	xxx
14.	Budgetary offsetting collections and receipts that do not affect net cost of operations		
	14a. Credit program collections which increase liabilities for loan guarantees or allowances for subsidy	xxx	xxx
	14b. Other	xxx	xxx
15.	Resources that finance the acquisition of assets	xxx	xxx
16.	Other resources or adjustments to net obligated resources that do not affect net cost of operations (+/–)	xxx	xxx
17.	*Total resources used to finance items not part of the net cost of operations*	xxx	xxx
18.	*Total resources used to finance the net cost of operations*	x,xxx	x,xxx

		_20X2_	_20X1_
Components of the net cost of operations that will not require or generate resources in the current period:			
Components requiring or generating resources in future periods:			
19.	Increase in annual leave liability	xxx	xxx
20.	Increase in environmental and disposal liability	xxx	xxx
21.	Upward/downward reestimates of credit subsidy expense (+/–)	xxx	xxx
22.	Increase in exchange revenue receivable from the public	xxx	xxx
23.	Other (+/–)	xxx	xxx
24.	Total components of net cost o operations that will require or generate resources in future periods	xxx	xxx
Components not requiring or generating resources:			
25.	Depreciation and amortization	xxx	xxx
26.	Revaluation of assets or liabilities (+/–)	xxx	xxx
27.	Other (+/–)	xxx	xxx
28.	Total components of net cost of operations that will not require or generate resources	xxx	xxx
29.	_Total components of net cost of operations that will not require or generate resources in the current period_	x,xxx	x,xxx
30.	_Net cost of operations_	$x,xxx	$x,xxx

Financial measures based on cost and accrued or applied costs are essential to measuring performance and determining total financial resources needed to achieve a particular output or outcome. However, for planning and financing decisions by the President and Congress, data on the budgetary basis are equally important.

The Statement of Net Cost (Exhibit 6.2) uses one financial basis—cost based. The Statement of Budgetary Resources (Exhibit 6.4) uses another basis—budgetary based.

The Statement of Financing reconciles the obligations derived from the entities' budgetary accounts (and reported on the Statement of Budgetary Resources) to the entities' net cost of operations derived from their proprietary accounts and included on the Statement of Net Cost. Most transactions recorded by a federal entity contain both proprietary and budgetary components. However, due to the different accounting bases used for budgetary and proprietary accounting and the many unique rules that exist for federal budgetary accounting, some transactions appear in only one set of books (i.e., the accrual of an environmental liability is only recorded on the proprietary books) or are recorded differently under proprietary and budgetary rules (the purchase of a fixed asset is capitalized and depreciated over its estimated useful life under proprietary accounting but is obligated and outlayed in the year acquired under budgetary accounting rules). The statement of financing is designed to provide the reader with information on linking these two federal accounting bases and is divided into five separate sections

Obligations and nonbudgetary resources. The first section of the Statement of Financing identifies the total resources used by the reporting entity. Total resources include both budgetary resources and other available resources. The other resources should agree to the amounts reported in the Other Financing Resources section of the Statement of Changes in Net Position.

Resources that do not fund net cost of operations. The second section of the Statement of Financing adjusts total resources to account for items that were included in net obligation and other resources, but are not part of the entity's net cost of operations for the reporting period. An example of an item in this section would be an expense that was recognized in a prior period, but the liability was liquidated with budgetary resources provided in the current period (i.e., the accrual of an unfunded environmental liability). Another example would be items in which a budgetary resource is utilized in the current period, but the item does not affect current period net cost (the purchase of a fixed asset).

Costs that do not require (current) resources. This section reflects items that are recognized as a component of net cost in the current period but do not require a current period obligation. Typical examples would include an increase in the annual leave liability, an increase in environmental liability, and the upward/downward reestimates of credit subsidy expense.

Financing sources yet to be provided. Another section reflects items that are part of the current period net cost of operations, but that will never require the use of a budgetary resource. The two most common note disclosures related to the Statement of Financing are:

1. An explanation of the relationship between liabilities not covered by budgetary resources on the balance sheet and the change in components requiring or generating resources in future periods.
2. A description of transfers that appear as a reconciling item on the Statement of Financing. This would occur when budget authority and other resources are allocated to another reporting entity.

This section identifies costs of a federal entity that have not been funded by Congress. Common examples include unfunded capitalized lease liabilities and earned but unused annual leave of federal employees. These costs are typically funded on a "pay-as-you-go" basis. Since these costs are unfunded, an offsetting financing source (i.e., financing sources to be provided) is required in calculating the net cost of operations for a fiscal period.

Net cost of operations. The net cost of operations reported on this statement must be the same amount that appears as the "net cost of operations" on the Statement of Net Cost and on the Statement of Changes in Net Position for the same fiscal period.

Statement of Custodial Activity

The Statement of Custodial Activity is not required for all federal entities, only for those agencies that collect nonexchange revenue for the General Fund of the Treasury, a trust fund, or other recipient entities. An additional exception to the preparation of the Statement of Custodial Activity is made for entities whose custodial collections are immaterial and incidental to their primary mission. In these instances, the collections are identified in the footnotes to the entity's financial statements. In addition, entities preparing a Statement of Custodial Activity for nonexchange revenue should disclose the:

- Basis of accounting
- Factors affecting the collectibility and timing of the nonexchange revenue
- Cash collections and refunds

Agencies required to prepare a Statement of Custodial Activity include the Internal Revenue Service, Customs and Border Protection, and the Federal Communications Commission.

To account for custodial activity, the collecting entities do not recognize as revenue those collections that have been, or should be, transferred to others as revenue. Instead, the collection and disbursement of funds is reported on the statement of custodial activity. If some of the nonexchange revenue is transferred to others and some is retained by the collecting entity to offset the cost of collections, both amounts are reported on the Statement of Custodial Activity and the amounts retained are also reported on the Statement of Net Cost. (See Exhibit 6.6.) In all cases, the total sources of collections section (total revenue) must equal the total of the disposition of collections section (total disposition of revenue). The net custodial activity must always be zero. These requirements are described in SFFAS 7, *Accounting for Revenue and Other Financing Sources.*

Exhibit 6.6: Statement of custodial activity

Department/Agency/Reporting Entity
Statement of Custodial Activity
For the Years ended September 30, 20X2 and 20X1
(in dollars/thousands/millions)

	20X2	*20X1*
Revenue activity:		
Sources of cash collections:		
1. Individual income and FICA/SECA taxes	$ xxx	$ xxx
2. Corporate income taxes	xxx	xxx
3. Excise taxes	xxx	xxx
4. Estate and gift taxes	xxx	xxx
5. Federal unemployment taxes	xxx	xxx
6. Customs duties	xxx	xxx
7. Miscellaneous	<u>xxx</u>	<u>xxx</u>
8. Total cash collections	x,xxx	x,xxx
9. Accrual adjustments (+/–)	<u>xxx</u>	<u>xxx</u>
10. Total custodial revenue	x,xxx	x,xxx
Disposition of collections:		
11. Transferred to others (by recipient)	xxx	xxx
Recipient A	xxx	xxx
Recipient B	xxx	xxx
Recipient C	xxx	xxx
12. (Increase)/decrease in amounts yet to be transferred (+/–)	xxx	xxx
13. Refunds and other payments	xxx	xxx
14. Retained by the reporting entity	<u>xxx</u>	<u>xxx</u>
15. Net custodial activity	$ 0	$ 0

Management Discussion and Analysis

Every agency's annual audited financial statement must include a section devoted to Management's Discussion and Analysis (MD&A) of the financial statements and related information. The MD&A section is designed to help readers better understand the entity's financial position and operating results and to answer questions more directly related to a federal entity's activities. Examples include:

- What is the entity's financial position and condition and how did these occur?
- What were the significant variations from prior years, from the budget, from performance plans in addition to the budget?
- What is the potential effect of these factors, of changed circumstances, and of expected future trends?
- Will future financial position, condition, and results, as reflected in future financial statements, probably be different from this year's, and if yes, why?
- Are the systems of accounting and internal administrative controls adequate to ensure that transactions are executed in accordance with budgetary and financial laws, assets are properly acquired and used, and performance measurement information is adequately supported?

The content of the MD&A is the responsibility of management. Its preparation should be a joint effort of both the Chief Financial Officer and the program offices. The MD&A should be a fair and balanced presentation of information. It should include both positive and negative performance information, as necessary, to accurately portray the results of the agency. The information presented should be consistent with information presented in the performance plans and reports and the budget information. The auditor will not opine on the information presented in the MD&A, but must perform certain limited procedures. The procedures consist principally of inquiries of the agency's management regarding the methods of measurement and presentation of the information.

In 1998, FASAB recommended that the MD&A be treated as required supplementary information to federal financial statements.[7] FASAB desired that the MD&A section of federal financial statements section address an entity's:

- Mission and organizational structure
- Performance goals and results
- Financial statements
- Systems and controls
- Possible future effect on the entity's current demands, risks, uncertainties, events, conditions, and trends

FASAB states that the subjects in the MD&A could be based on information in other sections of the entity's general-purpose financial report or other reports that may be separate from the general-purpose financial report.

Required Supplementary Stewardship Information

Some federal entities are entrusted with responsibilities for stewardship assets: (1) stewardship property, plant & equipment (PP&E), for example, heritage assets (monuments, memorials, historical cultural), mission PP&E (defense and space), and

---

[7] FASAB, *Concepts for Management's Discussion and Analysis*, Washington, DC, November 1998.

stewardship land (not for, or in connection with, general PP&E); (2) stewardship investments; and (3) other stewardship responsibilities.

The reporting and disclosure of these assets may be in terms of physical units rather than cost, fair value, or other monetary values. While discussed in some detail in FASAB publications and by OMB, reporting of stewardship assets is largely experimental at this time.

GOVERNMENT-WIDE FINANCIAL STATEMENTS

In the spring of 1998, the first consolidated and audited financial statements were issued for the United States government covering its fiscal year ended September 30, 1997. The secretary of the Treasury proclaimed it a historic event, stating "never before has the United States government attempted to assemble comprehensive financial statements covering all of its myriad activities and to subject those financial statements to an audit."

Format of Consolidated US Statements

The consolidated government-wide financial statements differed somewhat from those prescribed and used by individual federal entities in order to reflect the different reporting perspective for the entire government. Those initial government-wide consolidated statements were comprised of:

- A Management Discussion and Analysis section by the secretary of the Treasury
- A disclaimer of audit opinion on the government-wide consolidated financial statements, a report on internal controls, a report on compliance with laws and regulations related to financial reporting, plus other information transmitted by the chief accountant of GAO
- A consolidated Balance Sheet for the United States government
- A consolidated Statement of Net Cost for the United States government
- A consolidated Statement of Changes in Net Position for the United States government
- Notes to these financial statements
- A consolidated stewardship reporting for the United States government
- A consolidated stewardship reporting that reconciled changes in net position reported on a cost basis to the deficit position reported on the budgetary basis

Content of Consolidated US Statements

The notes to the 2004 financial statements of the government (i.e., the consolidated financial statements of the United States) included the financial activities of the executive, legislative, and judiciary branches, with these exceptions (or deviations from GAAP):

- The Senate and the House of Representatives report on the cash basis.
- The judiciary branch reports on a limited basis (this branch is not required by law to submit financial statements to the Department of the Treasury), and what is reported is reported on the cash basis.

- Government-sponsored enterprises (i.e., Fannie Mae, Freddie Mac) are not included.
- Entities with activities not included in the federal budget's total are also excluded. Examples include the Board of Governors of the Federal Reserve and the Thrift Savings Fund.

Basis of Accounting for US Statements

The consolidated financial statements are prepared in accordance with the form and content guidance specified by OMB that incorporates the recommendations of the Federal Accounting Standards Advisory Board. Under this basis of accounting, expenses are recognized when incurred and nonexchange revenues are recognized on a modified cash basis. Cash remittances are recognized when received, and any related receivables are recognized when measurable and legally collectible by the federal government. Exchange revenues are recognized when earned.

Financial Reporting Checklist

In performing the audit of a federal entity, the auditor should complete, or have completed by the auditee, GAO/PCIE's *Financial Audit Manual Checklist for Reports Prepared under the CFO Act*. The checklist has been incorporated in GAO's Financial Audit Manual (Section 1050).

APPENDIX

Financial Statement Account Balances Checklist

The items below set forth certain relationships between the line items in the basic financial statements. As part of his/her closing procedures, the auditor should ensure that the basic financial statements and accompanying footnotes follow these relationships.

Yes   *No*   *Explain*

1. The Total Net Position (Line 31) on the Consolidated Balance Sheet will agree with the Ending Balance (Line 18) as reported on the Consolidated Statement of Changes in Net Position.

2. The Net Cost of Operations (Line 10) on the Consolidated Statement of Net Cost will agree with both the Net Cost of Operations (Line 17) as reported on the Consolidated Statement of Changes in Net Position and the Net Cost of Operations (Line 30) as reported on the Consolidated Statement of Financing.

3. The Other Financing Sources: donations and forfeitures of property (Line 12) on the Consolidated Statement of Changes in New Position will agree with Other Resources: donations and forfeitures of property (Line 6) as reported on the Consolidated Statement of Financing.

4. The Other Financing Sources: Transfers-in/out without reimbursement (Line 13) on the Consolidated Statement of Changes in New Position will agree with other resources: Transfers-in/out without reimbursement (Line 7) as reported on the Consolidated Statement of Financing.

5. The Other Financing Sources: Imputed financing from Costs Absorbed by Others (Line 14) on the Consolidated Statement of Changes in New Position will agree with Other Resources: Imputed financing from costs absorbed by others (Line 8) as reported on the Consolidated Statement of Financing.

6. The Other Financing Sources: Other (Line 15) on the Consolidated Statement of Changes in New Position will agree with Other Resources: Other (Line 9) as reported on the Consolidated Statement of Financing.

7. The sum of Spending authority from offsetting collections: Subtotal (Line 3e) and Recoveries of prior year obligations (Line 4) on the Combined Statement of Budgetary Resources will agree with Less: Spending authority from offsetting collections and recoveries (Line 2) as reported on the Consolidated Statement of Financing.

8. The Obligations incurred: Subtotal (Line 8c) on the Combined Statement of Budgetary Resources will agree with Obligations incurred (Line 1) as reported on the Consolidated Statement of Financing.

Yes   *No*   *Explain*

9. The Less: Offsetting receipts (Line 16) on the Combined Statement of Budgetary Resources will agree with Less: Offsetting receipts (Line 4) as reported on the Consolidated Statement of Financing.

Note Disclosures Related to the Consolidated Balance Sheet

10. The Total Assets disclosed in Note 2 will agree with the Total Assets (Line 15) as reported on the Consolidated Balance Sheet.

11. The Total Fund Balance with Treasury disclosed in Note 3 will agree with the Fund Balance with Treasury (Line 1) as reported on the Consolidated Balance Sheet.

12. The Total Cash and Other Monetary Assets disclosed in Note 4 will agree with the Cash and Other Monetary Assets (Line 7) as reported on the Consolidated Balance Sheet.

13. The Total Investments (Section A and B) disclosed in Note 5 will agree with the Intragovernmental: Investments (Line 2) and Investments (Line 8) as reported on the Consolidated Balance Sheet.

14. The Accounts Receivable, Net disclosed in Note 6 will agree with the Intragovernmental: Accounts receivable (Line 3) and Accounts receivable, net (Line 9) as reported on the Consolidated Balance Sheet.

15. The Taxes Receivable, Net disclosed in Note 7 will agree with the Taxes Receivable, Net (Line 10) as reported on the Consolidated Balance Sheet.

16. The Direct Loans and Loan Guarantees, Nonfederal Borrowers disclosed in Note 8 will agree with the Loans Receivable and related foreclosed property, net (Line 11) and Loan guarantee liability (Line 21) as reported on the Consolidated Balance Sheet.

17. The Inventory and Related Property, Net disclosed in Note 9 will agree with Inventory and Related Property, net (Line 12) as reported on the Consolidated Balance Sheet.

18. The General Property, Plant, and Equipment, Net disclosed in Note 10 will agree with General Property, Plant, and Equipment, net (Line 13) as reported on the Consolidated Balance Sheet.

19. The Total Intragovernmental (A.1.) and Total Other Assets disclosed in Note 11 will agree with the Intragovernmental: Other (Line 5) and Other (Line 14) as reported on the Consolidated Balance Sheet.

20. The Total liabilities disclosed in Note 12 will agree with the Total liabilities (Line 27) as reported on the Consolidated Balance Sheet.

21. The Debt disclosed in Note 13 will agree with the In-tragovernmental: Debt (Line 17) and Debt held by the public (Line 22) as reported on the Consolidated Balance Sheet.

22. The Federal Employee and Veterans' Benefits disclosed in Note 14 will agree with Federal employee and veterans' benefits (Line 23) as reported on the Consolidated Balance Sheet.

23. The Environmental and Disposal Liabilities disclosed in Note 15 will agree with Environmental and Disposal Liabilities (Line 24) as reported on the Consolidated Balance Sheet.

24. The Other Liabilities (Note 16), Leases (Note 17) and Life Insurance Liabilities (Note 18) as disclosed will agree with the Intragovernmental: Other (Line 18) and Other (Line 26) as reported on the Consolidated Balance Sheet.

25. The Commitments and Contingencies disclosed in Note 19 will agree with Commitments and Contingencies (Line 28) as reported on the Consolidated Balance Sheet.

Note Disclosures Related to the Statement of Net Cost

26. The Suborganization Program Costs/Program Costs by segment disclosed in Note 21 will act as a supporting schedule to fully display the entity's suborganizations. The Consolidated Total Net Cost of Operations will agree with the Net Cost of Operations (Line 10) as reported on the Consolidated Statement of Net Cost.

Note Disclosures Related to the Statement of Changes in Net Position

27. The Cleanup Cost Adjustments disclosed in Note 26 will be included in the Prior period adjustments (Line 2) as reported on the Consolidated Statement of Changes in New Position.

Note Disclosures Related to the Statement of Budgetary Resources

28. The Apportionment Categories of Obligations Incurred disclosed in Note 27 will agree with Obligations Incurred: Direct (Line 8a) and Reimbursable (Line 8b) as reported on the Combined Statement of Budgetary Resources.

PART III

Auditing in the Federal Government

7 THE FEDERAL AUDIT MODEL

The acquisition of audit evidence and reporting the results of a federal audit requires a particular diligence, as data from the audit of a federal agency's financial statements find their way into other related sources of information. Among these outlets are reports to senior executives of the federal cabinet and other agencies, the Executive Office of the President of the United States, responsible committees of Congress, and, with some frequency, "sound bites" by television's talking heads or more extensive reporting by the print media.

AUDIT CHECKLISTS AND MODELS

Over the years, virtually every accounting firm and federal agency involved in the execution of financial statement audits has developed an audit model along with supporting "audit checklists" and audit programs to guide the efforts of their staff. The GAO, with PCIE, has compiled three manuals directly relevant to the conduct of federal audits:

- *Financial Audit Manual (FAM)*
- *Federal Information System Controls Audit Manual (FISCAM)*
- *Standards for Internal Control in the Federal Government*

These documents, superbly researched and the labor of many months, are comprehensive (the two-part FAM being nearly 800 pages and FISCAM, another 280 plus pages) guides covering virtually every possible aspect of a federal financial audit. The availability of such guidance may beg the question of why any planning must be done when such working models and well-defined audit procedures are readily available.

Every audit is unique. Applied audit procedures must be tailored to the conditions and circumstances encountered, which not only differ from agency to agency, but within a single agency from one year to the next. Models are very useful in planning, but it does not follow that every audit consists of the execution of predetermined steps or procedures.

Audit manuals are not a substitute for audit judgment. The circumstances and conditions specific to a particular agency may deem application of the FAM guidance as entirely appropriate. However, the FAM's audit model notes that judgment must be exercised in applying the model. It is expected that the tasks and activities suggested will require modification, refinement, and/or supplementation. Many of the recent audit failures have marred commercial audits with resultant shortcomings in the applied audit approaches and possible applications of inappropriate accounting principles.

AUDITING DEFINED

In its codification of statements on auditing standards, the AICPA provided this definition of an audit:

> *An examination of financial information of any entity, whether profit-oriented or not, and irrespective of its size, or legal form, when such an examination is conducted with a view to expressing an opinion thereon.*
>
> *The objective of this examination is the expression of an opinion on the fairness with which the financial statements present an entity's financial position, results of operations, and changes in financial position and cash flows in conformity with generally accepted auditing standards.*

Historically, and to this date, this definition and the AICPA's generally accepted auditing standards are the principal audit criteria underlying the examinations of financial statements made by auditors and accepted by users of the resulting audit reports. These standards, while applied earlier to audits of corporate and private entities, have been adopted for the performance of audits at all levels of government and of all types of public entities and nonprofit organizations.

In the 1970s, GAO declared audits of governments to be different, more comprehensive, and requiring, if not different standards, then the application of additional standards to address issues other than financial that are important to everyone interested in the accountability of governments and other public bodies. Thus, GAO's generally accepted government auditing standards defined *audit* as:

> *A term used to describe, not only work done by accountants in examining financial statements, but also work done in reviewing (1) compliance with laws and regulations, (2) economy and efficiency operations, and (3) effectiveness in achieving program results.*
>
> *The objective of such an examination includes an expression of the fairness of the presentation of an entity's financial statements, but additionally a reporting, or an audit opinion, if sufficient audit work was performed, on the nature of tests made and results of those tests with respect to an entity's system of internal controls and its compliance with laws and regulations and provisions of contract and grant agreements.*

In the 1980s, with the passage of the Single Audit Act of 1984, the nature of government audits was refined further to encompass an annual comprehensive audit of any government. By the initial act, and amendments in 1996, a single annual audit was to be made, ideally, by one audit organization once a year. The scope of a *single audit* was defined as:

> *The single audit is to encompass the entirety of the financial operations of state and local government operations, or such departments, agencies, and establishments as applicable, and to report on: (1) whether the financial statements were presented fairly; (2) whether the state and local governments' operations or such departments, agencies, and establishments complied with laws and regulations that could have an effect on those financial statements and on each major federal program; (3) whether the state and local governments' operations or such departments, agencies, and establishments had internal control systems to provide reasonable assurance that federal programs were managed in compliance with laws and regulations.*

The comprehensiveness of the scope of a single audit requires an auditor to simultaneously apply the generally accepted auditing standards (of the AICPA), the *Government Auditing Standards* (of GAO), and federal regulations (of OMB) to these comprehensive audits of federally assisted programs.

FEDERAL AUDIT MODEL

The federal audit model outlined in the *Financial Audit Manual* provides a framework for performing financial statement audits in accordance with *Government Auditing Standards,* integrating the requirements of the federal accounting standards, and assessing compliance with laws and regulations. The *Government Auditing Standards* incorporate, by reference, all of the generally accepted field auditing standards, audit reporting standards, and attestation standards established by the AICPA.

The methodology outlined in the government's FAM audit model was also designed to meet compliance requirements prescribed by several other federal-wide criteria and guidance, such as those prescribed by the

- FMFIA
- CFO Act
- PCIE
- FFMIA
- FASAB[1]
- OMB

PHASES OF FEDERAL AUDITS

At the outset of any audit, the auditor must have a clear idea of the objectives of the audit in order to identify an audit scope, audit process, and audit procedures that will achieve those objectives. Naturally, it helps to have a model.

For financial audits, several useful models exist. One such model, applied in the execution of financial audits of federal agencies, is the model jointly developed by GAO and the PCIE (i.e., the federal government's Council of Inspectors General). Their audit model, as detailed in the FAM and FISCAM, describes an audit of a federal agency's financial statements that is comprised of four phases:

- Phase I: Planning the audit and assessing financial processes and systems
- Phase II: Understanding and evaluating the internal controls
- Phase III: Testing controls and substantive audits of transactions, accounts, and account groups
- Phase IV: Reporting audit conclusions, audit results, auditor's opinion, and other assurances

---

[1] *In October 1999, the AICPA recognized FASAB as the accounting standards setter and dictated its standards to be the generally accepted accounting principles for federal entities. FASAB standards allow government corporations and certain other federal entities to report using GAAP issued by the Financial Accounting Standards Board, the recognized promulgator of GAAP for entities in the private sector.*

Phase I: Planning the Audit

The purpose of Phase I is to develop a preliminary understanding of the operations of the auditee, the auditee's internal controls, and financial systems, including an initial review of the auditee's computer-based support systems. The auditor's initial understanding of these systems is augmented during each subsequent phase of the audit, as control systems are further evaluated and tested. It is important to realize that planning a financial audit is not a one-time-only task, but rather a process.

An objective of this initial phase of planning is to identify significant areas of risks and issues required by law and regulations to be examined and to design appropriate evaluative audit procedures. To accomplish this, the auditor must conduct a review early on to rapidly acquire an understanding of the federal agency's operations, organization, management style and systems, applied internal controls, and external factors that influence its operations. In this phase, it is imperative that the auditor also identify all significant accounts, accounting applications, the key financial management systems, material appropriation restrictions and budget limitations, and provisions of applicable laws and regulations.

The planning phase is where the auditor must assess and acquire an understanding of the relative effectiveness of both an agency's systems of internal financial controls and its information systems controls, with the objective of identifying high-risk areas, potential risks of fraud, and possible abuses of financial resources.

Phase II: Understand and Evaluate Internal Controls

The purpose of Phase II is to assess and obtain a comprehensive working knowledge of the current state and operating efficiency of the internal control systems and work flows of a federal agency's significant systems. This includes such systems as budget, financial reporting, procurement, revenue/cash receipts, cash disbursements, payroll, and data processing. At this phase's conclusion, the auditor should have evaluated the system's design and related internal financial controls and identified the system's design strengths and weaknesses and potential audit obstacles that will require refinement of the planned audit approach.

This phase requires internal controls to be assessed to support the auditor's initial evaluations about the:

- *Reliability of financial reporting:* Whether transactions are properly recorded, processed, and summarized to permit the preparation of the principal statements and required supplementary stewardship information (RSSI) in accordance with GAAP, and assets are safeguarded against loss from unauthorized acquisition, use, or disposition.
- *Compliance with applicable laws and regulations:* Whether transactions are executed in accordance with: (a) laws governing the use of budget authority and other laws and regulations that could have a direct and material effect on the agency principal statements or RSSI, and (b) any other laws, regulations, and government-wide policies identified by OMB in its audit guidance.

The AICPA's attestation standards, incorporated by reference into the government's auditing standards, permit an auditor to give an opinion on internal control or on management's assertion about the effectiveness of internal control. There is an exception if material weaknesses are present; then the opinion must be limited to internal controls and not management's assertion. Additionally, OMB's audit guidance includes a third objective of internal control related to performance measures.

Thus, an evaluation of internal controls requires the auditor to identify and understand the relevant controls and assess the relative effectiveness of the controls, which will then be tested later in the audit. Where controls are considered effective, reliance may be placed on such controls and the extent of later substantive testing (e.g., detailed tests of transactions and account groups) can be reduced. The FAM model methodology includes relevant guidance to:

- Assess specific levels of control risk.
- Select the financial controls to be tested.
- Determine the effectiveness of information systems controls.
- Test the controls, including the coordination of the more extensive control tests to be conducted in the later testing phase.

During the internal control phase, the auditor should understand the entity's significant financial management systems and test systems compliance with FFMIA requirements.

Phase III: Test Controls, Transactions, Account, and Account Groups

Phase III encompasses tests of controls and the performance of substantive testing (e.g., tests of the transactions and accounts and the conduct of analytic review procedures).

Upon conclusion of internal control testing, the auditor will have either verified the initial control evaluation or identified conditions which require a revision of the initial evaluation.

Internal control testing will be followed by substantive testing. The extent of substantive testing will depend on the auditor's (revised, if applicable) final evaluation of internal controls. Evidence acquired from performing substantive audit procedures, when considered in conjunction with the results of internal control testing, is a critical determinant as to whether an agency's financial statements are free of material misstatements. Some important audit objectives of the testing phase are to:

- Obtain reasonable assurance about whether the financial statements are free from material misstatements.
- Determine whether the entity complied with significant provisions of applicable laws and regulations.
- Assess the effectiveness of internal control through actual testing of the controls applied and practiced by agency employees.

To do this, the FAM model audit methodology includes guidance on the:

- Design and performance of substantive, compliance, and control tests
- Design and evaluation of evidence obtained in audit samples
- Correlation of risk and materiality with decisions on the nature, timing, and extent of substantive audit tests

- Design of multipurpose tests, using a common sample to test several different controls, transactions, and specific accounts
- Execute tests, and based on test results, validate or revise the initial evaluation developed during Phase II.

Phase IV: Reporting Audit Conclusions, Audit Results, and the Auditor's Opinion

During Phase IV, the auditor considers the evidential result of testing tasks and other audit activities, completes a number of end-of-audit procedures, makes a final technical review of the audit procedures performed, and concludes whether sufficient evidential matter has been obtained to support the audit opinion and other assurances the auditor must provide on an agency's financial statements and other information included in the auditor's report.

Key audit tasks and procedures of this phase involve preparation of the auditor's report on an agency's:

- Financial statements (i.e., the principal statements)
- Other information, such as MD&A
- Other required supplementary information and accompanying information required by the GAAP issued by FASAB
- Results of audit tests made of internal controls
- Financial management systems employed by the agency to substantially comply with Federal Financial Management Improvement Act requirements[2]
- The results of audit tests for compliance with laws and regulations.

Exhibit 7.1 is an overview of the numerous audit tasks, activities, and audit procedures suggested by GAO and the PCIE in the *Financial Audit Manual* that should[3] be performed for most federal financial statement audits. Several of the following chapters contain additional discussions of some audit tasks and activities most often applied in practice. It is important to recognize that, in practice, an audit is a continuum of tasks and activities that must be completed within a finite budget and in a coordinated manner to permit the timely communication of the audit results to the government.

The federal audit model (FAM) and the execution of federal audits are influenced by standards, concepts, guidelines, manuals procedures, and techniques as

---

[2] *The Federal Financial Management Improvement Act of 1996, Congress required that "each agency shall implement and maintain financial management systems that comply substantially with (1) federal financial management systems requirements, (2) applicable federal accounting standards, and (3) the United States Government Standard General Ledger at the transaction level."*

[3] *With respect to federal audits, words have very definite meanings, for example:*

- *Must: Compliance with a "must" policy or procedure is mandatory unless an exception is approved in writing by the reviewer of the audit, as in certain instances when a disclaimer of opinion is anticipated.*
- *Should: Compliance with a "should" policy or procedure is expected unless there is a reasonable basis for departure from it. Any such departure and the basis for the departure is required to be documented in a formalized memorandum, approved by the appropriate designated level in the audit management organization.*
- *Generally should: Compliance with a "generally should" policy or procedure is strongly encouraged. Departure from such a policy or procedure should be discussed with the appropriate designated level in the audit management organization.*
- *May: Compliance with a "may" policy or procedure is optional.*

well as specific circumstances encountered during the performance of the audit itself. These factors and their effect(s) on the audits of federal entities are detailed in the following sections.

GOVERNMENT AUDITING STANDARDS:
NOT STAND-ALONE STANDARDS

The *Government Auditing Standards* are not a stand-alone set of auditing standards. For prescribed audits, both GAGAS and GAAS of the AICPA must be applied for an audit to comply fully with the GAGAS criteria. Each revision of GAGAS contains references to the fact that GAGAS incorporates all of the AICPA's GAAS and all the AICPA's Statements on Auditing Standards, unless specifically exempted by GAO. Since the initial edition of GAGAS in 1972, GAO has not exempted an AICPA auditing standard. The beginnings of *Government Auditing Standards* can be traced to meetings as early as 1968 between state auditors and the comptroller general at which the case was made to GAO that state and federal auditing practices left much to be desired and that a unique body of auditing standards was needed to rectify this deficiency.

GAO's audit and investigatory authority permitted audits and examinations to be made of federal and nonfederal entities, as well as federal contractors, grantees, not-for-profits, educational institutions, and others receiving federal financial assistance. Subsequent federal legislation, particularly several laws passed in the 1990s, required that audits of federal agencies, programs, and activities conform to the *Government Auditing Standards. Government Auditing Standards* are to be applied by any auditor, regardless of their employer, when these standards are required by federal law, regulation, agreement, contract, grant, or federal governmental policy, including

- Federal, state, and local governmental internal auditors
- Governmental Inspectors General and auditors
- Accounting firms under contract to federal departments and agencies and programs of federal financial assistance
- Certified public accountants and non-CPA auditors
- Nonaudit personnel on federal audit teams

Further, GAGAS are not auditing standards imposed only on governmental entities. GAGAS are the auditing standards applied to audits of all federal entities and nonfederal organizations that receive a designated level of federal financial assistance, whether that assistance is obtained under a federal contract or grant, loans or loan guarantees, federal insurance programs, or federal government food commodity initiatives. With respect to the nonfederal entities, this universe of potential auditees includes organizations such as contractors, grantees, nonprofit organizations, colleges and universities, Indian tribal nations, public utilities and authorities, financial institutions, hospitals, and more.

Exhibit 7.1: Federal audit model

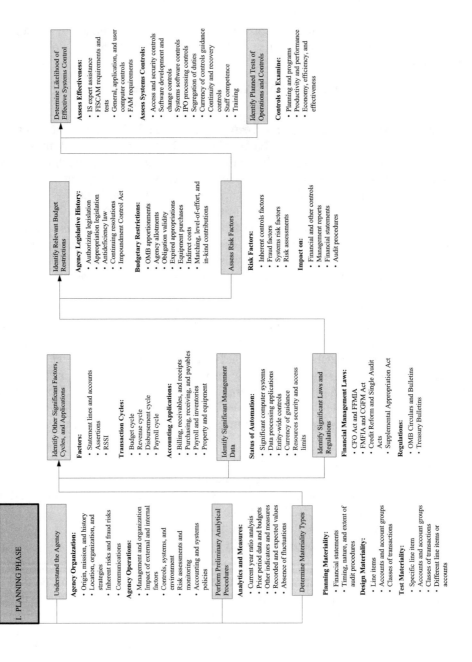

I. PLANNING PHASE

Understand the Agency

Agency Organization:
- Origin, mission, and history
- Location, organization, and strategies
- Inherent risks and fraud risks
- Communications

Agency Operations:
- Management and organization
- Impact of external and internal factors
- Controls, systems, and environment
- Risk assessments and monitoring
- Accounting and systems policies

Perform Preliminary Analytical Procedures

Analytics and Measures:
- Current year ratio analysis
- Prior period data and budgets
- Other indicators and measures
- Recorded and expected values
- Absence of fluctuations

Determine Materiality Types

Planning Materiality:
- Financial statements

Design Materiality:
- Line items
- Accounts and account groups
- Classes of transactions

Test Materiality:
- Specific line item
- Accounts and account groups
- Classes of transactions
- Different line items or accounts

Identify Other Significant Factors, Cycles, and Applications

Factors:
- Statement lines and accounts
- Assertions
- RSSI

Transaction Cycles:
- Budget cycle
- Revenue cycle
- Disbursement cycle
- Payroll cycle

Accounting Applications:
- Billing, receivables, and receipts
- Purchasing, receiving, and payables
- Payroll and inventories
- Property and equipment

Identify Significant Management Data

Status of Automation:
- Significant computer systems
- Data processing applications
- Entity-wide controls
- Currency of guidance
- Resources security and access limits

Identify Significant Laws and Regulations

Financial Management Laws:
- CFO Act and FFMIA
- FMFIA and CGFM Act
- Credit Reform and Single Audit Acts
- Supplemental Appropriation Act

Regulations:
- OMB Circulars and Bulletins
- Treasury Bulletins

Identify Relevant Budget Restrictions

Agency Legislative History:
- Authorizing legislation
- Appropriation legislation
- Antideficiency law
- Continuing resolutions
- Impoundment Control Act

Budgetary Restrictions:
- OMB apportionments
- Agency allotments
- Obligation validity
- Expired appropriations
- Equipment purchases
- Indirect costs
- Matching, level-of-effort, and in-kind contributions

Assess Risk Factors

Risk Factors:
- Inherent controls factors
- Fraud factors
- Systems risk factors
- Risk assessments

Impact on:
- Financial and other controls
- Management reports
- Financial statements
- Audit procedures

Determine Likelihood of Effective Systems Control

Assess Effectiveness:
- IS expert assistance
- FISCAM requirements and tests
- General, application, and user computer controls
- FAM requirements

Assess Systems Controls:
- Access and security controls
- Software development and change controls
- Systems software controls
- IPO processing controls
- Segregation of duties
- Currency of controls guidance
- Continuity and recovery controls
- Staff competence
- Training

Identify Planned Tests of Operations and Controls

Controls to Examine:
- Planning and programs
- Productivity and performance
- Economy, efficiency, and effectiveness

Exhibit 7.1: Federal audit model (continued)

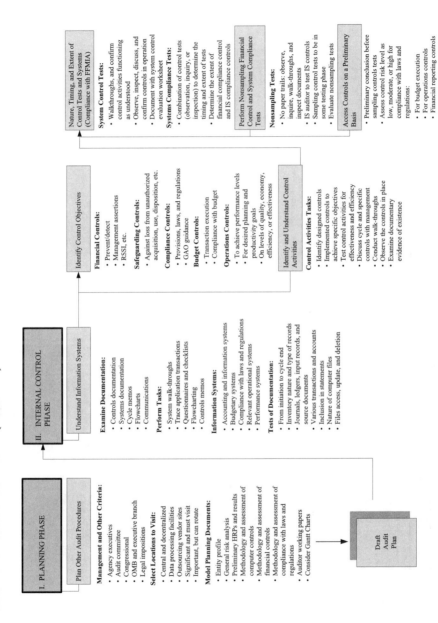

I. PLANNING PHASE

Plan Other Audit Procedures

Management and Other Criteria:
- Agency executives
- Audit committee
- Congressional
- OMB and executive branch
- Legal impositions

Select Locations to Visit:
- Central and decentralized
- Data processing facilities
- Outsourcing vendor sites
- Significant and must visit
- Important, but can rotate

Model Planning Documents:
- Entity profile
- General risk analysis
- Preliminary HRP's and results
- Methodology and assessment of computer controls
- Methodology and assessment of financial controls
- Methodology and assessment of compliance with laws and regulations
- Auditor working papers
- Consider Gantt Charts

Draft Audit Plan

II. INTERNAL CONTROL PHASE

Understand Information Systems

Examine Documentation:
- Controls documentation
- Systems documentation
- Cycle memos
- Flowcharts
- Communications

Perform Tasks:
- System walk-throughs
- Trace application transactions
- Questionnaires and checklists
- Flowcharting
- Controls memos

Information Systems:
- Accounting and information systems
- Budgetary systems
- Compliance with laws and regulations
- Relevant operational systems
- Performance systems

Tests of Documentation:
- From initiation to cycle end
- Inventory nature and type of records
- Journals, ledgers, input records, and source documents
- Various transactions and accounts
- Inclusion in statements
- Nature of computer files
- Files access, update, and deletion

Identify Control Objectives

Financial Controls:
- Prevent/detect
- Management assertions
- RSSI, etc.

Safeguarding Controls:
- Against loss from unauthorized acquisition, use, disposition, etc.

Compliance Controls:
- Provisions, laws, and regulations
- GAO guidance

Budget Controls:
- Transaction execution
- Compliance with budget

Operations Controls:
- To achieve performance levels
- For desired planning and productivity goals
- On levels of quality, economy, efficiency, or effectiveness

Identify and Understand Control Activities

Control Activities Tasks:
- Identify designed controls
- Implemented controls to achieve specific objectives
- Test control activities for effectiveness and efficiency
- Discuss cycle and specific controls with management
- Conduct walk-throughs
- Observe the controls in place
- Examine documentary evidence of existence

Nature, Timing, and Extent of Control Tests and Systems (Compliance with FFMIA)

System Control Tests:
- Walkthroughs, and confirm control activities functioning as understood
- Observe, inspect, discuss, and confirm controls in operation
- Document with system control evaluation worksheet

Systems Compliance Tests:
- Combination of control tests (observation, inquiry, or inspection) to determine the timing and extent of tests
- Determine the extent of financial compliance control and IS compliance controls

Perform Nonsampling Financial Control and System Compliance Tests

Nonsampling Tests:
- No paper trails: observe, inquire, walk-throughs, and inspect documents
- IS auditor to test IS controls
- Sampling control tests to be in some testing phase
- Evaluate nonsampling tests

Access Controls on a Preliminary Basis
- Preliminary conclusion before sampling controls tests
- Assess control risk level as low, moderate, or high for compliance with laws and regulations:
  - For budget execution
  - For operations controls
  - Financial reporting controls
- Determine if results are contrary to the preliminary controls assessments

Exhibit 7.1: Federal audit model (continued)

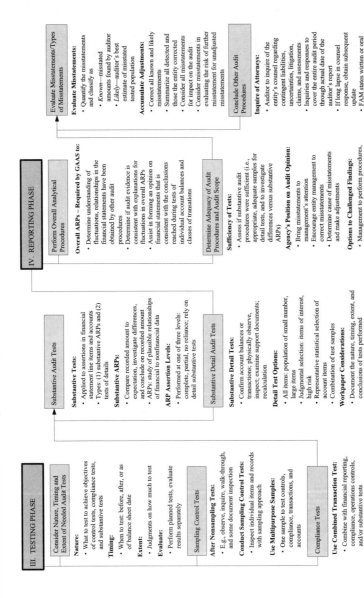

III. TESTING PHASE

Consider Nature, Timing and Extent of Needed Audit Tests

Nature:
- What to test to achieve objectives of control tests, compliance tests, and substantive tests

Timing:
- When to test: before, after, or as of balance sheet date

Extent:
- Judgments on how much to test

Evaluate:
- Perform planned tests, evaluate results separately

Sampling Control Tests

After Nonsampling Tests:
- E.g., observe, inquire, walk-through, and some document inspection

Conduct Sampling Control Tests:
- Inspect individual items and records with sampling approach

Use Multipurpose Samples:
- One sample to test controls, compliance, transactions, and accounts

Compliance Tests

Use Combined Transaction Test:
- Combine with financial reporting, compliance, operations controls, and/or substantive tests

Test Transactions Amounts with/for:
- Validity criteria, completeness, cutoff, recordation, classification, and summarization criteria

Substantive Audit Tests

Substantive Tests:
- Applied to assertions in financial statement line items and accounts
- Types: (1) substantive ARPs and (2) tests of details

Substantive ARPs:
- Compare recorded amount to expectation, investigate differences, and conclude on recorded amount
- ARPs: study of plausible relationships of financial to nonfinancial data

ARP Assertion Levels:
- Performed at one of three levels: complete, partial, no reliance; rely on detail substantive tests

Substantive Detail Audit Tests

Substantive Detail Tests:
- Confirm account balances or transactions; physically observe, inspect; examine support documents; recalculation

Detail Test Options:
- All items: population of small number, large items
- Judgmental selection: items of interest, high risk
- Representative statistical selection of account items
- Combination of test samples

Workpaper Considerations:
- Document the nature, timing, extent, and conclusions of tests performed
- Document sample method, selection factors, sample size, and method of determination
- Document audit procedures performed, results, evaluations, and conclusions

Tests of Budget and Expended Budget Authority:
- End-of-period tests: transaction validity, cutoff, amount recordation, fund classification, completeness, and cutoff procedures

IV. REPORTING PHASE

Perform Overall Analytical Procedures

Overall ARPs – Required by GAAS to:
- Determine understanding of fluctuations, relationships in the financial statements have been obtained by other audit procedures
- Determine if audit evidence is consistent with explanations for fluctuations in overall ARPs
- Assist in forming an opinion on financial statements that is consistent with the conclusions reached during tests of individual account balances and classes of transactions

Determine Adequacy of Audit Procedures and Audit Scope

Sufficiency of Tests:
- Assess if substantive audit procedures were sufficient (i.e., appropriate, adequate samples for detail tests, and to investigate differences versus substantive ARPs)

Agency's Position on Audit Opinion:
- Bring misstatements to management's attention
- Encourage entity management to correct misstatements
- Determine cause of misstatements and make adjustments

Options to Challenged Findings:
- Management to perform procedures, as reviewing all or substantially all of the items to refine estimated misstatements
- Auditor increase assurance of misstatement by testing additional items

Evaluate Misstatements/Types of Misstatements

Evaluate Misstatements:
- Quantify the misstatements and classify as
- *Known*—misstated amounts found by auditor
- *Likely*—auditor's best estimate of misstated tested population

Accumulate Adjustments:
- Correct all known and likely misstatements
- Summarize all detected and those the entity corrected
- Consider all misstatements for impact on the audit
- Consider misstatements in evaluating the risk of further misstatement for unadjusted misstatements

Conclude Other Audit Procedures

Inquire of Attorneys:
- Auditor to inquire of the entity's counsel regarding contingent liabilities, uncertainties, litigation, claims, and assessments
- Inquiries and responses to cover the entire audit period through actual date of the auditor's report
- If long lapse in counsel response, obtain subsequent update
- FAM states written or oral responses; GAAS requires written responses
- Consider if refusal to respond could be a scope limitation
- Document in workpapers

Consider Subsequent Events or Transactions:
- Occur after the balance sheet date, but before audit report issued
- If material, statements must be adjusted or disclosures made

Exhibit 7.1: Federal audit model (continued)

IV. REPORTING PHASE

Conclude Other Audit Procedures (continued) → Draft Reports

Obtain Management Representations:

- Written representations are to supplement audit procedures, *not* a substitute for them
- Corroborating evidence for representations may not be available, involving management's intent, future transactions, or business decisions
- Representations to be signed by responsive, knowledgeable, management
- Representation letter to be signed as of the date of the auditor's report
- Consider that a refusal to respond could be a scope limitation
- Document workpapers
- Federal government auditors should obtain representations in addition to those required by GAAS, as:
  - Management assertions on effectiveness of internal control
  - Substantial compliance of systems to the three FFMIA requirements

Consider Related-Party Transactions:

- Existence of related parties and related-party transactions could affect the financial statements
- Require identification and examination of related-party transactions
- Disclosure of amounts and other considerations

Determine Conformity with GAAP/ GAAS:

- GAAP developed by FASAB
- GAAP if no objections by OMB, GAO, and Treasury Department
- Determine if hierarchy of federal GAAP should be applied
- Confirm GAAS procedures of AICPA, GAO and OMB

Auditor's Conclusions on:

- Financial statements
- Internal controls
- Whether the financial management systems comply with:
  - FFMIA systems requirements
  - Federal accounting standards (GAAP)
  - SGL at the transaction level
- Compliance with laws and regulations
- MD&A
- Other information in the Accountability Report, including RSSI

Issue Audit Reports, Opinions, and Assertions

Government Auditing Standards (the yellow book) were initially promulgated by GAO in 1972 and have been revised and refined over the years and could be changed more as a result of the Sarbanes-Oxley governance legislation and regulations of 2002 and later years. The June 2003 revision of the yellow book incorporates all of the fieldwork audit and audit reporting standards and subsequent statements of auditing standards issued by the AICPA.

With passage of the Sarbanes-Oxley Act in 2002 by Congress, the newly created Public Company Accounting and Oversight Board (PCAOB) became the legally empowered organization to set the auditing standards to be used by registered public accounting firms in preparing and issuing audit reports for publicly traded companies. When PCAOB promulgates these auditing standards, GAO has stated that it will monitor both the AICPA and PCAOB and clarify the GAGAS, as necessary.

MANAGEMENT'S ASSERTIONS

Under the federal audit model and its *Financial Audit Manual*, a condition precedent to forming an audit opinion on financial statements is that the auditor must first obtain and evaluate evidential matter concerning the fairness of several management assertions that are implicit or explicit in the agency's financial statements and other reporting. Audits of financial statements, financial reports, and financial data provided by an agency's management are a process of independently examining, assessing, and reporting on several assertions by that agency's management with respect to evidence supporting underlying classes of financial transactions, individual accounts, account groupings, and line items in financial statements and other financial reportings.

In presenting its financial statements, transactions, and accounts for audit, agency management explicitly and implicitly makes or warrants that several assertions are true with respect to the reported data. For example, an agency's management assertions relate to:

- *Existence or occurrence*: By this assertion, management warrants that all assets, fund balances, appropriation balances, and so on, are a true representation of real, valid, existing agency assets, rights, and resources as of the date of the financial statement or other report. Further, this assertion warrants that all events, transactions, and accounts represented in financial statements and other financial reports are real; that is, these events occurred.
- *Completeness:* By this assertion, management warrants that no amounts, balances, transactions or disclosures are omitted from the financial statements and other financial reports, that is, the submitted data are complete and reflect "the whole truth and nothing but the truth."
- *Rights and obligations:* By this assertion, management warrants that all reported assets are owned by the agency and that all liabilities represent amounts properly owed, that will be owed, or for which a contingent liability and a future claim against the agency is probable.
- *Valuation or allocation:* By this assertion, management warrants that the values of all assets, liabilities, fund and budget authority balances, expenditures, expenses, and receipts are values and reported pursuant to federal GAAP, as

promulgated by FASAB, and that amounts have been fairly allocated (through depreciation or amortization or direct write-off, etc.) between the agency's statements.

- *Presentation and disclosure:* By this assertion, management warrants that the accounting classifications (i.e., presentations in the financial statements and other reporting) between current versus noncurrent, asset versus expenses, liabilities versus expenditures, and receipts versus revenues are properly reflected pursuant to the federal GAAP, as promulgated by FASAB. Further, it warrants that all footnotes and other disclosures are adequate, not misleading, and not misstated by either the inclusion or the omission of significant or material facts.

Thus, the auditor must determine, through the audit evidence obtained and examined for each class of financial transactions, individual accounts, account groupings, and line items in financial statement and other financial reportings, whether these assertions are fair representations. Through audit tests and procedures, the auditor must examine evidence that supports or rebuts each of these assertions.

AUDIT TESTS, PROCEDURES, AND ACTIVITIES

To obtain and evaluate evidential matter concerning the fairness of management assertions implicit or explicit in the agency's financial statements and other reporting, the federal audit model and its *Financial Audit Manual* require the auditor to employ or conduct a variety of audit procedures.

Some audit procedures are more appropriate for evaluating and testing controls; others are better suited to test the fairness of transactions, account balances, and account groupings. Also, various authorities have described and grouped audit procedures and tasks by different categories. A listing of commonly applied audit procedures, audit tasks, or audit activities, all of which are required at some time by the federal audit model and its *Financial Audit Manual*, includes:

- *Examine:* a reasonably detailed study by the auditor of documents or records to determine specific facts about the evidence
- *Scan*: a less detailed examination by the auditor of documents or records to determine whether there is something unusual that warrants further investigation
- *Read:* an examination by the auditor of written information to determine facts pertinent to the audit
- *Compute:* calculation by the auditor, independent of the auditee
- *Recompute:* recalculation by the auditor to determine the correctness of an auditee's earlier calculation
- *Foot:* the addition of columns of numbers by the auditor to determine whether the total is the same as the client's amounts
- *Trace:* the validation of details, as documents and transactions, in support of amounts recorded in ledger accounts and statements; a testing of details to summary data

- *Vouch:* the validation of transaction amounts recorded in ledger accounts and statements back to details, as underlying documents and supporting records; a testing of data from the summary back to details
- *Count:* a determination of assets or other items by the auditor through physical examination
- *Compare:* a comparison of information in two different locations by the auditor
- *Observe:* the personal witnessing of events, resources, or personnel behavior by the auditor
- *Inquiry:* discussions or questioning by the auditor to obtain audit evidence
- *Confirm:* the receipt, by the auditor, of a written or oral response from an independent third party to verify information requested about the auditee by the auditor
- *Analytical review procedures:* the auditor's evaluation of financial information by a study of plausible relationships among financial and nonfinancial data, involving comparison of recorded amounts to expectations developed by the auditor[4]

Generally, or with few exceptions, the auditor's application or use of only one of these audit procedures to confirm or validate a particular management assertion would not be sufficient in itself. For the most part, more than one, and even several, of the above procedures would be applied in a financial statement audit to confirm or validate a particular management assertion.

The determination of which audit procedure or combination of audit procedures should be employed by the auditor to most efficiently and effectively acquire necessary and sufficient audit evidence requires that decisions be made with respect to the *timing, nature*, and *extent* of the audit procedures required. These terms, used extensively throughout the *Financial Audit Manual* for a variety of testing and validation efforts, are generally defined in these ways:

- *Timing* of an audit procedure or audit tests relates to the decision as to *when* audit procedures and audit tests will be applied: for example, (1) at various interim dates of the period to be audited, (2) at the end of the period to be audited, (3) after the close of the period undergoing audit, or (4) at some combinations of these times.
- *Nature* of an audit procedure or audit tests relates to the decision as to *what* audit procedures or combination of audit procedures should or will be applied.
- *Extent* of an audit procedure or audit tests relates to the decision as to specific *number* of transactions, documents, actions, and/or events that will undergo scrutiny by application of one, several, or the majority of the cited audit procedures.

In most instances, the FAM identifies the timing, nature, and type of audit procedures to be applied in the audit of a federal financial statement. However, the

---

[4] Arens, Loebbecke, **Auditing: An Integrated Approach**, 8th ed. (Saddle Brook, NJ: Prentice Hall 2000).

federal audit model and other models are somewhat less forthcoming with respect to prescribing the extent of, how much, or how many transactions, documents, actions, and events should be specifically tested. Decisions regarding the extent of testing are better left to the judgment of the auditor and the conditions and circumstances that the auditor encounters during the audit of a particular entity.

AUDIT EVIDENCE

Audit evidence must pass several tests to be acceptable in support of an auditor's conclusions and opinion. Such tests include relevance, validity, timeliness, lack of bias, objective compilation, and sufficiency. With respect to the sufficiency of audit evidence, this characteristic is judgmental and directly related to audit materiality, the adequacy of an agency's systems of internal controls, and the conditions and circumstances encountered during the audit.

In large audit entities such as federal agencies, evidence can be manually or electronically prepared, or be a combination of both data processes. Also, the evidence may have been compiled by the federal agency or outsourced to a contractor, or be a combination of both methods.

From an auditor's perspective, the various types of audit evidence gathered can generally be categorized as:

- *Confirmation:* evidence obtained by the auditor through direct written or oral confirmation with a party external to the auditee
- *Observation:* evidence obtained through direct, personal observations by the auditor
- *Documentary:* evidence obtained by the auditor's review of underlying accounting data and other corroborating forms and documents
- *Mathematical:* evidence developed by the auditor through the auditor's independent calculations and computations
- *Analytical:* high-level comparisons of current year data. These comparisons may include expected relationships between account balances and comparisons to prior years' balances. The comparisons typically take the form of ratios, trends, and time series analyses.
- *Hearsay:* evidence obtained by auditor inquiry, perhaps even in the form of hearsay and "gossip," that must be corroborated by other evidence

The sheer size of federal agencies dictates that audit evidence be obtained through sampling in order to conduct an efficient audit. Thus, the federal audit model and the federal audit manual describe both statistical and nonstatistical sampling, with considerable guidance being provided on statistical sampling approaches. Ultimately, the sampling approach must be dictated by the circumstances and conditions encountered in each audit. Both approaches do have their merits and demerits.

SAMPLING

When performing the audit of an entity, examining a selected number of transactions, generally referred to as sampling, is by far the most common audit technique. Sampling can take any of several forms, including statistical, nonstatistical, or judgmental. These sampling forms are discussed in further detail in later chapters.

The scientific statistical approach, quantitatively based, and premised on theory of probability, is best when applied to:

- Populations of infinite size
- Populations with minimal variances in size, in frequency, or periodicity
- Populations that are relatively homogeneous
- Populations with known errors or attributes

A subjective or judgmental sampling approach is premised on auditor expertise in relation to what may be considered an adequate or sufficient sample. Subjective sampling is most efficient when a relatively large portion of the universe can be tested through the review of a small number of transactions.

MATERIALITY

Materiality, a basic important audit concept, is a concern to an auditor from two viewpoints: (1) when assessing an auditee's compliance with generally accepted accounting principles and (2) when planning, conducting, and reporting the results of an audit made pursuant to generally accepted auditing standards and the *Government Auditing Standards*.

Some standard setters have suggested specific dollar amounts, or a percentage criteria, or specific conditions as being material. However, while these standards provide useful guidance, materiality remains a subjective concept requiring the exercise of auditor judgment in virtually every audit. Typically, these materiality issues warrant a separate examination, separate reporting, or different accounting and auditing emphasis, but these attempts to quantitatively proscribe materiality are admittedly arbitrary. In short, for accounting and auditing purposes, to be material, an item or issue must be significant, important, or big enough to make a difference.[5]

Accounting Materiality Defined

Financial statements can be materially misleading on two fronts: (1) for misstated amounts and facts appearing in the statements, or (2) for amounts and facts that have been omitted from those statements. FASB's working definition of *materiality* (also cited by the AICPA, FASAB, and GAO) is:

> *Materiality: The magnitude of an omission or misstatement of accounting information that, in the light of surrounding circumstances, makes it probable that the judgment of a reasonable person relying on the information would have been changed or influenced by the omission or misstatement. (FASB Concept Statement 2)*

---

[5] *See W. Holder, K. Shermann, and R. Wittington, "Materiality Considerations," **Journal of Accountancy** (November 2003), for an excellent discussion of the importance of materiality considerations in financial reporting and auditing and the profound impact or complications arising from FASB 34 concerning the application of materiality to audits of governments.*

Materiality is not constant, but relative, dependent on circumstances, and affected by the environment or industry within which the auditee operates. Amounts or factors material to the financial statements of one entity may not be material to another entity of a different size, with a different mission, or even for the same entity, but for two different fiscal periods. The concept of materiality is based on the premise that some amounts, matters, or issues, individually or in aggregate, are important enough to be fully disclosed and fairly presented in order for an entity's statements to conform with GAAP. Implicit in this concept of materiality is that lesser amounts and other matters and issues are not as important and therefore are immaterial for the purpose of an audit.

The AICPA, in its guidance relating to materiality, states "the auditor's consideration of materiality is a matter of professional judgment and is influenced by the auditor's perception of the needs of a reasonable person who will rely on the financial statements" (AICPA Sec. 312). Materiality, within this context, encompasses both a quantitative materiality (e.g., measured in absolute dollar amounts or percentage variances) and a qualitative materiality (e.g., an illegal payment, of minimal quantitative materiality, but that could have significant legal and ultimately large dollar consequences).

Materiality (of errors, misstatements, variances, changes, weak or overridden controls, etc.) is a concern in various phases of an audit and must be considered when:

- Planning an audit and designing the timing, nature, and extent of auditing procedures to be applied in an audit of financial statements
- Performing and assessing the results of audit tests of controls, transactions, and classifications of transactions, accounts and account groupings, and line items of a financial statement
- Evaluating the results of an audit to assess whether the audited financial statements, taken as a whole, are fairly presented in conformity with generally accepted accounting principles

For audits made in conformity with GAAS and audit opinions on whether the financial statements are presented fairly in accordance with GAAP, the auditor must consider the effects of material misstatements and material omissions, individually and in aggregate, that have not been corrected by the auditee.

Pervasiveness of Materiality

References to when and to what preparers and auditors of financial statements must apply the materiality criteria permeate *Government Auditing Standards* (by the AICPA and GAO). Some examples include:

- *GAAS for governments:* When evaluating whether financial statements are presented fairly, in all material respects, in conformity with GAAP, auditors must consider the effects, individually and in aggregate, of misstatements not corrected by the entity.
- *GAAS for governments:* The auditor must assess the risk of material misstatements (by fraud or error) and omissions during the planning phase of the audit.

- *GAAS for governments:* Auditors must consider material misstatements and omissions of financial statements when determining the timing, nature, and extent of applied audit procedures, assigned audit team staff, and appropriate levels of supervision.
- *GAAS for governments:* Auditors must plan the audit to obtain reasonable assurance about whether the financial statements are free of material misstatements arising from illegal acts that have a direct and material effect on the determination of financial statement amounts.
- *GAAS for governments:* In determining the nature, timing, and extent of audit procedures and testing required to obtain reasonable assurances about detecting misstatements in these data, auditors are required to make preliminary judgments about what they consider to be material, individually or in aggregate with other misstatements, in relation to the financial statements taken as a whole.
- *GAAS for governments:* Auditors shall make separate materiality determinations for planning, performing, and evaluating results, and reporting for each of the government's opinion units.
- *Government Auditing Standards:* Auditors should design the audit to provide reasonable assurance of detecting material misstatements resulting from violations of provisions of contracts or grant agreements that have a direct and material effect on the financial statements.
- *Government Auditing Standards:* Auditors shall report significant (i.e., material) findings including fraud, abuse, illegal acts, and violations of provisions of contracts or grant agreements.
- *Government Auditing Standards:* When reporting deficiencies in internal control, auditors must identify reportable conditions that are, individually or in aggregate, considered to be material weaknesses.
- *Government Auditing Standards:* When circumstances call for the omission of certain information in the auditors' report, auditors must consider whether the omitted information distorts (i.e., is the included or excluded information material to report users?) the reported results or conceals improper or illegal acts.

Qualitative Materiality

Generally accepted auditing standards are rather specific in that auditors are instructed to conduct tests of controls, transactions, and account balances with the objective of detecting material quantitative misstatements. For audits involving governments and other public entities, often the qualitative issues emphasized by oversight boards and commissions create media focus.

Planning audit procedures with the objective of detecting material qualitative misstatements or material omissions in financial statements may not be cost-beneficial or practical. Alternatively, GAAS instructs the auditor to *consider* qualitative factors that could cause seemingly quantitatively immaterial items to take on immense significance, or, in the language of GAAS, have qualitative materiality. Examples of qualitative issues having the potential to rise to a material quantitative matter might be noted or presumed instances of errors, illegal acts, fraud, thefts, misappropriation of funds and assets, defalcations, abuses, conflicts of interest, contract and grant terms, bond covenants, and the like.

DISCREDITABLE ACTS

AICPA members must justify departures from governmental GAAS, as defined and described in the AICPA's auditing and accounting guidance for governmental entities. In the case of audits of governmental financial statements, a specific Ethics Interpretation, 501-3, of the AICPA applies:

> *If a member [of the AICPA]...undertakes an obligation to follow specified government audit standards, guides, procedures, statutes, rules, and regulations in addition to generally accepted auditing standards, he or she is obligated to follow such requirements. Failure to do so is an act discreditable to the profession in violation of Rule 501 of the AICPA **Code of Professional Conduct**, unless the auditor discloses in his or her report the fact that such requirements were not followed and the reason therefor.*

The AICPA's GAAS standards describe measures of quality of audit performance, quality of exercised judgment during the audit, and the quality of audit objectives. In its many other promulgations for auditors, the AICPA continues to further define, describe, and illustrate these measures by delineating audit procedures, providing illustrations, suggesting audit programs, and offering guidance by many specific industries.

8 PLANNING THE AUDIT

As briefly described in Chapter 7, the federal audit model is comprised of four phases.

Phase I: Plan the audit and preliminarily assess financial processes and systems
Phase II: Understand and evaluate the internal controls
Phase III: Test controls and conduct substantive tests of transactions, accounts, and account groups
Phase IV: Report audit conclusions, audit results, auditor's opinion, and other assurances

At the outset of an audit, the auditor must have a clear idea of the audit scope to identify a process that will achieve audit objectives. Chapter 7 provided a summary of the Federal Audit Model that was jointly developed by GAO, PCIE, and OMB. Exhibit 7.1 displays the audit phases, procedures, and tasks for this model that are described in some 1,100 pages of federal guidance appearing in the *Financial Audit Manual*, *Federal Information System Controls Audit Manual*, and the *Standards for Internal Controls in the Federal Government*. Models and checklists are useful tools and can assist in the development of an effective audit approach and audit procedures; however, a model is not a plan.

The first auditing standard of fieldwork states, in part: "The work is to be adequately planned...." This simple, straightforward, and patently obvious statement, however, is no mere tautology. Planning is at the core of every successful audit; and conversely, failed audits can often be attributed to a poor, minimal, or partial plan. The breadth, depth, duration, and effectiveness of the planning phase is directly dependent on the auditor's access to the federal auditee's personnel, the agency's underlying data and information sources, and the experience of the audit team in conducting federal financial audits. Indeed, as implied by the title of this chapter, an audit approach that is the product of a properly executed planning process is likely to be successful.

The focus of this chapter is planning. Exhibit 8.1 is a graphic depiction of the nature and specificity of the understanding that is needed to ascertain the conditions and circumstances related to understanding the "business" of a federal agency. The exhibit lists many facts and characteristics of an auditee that, if known to the auditor, will provide a sound base to plan and execute an audit that addresses the accountability concerns of the government.

THE PLANNING PHASE: DO IT EARLY, DO IT CONTINUOUSLY

If an audit is to be properly planned, the auditor must have a sound understanding of the objectives of the audit and the general nature of the audit process. The purpose of Phase I, planning, is to develop a preliminary understanding of the op-

Exhibit 8.1: Audit planning phase

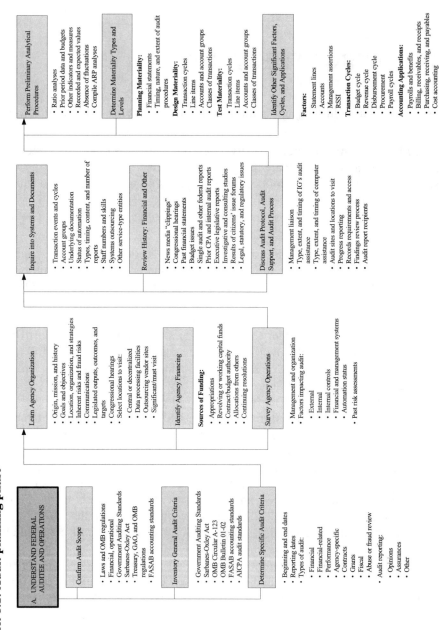

A. UNDERSTAND FEDERAL AUDITEE AND OPERATIONS

Confirm Audit Scope
- Laws and OMB regulations
- Financial, operational
- Government Auditing Standards
- Sarbanes-Oxley Act
- Treasury, GAO, and OMB regulations
- FASAB accounting standards

Inventory General Audit Criteria
- Government Auditing Standards
- Sarbanes-Oxley Act
- OMB Circular A-123
- OMB Bulletin 01-02
- FASAB accounting standards
- AICPA audit standards

Determine Specific Audit Criteria
- Beginning and end dates
- Reporting dates
- Types of audit:
  - Financial
  - Financial-related
  - Performance
  - Agency-specific
  - Contracts
  - Grants
  - Fiscal
  - Abuse or fraud review
- Audit reporting:
  - Opinions
  - Assurances
  - Other

Learn Agency Organization
- Origin, mission, and history
- Goals and objectives
- Location, organization, and strategies
- Inherent risks and fraud risks
- Communications
- Legislated outputs, outcomes, and targets
- Congressional hearings
- Select locations to visit:
  - Central or decentralized
  - Data processing facilities
  - Outsourcing vendor sites
  - Significant/must visit

Identify Agency Financing

Sources of Funding:
- Appropriations
- Revolving or working capital funds
- Contract/budget authority
- Allocations from others
- Continuing resolutions

Survey Agency Operations
- Management and organization
- Factors impacting audit:
  - External
  - Internal
  - Internal controls
  - Financial and management systems
  - Automation status
  - Past risk assessments

Inquire into Systems and Documents
- Transaction events and cycles
- Account groups
- Underlying documentation
- Status of automation
- Types, timing, content, and number of reports
- Staff numbers and skills
- Systems outsourcing
- Other service-type entities

Review History: Financial and Other
- News media "clippings"
- Congressional hearings
- Past financial statements
- Budget issues
- Single audit and other federal reports
- Prior CPA and internal audit reports
- Executive legislative reports
- Investigative and consulting studies
- Results of citizens' issue forums
- Legal, statutory, and regulatory issues

Discuss Audit Protocol, Audit Support, and Audit Process
- Management liaison
- Type, extent, and timing of IG's audit assistance
- Type, extent, and timing of computer assistance
- Audit sites and locations to visit
- Progress reporting
- Records requirements and access
- Findings review process
- Audit report recipients

Perform Preliminary Analytical Procedures
- Ratio analyses
- Prior period data and budgets
- Other indicators and measures
- Recorded and expected values
- Absence of fluctuations
- Compile ARP analyses

Determine Materiality Types and Levels

Planning Materiality:
- Financial statements
- Timing, nature, and extent of audit procedures

Design Materiality:
- Transaction cycles
- Line items
- Accounts and account groups
- Classes of transactions

Test Materiality:
- Transaction cycles
- Line items
- Accounts and account groups
- Classes of transactions

Identify Other Significant Factors, Cycles, and Applications

Factors:
- Statement lines
- Accounts
- Management assertions
- RSSI

Transaction Cycles:
- Budget cycle
- Revenue cycle
- Disbursement cycle
- Procurement
- Payroll cycles

Accounting Applications:
- Payrolls and benefits
- Billing, receivables, and receipts
- Purchasing, receiving, and payables
- Cost accounting
- Inventories
- Property and equipment

Exhibit 8.1: Audit planning phase (continued)

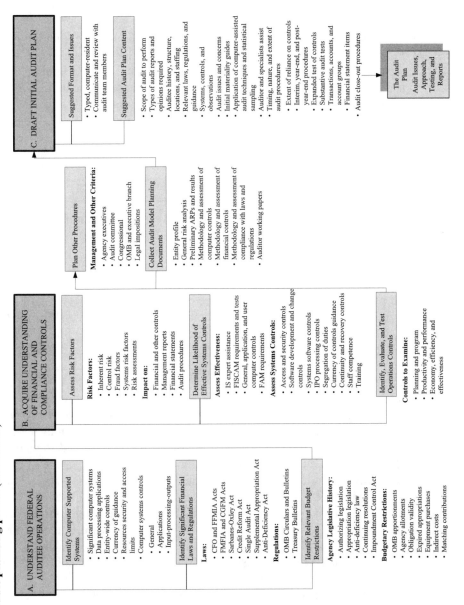

erations of the auditee, including an initial review of the auditee's underlying systems of controls, accounting, and information, with particular emphasis on the level of the computerized state of these systems. The auditor's understanding of these systems is augmented further during each succeeding phase of the audit. During the planning phase, the auditor begins to determine the general information needed for the audit. It is important to understand that audit planning is an iterative process. The auditor must be ready to reassess the audit strategy and, if necessary, revise the planned approach as new information on the audit or auditee surfaces as a result of audit procedures.

The availability of models such as that developed by GAO may beg the question as to why planning is so important when working models and well-defined audit procedures are so readily available. The easy answer is that planning is required by OMB, GAO, *Government Auditing Standards*, and GAAS of the AICPA. These criteria and guidance aside, sound planning is simply good auditing.

Poor planning, or lack of planning entirely, will most likely result in duplicate audit work, auditing the wrong data, delays in the audit itself, and the omission of critical and possibly legally mandated procedures. In all likelihood, it will result in excessive audit costs. Another important reason to plan is audit risk mitigation or avoidance. Understandably, when any organization undertakes an initial audit of an auditee, the most experienced audit managers must be involved in the planning. No lesser commitment of audit management should be applied to each subsequent audit of that same auditee. Assuming that one year's audit will be the same as the prior year's is highly risky and poor strategy. Prudence, legal and statutory requirements, and professional standards all dictate that each year's audit must be planned anew.

Models are useful. But, as with any model, it does not follow that the audit of every federal agency will conform to the execution of predetermined steps or procedures of a hypothetical model for application to a model federal agency. Rote execution of checklist procedures may leave the auditor with the false impression that a successful audit was performed. Model manuals, programs, and checklists are not a substitute for the audit judgment that is applied based on the conditions and circumstances of a particular federal audit, each with characteristics different from other federal audits.

Finally, in the interest of full disclosure, the authors acknowledge that this and the remaining chapters on financial audits can provide the reader only with a conceptual road map—a model—of a process to conduct an audit of a federal agency. This text is qualified with the caveat that audit judgment must be prevalent and exercised at all times.

AUDIT MODELS, AUDIT CHECKLISTS

Every audit is unique, and audit procedures must be tailored to distinct circumstances. It is not possible to develop the perfect audit model or a universal checklist for all audit situations. Although models are useful in planning, it does not follow that every audit will consist of the execution of predetermined steps or procedures through each phase of the federal audit model. Manuals, programs, and checklists are not a substitute for audit judgment. Many believe the recent audit failures that have marred commercial audits are at least partly due to a failure to exercise the audit judgment that should have alerted the auditor to shortcomings in audit planning, execution of the audit approach, or in application of appropriate accounting principles. Thus, the auditor should consult manuals such as those developed by GAO and even develop his or her own internal checklists to assist in the execution of audit procedures, so long as there is an understanding that the specific circumstances of the auditee will dictate what procedures are applicable (or whether any of the procedures in the checklist apply).

Planning an audit is not a one-time-only undertaking. Even the best plans must be refined, revised, and sometimes changed completely, as the audit progresses and unanticipated activities, circumstances, and conditions are disclosed. This is particularly true for audits of the federal government, where, in addition to these factors, Congress could change its mind with respect to the desired goals, objectives, funding limitations, and even the programs of a federal agency from one year to the next.

UNDERSTAND EACH FEDERAL AUDITEE

Armed with an understanding of the audit process, as discussed in Chapter 7, the auditor can proceed to understand the unique characteristics of the auditee to plan an audit approach that addresses the specific circumstances of the auditee.

Learn the Agency's "Business"

The need to understand the auditee's "business" is a well-established concept in commercial auditing. Clearly, if the auditor does not understand the auditee's business, how can the auditor understand how the business operates, earns its revenues, invests its resources, and makes money? Further, without this understanding, how can the auditor identify significant accounting cycles and processes involved in the production of the financial statements that are the subject of the auditor's assertion?

To some, however, the use of the term *business* as a reference to a federal agency may seem inappropriate or strange, as almost no federal agency earns revenues, and there is usually no profit motive. Many think of federal agencies in terms of missions, goals, and objectives that are subsets of the overall mission (e.g., good health, national defense, social security); but commercial enterprises can also be defined in terms of mission, such as maximization of shareholder wealth or profits or the more "politically correct" optimization of customer service. Additionally, the mission itself has supporting goals, such as sales goals, investments in product research, human resource quality of life issues, and participation in community-related social programs, all of which ultimately contribute to the achievement of the enterprise's mission.

But, as used in this text, the term *business* encompasses not only missions, goals, and objectives, but also the processes, both logical and physical, that enable any organization to achieve its mission. Thus, as in audits of a commercial enterprise, by understanding the agency's business, the auditor will understand:

- How the federal auditee operates
- How the agency is funded (e.g., appropriation, budget or contract authority, payment for services rendered, third-party fees, etc.)
- How the agency invests its resources (and existing restrictions on the expenditure of resources)
- How the agency measures performance
- How the combination of these factors is likely to motivate agency management

Perform General Risk Analysis

Closely related to the understanding of the auditee's business is the need to understand the auditee's control environment. The control environment reflects the overall attitude, awareness, and actions of management and others concerning the importance of control and the emphasis given to control in the auditee's policies, procedures, methods, and organizational structure. The control environment reflects management's attitude toward the development of accounting estimates and its financial reporting philosophy, and is the context in which the accounting system and internal controls operate.

Obtaining an understanding of the auditee's control environment assists in the identification of factors that may have a pervasive effect on the risk of errors of audit importance in the processing of transactions and on the judgments management makes when preparing financial statements. An earlier understanding of the auditee's business facilitates the identification of factors to look for in the assessment.

Although the existence of a satisfactory control environment does not guarantee the effectiveness of specific application controls over the processing of data, it can be a positive factor in assessing the risk of errors. An effective control environment provides a basis for expecting that accounting systems tested at an interim date will continue to function properly during the entire period under audit. Conversely, perceived weaknesses in the control environment may undermine the effectiveness of specific controls and can thus be a negative factor in the assessment of the risk of errors of audit importance. Therefore, assessing the overall effectiveness of the control environment helps to establish the level of professional skepticism required for the audit, influences the likely nature and extent of audit testing, and is a factor in determining how early in the year tests can be performed. The control environment is determined by a combination of:

- Management's control consciousness and operating style
- Control mechanisms established by management that provide the framework in which specific controls and accounting processes operate
- Those factors that influence management's attitude about the conduct and reporting of operations and the importance of controls

In order to understand and assess the control environment, each of the elements listed above, and their interrelationships, must be considered. Significant deficiencies in any one of the elements may undermine the effectiveness of the others.

ACHIEVE AN UNDERSTANDING OF THE AGENCY

As every auditee is unique, how the auditor develops an understanding of the auditee depends on the nature or purpose of the federal agency, as well as information and data about the agency that is readily available. In general, sources of information will fall into one of these categories.

- External guidance issued by standard-setting organizations
- Internally developed guidance issued by the federal agency (including both cabinet and subcomponent levels)
- Audit and consulting reports and working papers
- Internally developed documentation
- Historical and interim accounting information
- Management and operating personnel

External Guidance: By Regulators and Standard Setters

Every agency must comply with rules issued by third parties. With respect to federal agencies, the nature of the third-party rules is extremely diverse, emanating from constitutionally created executive, legislative, and judiciary branches of government and from nongovernmental trade organizations, such as the AICPA. In developing an understanding of the auditee, an auditor will typically consult

- Agency = enabling legislation
- Current budgetary guidance
- Oversight agency and standard-setting organization guidance including
  - OMB
  - GAO
  - Department of the Treasury
  - FASAB
  - FASB
  - AICPA

In general, external guidance is designed to define the parameters and boundaries within which the auditee must function, and will identify accounting principles and internal control practices and procedures that the auditee must follow. As a general rule, noncompliance with this external guidance will likely affect one or more of the three auditor's reports (financial statements, internal controls, and/or compliance with laws and regulations).

Internal Guidance: By the Agency, Cabinet, and Subcomponents

Most federal agencies issue additional guidance related to their own accounting procedures and internal controls and data processing, be it a manual or computerized process. Although this guidance is frequently reflective of higher (i.e., external to the agency) authority or guidance, the agency-generated guidance is often useful in informing the auditor of unique characteristics and concerns of the auditee.

Noncompliance with this guidance is likely to affect the auditor's report on compliance with laws and regulations (depending, of course, on the magnitude of noncompliance and the likely impact on the financial statements).

Audit Reports, Consulting Reports, and Working Papers

Not to be overlooked when attempting to understand an agency's financial, compliance, and computer processing controls are reports by organizations such as GAO and the Office of Inspector General, which report on issues and problems affecting the auditee. In addition, the auditor should consult prior years' financial audit reports and the supporting working papers. A review of records, when available, is an invaluable source of information to any auditor. Although it is important to note that a review of these reports is not a substitute for the auditor's own compliance with the second standard of fieldwork (developing an understanding of internal controls), these reports are, nevertheless, of invaluable assistance in improving audit efficiency, guiding the audit effort, and identifying audit and accounting issues that may significantly impact the auditor's assertions.

Like audit reports, consulting reports can also provide valuable insights on issues affecting the auditee, particularly in regard to the development of new systems, planned system enhancements, and progress achieved in addressing internal control weaknesses identified in prior audits. However, the auditor should also consider that, while subject to professional standards, consulting reports are not governed by the same independence rules as audit reports.

Internally Developed Documentation

The previously addressed sources of information assist the auditor in identifying the rules that the auditee is subject to, as well as internal control and accounting issues that may affect the audit. Internally developed documentation, such as accounting and users' manuals, policy and procedures manuals, and desk instructions, provide information on how (or whether) the auditee complies (or attempts to comply) with rules and regulations and provides (or attempts to provide) adequate accounting and operating controls to support the development of financial statements in accordance with generally accepted accounting principles.

By providing information on relevant accounting cycles and processes, as well as existing controls, this documentation is essential to the auditor in developing a sufficient understanding of internal controls to guide planning, development, and later execution of relevant audit procedures, as required by the second standard of fieldwork.

Interim Accounting Information

A review of interim financial information (preferably at the trial balance level) provides the auditor with immediate insight into a number of audit-related considerations including:

- What accounts are material/significant to the audit
- What systems are likely to impact those accounts and, therefore, merit careful documentation and audit consideration

- The types of processes (e.g., recurring or routine, nonrecurring or nonroutine, and processes requiring estimates) that are likely to support the accounting cycle for each of these accounts (and thus the type of audit procedures that are likely to be required)
- Where audit issues are likely to surface and what internal control practices (e.g., reconciliation procedures, segregation of duties) the auditor should look for, as the presence (or absence) of these procedures will directly impact internal control and audit risk

In addition, the review of interim data is essential to the execution of analytical procedures, as required by GAAS, during the planning phase of the audit. Analytical procedures will quickly reveal areas of potential audit significance by highlighting, for example, major changes in account balances from prior years or a reversal in expense or revenue trends.

The AICPA, in its GAAS, and GAO, in its *Government Auditing Standards*, mandate that auditors perform analytical review procedures (e.g., make comparisons and trend and variance analyses, perform modeling, etc.) of financial statements, portions of financial statements, funds, group of accounts, individual accounts, and financial transactions. Analytical procedures consist of the evaluation of financial information by a study of plausible relationships among both financial and nonfinancial data. As a rule, the auditor applies these techniques four times during an audit:

1. To assist the auditor in planning the nature, timing, and extent of other audit procedures to obtain evidential matter for specific statements, reports, accounts, or classes of transactions
2. As a substantive audit test to obtain evidential matter about particular assertions related to classes of transactions
3. As a substantive audit test to obtain evidential matter about particular assertions related to account balances
4. As an overall review of the financial information during the final review stage of an audit

When well executed, analytical review procedures will, in most instances, identify conditions such as unusual transactions and events, material accounting changes, significant operational changes, large random fluctuations, and material misstatements, all of which should be known to the auditor as early as possible. Analytical review procedures should not be limited to financial data. Revealing, informative conclusions that could impact the audit could result from analyses of numbers and grade levels of employees, organization charts, square footage and equipment statistics, persons or organizations on tax rolls, populations of citizens served, numbers and types of computers, other equipment, and inventories owned, and the like. In short, analytical procedures, combined with the review of interim accounting information, are an efficient means of identifying areas that bear immediate attention by more senior audit personnel.

Management and Operating Personnel

In theory, an auditor could obtain all necessary information from formal guidance and/or documentation and reports, as discussed above. However, in practice, there is no substitute for the additional insight into current operating conditions that can only be obtained directly from the management and operating personnel responsible for the daily execution of the accounting function and other activities that ultimately impact the process of developing financial statements that are fairly presented.

As with any other audit activity, the auditor must exercise judgment in achieving a proper balance of formal documentation and information obtained directly from the auditee's personnel. At all times, the auditor must be cognizant that the auditee's employees have daily duties and responsibilities that must be accomplished no matter how pressing the information needs of the audit are. Thus, ideally, the auditor should obtain as much information as possible from existing formal documentation and consult auditee personnel only to fill in documentation gaps and obtain a final verification of the auditor's understanding of the systems, as documented in the auditor's working papers.

Historically, formal written documentation was often outdated or fragmented, consisting of operational memos and desk instructions that have not been properly controlled or compiled, or both; had significant gaps in connection with the documentation of internal controls; or, sadly, was too illegible and/or too hard to follow to be effectively utilized by an auditor who had not spent years working with the auditee's systems. The recently issued A-123 revision addresses the need for proper, formal written documentation. Compliance with the revised guidance should avert or mitigate this issue.

The auditor's need to consult auditee personnel to complete the documentation of systems is frequently a source of friction between auditor and auditee. It is the auditor's responsibility to explain plainly, but diplomatically, why, despite the existence of formal documentation, it is necessary to interview accounting and operating personnel to complete the documentation and assessment of internal controls.

A later discussion in this chapter addresses other matters of importance in connection with direct dealings with any auditee's personnel.

DOCUMENT THE UNDERSTANDING

The information discussed above is essential for the development of an audit approach that will be outlined in an audit plan. It is also necessary for documenting the auditor's compliance with the government's requirements on assembly of working papers related to planning and the auditor's internal controls assessment, posed by both the AICPA's GAAS and GAO's *Government Auditing Standards*.

Documentation can take the form of narratives or flowcharts, completed control decision trees, control questionnaires and checklists, and the like. Narratives consist of memos summarizing key aspects of the systems of internal controls. Flowcharts and decision trees are graphic depictions of the flow and the controls that transactions are subjected to as they proceed through applicable accounting cycle or process. The documentation will also include copies of critical control features (e.g., computer input screens, purchase orders, time sheets) and may also include copies of selected sections of user's and policy manuals.

A more detailed discussion of the documentation of accounting cycles is addressed in Chapter 9 with the evaluation of internal controls and the execution of detailed risk assessments.

DEVELOP THE INITIAL AUDIT APPROACH

At this point in the planning process, the auditor should have obtained the necessary information to develop an initial audit plan to guide future audit efforts. In summary, the procedures discussed above should enable the auditor to achieve these planning objectives:

- Identify areas of audit significance, including potential problem areas.
- Catalog all applicable federal requirements, including OMB circulars/bulletins, as appropriate.
- Consider, catalog, and update the auditor's understanding of the auditee's internally developed standards and procedures used to monitor compliance with internal requirements and federal standards.
- Assess the degree of risk and the nature of errors that could result from accounting estimates and other subjective areas.
- Identify unusual or unexpected transactions.
- Identify significant accounting issues.
- Assess the degree of difficulty that may be encountered in gaining sufficient audit evidence.

Certain areas of significance to the development of the audit plan are discussed in more detail below.

Establishing Materiality

Although materiality is often thought of as an amount or percentage, the accounting literature, including that of GAO and FASB, defines materiality in terms of magnitude and a threshold. Materiality refers to an error beyond a certain level or threshold that would likely result in the users of the financial statements being misled.

There is a reason why the terms *magnitude* and *threshold* are used instead of an absolute amount in defining materiality. All authoritative guidance agrees that absolute amounts alone cannot define materiality. Rather, other facts and disclosures could, if misstated beyond a tolerable threshold, also mislead the reader of the financial statements. In the case of federal financial statements, GAO adds a new dimension by stating that the nature of government and the public trust will often require that the auditor consider a lower materiality threshold than would apply to a commercial enterprise.

In practice, auditors will usually quantify materiality at two levels:

1. An overall level, as it relates to the financial statements taken as a whole, and typically referred to as planning materiality

2.   An individual account or group of accounts level—where the auditor will typically allocate a lower materiality threshold covering these items

Planning materiality is the auditor's preliminary judgment of what amount or variance would be significant to an agency's financial statements, keeping in mind GAO's more stringent threshold. Planning materiality judgments are used to develop the initial overall audit approach, probable audit procedures, and possible audit tasks, but must be reevaluated at the conclusion of the audit to consider whether the total effect of the audit differences identified (and not corrected) was material to the fair presentation of the financial statements.

As a general rule, materiality at the account level is set so that the probability is remote that the total of audit differences in all accounts will exceed the auditor's initial judgment regarding planning materiality. By allocating a lower materiality threshold to individual accounts or groups of accounts, the auditor is able to determine the extent of testing necessary at the account balance level. The auditor is required to document the steps taken to consider materiality. GAO's *Financial Audit Manual* suggests that planning materiality should be set at 3% of the materiality base (FAM paragraph 230.11) and that design materiality (e.g., materiality at the account level) be set at one-third of planning materiality (FAM paragraph 230.11). The materiality base is defined as either total assets or total expenses, depending on the nature of the auditee's operations/mission and the auditor's judgment (FAM paragraph 230.09).

Identifying Significant Accounts

Planning an effective audit approach requires an accurate assessment of the likelihood that errors of audit importance may have occurred in the information subject to audit. This requires the auditor to identify the significant accounts or groups of accounts, which would be any account or group of accounts that could contain errors of audit importance. *Errors of audit importance* include:

- Those that individually or collectively could have a material effect on the financial statements being examined
- Other matters that, though not material from a dollar aspect, could adversely affect the audit if such matters were to remain undetected or not be reported by the auditor (e.g., illegal acts, conflicts of interests, unauthorized management actions, antideficiency violations, and fiscal improprieties)

It is critical that the auditor identify the significant accounts and account groups and related audit risks that must be examined in greater detail during the audit. This technique of quick, early identification of potential audit issues and risks provides for the optimal allocation of junior, senior, and management personnel and provides essential input into a more strategic planning of the audit approach. But, these early determinations should not be viewed as final, never to be revisited or changed. On the contrary, these determinations should be examined and reexamined through the date the audit report is completed.

Administering and Managing the Audit

Despite the auditor's best intentions, the auditor is in an adversarial role during the execution of the audit. To this end, the auditor must strive to establish, as early as possible, well-defined channels of communications and working relationships with executives, managers, and staff of the federal agency. To minimize friction, it is important that agreement be reached with the auditee regarding the protocol to be followed during audit execution. In general, it is recommended that the auditor:

- Hold early protocol governing discussions and conduct interviews of top agency management, the senior and technical accounting, systems, and other operating personnel.
- Discuss, to the extent permitted by those arranging for the audit, the audit approach and procedures that will likely be followed to verify audit findings.
- Identify the protocol or process to be followed for documentation requests.
- As soon as possible in the planning phase, obtain a listing of documentation and other supporting competent evidential matter that will be required for the audit. This documentation list should be as detailed and exhaustive as possible to assist the auditee in the execution of the audit plan. Developing a truly comprehensive list may be virtually impossible during first-time audits. First-time audits of large, complex organizations are, arguably, unique to the federal government. It is important to note that a first-time audit refers to the auditee being audited for the first time and not to the first time a particular auditor audits the auditee. (The latter is the more common first-time audit condition in both the private and federal sectors.) When auditing an entity previously audited by a predecessor auditor, the successor auditor will have access to prior years' working papers and prior years' audit history, thus significantly reducing the uncertainties surrounding a true first-time audit by the new auditor.
- Establish an agreed-on timetable to execute the audit, including the timing of audit procedures, expected availability of auditee personnel, and agency production of required documentation for auditor examination.
- Introduce the audit professionals who will participate in the audit and protocol to be followed in introducing newer auditors to the team. Given the current risks and security concerns faced by the federal government, this is a critical consideration in all federal audits.
- Set and adhere to a schedule of timing and frequency for progress meetings, status meetings, and reporting to keep the auditee apprised of progress, as well as of potential problems.
- Disclose and dispose of findings including procedures to be followed to enable the auditee to validate the factual understanding of audit and accounting issues.
- When applicable, review the procedures and requirements established or desired by the auditee's audit committee.
- Review representations that must, and will, be requested of auditee management, its accounting, and legal counsel.

The above listing is not all-inclusive, and once again a warning of the need to tailor procedures to the specific characteristics/circumstances of the auditee is appropriate. An audit approach that is appreciative of and responsive to the auditee's operating needs is essential to the successful execution of an audit.

When developing a communications protocol, the auditee may pose restrictions and requests that information or meetings with operating personnel be routed through a member of management. This is not unusual, as auditee personnel have always been leery of auditors acting on incomplete or misleading information. But, in general, management is probably best suited to point the auditor to those individuals who are most able to provide accurate, up-to-date information. When auditing federal agencies, the audit team must continually recognize the agency's need to comply with legally imposed security regulations and restrictions.

Thus, the auditor should not always be distrustful of restrictions imposed by an agreed-on protocol. Yet the auditor also must be careful that, in practice, the audit administrative protocol does not result in restrictions to the required audit scope. There will always be certain individuals or aspects of the audit that require direct auditor access, and the protocol cannot limit this access. Once again, the auditor must exercise judgment to achieve a proper balance between audit needs and the need to avoid disruption of the auditee's operations.

DEVELOPING THE AUDIT PLAN

There is a purpose to the survey, inquiry, limited tests, walk-through, and data-gathering efforts: It is the writing of the initial audit plan. The final output of the planning phase is the initial audit plan describing the proposed audit approach. The audit plan, the product of the planning phase, must describe both technical audit requirements and engagement execution/administration issues. The audit plan assists in providing a consistent framework or thought process, a strategy, to be applied throughout the audit. The audit plan will describe the financial conditions and operating environment of the auditee and highlight potential audit issues, while incorporating relevant input from prior audits and from management. The audit plan will identify staffing requirements, including specialists, and provides for the timely involvement of more senior personnel responsible for the execution of the more technical aspects of the audit, as well as quality control.

Typical contents of the audit plan include:

- A description of the auditee's operations including:
  - Mission
  - Location(s)
  - Interim financial information
  - Current-year budget information
  - Number of employees
  - Organization chart

- Laws and regulations including specific requirements identified by OMB for all federal entities being audited, as well as laws and regulations that may apply specifically to the auditee

- Descriptions of accounting cycles and systems memorandum
- Identification/definition of materiality (usually in total and at the financial statement line item or account level)
- General risk analysis and preliminary risk assessments
- Account risk analysis
- Identification of potential audit issues considering:

  - Significant accounts
  - Potential high-risk areas
  - Significant nonroutine and estimation processes involved in the development of the financial statements
  - Unique accounting requirements
  - New or developing accounting systems
  - When applicable, progress made in addressing internal control issues identified in past audits

- Application of computer-assisted audit techniques and statistical sampling
- Planned audit procedures, including initial audit programs and sampling plans, as applicable to:

  - Internal controls
  - Risk assessment procedures
  - Compliance testing
  - Substantive testing
  - Planned analytical procedures

- Staffing requirements, including specialists
- Milestones, deadlines, and audit administration/coordination protocol developed with the auditee

In developing an audit plan, the auditor must design an audit approach that, of necessity, will and must include assumptions regarding the auditee's internal control environment and internal control structure. Once again, one of the realities of auditing must be underscored: Audit planning is present in every phase of the audit. The initial phase of the audit is planning-intensive, but the completion of phase I does not mark the end of planning.

In fact, during the conduct of an audit, the audit plan is continuously reexamined, refined, revised, and changed as the specific audit procedures performed shed additional light on existing conditions and circumstances, and particularly those related to the internal control structure and significant accounting, auditing, and financial reporting issues. The technical audit approach must provide for planning throughout the execution of the audit and allow for the flexibility to alter plans as the audit progresses.

This is particularly true of a first-time audit, where there is no history to guide the initial planning effort. In fact, in a first-time audit, with only preliminary and limited information on internal controls, there is no clear distinction between the planning phase and the initial procedures of the internal control phase, where the auditor obtains additional information about the auditee as the auditor proceeds to a more in-depth documentation of accounting cycles and the related systems of internal control. The auditor must accept that conditions are bound to change during the course of an audit and must be flexible enough to handle departures from plans to address changing requirements.

GANTT CHART: THE AUDIT APPROACH

The drafting of a written audit plan is essential for compiling, consolidating, and then communicating the essentials of the planning phase to the audit team, and the audit plan should be required reading by each team member. However necessary and required (by auditing standards and federal regulations), the written plan has limitations and some inherent difficulty in succinctly describing important audit management concern, phasing considerations, and staff assignments that, if not confronted by the audit directors and team managers, will consume time and resources, and may result in a less-than-optimal audit.

In addition to the written plan, audit management, in fact the entire team, will benefit from the knowledge of knowing audit-related facts such as:

- How are the audit phases integrated with prescribed audit procedures?
- What are the audit procedures and audit tasks that must be performed?
- What is the start date, the duration, and end date for each audit procedure and task?
- Who is to perform each audit procedure and task?
- What is the "critical path," the "critical procedures," and the "critical success factors" of the audit?
- What procedures and tasks must be completed on time to keep from jeopardizing the audit completion date?
- When and what interim or periodic reporting is to be made to the federal agency?
- What reviews, how often, and when will audit management review the audit progress?
- What is the level and hours of staffing committed to performance of which audit procedures and related audit tasks?
- How are the audit team and its individual members to be scheduled to level out, coordinate, and complement the audit as a whole?

All of these are essential issues, but not easily illustrated, portrayed, or communicable to audit team members by words in a written plan. A management tool widely used by industrial engineers and the major management consulting firms, but used to a lesser degree by the audit profession, is charting. More specifically, a well-planned audit would benefit by the construction and use of Gantt charting.[1] The Gantt chart (for purposes of naming, there are more than a few variations of the techniques) permits the graphic display of audit milestones, significant events, and audit tasks and procedures that must be accomplished, along with key approval and reporting points and audit completion dates, while at the same time informing mem-

---

[1] *See Steve M. Erikson, **Management Tools for Everyone: Twenty Techniques** (Princeton, NJ: Petrocelli Books, 1981), for an excellent "quick read."*

bers of the audit team who is to do what and when. The process requires audit management to approach the "Gantting" from two viewpoints:

1. Determine and schedule each audit procedure and audit task required to be completed. Begin at the starting point in the written audit plan and proceed to the completion of the last task of the audit (i.e., deliver the audit report[s] and audit assertions) on time.
2. Determine and schedule the estimated time to complete each audit procedure and task. This time, however, begin with the end dates for (a) the audit, (b) each required audit procedure, and (c) each audit task, and work backward, fixing the estimated completion times for each audit procedure and audit task.

As may be evident, the "Gantting" exercise has the potential for providing another advantage: the identification of gaps, duplications, omissions, and other issues within the audit plan and audit approach that may have to be reexamined before the full audit team arrives at the audit site.

9 DOCUMENTING INTERNAL CONTROLS: WHAT, WHO, WHERE, WHY?

As noted earlier, the auditor must have a clear idea of the audit scope to identify a process that will achieve the audit objectives. According to the federal audit model introduced in Chapter 7 and as discussed in greater detail in Chapter 8, the auditor's effort to understand controls is initiated during the planning phase of the audit and continues to be reexamined, refined, and revised during the entire internal control phase.

The second auditing standard of fieldwork states: "A sufficient understanding of internal controls is to be obtained to plan the audit to determine the nature, timing, and extent of tests to be performed." This chapter addresses internal control documentation, internal control definitions and requirements, and selected evaluation aspects of internal controls. Exhibit 9.1 is a graphic depiction of audit procedures and tasks to assist the auditor in grasping the conceptual nature, understanding, and importance of internal controls within a federal agency. This chapter underscores the priority that must be given to this phase of the federal audit model, as required by federal law, regulations, and auditing standards.

INTERNAL CONTROLS, DEFINITIONS, AND REQUIREMENTS

The most relevant AICPA source on internal controls and the relationship to audit is SAS 55, as amended by SAS 78, which adopted the definitions of controls and COSO's *Internal Control—Integrated Framework*. In accordance with the COSO definition, AICPA defines internal control

> *...as a process instituted by an entity's board of directors, management, and other personnel for the purpose of providing reasonable assurance of achieving objectives in the following three general categories: financial reporting, efficiency of operations, and compliance with laws and regulations.*

It is important to note that, although the AICPA adopted the broader definition of internal controls, as a general rule (and depending on the audit scope), the auditor is not required to consider efficiency of operations and compliance with laws and regulations in connection with an audit of financial statements conducted pursuant to the AICPA's generally accepted auditing standards.

Congress and OMB define the internal control structure for government purposes more broadly than COSO. This expansion allows for the encompassing of nonaccounting and nonfinancial factors as the plan of organization and methods and procedures adopted by management to ensure that the agency's resource use is consistent with legal criteria and that resources are safeguarded against waste, loss, and misuse.

Exhibit 9.1: Internal control phase of the audit

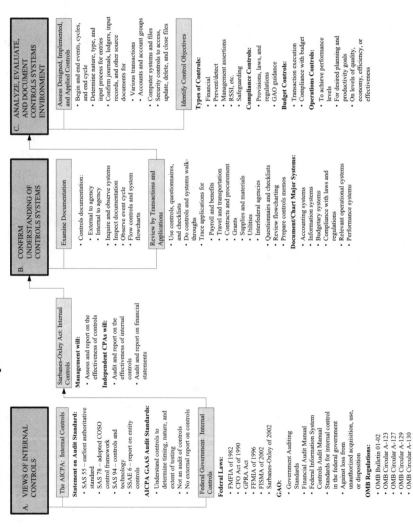

A. VIEWS OF INTERNAL CONTROLS

The AICPA: Internal Controls

Statement on Audit Standard:
- SAS 55 – earliest authoritative standard
- SAS 78 – adopted COSO control framework
- SAS 94 – controls and technology
- SSAE 6 – report on entity controls

AICPA GAAS Audit Standards:
- Understand controls to determine timing, nature, and extent of testing
- Not an audit of controls
- No external report on controls

Federal Government: Internal Controls

Federal Laws:
- FMFIA of 1982
- CFO Act of 1990
- GPRA Act
- FFMIA of 1996
- FISMA of 2002
- Sarbanes-Oxley of 2002

GAO:
- Government Auditing Standards
- Financial Audit Manual
- Federal Information System Controls Audit Manual
- Standards for internal control in the federal government
- Against loss from unauthorized acquisition, use, or disposition

OMB Regulations:
- OMB Bulletin 01-02
- OMB Circular A-123
- OMB Circular A-127
- OMB Circular A-129
- OMB Circular A-130

Sarbanes-Oxley Act: Internal Controls

Management will:
- Assess and report on the effectiveness of controls

Independent CPAs will:
- Audit and report on the effectiveness of internal controls
- Audit and report on financial statements

B. CONFIRM UNDERSTANDING OF CONTROLS SYSTEMS

Examine Documentation
- Controls documentation:
  - External to agency
  - Internal to agency
- Inquire and observe systems
- Inspect documentation
- Observe event cycle
- Flow controls and system flowcharts

Review by Transactions and Applications
- Use controls, questionnaires, and checklists
- Do controls and systems walk-throughs
- Trace applications for
  - Payroll and benefits
  - Travel and transportation
  - Contracts and procurement
  - Grants
  - Supplies and materials
  - Utilities
  - Interfederal agencies
- Questionnaire and checklists
- Review flowcharting
- Prepare controls memos

Document/Chart Major Systems:
- Accounting systems
- Information systems
- Budgetary systems
- Compliance with laws and regulations
- Relevant operational systems
- Performance systems

C. ANALYZE, EVALUATE, AND DOCUMENT CONTROLS SYSTEMS ENVIRONMENT

Assess Designed, Implemented, and Applied Controls
- Begin and end events, cycles, and end cycle
- Determine nature, type, and input process for entries
- Confirm journals, ledgers, input records, and other source documents for
  - Various transactions
  - Accounts and account groups
- Computer systems and files
- Security controls to access, update, delete, and close files

Identify Control Objectives

Types of Controls:
- Financial
- Prevent/detect
- Management assertions
- RSSI, etc.
- Safeguarding

Compliance Controls:
- Provisions, laws, and regulations
- GAO guidance

Budget Controls:
- Transaction execution
- Compliance with budget

Operations Controls:
- To achieve performance levels
- For desired planning and productivity goals
- On levels of quality, economy, efficiency, or effectiveness

Exhibit 9.1: Internal control phase of the audit (continued)

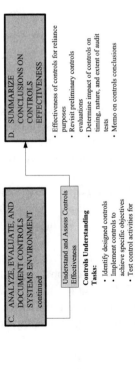

C. ANALYZE, EVALUATE, AND DOCUMENT CONTROLS SYSTEMS ENVIRONMENT continued

Understand and Assess Controls Effectiveness

Controls Understanding Tasks:

- Identify designed controls
- Implement controls to achieve specific objectives
- Test control activities for effectiveness and efficiency
- Discuss cycle and specific controls with management
- Execute walk-throughs
- Observe controls in place and applied
- Examine documentary evidence of existence

Inquire, Observe, Flowchart, and Evaluate Controls:

- Designed controls
- Implemented controls
- Applied controls
- Document with system control evaluation worksheet

Systems Compliance Test:

- Combination of control tests
  - Observation
  - Inquiry
  - Inspection
  - Walk-throughs
- Determine financial compliance control to test
- Determine IS compliance controls to test
- Determine the timing and extent of audit tests to perform

D. SUMMARIZE CONCLUSIONS ON CONTROLS EFFECTIVENESS

- Effectiveness of controls for reliance purposes
- Revisit preliminary controls evaluations
- Determine impact of controls on timing, nature, and extent of audit tests
- Memo on controls conclusions

GAO, in its standards for performance audits, requires auditors to understand management controls including the plan of organization, methods, and procedures adopted by management to ensure that its goals are met.

Over the years, increasing attention and concern has been directed by Congress in its laws and by federal agencies in their regulations to the importance of an agency's internal control structure. Within the federal government, many executives support the premise that audits of controls are quite possibly, from a management and oversight perspective, as important as the detailed auditing of financial information. These views have been volunteered and also endorsed by members of the accounting profession, independent commissions, Congress, and Comptrollers General of the United States.

Even prior to the implementation of the Sarbanes-Oxley Act, an auditor's scope for assessing and reporting on internal controls was greater for audits of governmental entities than for audits of corporate entities. *Government Auditing Standards* required the auditor to issue reports on internal controls every audit of a federal agency, while the AICPA standards required only that reportable conditions and material weaknesses be brought to the attention of the audit committee or other appropriate executive/management level, which kept this information within the corporate family.

The Sarbanes-Oxley Act changed internal control requirements (for publicly traded companies and companies opting to comply with PCAOB standards). Passage of Sarbanes-Oxley was precipitated by recent developments and scandals; however, general concern over the lack of priority given to internal controls during the course of an audit has been building for years. Some examples include:

- In April 1988, the AICPA issued 10 SASs, referred to as the "expectation" SASs. At least four of these SASs outlined new auditor responsibilities or defined with more specificity the auditor's responsibility for internal controls and for communicating the results of tests of controls under certain adverse conditions.
- A 1991 article entitled by the former chairman of the AICPA's Auditing Standards Board argued that auditors should work to place greater value on internal controls and that such work should provide an early warning of potential problems.[1]
- The Committee of Sponsoring Organizations of the Treadway Commission developed an expanded definition of internal controls emphasizing that increased importance be given to controls. The 1992 COSO report identified five prerequisites of an effective internal control structure to include (1) the control environment, (2) risk assessment, (3) control activities, (4) information and communications, and (5) monitoring.
- A former member of the AICPA's board of directors, in an article entitled "Reinventing the Audit," addressed the matter that the public expects assurances that audited entities are well controlled and in compliance with laws and

---

[1] *CPA Journal* article "Addressing Early Warning and the Public Interest: Auditor Involvement with Internal Control", NY, NY. 1991.

regulations. In addition, auditors should be providing these assurances rather than opining only on whether the historical numbers are in accordance with GAAP at a particular moment in time.

- GAO reported on a survey of major bank audit committees, asking what they desired from an audit and what they felt was lacking. The survey revealed that audit committee members desired more reporting on internal controls and compliance with laws and regulations—the financial statement, audit, and some "boilerplate" reports on controls were not meeting the needs of audit committee members.

- An independent auditor's report of GAO for the year ended September 30, 1992, included both an opinion on the agency's financial statements as well as an opinion on its system of internal control in effect on that date. In rendering the control opinions, auditors used criteria established by the COSO of the Treadway Commission.

- A shift in the historic audit "paradigm" was proposed by GAO in 1993 when the Comptroller General recommended that changes in auditing standards give increased audit coverage to controls. This broader draft audit standard supported GAO's thesis that audits of internal controls were at least as important as the auditing and reporting of the historical financial information.

- The 1993 changes proposed by GAO would affect several areas: (1) an expansion of the scope of the controls reviewed beyond the internal accounting and administrative controls now envisioned by GAAS; (2) an elevation of the objective of auditing controls to a level of emphasis commensurate with the audit of financial data; and (3) requiring a separate reporting—that is, a separate opinion on the effectiveness of controls—by the auditor. (These changes to the *Government Auditing Standards*, offered years before Sarbanes-Oxley, were not implemented at the time.)

The second half of the 1990s and the years preceding the passage of Sarbanes-Oxley in July of 2002 produced a significant number of pronouncements by the AICPA affecting internal controls. Notable examples include:

- SAS 78, *Consideration of Internal Control in a Financial Statement Audit: An Amendment to Statement on Auditing Standards No. 55*

- SAS 82, *Consideration of Fraud in a Financial Statement Audit* (which was superseded in October 2002 by SAS 99 bearing the same title)

- SAS 88, *Service Organizations and Reporting on Consistency* (which amended SAS 70, *Service Organizations*)

- SAS 90, *Audit Committee Communications*

- SAS 94, *The Effect of Information Technology on the Auditor's Consideration of Internal Control in a Financial Statement Audit*

- SSAE 10, *Attestation Standards: Revision and Recodification* (which amended SSAE 6, *Reporting on an Entity's Internal Control over Financial Reporting: An amendment to Statement on Standards for Attestation Engagements No. 2*)

In short, the concept of increasing the audit attention given to internal controls has been gaining momentum, and today, the private sector subject to PCAOB requirements is placing an importance on internal controls and related reporting that is greater than that of the federal government. Whether the federal government should match PCAOB's requirements is and will be subject to debate, with congressional action likely during the federal fiscal year 2006 or 2007.

FEDERAL STANDARD SETTERS

The need for strong, effective internal controls cannot be overemphasized. The importance, as noted is recognized by GAAS and, in the light of recent accounting scandals, the consequences of deficient internal controls of publicly traded companies have been made all too obvious to the public.

Besides laws of Congress, federal regulations and guidance on management reporting assurances concerning internal controls and related controls reporting requirements include:

- *Office of Management and Budget:* OMB provides guidance on the implementation of, and compliance with, congressional legislation affecting internal controls. Guidance is typically issued in the form of OMB circulars, although internal control-related guidance can also be found in OMB bulletins.
- *Government Accountability Office:* GAO is required by law (FMFIA) to develop the internal control standards that apply to the federal government, which it has done and which have been implemented and are being applied by federal agencies.

In addition, these agencies also have a direct impact on federal internal controls:

- *Department of the Treasury:* Through its *Treasury Financial Manual* and other guidance, the Treasury Department is responsible for defining the fiscal responsibilities of federal agencies by providing internal control-related policies, procedures, and instructions. In addition, the department's Financial Management Services (FMS) is responsible for the consolidation of the annual financial statements of the federal government. As such, FMS is responsible for developing the controls and procedures governing the financial statement consolidation process.
- *Office of Personnel Management:* Through the issuance of policies affecting all aspects of human resources within the federal government, OPM is responsible for issuing controls that affect the most important resource in the federal government: its human capital.

Arguably, these four central federal agencies have had the greatest impact on internal controls. Together, these agencies comprise the principals of the Joint Financial Management Improvement Program (JFMIP).

The mission of JFMIP was to improve federal financial management practices. To that end, JFMIP has issued its *Framework for Federal Financial Management Systems*, as well as requirements documentation covering a variety of federal financial systems. In December 2004, the principals of JFMIP voted to realign the program, meaning that JFMIP would no longer be a stand-alone organization.

Although the newer role of JFMIP has not yet been clarified, it is expected that JFMIP's efforts will likely continue.

Other organizations that deserve mention when identifying the developers of federal internal controls and audit-related controls policy and guidance include:

- *Chief Financial Officers Council (CFOC):* This council consists of the CFOs and deputy CFOs of the largest federal agencies, as well as senior managers from OMB and the Department of Treasury. The council was created by the CFO Act of 1990 and charged with the task of improving federal financial management. In addition, CFOC was responsible for coordinating the activities of federal agencies in connection with financial practices including systems and internal controls. Considering the recent realignment of JFMIP, as discussed above, it is anticipated that CFOC will play an increasing role in federal internal controls guidance and requirements in the future. The current plan is that JFMIP will report to a newly created CFOC committee, chaired by the chief of OMB's Office of Federal Financial Management.

- *President's Council on Integrity and Efficiency* and the *Executive Council on Integrity and Efficiency (ECIE):* Among other goals the PCIE and ECIE were established by executive order to consider agency efficiency and integrity issues affecting government agencies. Both organizations are primarily concerned with federal auditing issues and are comprised of Inspectors General (IGs) tasked with increasing the effectiveness of the IG function. The PCIE/ECIE and individual Offices of Inspector General are often involved in the determination of internal control requirements at the agency level. In addition, due to the nature of their mission, IGs often uncover internal control weaknesses and are responsible for recommending internal control standards, policies, and procedures to be followed by federal agencies.

- *Chief Information Officers Council (CIOC):* This council was established by executive order in 1996 to promote the efficient and effective utilization of federal information resources. Although the emphasis is on modernization and the effective application of advanced information technology, the council is involved with significant federal systems security and internal control issues.

- *Federal Accounting Standards Advisory Board:* FASAB is primarily responsible for developing accounting principles, not internal controls, for the federal government. But, in the first document issued by FASAB, Statement of Federal Financial Accounting Concepts 1 (SFFAC 1), *Objectives of Federal Financial Reporting,* FASAB identified four major reporting objectives: (1) budgetary integrity, (2) operating performance, (3) stewardship, and (4) systems and control. Two of these objectives, budgetary integrity and systems and control, address internal controls that promote compliance with laws and regulations, safeguarding of assets, and fairness of presentation.

While it is clear that FASAB's role is not as broad as that of OMB or GAO with regard to internal controls, FASAB since 1990 has played a role in the development of standards promoting internal controls within the federal government.

In addition to the above, many other organizations are involved in the development of internal control guidance for the federal government. Virtually all cabinet-level agencies (and many of their departmental components) have developed their own internal control guidance addressing the unique requirements of each agency. In practical terms, the auditor will look to OMB and GAO for guidance on internal controls; however, it is important that the auditor be aware of other organizations that play significant roles.

This section has addressed guidance relative to internal controls developed by the federal government and federal agencies. Internal control guidance can, of course, be found in sources outside of the federal government not directly responsible for issuing federal internal controls guidance. One such source is the *Internal Control—Integrated Framework* developed by COSO. The COSO controls framework contains an extremely comprehensive discussion of internal controls and has been adopted by GAO in its *Standards for Internal Control in the Federal Government*. Other sources of authoritative, reputable guidance include the PCAOB and COSO itself, whose guidance is discussed further in other chapters of this text.

FEDERAL GUIDANCE

Congress, OMB, GAO, and the other standard setters discussed earlier all play significant roles in the development of internal controls requirements. Key laws and other legislation are discussed further next.

Laws of Congress

The most authoritative internal control guidance of the federal government is the body of laws and regulations passed by Congress. Each law is supplemented by provisions in OMB pronouncements (typically in the form of OMB circulars and bulletins), which serve as the regulatory implementation guidance that federal executive agencies must follow. This section provides an overview of the most significant laws, regulations, and OMB guidance affecting internal controls, as well as selected guidance from GAO and JFMIP.

Addressing agency-specific controls guidance is beyond the scope of this book, but auditors should be aware of these particular externally imposed controls requirements during the planning phase of an audit. No agency is permitted to implement guidance that is in opposition to laws of Congress or regulations of OMB. More important, as evidenced by the volume of financial management legislation since 1990, the reader is warned that internal control guidance in the federal government is an ever-changing process. Further, developments in the private sector, such as Sarbanes-Oxley and PCAOB, may very well affect future federal internal control guidance, including agency financial reporting requirements and scopes of mandated financial audits. A committee of Congress has stated that a position relative to audit coverage and reporting on an agency's internal controls over financial reporting will be forthcoming during the federal government's fiscal year 2006 or 2007. An auditor must be cognizant of the imminence of change at all times and follow the development/enactment of any new federal internal controls and related audit guidance.

The 1990s witnessed the issuance of more financial management legislation than any preceding decade in the country's history. Congress has been involved in the promotion of competent financial management and sound internal controls virtually since the creation of the republic, but some of the more recent significant legislative actions have included:

- *Inspector General Act of 1978 (IG Act):* This act was a major congressional initiative to create independent and objective units within departments and agencies to conduct and supervise audits and investigations and to promote internal controls to ensure operating efficiency and effectiveness and prevent and/or detect fraud.
- *Federal Managers' Financial Integrity Act of 1982:* FMFIA was, and arguably still is, the most significant congressional legislation addressing the existence and effectiveness of systems of internal controls. FMFIA amended the Accounting and Auditing Act of 1950 and makes it clear that effective controls (both accounting and administrative) are essential. The act identifies general criteria that must be adhered to in the design and maintenance of accounting systems in compliance with the standards for internal controls to be developed by the Comptroller General. In addition, the act assigned to OMB (in consultation with GAO) the responsibility of developing guidelines for implementation of the FMFIA legislation (see the OMB Circular A-123 discussion later in this section). An important feature of FMFIA is the requirement that the heads of each executive branch agency issue annual reports to the President and Congress on whether the agency's internal controls comply with federal standards.
- *Chief Financial Officers Act* and *Government Management and Reform Act:* The CFO Act of 1990 provides for the production of audited financial statements and addresses the need for strengthened financial management leadership, long-range planning, and improved financial reporting. The need for sound internal controls is clearly supported by the CFO Act, which requires audits to comply with the federal *Government Auditing Standards* and include reports on tests required of internal controls and other tests required of compliance with laws and regulations. The scope of the CFO Act was later expanded by the GMRA in 1994 that significantly increased the number of federal agencies subject to annual audits.
- *Government Performance and Results Act:* GPRA requires the development of a long-range strategic plan addressing performance, including the identification of specific goals and objectives. Actual performance is to be reported and compared to the plan.   GPRA reporting is, by itself, a significant administrative control that forces federal agencies to focus on performance. Internal controls are also important to the achievement of GPRA objectives, and OMB requires that controls promoting the fair presentation of performance be reviewed by the agency's auditors (although there is currently no requirement to express an opinion on the effectiveness of controls).
- *Clinger-Cohen Act:* Also known as the Information Technology Management Reform Act (ITMRA), the Clinger-Cohen Act promotes IT compliance with

GPRA by promoting, among other objectives, effective management and controls over the IT acquisition process and ensuring that IT planning and investing is tied directly to the federal agency's mission and goals.

- *Federal Financial Management Improvement Act of 1996:*   FFMIA established certain financial management system requirements to be followed by federal agencies. It also requires an auditor to report on compliance with laws and regulations, and state whether an agency's financial management systems comply with:

  - Federal financial management systems requirements
  - Applicable federal accounting standards
  - US government standard general ledger, at the transaction level

- *Federal Information Security Management Act:* FISMA was passed into law in 2002, replacing the Government Information Security Reform Act of 2000 (GISRA).   FISMA requires the development of minimum standards for agency systems and dictates federal agencies to conduct annual IT security reviews and to have IGs perform annual independent evaluations of agency programs and systems. The results of these reviews and evaluations are to be reported annually to OMB and Congress. FISMA also includes provisions aimed at further strengthening the security of the federal government's information and information systems. Under FISMA, additional guidance is provided regarding configuration management, continuity of operations, and the maintenance of an inventory of major information systems providing for the identification of the interfaces between all systems.

Office of Management and Budget

OMB is responsible for the development of instructions and guidance to assist federal agencies in their efforts to comply with congressional legislation. OMB guidance is issued in the form of circulars, bulletins, or memoranda.

Regarding internal controls, the most significant controls guidance available to federal agencies is contained in OMB Circular A-123, *Management Responsibility for Internal Control*. OMB Circular A-123 implements FMFIA, and compliance is required of all executive branch agencies. The circular is updated periodically to reflect evolving views and techniques relating to internal controls and to promote the effectiveness and efficiency of government. The most recent revision is dated December 2004 and is effective starting in fiscal year 2006. The prior revision was dated 1995. The most recent revision was issued in response to new requirements imposed on the commercial sector by Sarbanes-Oxley. The purpose of the revised circular is to provide guidance to federal managers addressing:

- Management's responsibility for internal control
- The process for assessing internal control effectiveness and new requirements for conducting the assessment
- Updated internal control standards
- The integration and coordination of internal control assessments

OMB has issued draft implementation guidance which is currently being reviewed by affected stakeholders. Other circulars and bulletins with significant internal control implications include:

- OMB Circular A-127, *Financial Management Systems:* This circular prescribes policies and standards for executive departments and agencies to follow in developing, operating, evaluating, and reporting on financial management systems. It provides guidance in connection with the acquisition of system software and was revised in December of 2004 to reflect the realignment of JFMIP.
- OMB Circular A-129, *Managing Federal Credit Programs:* This circular prescribes policies and procedures in connection with the accounting, management, and control of federal credit programs. The circular provides guidance to comply with the Federal Credit Reform Act and financial system standards designed to properly account for and control federal credit programs. With loans, loan guarantees, and other financial transactions, such as certain long-term leases, being subject to credit reform, virtually every federal agency must comply with the accounting and control requirements of the act.
- OMB Circular A-130, *Management of Federal Information Resources:* This circular prescribes policy for the management of federal information resources including specific implementation guidelines. The circular is issued pursuant to several laws including the Information Technology Management Reform Act of 1996 (Clinger-Cohen) and the CFO Act. The circular addresses several control issues including security and controls over information technology investments.
- OMB Bulletin 01-02, *Audit of Federal Financial Statements:* This bulletin is primarily designed to provide audit-related guidance to federal agencies and the auditors of federal agencies. However, it also includes internal control guidance and definitions for material weaknesses and reportable conditions.
- OMB Memoranda and Reports: Memoranda and reports with internal control requirements and implications are routinely issued by OMB and may impact the audit of federal agencies.

Government Accountability Office

Although GAO is usually associated with federal investigations and federal auditing, including the development of *Government Auditing Standards* ("yellow book"), GAO is also a primary source of guidance concerning internal controls and related best practices. The most influential sources of GAO internal control guidance include:

- *Standards for Internal Control in the Federal Government* ("green book"): This document was developed by GAO as mandated by Congress in passage of the Federal Managers' Financial Integrity Act of 1982. In the act Congress required GAO to issue standards for internal control in government. The document closely parallels COSO controls framework standards and provides a general financial internal controls framework and considers controls related to computer technology. As stated by GAO, the purpose of its *Standards for Internal Controls* is to assist in establishing and maintaining internal controls in the federal government and to enable agency managers to identify and address "major performance and management challenges and areas at greatest risk of fraud, waste, abuse, and mismanagement."

- GAO/PCIE *Financial Audit Manual:* GAO's *Financial Audit Manual* is clearly designed to assist the federal auditor in the execution of his or her audit procedures, and not as a statement of sound internal controls. However, the nature of *FAM,* particularly sections 200, Planning, and 300, Internal Control, is such that the manual, by guiding the auditor in what to do and look for, can function as a very helpful source of best practices in internal controls.
- *Federal Information System Controls Audit Manual:* Like *FAM*, FISCAM is designed to assist in the audit of federal agencies and is not meant as a briefing on internal controls. However, by discussing control objectives and providing relevant examples of the control techniques followed by federal agencies, *FISCAM,* like *FAM,* is an invaluable source of best practices in internal controls.
- *Joint Financial Management Improvement Program:* As noted earlier, JFMIP is a joint project of the Department of Treasury, OMB, GAO, and OPM. JFMIP was recently realigned and is no longer a stand-alone agency. The future influence of JFMIP is currently unclear, however, as, in the past, JFMIP has been responsible for the issuance of systems requirements (including internal controls). Auditors of federal agencies are well advised to consult JFMIP guidance when relevant to the systems they are auditing. Selected systems requirements/guidance issued by JFMIP includes general controls as well as systems control requirements. The *general guidance* addresses subjects such as:

  - Framework for federal financial management systems
  - Financial requirements source matrix document
    Core financial system requirements
    Core financial system requirements
  - Addendum to core financial system requirements
    JFMIP plan for an integrated requirements database
  - Managerial cost accounting implementation guide

The JFMIP's *systems control requirements* include topics such as:

- System requirements for managerial cost accounting
- Human resources and payroll system requirements
- Direct loan system requirements
- Travel system requirements
- Seized property and forfeited assets system requirements
- Guaranteed loan system requirements
- Grant financial system requirements
- Property management system requirements
- Benefit system requirements

- Revenue system requirements document
- Acquisition financial system requirements
- Inventory, supplies, and materials system requirements

It is essential that an auditor be aware of relevant requirements prior to the initiation of any audit in order to properly define the audit scope and plan the audit in accordance with GAO standards and all other requirements (including agency-specific requirements, which are not covered above).

Fortunately, OMB, GAO, and most federal agencies, in general, are very efficient in disseminating requirements information. In addition, agency Web sites are usually current. The auditor is well advised to consult these Web sites prior to initiating the audit.

EVALUATING INTERNAL CONTROLS

So far, definitions, oversight agencies, and guidance have been discussed. This is important, useful information on what constitutes sound internal controls, but little has been said about how one evaluates internal controls to determine whether the agency-applied controls comply with guidance and, given the unique circumstances of a governmental auditee, whether the controls are effective. The ensuing discussion addresses the evaluation of internal controls.

The effective evaluation of internal controls hinges on the successful execution of risk analysis techniques, discussed later. However, risk analysis requires relevant documentation of accounting cycles, processes, systems, and accounts.

During the internal control phase, the auditor reviews documentation developed during the planning phase to conduct the evaluation. For audits that are not first-time audits, the documentation needed for evaluation will usually be available after the completion of the planning phase, where the auditor should have noted changes (if any) from prior years.

In recurring audits, the auditors will execute walk-throughs of transactions (if not completed during the prior phase) to confirm their understanding of the system/cycle, and will proceed to the execution of evaluation procedures.

For first-time audits, however, it is not likely that the auditor could fully document an agency's financial systems/cycles during the planning phase of the audit. In practice, some of this audit effort will necessarily overlap with the internal control phase of the audit process. As long as documentation is properly completed prior to the auditor's execution of risk assessment audit procedures, it matters little whether the documentation is completed during phase I or II of the audit. The following discussion illustrates an approach to evaluate and test an agency's systems of internal controls.

Documentation of financial management systems must include a detailed examination of the agency's system of internal controls and other aspects of its financial management system. The objective is to determine whether adequate control measures exist and whether the controls have been implemented to prevent or minimize risk and/or detect the occurrence of erroneous and/or unauthorized transactions/events in a timely, cost-effective manner. Systems documentation, the evaluation of the systems of controls, and actual testing of the controls applied in practice are performed during the execution of the first three phases of the audit. The results of these audit procedures include findings, observations, and determination of audit risk. These audit procedures and tasks will provide the inputs and knowledge necessary to conclude on the relative effectiveness of controls and to confirm the efficacy of the auditor's decision to rely or not rely on the controls when determining the timing, nature, and extent of audit procedures to apply in the audit. Such an audit approach would include several steps:

Step 1: Identify and document the event cycle. Event cycles are the processes used to initiate and perform related activities, create the necessary documentation, and gather and report related data. In other words, an event cycle is a series of steps taken to get something done (e.g., pay personnel, contract for services, issue grants, etc). Event cycles are the focal points for documenting and understanding the financial management systems and related internal controls. Accordingly, the first step in the procedure is to identify these event cycles for the particular program or administrative function being reviewed. The initial documentation of event cycles takes place during Phase I (the planning phase) of the audit, and the cycle documentation is completed during Phase II (the controls phase). The identification of the event cycles is based on information collected from several different sources and a variety of evidence-gathering techniques, as discussed in Chapter 8.

Step 2: Analyze and evaluate the general systems of controls and controls environment. The effectiveness of a system of internal control depends largely on the environment in which it operates. A cycle/process with strong internal controls operating in a weak control environment is likely to have overall weak controls in practice. Conversely, a process with weaker system controls that operates in a sound/strong general control environment can very well have strong controls overall. In the case of a sound system of controls operating within a weak environment, it is likely that controls will be disregarded. On the other hand, control weaknesses can be overcome, or even negated, when a system operates within a strong internal control environment.

General systems evaluation, acquiring an understanding of the systems of controls, and making a preliminary assessment of the controls environment are performed during the earlier planning phase of the audit. In this phase, the specific attributes of the internal control environment, such as management attitude and policies and procedures, are identified, initially documented, and possibly confirmed on a limited basis. These audit concerns and tasks were discussed more in Chapter 8.

Step 3: Identify and document the individual processing events/activities for each event cycle. In this step, each of the individual processing events/activities for each event cycle identified in Step 1, above, must be noted and documented. The division into individual events/activities facilitates the evaluation of the internal controls for each event cycle. The auditor's documentation for this audit phase will include narrative descriptions and flowcharts

for each of the event cycles and significant events and other observed activities.

Step 4: *Evaluate the internal controls within each event cycle.* For the data related
to the internal control environment and additional information on relevant
transactions, events/cycles, and the activities occurring within each cycle,
the auditor is in a position to evaluate the controls being used for the various
event cycles. This evaluation of internal controls and determination of related risk assessment is a significant procedure of the controls phase of the
audit.   By reviewing the documentation, the auditor can acquire an
indication of the extent to which the system is documented, may be relied on
to safeguard the auditee's assets, complies with laws and regulations, and is
capable of producing financial data that are fairly presented in accordance
with GAAP. This evaluation enables the auditor to characterize the level of
control risk and the extent of reliance that may be placed on internal
controls, and to make auditor judgments on the combination of internal
control and substantive testing (i.e., the actual timing, nature and extent of
auditor tests of transactions and account balances). The substantive tests are
conducted to obtain sufficient competent evidential matter that will be
supportive of the auditor's opinions that must be provided to the agency at
the conclusion of the audit.

Step 5: *Evaluate tests of internal controls.* As noted, the documentation gathered in
the prior steps enables the auditor to: (1) evaluate the effectiveness of the
design of the system of internal controls, (2) make *initial* preliminary assertions regarding the reliance that may be placed on the system (subject to the
actual detailed test of applied controls that has yet to be done), and (3) determine the extent to which audit efficiency can be achieved by testing internal controls in contrast to conducting more extensive, time-consuming,
and costly substantive audit tests of transactions and accounts.

Step 6: *Develop preliminary observations and recommendations.* The auditor's
conclusions, to this point in the audit, should be communicated to the
auditee in order to confirm or refute information or perceptions relative to
controls that were acquired earlier and to obtain management's views on the
auditor's findings up to this point. The timely communication of audit find-
ings/observations on internal controls and related recommendations is essential to support ongoing efforts to improve federal government financial
management.   Thus, auditors should not wait until the completion of
Phase III, the testing phase, to report facts of financial management and
internal control significance.

During Phase III, the results of the tests developed during Phase II will either
validate or disprove the auditor's initial assertions relative to the operating effectiveness of the agency's system of internal controls. Depending on the auditor's conclusions concerning the operating effectiveness of the internal controls over financial
reporting and the controls over compliance with laws and regulations, the auditor
will either proceed to complete the planned substantive auditing procedures or, if

indicated by test results, revise and increase the extent of previously planned substantive auditing procedures to reduce audit risks to a more tolerable level.

INTERNAL CONTROL EVALUATION REQUIREMENTS

SAS 55, as amended by SAS 78 (which essentially represents the AICPA's adoption of COSO's *Internal Control—Integrated Framework*), defines the auditor's responsibility in connection with internal control in terms of:

1. Understanding the components of internal control
2. Establishing whether controls are in place
3. Assessing control risks
4. Documenting the understanding and the risk assessment

Items 1 and 2 are directly related to assessing control risk. This essentially means that, first, the auditor must understand the five components of internal control identified by SAS 55 and further refined by SAS 78:

1. *Internal control environment:* This refers to the overall "tone at the top," established and confirmed daily to agency personnel by management's actions and demonstrated concerns for effective controls.
2. *Risk assessment:* Assessments or evaluations of controls identify potential risks to the organization and lead to the direct development of policies and procedures to mitigate/negate this control risk.

   NOTE: This is an ongoing assessment that is an agency's responsibility. This distinction is important to avoid a misunderstanding between management's assessment of controls and the risk assessment and the control evaluation and testing required of the auditor in the performance of a financial audit pursuant to federal audit guidance.
3. *Control activities:* These are the actual control practices and procedures that are in place and used to execute management's control policies. This control component includes obvious control activities such as transaction authorizations and approvals, processing of financial data, and segregation of duties, as well as less obvious activities such as personnel reviews and training of the agency personnel.
4. *Information and communication practices:* These practices include the accounting and information systems, plus related procedures, manuals, books, and underlying records, as well as management's communications and promotion of internal controls policies and publication and enforcement of employee responsibilities for observing and assessing procedures and rules for the implemented controls.
5. *Monitoring:* This control component is directed toward how management promotes/enforces compliance with its control policies, including oversight functions. Although emphasis is typically placed on an agency's Office of Inspector General and/or internal auditor, plus the independent audit function, this does not need to be the extent of management's monitoring. Other evaluations by agency teams and external consultants and ongoing assess-

ments by agency program management are equally valid indicators of the effectiveness of controls monitoring.

The auditor's understanding of these basic components of an effective internal controls structure should be followed by the auditor's determination as to whether these controls components have actually been placed into operation and are being complied with on a day-to-day basis. Most often this determination is made through auditor inquiries of agency management and operating personnel, personal observations by the audit team, and walk-throughs of offices and agency activity locations to personally witness controls in operation.

Once items 1 and 2 are completed, the auditor can proceed to evaluate internal controls (item 3) and test and assess the practices employed in operations of the accounting and financial management systems (item 4).

The discussion that follows highlights techniques that should prove useful in evaluating the effectiveness of the components of internal control and in completing the auditor's risk assessment, as discussed later in Chapter 10.

During Phases I and II of the audit, the auditor identifies significant accounts and any perceived audit risks. This should be followed by the identification of the various sources of information and relative reliability of these information sources.

In general, each account will be affected by a variety of accounting processes, and it is important that the auditor realize that the likelihood of errors of audit importance will depend on the type of process or processes affecting the account. Thus, auditors will find it useful to classify sources of information by processes:

- *Recurring/routine processes*: These are accounting applications that process routine financial data (the detailed information about transactions) recorded in the books and records (e.g., cash receipts, procurement and accounts payable, cash disbursements, payroll), which are generally well supported by use of government-wide standard forms.
- *Nonroutine processes*: These are other, less frequently used processes, possibly those used in conjunction with the preparation of financial statements (e.g., involving reconciliations, physical inventories, aging of outstanding receivables, calculating depreciation expense, recording year-end liabilities), that require consideration of costs and activities not recordable or resulting from a standard routine data process and for which government-wide standards forms do not exist.
- *Estimation processes*: These processes reflect the numerous judgments, decisions, and choices made by the auditee in preparing financial statements (e.g., determining allowances for losses, valuing off-balance-sheet risk for contingencies such as environmental liabilities, contingent liabilities, credit reform estimates).

This distinction is useful, but auditors should anticipate that certain processes will combine attributes of other processes. For example, the proper determination of accounts payable at the end of a fiscal year will typically include nonroutine activities and procedures in an attempt to obtain a proper transaction cutoff and to ensure that all available information on accounts payable is recorded (e.g., invoices received by operating personnel and not forwarded to the accounts payable department must be inventoried and recorded at year-end).

COMPLETING AND DOCUMENTING THE AUDITOR'S UNDERSTANDING OF INTERNAL CONTROLS

At this point in the audit, the auditor would have:

- Identified and documented significant accounts (Phase I of the audit)
- Identified and documented significant accounting/event cycles, including the processes and activities included in the cycle (Phases I and II of the audit)
- Determined which accounting/event cycles and transactions affect each of the significant accounts (Phase II of the audit)
- Considered the types of processes comprising the accounting/event cycle, such as routine, nonroutine, and estimated sources (Phase II of the audit)

The information above enables the auditor to execute his/her risk assessment by:

- Identifying the types of errors that potentially threaten or impact each accounting/event cycle affecting all accounts or account groupings
- Identifying system characteristics, controls, procedures, or practices may prevent, mitigate, or detect the occurrence of these threats (e.g., relevant internal controls)
- Considering how the risk inherent in each accounting/event cycle could affect each significant account

Once the auditor determines the internal control risk, as it affects each of the significant accounts, he/she will be in a position to determine whether the system of internal controls can be relied upon. The concept of risk assessment is expanded in the next chapter to illustrate how, following completion of the risk assessment, the auditor develops detailed audit programs combining, as necessary, tests of internal controls with substantive audit tests, including analytical procedures.

10 ASSESSING AND EVALUATING CONTROL RISKS

The third standard of fieldwork states: "Sufficient competent evidential matter is to be obtained through inspection, observation, inquiries, and confirmations to afford a reasonable basis for an opinion regarding the financial statements under audit."

Consistent with the audit model introduced earlier, during the internal control phase the auditor must determine whether controls appear to be in place to provide reasonable assurance that the financial data to be reported on is fairly stated.[1] Depending on the results of this evaluation, the auditor decides the extent to which controls are to be tested to provide the "competent evidential matter."

This chapter expands on the internal control evaluation process introduced earlier and provides a controls risk assessment model, which has proved useful in the execution of federal audits. This chapter concludes the discussion of the control phase of an audit that began in Chapter 9. An important output of this phase of the audit is the development of the audit approach and accompanying detailed audit programs to guide the execution of both tests of internal control and the substantive testing of accounts balances.

ASSESS CONTROL RISKS

The auditor must formally *assess control risks*, that is, the risk that a material misstatement could occur in a financial statement assertion and not be prevented or detected on a timely basis by the system of internal control. In assessing control risks, the auditor is making an estimate of the relative effectiveness of the existing internal control system.

Levels of Control Risks

In assessing control risk, the auditor's interest must be focused on the extent to which the government's control system is preventing or detecting incomplete, inaccurate, or invalid transactions. Guidance of the AICPA states that control risks may be expressed in quantitative terms, such as percentages, or, more commonly, in non-quantitative terms. AICPA guidance also uses the terms *maximum risk* (controls are totally or nearly 100% ineffective) and *below the maximum risk* (controls are effective to some extent, as determined by the auditor's judgment). GAO guidance provides degrees for assessing control risk at one of three levels: low, moderate, and high.

---

[1] *The GAO's guide, **Federal Information System Controls Audit Manual**, is not an audit standard; its purpose is to: (1) inform financial auditors about computer-related controls and related audit issues so that they can better plan their work and integrate the work of information systems (IS) auditors with other aspects of the financial audit; and (2) provide guidance to IS auditors on the scope of issues that generally should be considered in any review of computer-related controls.*

AICPA guidance provides that the auditor must document conclusions regarding assessed levels of control risk for each relevant system/cycle, group of transactions, and/or account balance. With respect to documenting conclusions, AICPA provides this guidance in AU 319.83:[2]

- For financial statement assertions where control risk is assessed at the maximum level (i.e., 100% or total risk), auditors should document that fact, but need not document the basis for that conclusion.
- For financial statement assertions where the assessed level of control risk is below the maximum level (i.e., less than 100 % or total risk), auditors should document the basis for their assessed risk level.

For levels of the assessed control risk below the maximum levels, more audit evidence is needed to support the lower risk level assessment. Prior to testing, the auditor's assessment of risk is a preliminary estimate and subject to change if later tests disclose circumstances, conditions, and events indicating that the assessed level of risk was too low or that control deficiencies may have led to misstated financial statements.

Definitions and Classifications of Internal Control

In some circumstances, internal control deficiencies may be significant enough to be classified as reportable conditions or material weaknesses. The GAO, in its *Government Auditing Standards*, adopts the AICPA definition of reportable condition (paragraph 5-13) and material weakness (paragraph 5-14). OMB Bulletin 01-02 adopts this definition for reportable conditions:

...matters coming to the auditor's attention that, in the auditor's judgment, should be communicated because they represent significant deficiencies in the design or operation of internal control that could adversely affect the organization's ability to meet the objectives in paragraph 2.g. of this Bulletin.

Paragraph 2.g of Bulletin 01-02 describes internal controls as a process affected by agency management and other personnel, designed to provide reasonable assurance that the following three objectives are met:

(1) Reliability of financial reporting—transactions are properly recorded, processed, and summarized to permit the preparation of the Principal Statements and Required Supplementary Stewardship Information in accordance with generally accepted accounting principles, and assets are safeguarded against loss from unauthorized acquisition, use, or disposition;

(2) Compliance with applicable laws and regulations—transactions are executed in accordance with (a) laws governing the use of budget authority and other laws and regulations that could have a direct and material effect on the Principal 3 Statements or Required Supplementary Stewardship Information, and (b) any other laws, regulations, and government wide policies identified by OMB...;

---

[2] *AU citations refer to sections of the AICPA's annual publication of its **Professional Standards**, the U. S. Auditing Standards, NY, NY.*

(3) Reliability of performance reporting—transactions and other data that support reported performance measures are properly recorded, processed, and summarized to permit the preparation of performance information in accordance with criteria stated by management.

OMB's definition of internal control essentially parallels AICPA's definition, as set forth in AU 325.02, but differs in four ways:

1. OMB excludes the need to communicate specifically to an audit committee as currently very few federal agencies have formal audit committees.
2. OMB's reliability financial reporting objective is consistent with the AICPA's objective in connection with data included in the financial statements. But a notable difference is the specific OMB reference to the reporting of required supplementary stewardship information, which is not present in the AICPA's guidance.
3. OMB specifically includes compliance with laws and regulations as an objective. In the AICPA definition, noncompliance with laws, when such noncompliance could materially affect the financial statements, is implied in the AICPA's financial reporting objective, with the decision as to materiality being judgmental on the part of the auditor. However, OMB expands on the definition by, in essence, reserving the right to identify specific laws and regulations that should be supported by effective controls, removing the option for auditor judgment as to which laws and regulations will be tested.
4. OMB includes a need for effective controls over performance reporting.

For material weaknesses for federal audits, OMB Bulletin 01-02 adopted this definition:

...reportable conditions in which the design or operation of the internal control does not reduce to a relatively low level the risk that errors, fraud, or noncompliance in amounts that would be material in relation to the Principal Statements or Required Supplementary Stewardship Information being audited, or material to a performance measure or aggregation of related performance measures, may occur and not be detected within a timely period by employees in the normal course of performing their assigned functions.

Again, the OMB definition is close to the AICPA definition, in section AU 325, but not identical. Notable differences include

- OMB's substitution of the phrase "errors, fraud, or noncompliance" for "material misstatements," the term used by AICPA in AU 325.

OMB added references to material noncompliance in reference to required supplementary stewardship information and material noncompliance in reference to a performance measure. More recently, in 2002, PCAOB further changed the definition of the "internal control weakness," dropping the use of the term *reportable condition* and introducing its concept of the "significant deficiency." In its Auditing Standard 2, *An Audit of Internal Control over Financial Reporting Performed in Conjunction with an Audit of Financial Statements*, PCAOB defined a *significant deficiency* as:

> *...a control deficiency, or combination of control deficiencies, that adversely affects the company's ability to initiate, authorize, record, process, or report external financial data reliably in accordance with generally accepted accounting principles such that there is more than a remote likelihood that a misstatement of the company's annual or interim financial statements that is more than inconsequential will not be prevented or detected.*

PCAOB goes on to state that "remote" is defined as it is in Statement 5 of the Federal Accounting Standards Advisory Board (FASAB), which provides this guidance in relation to loss contingencies and the proper accounting and disclosure of those contingencies. The PCAOB standard suggests three terms to define the degrees of likelihood that the contingency will result in a loss:

1. *Probable:* The future event(s) is likely to occur.
2. *Reasonably possible:* The chance of the future event(s) occurring is more than remote, but less than likely.
3. *Remote:* The chance of the future event(s) occurring is slight.

PCAOB concludes "an event is 'more than remote' when it is either reasonably possible or probable." PCAOB proceeds to define the meaning of inconsequential by stating:

> *...a misstatement is **inconsequential** if a reasonable person would conclude, after considering the possibility of further undetected misstatements, that the misstatement, either individually or when aggregated with other misstatements, would clearly be immaterial to the financial statements. If a reasonable person could not reach such a conclusion regarding a particular misstatement, that misstatement is more than inconsequential.*

PCAOB does retain the term *material weakness*, which it defines as:

> *...a significant deficiency, or combination of significant deficiencies, that result in more than a remote likelihood that a material misstatement of the annual or interim financial statements will not be prevented or detected.*

A definition of internal control weaknesses can also be found in OMB's circular A-123, which provides guidance on the annual reporting of material weaknesses to the President and Congress. The circular states that the OMB definition of *material weakness* is similar to that used by financial statement auditors, but that for reporting under FMFIA Act requirements, the term also includes weaknesses affecting the operation of federal programs and the agency's ability to comply with laws and regulations.

Note that the recently revised OMB Circular A-123 adopts the definitions set forth by PCAOB and uses the term *significant deficiency* instead of *reportable condition*. While this may indicate that OMB plans to revise guidance to auditors of federal agencies by adopting the term *significant deficiency* and accompanying PCAOB, it is not a certainty at publication time that OMB's current position will be the "final word." OMB Bulletin 01-02 has not been revised to institute such a change. For audit purposes, the definitions in Bulletin 01-02 should be followed unless later amended.

ASSESS CONTROL RISKS IN ACCOUNTING PROCESSES/CYCLES

A risk assessment is a thought-intensive judgment process requiring a careful consideration of documentation gathered earlier and the potential implications/effects of the processes, cycles, systems, or activities documented on internal control risk.

Evaluating the Processes/Systems—A Useful Methodology

The risk assessment methodology discussed in this section is summarized below.

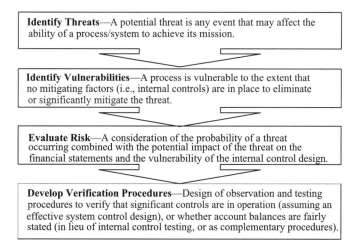

The first three activities depicted in the exhibit enable the auditor to define and document existing internal control risk, as required by AICPA and GAO guidance, and to develop an efficient audit approach that, where possible, capitalizes on existing system strengths (e.g., by testing controls) while focusing the auditor's efforts on those areas that may not be supported by strong controls.

The model departs from a more traditional audit approach by addressing process or system threats instead of internal control objectives. This is strictly a judgment call. Experience dictates that the identification of threats (the flip side of objectives) focuses the auditor's attention on the specific characteristics of the process/system being audited. All too often, identification of objectives becomes a recitation of "good characteristics" of any system that is the result of memorization and not the critical evaluation of the process or system. The model does not preclude the identification of objectives and, as will be seen in connection with the audit of account balances where objectives are typically more diverse, our recommended approach combines the identification of threats and objectives.

The ensuing discussion illustrates how risk assessments may be executed and includes techniques that have been found useful in the execution of financial statement audits.

Identify Threats

Risk can never be eliminated, but with proper controls it can be reduced to a reasonable level. The initial effort in our assessment is to identify what can go wrong in the operation of a given process or system. It is important that threats be identified initially without considering whether controls are already in place. This practice reduces the possibility of threats being prematurely eliminated from consideration without a full evaluation of mitigating controls and knowing the full implications of the threat on the financial statements. Further, it enables a reevaluation of the threat when subsequent testing indicates that the mitigating control is not fully operational or effective.

The identification of threats requires equal parts of imagination and experience. Extreme flights of fancy are not very productive, but neither is rigidity of thought. Risk assessments should be supervised by more senior members of the audit team, but should also include contributions of more junior personnel. Experience is invaluable when it comes to the identification of threats, but can sometimes hinder original thought. The identification of threats is facilitated by interactive discussions among audit team members with different levels of experience and assorted specializations.

In identifying threats, the auditor will find the concepts of routine, nonroutine, and judgmental processes very useful. In general, the less routine and more judgmental the process is, the higher the level of risk and the number of possible threatening events.

Identify Vulnerabilities

Having identified the possible threat, the auditor considers whether the process includes procedures that eliminate or mitigate the threat (i.e., whether internal controls are in place to effectively reduce internal control risk to a reasonable or tolerable level). Representative *general* internal controls that the auditor considers include

- Internal control environment
- Electronic data processing (EDP) practices
- Segregation of duties
- Audit trails
- Availability of competent evidential matter (e.g., invoices, receiving reports, purchase orders)
- Knowledgeable, trained personnel (particularly in connection with nonroutine and judgmental processes)
- Adequacy and completeness of documented operating policies and procedures

In identifying internal controls, the auditor often refers to "best practices" as documented in formal checklists and other guidance. Virtually every auditing firm or agency has developed (or adopted) an "internal control guide or checklist" in one form or another. In addition, accounting and auditing literature is filled with such checklists. Some of the most comprehensive checklists can be found in GAO publications, including systems requirements checklists and an Internal Control

Management and Evaluation Tool. There is, however, no substitute for audit judgment. As GAO stresses in every checklist or guidance issued, its documents are intended to serve as an aid to managers, not as a substitute for independent judgment.

Auditors are cautioned to consider the real impact of each control. Too often, the auditor assumes strong controls exist simply because of the existence of a procedure indicative of "best practices." For example, a time sheet is one such "best practice"; however, its mere existence does not lessen the threat of "phantom" or nonexistent employees, or prove that an employee actually worked the hours stated on the time sheet. The auditor must consider that a time sheet is but a sheet of paper that anyone can complete. Without a requirement that the time sheet be approved and/or reviewed by an appropriate member of management, there is no guarantee that an employee actually worked the hours stated on the time sheet. Further, without proper controls over authorization for the addition of new employees, including adequate segregation of duties of the approving manager, there is no guarantee that the employee actually exists. In addition, without proper audit trails (i.e., approving signatures, properly controlled time stamps), the auditor cannot test the control, although he or she may be able to observe compliance as part of a number of tests. Finally, in a poor internal control environment, the use of time sheets and the accompanying approval and audit trails could quite possibly provide no assurance that the threat has been mitigated.

By contrast, a process that is not supported by time sheets but that issues periodic and timely reports of payroll expense, including payee and hours worked, could be significantly better controlled. This would be the case if the report were issued to a well-motivated manager operating in a strong internal control environment with proper segregation of duties.

Evaluate Risk

The final determination of risk is generally based on the auditor's assessment of these factors affecting each threat:

- *The likelihood that the threat may occur.* For example, earthquakes may represent a threat to any process. However, a process operating in the state of New York is less susceptible to an earthquake than a process operating in the state of California. Thus, a weakness in ensuring continuity of operations in connection with the threat of a major earthquake is of greater consequence for processes in California, since the likelihood of occurrence is higher.
- *The impact of the threat on the financial statements.* In this case, weaknesses surrounding major cash disbursements, such as a payroll process, are clearly of more concern to the auditor than weaknesses surrounding petty cash disbursements.
- *The extent to which the threat is mitigated.* Having identified mitigating controls in the assessment of vulnerabilities, the auditor must determine the extent to which the threat can bypass existing controls.

The combined consideration of the threat's probability of occurrence, its potential impact, and the vulnerability of the process provides the basis for the auditor's assessment of internal control risk (i.e., high, moderate, or low, following GAO's classification).

ASSESS ACCOUNT LEVEL RISK

During planning and the early activities of the internal control phase, the auditor identifies significant accounts or groups of accounts. As was the case with accounting processes/cycles, these accounts are analyzed and the internal controls being applied by the agency must be evaluated. These accounts and groups of accounts evaluations are an extension of the risk assessment discussed earlier. Accounting cycles produce account balances by processing transactions, and the reliability of the account balance is affected by the internal controls associated with the accounting process/cycle or system.

Financial statements present data taken from account balances. Obviously, extending the risk assessment to include account balances is essential to obtaining competent evidential matter to support the auditor's assertions. The account-level risk assessment typically follows this pattern.

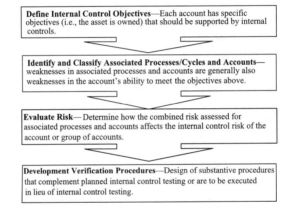

Define Internal Control Objectives—Each account has specific objectives (i.e., the asset is owned) that should be supported by internal controls.

Identify and Classify Associated Processes/Cycles and Accounts—weaknesses in associated processes and accounts are generally also weaknesses in the account's ability to meet the objectives above.

Evaluate Risk—Determine how the combined risk assessed for associated processes and accounts affects the internal control risk of the account or group of accounts.

Development Verification Procedures—Design of substantive procedures that complement planned internal control testing or are to be executed in lieu of internal control testing.

Define Internal Control Objectives

The first step in the evaluation consists of identifying the objectives (from a financial reporting perspective) of each account. The use of objectives to initiate the process instead of threats (as we did for processes/cycles) is a purely subjective one, but we believe that it is easier to relate an account objective to a financial statement assertion. In identifying control objectives, the auditor may find it helpful to consider:

- *Ownership and legitimacy*
  - The asset is real, representing the result of a legitimate transaction and supported by proof of ownership, such as a title or a contract supporting an account receivable.
  - The liability represents a legitimate obligation of the entity as a result of a reasonable, allowed, and legal transaction with the creditor.

- *Physical existence and safeguarding*
  - The asset currently exists and a process is in place to ensure that the asset is not stolen (if physical property) or otherwise rendered valueless (e.g., unauthorized or accidental record/data loss or write-off in the case of receivables).
  - The liability is removed when paid (or the obligation is otherwise fulfilled/terminated), and there is a process to ensure that all liabilities are recorded and protected against unauthorized or accidental additions, deletions, or data manipulation.
- *Fairness of classification.* Processes exist supported by documentation to ensure that transactions affecting the account are recorded in accordance with GAAP.
- *Fairness of account valuation.* Encompasses all of the above items, and usually requires processes and documentation that *periodically* assess the proper valuation of the account. Examples might include:
  - Estimation processes to revalue assets such as an account for bad debts or a reserve or write-off for obsolete or damaged inventory
  - Estimation processes to ensure that year-end accounts payable or periodic accruals are fairly stated

Identify Accounting Processes and Affected Accounts

In this step of the assessment, the auditor identifies processes and accounts that affect the specific account being evaluated. In general, the auditor considers:

- Routine accounting processes (e.g., cash disbursements, cash receipts, etc.)
- Nonroutine accounting processes (e.g., reconciliation procedures, supervisory monitoring procedures, etc.)
- Estimation processes (e.g., reserves for bad debts, reserves for contingencies, other valuation reserves, etc.)

The auditor will have already identified and documented most processes/cycles associated with the account; however, each general ledger account is subject to other (usually nonroutine or estimation) procedures designed to ensure the fair presentation of the account balance. Typical examples of nonroutine and estimation procedures that are unique to an account or group of accounts include:

- Reconciliation of account balances (e.g., cash, accounts payable/receivable, physical inventories)
- Periodic account reviews by management
- Availability and analysis of agings (e.g., for accounts receivable, accounts payable)
- Accruals and other period-end cutoff procedures (e.g., accrued salaries, accounts payable)
- Periodic physical inventory counts
- Computation of depreciation expense (or related analytical procedures if process is automated)

It is possible that these processes were not identified with the more routine accounting cycles during the planning and early stages of the internal control phases. Thus, this step in the risk assessment process should ensure that all relevant processes are identified.

Finally, the auditor should be aware of the relationship between accounts, as weaknesses or misstatements in an associated account may impact the account under evaluation. Thus, for example, a loss loan reserve (usually the result of an estimation process) is affected by the accuracy of data related to the associated loans (e.g., account balance, aging, terms, etc.). Similarly, an accrued interest payable account is affected by the details of the associated debt payable account (e.g., balance, interest rate, maturities).

Evaluate Account Risk

After defining the internal control objectives of the audited account and the related processes, the auditor will be in a position to establish whether these processes support the accomplishment of objectives identified. To the extent that the internal control risk of the associated processes was assessed as low, it may be possible simply to test relevant internal controls to support the auditor's assertions without executing any complementary substantive procedures (or by performing only minimal substantive procedures, such as selected analytical procedures). Conversely, where the controls of the supporting processes were assessed as high, internal control testing may serve no purpose and the audit of the account will require substantive auditing procedures to validate the account balance (or to ascertain the correct balance and propose audit adjustments). The development of an appropriate testing approach is discussed next.

DEVELOP AUDITING PROCEDURES

Having completed the risk assessment, the auditor is in a position to develop the audit approach. As addressed below, the optimal testing approach must consider specific federal requirements as well as audit efficiency.

Oversight Guidance

The AICPA requires that an auditor obtain an understanding of internal control. It does not, however, require that the auditor test internal controls regardless of whether the auditor evaluates internal control risk at a level below the maximum. GAO requirements in this regard are similar. However, OMB Bulletin 01-02 guidance (not GAO "yellow book" standards) is more specific than either the AICPA and GAO guidance. OMB guidance states, "For those internal controls that have been properly designed and placed in operation, the auditor shall perform sufficient tests to support a low assessed level of control risk."

Traditionally, AICPA guidance has stressed audit efficiency and allowed the auditor to bypass internal control testing if other procedures were more practical or efficient in the auditor's judgment. By contrast, both GAO and OMB have always stressed the importance of internal controls because of the fiduciary nature of government operations.

In requiring the testing of internal controls even when the internal control risk is below the maximum, OMB is simply asserting its belief that the public deserves reassurance that assets entrusted to federal agencies are properly safeguarded. Therefore, verifying that federal systems are free of significant internal control deficiencies is an important consideration in the execution of annual audits of federal agencies.

It is interesting to note that while current AICPA guidance still does not require testing of internal controls, the Sarbanes-Oxley Act does requires the issuance of an auditor's opinion on internal controls (as well as one on management's representation on the adequacy of internal controls). Thus, in effect, at least for public companies, there is a requirement for testing of controls.

Develop Test of Relevant Internal Controls

In developing the types of tests, an auditor must consider representative general internal controls such as:

- Entity-level controls including the control environment
- Information technology general controls, on which other controls are dependent
- Adequacy of cycle documentation (including both EDP systems and manual procedures)
- Segregation of duties
- Audit trails and availability of competent evidential matter (e.g., invoices, receiving reports, purchase orders) for transactions processed by the system/cycle
- Knowledgeable, trained personnel
- Adequacy and completeness of accounting policies and accounting principles to be applied (and supported by the systems/cycles)

General controls are important because, without them, there is little to be gained by testing more specific controls associated with each process/cycle. Although some general controls can be tested as part of a test of transactions (e.g., segregation of duties, presence of effective audit trails), many of the key controls, such as adequacy of documentation and availability of competent personnel, can be tested only through observation and the exercise of audit judgment.

After considering the effectiveness of general controls, the auditor proceeds to evaluate the individual controls affecting each subsystem/cycle and relevant to the audit assertions and significant accounts or groups of accounts. Auditors will generally address these controls within each major process/cycle or application:

- Controls over initiating, authorizing, recording, processing, and reporting significant accounts and disclosures embodied in the financial statements (e.g., authorization for purchases)
- Controls over the selection and application of accounting policies that are in conformity with GAAP (e.g., valuation and reserve accounts, depreciation)
- Antifraud programs and controls

- Controls over significant nonroutine and nonsystematic transactions, such as accounts involving judgments and estimates; this includes reconciliation procedures for balances with Treasury, accounts receivable, accounts payable, and physical inventories, among others
- Controls over the financial reporting process (e.g., how the individual process/cycle complies with federal guidance, such as OMB)

In addition, the auditor looks for the existence of more specific controls meeting the requirements of any given cycle. Thus, by way of example, in the case of processes and procedures related to accounts payable, the auditor will also determine whether sufficient controls are in place to achieve objectives such as:

- Purchases are made only from responsible parties authorized as vendors and in accordance with federal acquisition regulations.
- All cost expenses accruing are properly identified (including the name and address of the vendor).
- Disbursements are properly monitored and appropriate action is taken to ensure compliance with Prompt Payment Act requirements.
- Proper cutoff procedures are followed to ensure the fair presentation of payables and expenses.
- Costs and expenses are accounted for in accordance with GAAP.

In the case of revenue-related activities, the auditor will determine whether sufficient controls are in place to achieve objectives such as:

- All revenues, including taxes and fees, accruing to the auditee are properly identified.
- Collections are properly monitored and appropriate action is taken on delinquencies (e.g., dunning procedures).
- Revenues are accounted for in accordance with GAAP.

With the completion of these procedures, the auditor is in a position to determine:

- Whether guidance requires that the cycle process or system be tested (i.e., OMB Bulletin 01-02 requirements when the internal controls design is deemed to be effective and the internal control risk is low)
- Assuming controls warrant testing (or must be tested), which controls should be tested to validate the auditor's risk assessment and verify that account balances are achieving the objectives discussed earlier (i.e., ownership, legitimacy, existence, safeguarding, and fairness of classification and valuation)
- The nature of the tests (e.g., observation, inquiry, test of transactions)

FINALIZE AND DOCUMENT THE AUDIT APPROACH

Based on the risk assessment, and within the constraints imposed by guidance, the auditor develops an audit approach. Such an approach typically includes some or all of these tests:

- *Test of internal controls:* Generally, for systems where internal control risks are evaluated below the maximum, the auditor will find it efficient to test selected controls.
- *Substantive testing—tests of account balances:* Where control risk is at a high or moderate level, the auditor will typically develop auditing procedures with the intention of obtaining sufficient competent evidential matter to support the auditor's assertions on the financial statements. Where controls are assessed at a moderate or low level, these tests will likely complement test of control procedures.
- *Substantive testing—analytical procedures:* Analytical audit procedures require the auditor to look at certain relationships within financial data (e.g., analyzing trends; comparing financial data to the prior year's; comparing account balances and trends to similar entities; and considering the relationship between certain accounts, such as sales to inventory or accounts receivable, fringe benefit expense to payroll expense accounts payable as a percentage of total expenses, etc.). Analytical procedures are a requirement of the audit planning and review process, and can be used as substantive procedures, usually in combination with tests of internal controls and/or tests of account balances.
- *Combined test of controls and account balances:* In certain instances, the auditor will determine that the most efficient approach to auditing a given account or group of accounts is substantive (e.g., account balance) testing. However, it is also possible that these accounts are supported by a system of internal controls that was assessed by the auditor as effective (e.g., control risk assessed as low). In these instances, the best approach may be to combine the account balance testing with a related test of internal controls. This approach satisfies both the efficiency objective and the need to comply with OMB Bulletin 01-02 requirements.

Additional testing characteristics are discussed in the next chapter.

Upon completing the audit approach, the auditor will update the audit plan developed in Phase II (i.e., the understanding of controls and evaluation of controls phase). In addition, the more senior members of the audit team must develop audit programs covering the tests of controls and substantive procedures to be performed in the testing phase of the audit. The design of an effective audit program is essential to the execution of an effective and efficient audit. A well-designed audit program enables the effective utilization of more junior personnel, supports the development of relevant audit documentation, and facilitates the monitoring of audit team members.

Exhibit 10.1: Evaluate and plan to test internal controls

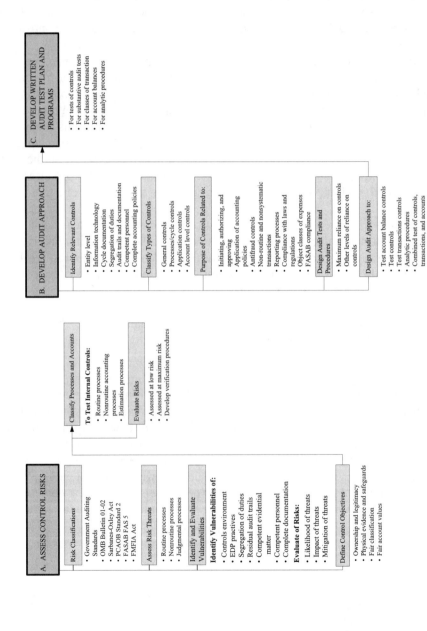

A. ASSESS CONTROL RISKS

Risk Classifications
- Government Auditing Standards
- OMB Bulletin 01-02
- Sarbanes-Oxley Act
- PCAOB Standard 2
- FASAB FAS 5
- FMFIA Act

Assess Risk Threats
- Routine processes
- Nonroutine processes
- Judgmental processes

Identify and Evaluate Vulnerabilities

Identify Vulnerabilities of:
- Controls environment
- EDP practives
- Segregation of duties
- Residual audit trails
- Competent evidential matter
- Competent personnel
- Complete documentation

Evaluate of Risks:
- Likelihood of threats
- Impact of threats
- Mitigation of threats

Define Control Objectives
- Ownership and legitimacy
- Physical evidence and safeguards
- Fair classification
- Fair account values

Classify Processes and Accounts

To Test Internal Controls:
- Routine processes
- Nonroutine accounting processes
- Estimation processes

Evaluate Risks
- Assessed at low risk
- Assessed at maximum risk
- Develop verification procedures

B. DEVELOP AUDIT APPROACH

Identify Relevant Controls
- Entity level
- Information technology
- Cycle documentation
- Segregation of duties
- Audit trails and documentation
- Competent personnel
- Complete accounting policies

Classify Types of Controls
- General controls
- Processes/cycle controls
- Application controls
- Account level controls

Purpose of Controls Related to:
- Initiating, authorizing, and approving
- Application of accounting policies
- Antifraud controls
- Non-routine and nonsystematic transactions
- Reporting processes
- Compliance with laws and regulations
- Object classes of expenses
- FASAB compliance

Design Audit Tests and Procedures
- Maximum reliance on controls
- Other levels of reliance on controls

Design Audit Approach to:
- Test account balance controls
- Test controls
- Test transactions controls
- Analytic procedures
- Combined test of controls, transactions, and accounts

C. DEVELOP WRITTEN AUDIT TEST PLAN AND PROGRAMS
- For tests of controls
- For substantive audit tests
- For classes of transaction
- For account balances
- For analytic procedures

11 TEST OF CONTROLS, TRANSACTIONS, AND ACCOUNTS

Audit procedures are designed to gather evidence and should be viewed as a process that continuously seeks to obtain and evaluate competent, relevant, evidential matter. However, in practical terms, the bulk of competent evidential matter supporting the auditor's financial statement assertions is the result of the testing conducted during Phase III of the federal government's audit model. The testing phase encompasses both internal control and substantive testing.

Throughout the audit process, the objective is the continual assessment and validation of the nature of *audit risk*, which is the risk of the auditor unknowingly issuing a clean audit opinion when the financial statements are materially misstated. AU 327 states that audit risk encompasses:[1]

- *Inherent risks* related to the susceptibility of a process or account to be misstated. For example, estimates such as those required by the Federal Credit Reform Act require complex calculations that are more likely to include errors, than, for example, simple payroll accrual estimates at the end of a reporting period. Similarly, certain assets, such as cash, are more susceptible to theft than others. Finally, certain assets are subject to spoilage unless consumed/disposed of on a timely basis. Inherent risks also arise from factors external to the agency such as changes in congressional funding levels and/or congressionally mandated change in the program's mission. Changes such as these could affect the value of, or render obsolete, assets such as inventories and other property that the agency had created for future use, but which was rendered valueless or nearly so as a result of the change in funding or program.

- *Control risks* relate to the possible occurrence of material misstatements that are not prevented or detected on a timely basis by the auditee's internal control processes. In other words, for some reason(s), the "prescribed" internal controls failed to work. Control risk also includes accounts, processes, cycles, or systems that are susceptible to certain threats that are not mitigated by the presence of effective internal control practices and procedures that reduce the likelihood of the threat to a reasonably low level. (Control risks cannot be reduced to zero, given the inherent limitations of any system of internal controls.)

- *Detection risks* relate to the auditor's failure to detect a misstatement. A sound audit approach executed by competent personnel with the requisite skills and experience necessary for the tests included in the approach should reduce this

---

[1] *AU citations refers to sections of the AICPA's annual publication of its **Professional Standards**, the US Auditing Standards, NY, NY.*

risk to a reasonable level. Since the auditor does not examine 100% of all transactions, this risk is always present. However, it is the auditor's responsibility to develop a sound audit approach to minimize detection risk.

Frequently, careful and informed interviews of agency executives, program managers, financial personnel, and data processing staffs provide early clues to client attitudes, pressures, problems, contingencies, and high-risk areas not readily apparent from examinations of general ledger accounts or not noted in tests of detailed transactions. Throughout the audit, but particularly with respect to the testing described in this chapter, the audit team must continually reflect on the impact of "projected" misstatements, not just "discoveries" and correction of specific errors.

Exhibit 11.1 highlights several aspects and issues concerning testing applications that should, and in some cases must, be used when conducting an audit pursuant to *Government Auditing Standards.*

TYPES OF TESTS

Audit testing traditionally takes one of two forms: internal control or substantive testing. In government auditing, federal guidance provides for a third type of testing: testing of compliance with laws and regulations.

Tests of Controls

Tests of internal controls are designed to verify whether the internal controls identified during the planning phase of the audit, in the auditor's evaluation of the system design, are, in fact, operating and/or being complied with in practice. As such, a test of internal controls is appropriate only (and can only be effective) if the auditor has evaluated control risk at below the maximum risk level.

Substantive Tests

Substantive tests are designed to validate an account balance by direct validation of the account (e.g., physical observation of property, review of documentation such as invoices to verify assigned costs, direct confirmation of balances with third parties, etc.) or by developing an independent estimate of what the account balance should be (e.g., by applying statistical techniques or executing analytical procedures) and comparing with the data recorded in the auditee's records.

Tests of Compliance with Laws and Regulations

Noncompliance with federal financial laws and regulations may have a direct impact on an entity's financial statements. For example, noncompliance with an environmental law may result in a contingent or possibly actual liability, which needs to be recorded or disclosed according to the specific circumstances. In this respect, governmental auditing is similar to commercial auditing, and this type of compliance can be considered in connection with specific internal controls and the internal control environment. However, OMB, and the agency itself, will also identify certain laws and regulations that may not have a material impact on the financial statements of the agency but that nevertheless should be considered by the auditor. It is important for the auditor to be aware of these regulations and to test compliance, as required by the guidance.

Exhibit 11.1: Test of controls, transactions, and accounts

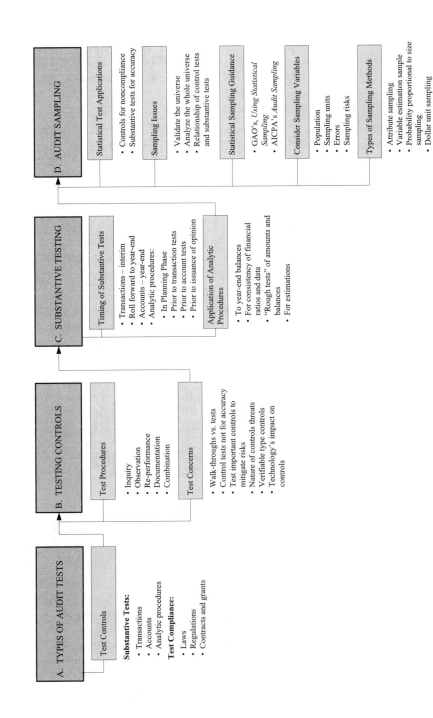

TESTING INTERNAL CONTROLS

Tests of controls require the application of audit procedures with the objective of validating (or disproving) the *operational effectiveness* of the internal controls. The test is designed to determine whether controls are, in fact, operating as designed. To the extent that testing confirms that controls are operating as described in the auditor's documentation of the system design, the auditor obtains the necessary support to validate the initial control risk assertion (e.g., moderate or low) and is in a position to continue with the execution of the audit approach developed during the internal control phase.

No definition of *operational effectiveness* exists in law, OMB or Treasury Department regulations, the accounting and audit guidance of GAO, or GAAS of the AICPA. However, auditors must establish the operational effectiveness of controls if reliance on internal controls is to serve as a "tool" in support of the audit assertions. In order to conclude that controls are *operationally effective*, auditors must consider whether the internal controls:

- Are an effective deterrent against theft, misuse, waste, or accidental destruction of physical assets (e.g., plant, property, and equipment) and nonphysical assets (e.g., financial and nonfinancial systems, software, other records supportive of financial and operational management and reporting)
- Are an effective safeguard over the collection, recording, processing, and ultimate reporting of financial and nonfinancial data (regardless of whether the systems are manual or electronic in nature, the information is recorded at remote sites or centrally, by professional or nonprofessional, financial or nonfinancial personnel, at the auditee's sites or at outsourced locations)
- Are effectively providing reasonable assurance of prevention or detection for instances of noncompliance with laws, regulations, contracts, and grants that have a direct and material effect in determining financial statement amounts or other data significant to the audit objectives

Conversely, where tests disclose that controls are not effective or were not fully operational throughout the year, the auditor must revise the audit approach. In other words, negative or unsatisfactory test results oblige the auditor to reassess the evaluation of internal control risk. To the extent that the auditor reduces the reliance on internal controls, the auditor must revise the audit approach accordingly.

Typically, when the initial assessment of control risk is proved wrong, the auditor will be required to develop additional substantive audit procedures to compensate for the newly determined internal control risk. However, in certain instances, the auditor may conclude that the magnitude of the internal control weakness or the nature of the transactions or accounts being tested is such that it would not be possible to execute sufficient substantive tests to compensate for the control weakness. When this is the case, the auditor will have to issue a qualified opinion or, if warranted, a disclaimer.

HOW TO TEST CONTROLS

Tests of controls must provide assurance on the operational effectiveness of the five control components, as defined by AICPA guidance in AU 319.07 (i.e., control environment, risk assessment, control activities, information and communication, and monitoring) in relation to each transaction cycle or accounting application of a government entity.

Audit procedures typically applied in testing the effectiveness of a government's controls over transactions and accounts include auditor inquiries, auditor document examinations, auditor observations, and auditor recalculation of auditee data. Common test procedures include:

- *Inquiry: Ask those who do it.* Governmental personnel with firsthand knowledge and who are directly responsible for implementing the designed controls must be interviewed. In conducting inquiries, it is important that the auditor interview those with operational knowledge as well as a sound "corporate or institutional memory" (i.e., an understanding of the entity's history based on years of experience working for the entity). Auditors consider inquiry to be an essential audit procedure. However, all knowledge acquired through inquiry must be corroborated by other audit procedures. Healthy skepticism is as necessary in the audit of government agencies as it is in the audit of commercial enterprises; reliance cannot be placed solely on inquiry.

- *Observation: Witness control-related activities.* The performance of certain control-related activities might only be noted by the auditor observing the actual act by auditee personnel. Examples could include learning of unauthorized personnel who routinely enter restricted computer spaces, or managers who consistently delegate check-signing responsibilities to subordinates, or supervisors who habitually sign off on time and attendance records days after payrolls are processed and backdate their actions. Experienced auditors recognize the importance of observation. Even the most well-intentioned employee will occasionally, and inadvertently, develop bad habits, such as failing to secure assets and information, not following restricted access rules, and the like. A competent auditor does not spend all of his or her time at a desk. Auditing by "walking around" (the combination of observation and inquiry) often discloses important facts and conditions that might otherwise be missed by the execution of more traditional documentation, evaluation, and testing techniques.

- *Reperformance: Repeat, recheck, and recalculate auditee work.* Sometimes recalculation and rechecking are the primary audit procedures for validating the operational effectiveness of certain control activities. For example, reperformance or recalculation is required by the auditor to validate the propriety of fees billed by a regulatory agency or amounts paid to vendors for goods or services received.

- *Documentation: Follow the paper trail.* In earlier phases, the auditor should have identified and obtained copies of the various forms that document the control process of each of the government's transaction groups or accounting applications (e.g., budgeting, tax billings, cash receipts, cash disbursements, payrolls, contract awards, debt issuance). Following the audit trail (often in combination with reperformance and the other techniques listed above) is an essential element in the execution of a sampling plan. Whether derived statistically or judgmentally, the sampling plan applied in the testing of controls requires that the audit trail be examined for a creditable number of transactions within each of the transaction groups or accounting applications. The objective is to confirm the timing, amount, purpose, quantities of recorded transactions, and appropriateness of accounts charged for the tested transactions are supported by documented authorizations, approvals, and sign-offs.

WALK-THROUGHS AND TESTS OF CONTROL

Determining what to test is one of the key audit decisions related to the testing of controls. At this point, it is important to make a distinction between the documentation developed during the planning phase and concluded during the internal control phase and the controls the auditors decide to test.

In documenting and assessing the system of internal control, the auditor obtains and documents information on all significant activities and procedures and, in his or her evaluation, considers all controls. This is essential to obtaining an understanding of internal controls and the risk assessment process. In obtaining and documenting his or her understanding, the auditor will execute "walk-throughs" of all, or nearly all, activities and obtain documentation on forms used for inclusion in the audit working papers. During the documentation, the auditor will typically examine a small number of transactions to document the auditor's performance of the walk-throughs.

In contrast, when later testing controls, these audit tests are usually limited to essential or key controls but require the review of a larger number of transactions. This is an important consideration in achieving audit efficiency. All too often, auditors have a tendency to test at the same level of detail as a walk-through, which not only increases the auditor's workload but may also detract from the auditor's ability to focus on issues of audit importance. The criteria for determining what controls to test is discussed later in this chapter.

TESTS OF CONTROLS ARE NOT EFFECTIVE TESTS FOR TRANSACTION ACCURACY

A recurring misconception, particularly among inexperienced auditors, is that a direct verification of the accounting accuracy of a transaction is a test of controls. During a test of internal controls, the auditor is primarily testing compliance with controls and not verifying the accuracy of the transactions tested.

For example, in a test of controls over cash disbursements, an auditor will typically examine documentation such as invoices to test compliance with internal controls. In these cases, the auditor may look for evidence that internal controls were followed in ordering the goods or services (e.g., a purchase order or similar documentation serving as an audit trail), that the invoice was approved for payment by an authorized individual, as required by the system design (audit trail documenting approval), and that the services or goods were received (audit trail documentation such as a receiving report), among others. Compliance or noncompliance with these processes provides information on the extent to which controls are operational.

In addition, the auditor will generally verify attributes of the transaction itself, such as whether the amount of the disbursement equals the amount on the invoice (or a discrepancy is properly explained by the audit trail documentation) and whether the invoice was properly coded. In conducting these tests, the auditor will determine whether the amount paid is correct (e.g., agrees with the invoice) and whether it was posted to the proper account (e.g., charged against the correct appropriation, element of expense account, properly capitalized if applicable, etc.). This is an important procedure because the auditor examines just a small fraction of all transactions and cannot afford to overlook any significant aspect of the transaction being tested. However, verifying this attribute is not a test of compliance with internal controls.

Even if the auditor finds no errors affecting accuracy or account classification, he or she cannot conclude by inference that controls promoting the correct payment and classification of expenses are operational. The controls could very well be working, and the accuracy of the transaction is indicative of this, but in these tests, the auditor was not testing any controls. Although reviewing the accuracy of the transaction is important, positive results do not directly support the auditor's prior assertion regarding internal controls. Conversely, if the auditor determines that an error has occurred, the error cannot be evaluated as another event of noncompliance. Audit judgment must be applied and the prior assessment of control risk (and the audit approach) revisited.

Tests of controls promote audit efficiency, in part, because the test recognizes that events of noncompliance will occur in even the best of systems supported by a strong control environment. As such, the auditor, using his or her judgment, identifies tolerable maximum noncompliance levels for controls. Thus, for example, the auditor may conclude that the universe of all transactions may include up to a 5 percent rate of noncompliance without forcing the reevaluation of the prior control risk assessment.

However, stating that a 5 percent noncompliance rate is tolerable is not the same as stating that the auditor is willing to accept that 5 percent of the transactions processed by the system are clerically inaccurate, inappropriate/fraudulent, posted to the wrong account, and/or improperly expensed or capitalized. Indeed, if the system produces data that can be up to 5 percent inaccurate, the data produced are very likely to exceed the materiality thresholds established by the auditor during the planning phase.

The reason that a 5 percent noncompliance rate may be tolerable, but a similar clerical accuracy error rate is not, is due to the objectives and assumptions behind testing internal controls. Stated simply, the fact that there was an event of noncompliance (e.g., no purchase order was issued, or one was issued after the fact, the invoice was not matched against the receiving report, etc.) does not necessarily result in an error. Correct transactions can be processed (and often are) by weak systems of internal controls. In addition, in many instances, threats to the processes identified in the auditor's risk analysis (see discussion in Chapter 10) are totally or partially mitigated by more than one control. To the extent that other compensating controls were operational, the noncompliance event may not be significant. A clerical error or improper payment, however, has different implications, possibly including:

- Internal controls are perfunctorily executed (e.g., invoices are signed and approved without appropriate review).
- The auditor has failed to identify all threats in his or her risk assessment.
- The auditor's assessment of the overall internal control environment was incorrect and needs to be downgraded.

At the outset of a test of internal controls, the auditor states what he or she considers to be a tolerable rate of noncompliance. The compliance benchmark may be expressed statistically or judgmentally and may take the form of an absolute number of errors or a percentage rate using statistical techniques. At the end of the test the auditor compares the actual results against the prior benchmark on compliance. If the benchmark is satisfactorily met (e.g., the error rate is below that which the auditor considered tolerable or acceptable), the auditor may reasonably conclude that the prior assessment of control risk was correct and proceed with the audit approach developed earlier, including, as appropriate, planned substantive testing. If the results are not within tolerable limits, the auditor must revisit his or her approach accordingly. The auditor cannot ignore the implications of an error uncovered by a test of controls simply because the test results fall within a tolerable internal control compliance error rate.

CONTROLS TO TEST AND HOW

There are a number of factors to consider when deciding what controls to test, including:

- *Importance:* A key consideration is how critical a control is. In practical terms, the more significant the threat a control mitigates, the more important the control.
- *Number of threats mitigated:* Testing a control that prevents or mitigates more than one threat can significantly increase audit efficiency.
- *Nature of the threat:* Just as one control may mitigate more than one threat, certain threats may be mitigated by more than one control. In general, the auditor may want to avoid testing controls that achieve the same objective. On the other hand, for significant threats, the auditor may want to test more than one mitigating control in order to add to his or her audit coverage and/or comfort level.
- *Verifiability:* In practical terms, to fulfill the auditor's purpose, a control must be verifiable. Disbursement approval, for example, is more easily verifiable if an audit trail (manual or electronic) is present. Without this trail, sampling is likely to be of little value, and observation may be the only option (but in this case, it may be of limited value to the audit). Faced with no audit trail, the auditor must seek alternative controls supported by appropriate audit trails, or

may be forced to drop the test of controls and execute extended substantive procedures with account balances.

- *Impact of information technology:* Advances in information technology often result in the loss of a visible audit trail or create other issues that the auditor must consider. For example, the transaction approval process may substitute passwords or encryption for a physical signature. Under these circumstances, the visible audit trail may consist of an indication in the transaction record or database that the transaction was approved at the proper level. Verifying that such a record exists is valid only if accompanied by audit testing procedures verifying controls over password access and encryption.

Selecting the controls to test along with the proper technique requires the exercise of judgment and the application of common sense. Common pitfalls include:

- *Testing every aspect of the system and giving every control equal significance.* All too often, auditors fall on the expedient of testing every aspect of a process, cycle, or system without considering the relationship between a specific procedure and a real threat. Thus, for example, in a poorly thought out test of payroll, the test of control may treat testing critical controls, such as controls over employee pay changes and adding new employees, as being of equal importance to lesser controls, such as controls over routine payroll forms such as W-4s, insurance elections, contributions, and so on.

- *Misinterpreting the purpose of a control.* The overabundance of internal control checklists often results in the auditor memorizing controls (and incorporating them in their tests) without considering their real purpose. In an example that is more common in the private sector, a typical control is the requirement that disbursements over a certain amount require two signatures. This control is effective in preventing (barring collusion) authorized check signers from unilaterally defrauding their employer of significant amounts of money and is commonly found in most commercial entities. In the absence of check signature stamps (and most medium- and larger-size organizations will use signature stamps), the dual signature requirement can also be considered as a control promoting the use of extra care in approving larger expenditures of funds. However, as is usually the case, when a signature stamp affixes the double signature, the only purpose of the control is the prevention of fraud. Further, the existence of a signature stamp raises control issues regarding the proper safeguarding of the stamp. In fact, if the stamp is not properly controlled, the presence of a signature stamp has simply transferred the opportunity to commit fraud from a management-level employee to lower-level personnel (or, in the absence of proper access controls, to anyone in the organization). In spite of this discussion, many audit tests include testing for dual signatures as a test, while ignoring the security issues and ignoring the possibility of exploring a simpler verification procedure. Such a procedure might be confirming directly with a bank that dual signatures are required and that the bank (and not the auditee) is responsible for any potential loss for failing to comply with this requirement.

- *Overestimating the control's positive impact.* Time sheets are another example of a control commonly associated with low control risk and often indiscriminately included in a test of controls over payroll. Yet a time sheet that is not subject to external validation such as a time clock (with controls preventing employees from punching other employees' time sheets) or the signature of a properly motivated management-level employee cannot effectively ensure that employees are paid only for hours actually worked. Further, in the absence of gatekeeping controls over new employees, the time sheet accomplishes little in preventing the presence of "phantom" employees.
- *Underestimating operating management monitoring controls.* Auditors often view sampling (discussed later) as the only effective means of obtaining competent evidential matter. This bias is often at the expense of testing other potentially strong controls, such as management's monitoring of its operations. Without denying or mitigating the critical importance of sampling in auditing, the auditor should be aware of the importance of monitoring controls in reducing control risk and the potential impact the testing of monitoring controls may have on the audit's efficiency. Monitoring controls also includes observation by both management and executives at all levels of operation as well as by an independent function as an internal audit function.

  While the auditor will seldom underestimate the usefulness of an effective, truly independent internal audit function, the same is not the case in connection with operating management's own monitoring activities. Yet monitoring activities by knowledgeable personnel who are held accountable for results (particularly if the financial records are part of the measuring criteria) are some of the most important aspects in ensuring the accuracy of financial data. It should be easy to see that the presence of operating personnel with a vested interest in how financial results are recorded provides great assurance that financial transactions are charged to the proper appropriation, organization, program, or activity and that all charges are legitimate. Further, monitoring is an activity that can be tested with sufficient objectivity through inquiry, observation, and inspection of records (although, admittedly, certain aspects of the test are, of necessity, more subjective than in audit sampling). Finally, the all-encompassing nature of the federal budget and the clear priority assigned to it by the Constitution and other laws of the land, politicians, federal executives, oversight agencies, and the American public ensure the presence (albeit not necessarily the effectiveness) of a monitoring function at all levels of the federal government.

Once the auditor decides what controls to test and, ideally, has avoided the potential pitfalls discussed earlier, the auditor would proceed with the execution of the different tests of internal controls. The next section discusses the most common form of testing—audit sampling—that is followed by a discussion of other types of tests the auditor considers in validating (or disproving) the prior assessment of control risk.

Substantive Testing: Is It True?

In general, tests of controls provide indirect evidence on the accuracy of account balances by testing whether the systems, processes, and cycles affecting an account are supported by an appropriate internal control design, which operates effectively in accordance with the design. If the controls are appropriate and operating effectively, the auditor concludes that the systems/processes/cycles affecting a particular account can be relied on to produce account balances that are fairly stated in all material respects in accordance with GAAP.

SUBSTANTIVE TESTS

Substantive testing provides direct evidence on an account balance regardless of the systems and/or controls interfacing with the account. *Substantive testing* may be defined as audit procedures designed to detect material misstatements of transaction groups or accounts. The AICPA has classified substantive audit tests into three groups:

1. *Test of transactions:* Best performed of a sampling of data during interim months of the period audited, with a confirmation of interim conclusions at year-end
2. *Test of account balance:* Performed at year-end with emphasis on debits/credit sides of accounts and interaccount relationships
3. *Analytic procedure:* To be performed four times in the audit: (1) in the planning phase, (2) prior to transaction testing, (3) prior to account balance testing, and (4) after the audit work is completed, but before the audit opinion is issued.

The development of substantive testing does not ignore the results of tests of internal controls. In fact, the extent and nature of substantive testing is usually dictated by the auditor's internal control evaluations and, when applicable, testing results.

The extent of substantive testing will, in most instances, be determined by these factors (or combinations thereof):

- The auditor's evaluation of internal controls. In general, the extent of testing is directly related to the auditor's final determination of audit risk on completion of audit testing (if audit testing was deemed appropriate). The need for substantive testing decreases as the auditor's confidence with, and reliance on, internal control increases.
- The specific weaknesses in internal controls identified during evaluation and/or testing.
- Audit efficiency when the auditor determines that substantive tests will require a lower level of effort than a test of internal controls, regardless of the auditor's risk assessment (but see OMB requirement below).
- The OMB requirement that internal controls be tested when the auditor concludes an effective internal control design is in place. If the auditor must comply with this OMB requirement even though a substantive test may be

more efficient, the auditor will usually develop a "hybrid" test combining substantive procedures with internal control testing.

Validating of Account Balances

Auditing the "existence" of account balances can be accomplished directly examining the documentation or other physical evidence substantiating the validity of the general ledger balance. Typical procedures include:

- Testing a sample of transactions posted to the account throughout the year or period under audit (audit sampling is discussed later in this chapter). This will typically include the examination of documents supporting the transaction (e.g., invoices). As a general rule, the auditor will:
  - Concentrate on large transactions to, in effect, "audit" a sufficient percentage of the total account balance.
  - Review the file for unusual transactions.
  - Develop projections from a sample usually applying statistical techniques.
  - Employ a combination of the procedures above.
- Physically inspecting the account components (e.g., physical inventory observations, verification of the physical existence of property such as buildings)
- Directly confirming the account components (usually in connection with accounts receivable, but may also be used in connection with inventories held by a third party and with accounts payable)
- Reviewing and verifying account reconciliations including:
  - Reconciliation of fund balance with Treasury (or cash held outside Treasury)
  - Reconciliation of detailed subsidiary ledgers (e.g., accounts receivable or payables) to the general ledger's control account
  - Reconciliation of property records kept by a custodian function (e.g., perpetual inventory records, property, plant, and equipment records) to the general ledger control account
  - Reconciliation of physical inventory counts to the general ledger control account
- Recomputing auditee estimates and other auditee-developed data to verify accuracy of estimate or computation (e.g., "footing" auditee prepared analysis, recomputing auditee's accruals)

Analytical Procedures

In general, analytical procedures compare different, but related, sets of financial data to assess whether the relationships and variances between the data is consistent with the auditor's expectations. Typical relationships that auditors consider include:

- *Comparing prior-year account balances to current-year balances:* In this procedure, the auditor looks for unusual variances in account balances from one year to the next. Unusual variances generally consist of significant increases or decreases that cannot be explained by other known variables (e.g., increases or decreases in programs and activities, new programs, program terminations, etc.). However, the auditor must consider that the lack of an increase or decrease in an account may also constitute an unusual variance. This would be the case, for example, if a program is terminated, but accounts related to the program remain unchanged from the prior year.

- *Considering the consistency of financial ratios:* In this procedure, the auditor considers whether relationships such as the relationship between the agency's budgetary and proprietary accounts, revenues to accounts receivable, expenses to accounts payable, and so on, are consistent with the entity's historical ratios. This is an important procedure because, for example, a decrease in the ratio of revenues to accounts receivable may be indicative of a deteriorating receivable. Similarly, if a working capital fund shows a decrease in the ratio of sales to inventory (inventory turn ratio), this condition may be indicative of obsolete or damaged inventory.

- *Performing "rough tests" of account balances:* Under this procedure, the auditor develops a simple estimate of what an account value should be and compares this value with the actual account balance. A typical example consists of developing an estimate of accrued salaries based on the last pay period of the year and comparing this estimate to the agency's recorded accrued salaries.

- *Projecting/estimating account balances:* This procedure is similar to developing "rough tests" of account balances (see discussion above). However, projections and estimates are usually more complex and often make use of statistical procedures including regression analysis to project/estimate account balances. Typical applications include:

  - *Estimates for uncollectible receivables*: This may include, for example, considering the aging of accounts receivable and developing a relationship (statistical or judgmental) between the aging and future write-offs to develop an estimate of uncollectible receivables.

  - *Grant accrual estimates*: A significant number of federal agencies are involved in the issuance of grants to individuals, institutions, and state and local agencies. For these agencies, the year-end grant accrual is material to the agency's financial statements. As the deadline for issuing federal financial statements tightens, the auditor cannot rely on more traditional procedures (e.g., review of grant activity/payments after year-end) and must rely on projections (statistical or judgmental) to validate the reasonableness of the grant accrual.

  - *Year-end liability estimates*: Before closing its books, each federal agency must consider outstanding debts and develop a reasonable estimate of the liability for services or goods received that have not been invoiced by vendors (or that have not yet been entered into the appropriate accounting system). In the past, the traditional audit procedure consisted of performing a "test for unrecorded liabilities" where the auditor examined post-closing disbursement/invoice vouchering activity for a number of months subsequent to year-end to test the reasonableness of the year-end estimate. As was the case with grants, the shortened reporting deadlines will often require the execution of analytical procedures to test/validate the reasonableness of the year-end balance for accounts payable.

Analytical procedures are not limited to the testing phase. In fact, as noted, AICPA guidance (SAS 56 and AU 329.04) requires that the auditor use analytical procedures in planning and in evaluating the audit engagement. It should be clear that procedures such as comparing balances from year to year and assessing the implications of financial ratios would quickly identify areas of potential audit significance, which should be considered during the planning phase and in the development/revision of audit programs.

The execution of analytical procedures is not a required substantive procedure. However, analytical procedures are often nonlaborious, time-saving procedures that can significantly increase the auditor's efficiency. Moreover, it should be apparent that the complexity and size of federal agencies, coupled with ever-tightening reporting deadlines, leave the auditor with no option but to make use of these techniques. AICPA guidance requires that when the analytical procedure is a significant substantive test, the expectations, results, and additional related procedures performed be documented.

Related procedures will usually include inquiries of the auditee (e.g., to explain unusual variances) and limited tests of accounting data. It is important that the auditor independently test information provided by the auditee and that he or she ensures the integrity and completeness of the universe from which accounting data are selected for testing. (The importance of ensuring data integrity and completeness is discussed in more detail later in this chapter.)

AUDIT SAMPLING

Sampling is a common audit procedure. The AICPA defines sampling as the execution of audit procedures to less than 100% of the items in the universe or account being audited (AU 350). At the outset, it should be understood that sampling encompasses judgmental, nonrandom procedures as well as statistical sampling. In practice, the auditor will often combine judgment and statistics in the execution of sampling-related procedures. This section discusses sampling as it relates to both tests of controls and substantive testing, goes over some dos and don'ts in the use of sampling, and concludes with a summary discussion of statistical sampling.

Sampling Applications

Sampling can be used in connection with the two types of audit tests discussed earlier. Sampling in connection with tests of controls and substantive tests will differ in terms of the information that the auditor will examine in the execution of his or her test.

Controls testing. In the execution of tests of controls, the auditor will look for evidence that a control was complied with. For example, the auditor will look at supporting documentation such as receiving reports, invoices, purchase orders, and management approvals to verify that goods and services were ordered and approved in accordance with the procedures and controls that were previously considered in the determination of control risk. Similarly, the auditor may look for approved time sheets and approved payroll registers (or evidence that the register was reviewed by management) to test key controls identified in the evaluation of the payroll cycle.

Substantive testing. In the execution of substantive procedures, the auditor is concerned with the accuracy of the account balance and not with the controls present in the processes/cycles that created the account balance. Again, the auditor will look at supporting documentation. However, in substantive testing, he or she is interested in establishing the accuracy of the transaction recorded in the account. Thus, the auditor may look at a vendor invoice to ensure that the account is properly valued or at a sales invoice to support an individual balance in accounts receivable.

SAMPLING CONSIDERATIONS

This section expands on some key issues that the auditor should consider when using sampling techniques.

Ensure Completeness of the Universe

The purpose of the sample is to make an assertion on the population being tested, such as whether internal controls are operational (in a test of controls) or whether account balances are fairly stated (in a substantive test). These assertions are the result of the auditor's examination of a (usually) small percentage of the population. Therefore, it is essential that the auditor ensure that the universe being audited includes all the transactions processed by the cycle or affecting an account balance for the period under audit.

Prior to selecting a sample, the auditor will obtain a record or database of all appropriate elements of the universe to be sampled. In general, the universe consists of

- *Test of controls.* In the case of a test of controls, the universe under audit will typically include all transactions processed by the cycle or system of internal controls such as all cash disbursements, all cash receipts, all payroll checks, and so on, for the period under audit.
- *Substantive test.* In a substantive test of an account balance, the universe is usually defined in terms of specific items, such as individual account receivables or payables, properties, inventory items, and the like that make up the account balance at the end of the year (or interim period under audit). The universe can also be defined in terms of all transactions that affected the account during the period under audit (e.g., beginning balance plus all debits and credits affecting the account). While this latter approach may be appropriate under certain circumstances (e.g., in the audit of property, plant, and equipment where the beginning balance was previously audited), defining the universe in terms of the specific items making up the account balance is often preferable.

The auditor is ultimately interested in being able to issue an opinion on the financial statements. The financial statements are derived from the books and records of the auditee (typically, the general ledger plus year-end adjustments). Therefore, to ensure the completeness of the universe, the auditor must ensure that the universe was, in fact, derived from the general ledger (including adjustments, if applicable).

In the case of an account balance audit, this procedure is relatively simple. The auditor will add the schedule of all items making up the balance (e.g., all accounts receivable) and will verify that the sum of these items agrees with the general ledger balance (including year-end adjustments, if applicable).

Under certain circumstances, agreeing the database to the accounting records in a test of controls may be rather straightforward. For example, in the case of a payroll test, the auditor may be able to agree the universe tested to a payroll expense account in the general ledger. Similarly, if the audit consists of testing benefit payments (e.g., in connection with the audit of an insurance or social benefit fund), the auditor may be able to relate the sum of these payments to a benefit expense account.

In practical terms, however, validating the universe in a test of internal controls will not be a straightforward procedure. Even in the simplified examples above, the auditor is likely to encounter difficulties in agreeing his/her database to the accounting records since it is almost certain that the payroll expense account and the benefit expense accounts, as well as the cash accounts, will include other transactions (e.g., journal entries, adjustments, accruals, etc.). Although validating the universe is not always a simple procedure, if the auditor has obtained a sound understanding of the accounting cycles and processes during the planning and internal control phases, he or she will be able to efficiently relate the universe being tested to the books of original entry.

The failure to validate the completeness of the universe being tested is a recurring problem with the quality of federal audits. Indeed, the authors of this book, on more than one occasion, have encountered situations where large samples were selected to test a critical process, but the database from which the sample was selected was never agreed to the accounting records. Moreover, some of the recent auditing failures can also be related, at least in part, to a failure to ensure the completeness of the universe. Selecting a sample without validating the universe from which the sample is selected renders the audit test meaningless.

Analyze the Universe

Information technology provides the auditor with ample opportunity to increase audit efficiency and ensure that the audit focuses on areas of potential audit significance. In most federal audits, the universe from which the sample is to be selected will consist of an electronic file or database, ideally including all of the elements to be tested.

Electronic files provide the auditor with the opportunity to analyze the characteristics of the universe and, in certain cases, even "audit" 100% of certain attributes. Typical procedures that can be performed to increase audit efficiency include

- *Obtain a frequency distribution of the file.* In testing disbursements of any kind (e.g., benefits, grants, payroll, vendors), a frequency distribution provides numerous opportunities to improve audit efficiency.

- *Identify large payments.* This procedure allows the auditor to concentrate on large payments (thus increasing audit coverage) and/or to identify unusual payments for follow-up.
- *Increase the efficiency of statistical applications.* Stratification of the universe often increases audit efficiency by reducing the impact of the variability of the population on the sample size.
- *Support the execution of analytical procedures.* For example, comparing the current year's frequency distribution to a prior year's may uncover unusual trends that could merit audit consideration.

- *Execute file matches.* It may be possible to test 100% of attributes by executing file matches. For example:

  - In a test of benefit payments, it is possible to match payments to beneficiaries with Social Security Administration's files to ensure that benefit checks do not continue to be issued after a beneficiary's death.
  - A match of this year's file to the prior year's can identify new payees and enable auditors to test gatekeeping controls.

- *Support exception testing.* The auditor may be interested in testing payments based on certain attributes in the file. In addition to large payments, the auditor may be looking for other characteristics, including, for example:

  - All disbursements charged to a specific element of expense account (e.g., all payments charged to a maintenance account or property, plant, and equipment to test for incorrect classifications)
  - All disbursements to a particular payee (e.g., to test for reimbursable travel expenses and/or advances to executives and other members of management)

In summary, databases and files provide the auditor with significant sampling opportunities to increase audit efficiency and properly focus the audit effort.

Relationship of Control Testing to Substantive Testing

An effective audit approach relates substantive testing to internal control testing. Substantive testing cannot take place in a vacuum. Substantive testing is derived entirely from the auditor's evaluation of internal control. The auditor will perform substantive testing for a variety of reasons, but the extent of substantive tests is always dependent on the state of an entity's internal controls. Weak or ineffective controls all result in the need to do more extensive and possibly different substantive tests, including a controls environment that:

- Lacks effective internal controls (either due to flaws in the design or noncompliance, as noted during internal control testing).
- Requires that the auditor compensate for certain weaknesses in internal controls.
- Mandates the auditor provide additional audit coverage on the large account balances.

- Notwithstanding the design of an efficient audit approach and proven effective controls, the auditor must perform sufficient control tests to comply with OMB's federal audit guidance.

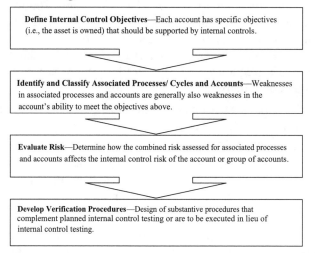

Define Internal Control Objectives—Each account has specific objectives (i.e., the asset is owned) that should be supported by internal controls.

Identify and Classify Associated Processes/ Cycles and Accounts—Weaknesses in associated processes and accounts are generally also weaknesses in the account's ability to meet the objectives above.

Evaluate Risk—Determine how the combined risk assessed for associated processes and accounts affects the internal control risk of the account or group of accounts.

Develop Verification Procedures—Design of substantive procedures that complement planned internal control testing or are to be executed in lieu of internal control testing.

Assuming the auditor properly performed the risk assessment during the prior phase of the audit, the verification procedures encompassed by substantive testing will ensure that the audit effort focuses on aspects of the account balance that are at risk of being misstated.

It would be erroneous to conclude that substantive testing results never have an impact on the auditor's evaluation of internal control. As noted earlier, planning and reevaluating the audit approach is a never-ending aspect of every audit. Thus, substantive testing will often provide additional information on internal controls that the auditor must take into account. Actions that the auditor considers include

- *Adverse results:* The execution of substantive procedures may disclose significant errors that will require audit adjustments. Depending on the circumstances, the auditor will

  - If control risk was evaluated at the maximum, consider whether the substantive procedures in the audit approach are sufficient to ensure that all material errors will be identified and corrected. Careful audit judgment must be exercised to ensure that conditions anticipated during the earlier evaluation are no worse than expected. If the auditor's worst expectations are exceeded, he or she must reconsider whether substantive procedures can overcome the risk that accounts are not fairly stated.
  - If control risk was evaluated below the maximum, consider whether errors disclosed by the procedures force the auditor to revise his or her evaluation of internal controls. In turn, this reevaluation will often result in additional substantive testing or, if the results are adverse enough, a reconsideration, as was the case above, of whether substantive procedures can overcome the risk that accounts are not fairly stated.

- *Positive results:* It is possible that substantive procedures disclose fewer errors than anticipated (or even no errors) based on the auditor's risk assessment. The auditor could, of course, ignore the positive results without increasing his or her audit risk (e.g., conclude that the account is fairly stated when, in fact, it is not). However, a careful evaluation of the results may lead the auditor to discover the presence or effectiveness of a control that was missed or not properly considered in the evaluation of internal controls. If this were the case, the auditor would be in a position to revise his or her audit approach. Although it is unlikely that this finding will increase the efficiency of the current year's audit, it may favorably impact the auditor's efficiency in future audits.

Statistical Sampling

Statistical techniques and statistical sampling are usually essential to the execution of an efficient audit strategy. Statistical sampling has the advantage of producing measurable results and, in many cases, will achieve audit objectives with a relatively small sample size. This section summarizes some key aspects of statistical sampling in auditing, but a full discussion of statistical sampling is beyond the scope of this book. There are a number of very helpful documents in this area that the reader may wish to consult, particularly:

- GAO's *Using Statistical Sampling* (May 1992 revision). A very helpful how-to document with insightful discussions on attribute sampling and variables estimation procedures
- AICPA's audit guide entitled *Audit Sampling* (April 1, 2001, edition). The document provides helpful guidance on statistical sampling including a very valuable discussion on the use of probability proportional to size sampling.

The successful application of statistical sampling in an audit requires the careful identification, definition, and evaluation of a number of variables. A discussion of some of these variables follows:

- *Population:* The universe of items from which a sample is taken (e.g., all disbursements, all receipts, all payroll payments).
- *Sampling unit:* Any of the individual items encompassed by the population (e.g., a check, a deposit, an invoice). In defining the sampling unit, the auditor must consider the attributes to be tested or account balance to be estimated, as well as the ease with which a sample can be selected.
- *Errors:* In attribute testing, an event of noncompliance with internal controls and/or clerical errors uncovered by testing procedures.
- *Sampling risk:* Relates to the possibility that the test includes a sample that will lead the auditor to reach an incorrect decision regarding the characteristics of the universe. In statistical sampling, risk can be expressed as:
  - Incorrectly concluding that the controls tested are being followed or complied with or that the account balance is not materially misstated. This risk may result from the auditor issuing an unqualified opinion when, in fact, such an opinion is not warranted.

- Incorrectly concluding that the controls tested are not being followed or complied with or that the account balance is materially misstated. In internal control testing, this may lead the auditor to perform additional substantive procedures, thus needlessly decreasing audit efficiency but not affecting the audit assertion (e.g., the auditor is guilty of "overauditing" but not of reaching the wrong conclusion and or type of opinion). However, in substantive testing, this type of error may lead the auditor to propose an audit adjustment that materially misstates the account balance under audit.

Statistical sampling supports both tests of controls and substantive tests. Types of tests or approaches typically used in auditing include:

- *Attribute sampling:* Most commonly used in tests of controls and tests of compliance with laws and regulations. Under attribute sampling, each unit tested will have one of two mutually exclusive characteristics (e.g., the control was complied with, or the control was not complied with). This procedure allows the auditor to develop an estimate of the universe's error rate (e.g., the extent to which a control is not being complied with expressed as a percentage of the total population). In this type of test, the auditor is concerned with the maximum error rate of the population (at a given confidence level). If the maximum error rate is within a predetermined compliance range (e.g., no more than 5 percent), the auditor will generally conclude that controls are effective. If the error rate is higher than the tolerable limit, then the auditor will revise the risk assessment and modify the audit approach, as necessary.

- *Variable estimation sampling:* Develops a projection within which the true audited value of the population lies. In this type of test, the auditor will develop a true or audited value for an item in the population (e.g., an invoice or a check) and from the audited value develop an estimate of the total population. The auditor's estimate is compared with the actual account balance, and (assuming the desired sampling precision was met) the auditor will either conclude that the account balance is fairly stated or propose an audit adjustment to correct the balance. Audited value relates to the correct amount of the sample item (e.g., a recorded invoice, check, individual account receivable or payable, etc.) regardless of the value at which it was recorded by the accounting cycle. Thus, the audited value can differ from the value recorded in the books and records of the auditee (i.e., because the transaction was incorrectly recorded).

  Variable estimation sampling encompasses direct, difference, and ratio estimations. Direct estimation consists of developing a projection of an account balance by utilizing the true or audited value of the sample items (e.g., an estimate of total accounts receivable from the audited value of all account receivables selected in the sample). A major problem with direct estimation is that obtaining the required precision for the estimate to be within tolerable limits often requires very large sample sizes. This problem can be overcome by the application of difference and/or ratio estimation techniques. Difference estimation consists of developing an estimate of the account balance by taking into account the difference between audited and recorded or book value. Ratio estimation develops the estimate based on the ratio of the audited value to the recorded value. In both cases, the approach is likely to significantly reduce the size of the sample required to develop projections that fall within tolerable limits.

Although difference and ratio estimation techniques can significantly increase the precision of the estimate, the technique should not be used unless a minimum number of errors are included in the randomly selected sample (GAO recommends a minimum of 10 errors and notes that some statisticians believe the number should be as high as 30).

- *Probability proportional to size sampling (PPS):* Combines characteristics of both attribute sampling and variable sampling. This approach is also known as dollar unit sampling because in PPS the sampling unit is each dollar included in the population or account. That is, each dollar in an account has an equal chance of being included in the sample (thus providing higher-value items/transactions with a proportionately greater chance of being selected). PPS allows the auditor to combine an attribute sampling approach with the ability to develop dollar projections. This approach is more informative than attribute sampling because it expresses results in terms of dollars. In addition, PPS is easier to apply than variables estimation sampling and will typically require a smaller sample size. As a result, PPS is, at least arguably, rapidly becoming the most often used statistical technique in auditing.

INFORMATION TECHNOLOGY CONSIDERATIONS

Information technology alters the fundamental manner by which transactional data are initiated, inputted, recorded, compiled, classified, and ultimately reported. In the interest of economy and efficiency, paper trails common to most manual systems disappear, the duties and responsibilities of computer-based systems personnel are different, and maximum segregation of duties of the old systems may no longer exist or be relevant. It is important to heed the AICPA's guidance with respect to technology and computerized data processing systems.

- Information technology provides the potential benefits of effectiveness and efficiency for an entity's internal control because the technology enables an entity to (AICPA, Section AU 319.18):
  - Consistently apply predefined business rules and perform complex calculations in processing large volumes of transactions or data.
  - Enhance the timeliness, availability, and accuracy of information.
  - Facilitate the analysis of information.
  - Enhance the ability to monitor the performance of the entity's activities and its policies and procedures.
  - Reduce the risk that controls will be circumvented.

- Enhance the ability to achieve effective segregation of duties by implementing security controls in applications, databases, and operating systems.

- But, on the other hand, information technology poses specific risks to an entity's internal controls, some of which include (AICPA, Section AU 319.19):

  - Reliance on systems or programs that are inaccurately processing data, processing inaccurate data, or both
  - Unauthorized access to data that may result in improper changes or the destruction of data, including the recording of unauthorized or nonexistent transactions or inaccurate recording of transactions
  - Unauthorized changes to data in master files
  - Unauthorized changes to systems or programs
  - Failure to make necessary changes to systems or programs
  - Inappropriate manual intervention
  - Potential loss of data

- The extent and nature of these internal control risks vary depending on the characteristics of the entity's information systems. Multiple users, external or internal, may access a common database that affects financial reporting. A lack of control at a single user point might compromise the security of the entire database, potentially resulting in improper charges or destruction of data (AICPA, Section AU 319.20).

OUTSOURCING ACCOUNTING AND DATA SERVICES

Outsourcing of data services does not eliminate, but rather aggravates, the data control risks by fundamentally altering the approach to testing and validating the data processes of an agency.

Whether data are processed, accounted for, and reported by a manual system, an in-house computer processing facility, or outsourced in whole or in part to an external provider of these services, the fundamental control issues and the responsibilities of the auditor do not change. Under each scenario, the auditor is required to acquire an understanding of each of the components of an agency's internal control structure (i.e., the controls environment; agency's regular risk assessments; the control activities, policies, and procedures for implementing management directives; the supportive information and communication systems for identifying, capturing, and reporting; and the monitoring process to assess the quality of controls).

When data services have been outsourced, the servicing entity could be responsible, under the outsourcing contract, for part or all of the original systems design and software as well as data input, processing, and reporting. Under these conditions, the outsourcing federal agency has limited or no data determinations, yet the quality of services provided by the servicing entity become controls and systems considerations for the auditor. The AICPA suggests that information concerning the servicing organization controls and systems be examined, tested, and validated from a wide variety of sources, including:

- The servicing organization's user manuals
- Systems documentation; technical manuals
- The terms, conditions, and scope of services of the outsourcing contract
- Reports issued by the servicing organization's independent auditor, internal auditor and retained consultants
- Reports of regulatory agencies

A specific section of the AICPA's Professional Standards (AU 324) provides considerable guidance on addressing the control risks associated with data processing, accounting, and reporting that have been outsourced to an organization external to the audited agency. Over the years, an increased use of service organizations has caused the AICPA to issue several related Statements on Auditing Standards:

- SAS 70, *Servicing Organizations*, 1992
- SAS 78, *Consideration of Internal Control in a Financial Statement Audit: An Amendment to SAS 55,* 1995
- SAS 88, *Service Organizations and Reporting on Consistency,* 1999
- SAS 94, *The Effect of Information Technology on the Auditor's Consideration of Internal Control in a Financial Statement Audit,* 2001
- SAS 98, *Omnibus SAS,* 2002

EVALUATING AND TESTING INFORMATION TECHNOLOGY SYSTEMS

The appendix to this chapter depicts and describes a methodology and notes considerations relative to computer-based systems that are of concern to auditors of most federal agencies. Although unique circumstances might require the chronology or sequencing of the described tasks to differ, for the most part, all of these tasks must be considered in a federal agency audit, as the auditor acquires an understanding of controls, then assesses, evaluates, tests, and reaches conclusions regarding the effectiveness of controls and the extent that the systems of controls may be relied on in the design of other audit procedures to test transactions and account balances.

APPENDIX

EVALUATION AND TESTING OF EDP SYSTEMS: A METHODOLOGY

During the audit of a federal agency, it is not unusual for an auditor to encounter various older, "legacy" systems operating in conjunction with some of the most complex and advanced information technology supported systems available. Although the procedures performed with electronic data processing (EDP) systems may appear similar to those of manually-based systems, computer-based systems environments merit additional discussion. In additional to fundamentally changing the controls and systems paradigm of an agency, there are other issues. As an example, there have been instances where an agency introduced computer technology into its data processing function by merely converting the manual system to electronic data processing, possibly speeding up the production of suspect information. Further, it would not be unusual to witness ineffective attempts to apply controls of the earlier manual system to the newly implemented computer-based data processing systems. Or, worse, that minimal or limited attention was given to instituting new controls to better address computer-based control risks.

The exhibit below and the ensuing discussion provide an overview of a methodology for the evaluation and testing of federal EDP systems. Additional information can be obtained by consulting the Government Accountability Office's (GAO) detailed and useful guidance included in its *Federal Information System Controls Audit Manual* (FISCAM). Auditors should note that the audit of EDP systems presents the audit team with a challenge which will require the use of computer specialists.

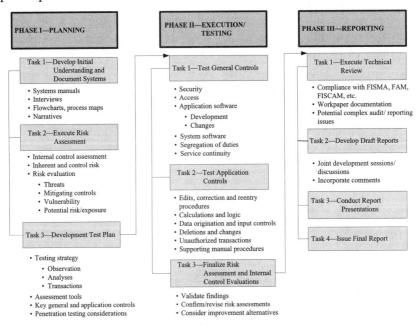

Phase I—Planning

Conceptually, the methodology to test and evaluate controls related to computer-based data processing systems are not dissimilar to those employed to test and evaluate controls for manual data processing systems. A plan must be developed to control and direct the efforts of the audit team; the initial phase requires the auditor to acquire an understanding and conduct tasks to document the computer systems. Once understood, the auditor must assess the relative risk that controls may not have been properly applied, or if applied, were not effective in achieving data control objectives. Conclusions reached at this point are the basis for the design of an audit test strategy for concluding on the effectiveness of key general controls and application controls.

Task 1—Develop Initial Understanding and Document Systems

During this task, the auditor will obtain documentation on:

- General and detailed functional requirements
- Descriptions and samples of input and output data
- Systems design and operating procedures manuals, system, and data flow diagrams
- System contingency and backup plans
- EDP plan project descriptions, system security, and test results
- Audit, inspection, and other review reports

This documentation is examined by the auditor to develop an understanding of the internal control environment and application systems, and to provide the perspective needed to conduct subsequent review activities. In addition, the auditor will perform the following tasks:

- Identify systems targeted for review (e.g., systems that process financial and accounting data and/or significantly affect the processing of financial and accounting data).
- Consider the availability of documentation.
- Discuss the proposed project work plan, schedule, milestones, and testing procedures with the auditee.
- Arrange for the agency and other support needed to complete the auditor's evaluations and assessments (e.g., interviewees, supporting documentation, access to computers, etc.).

Based on the information obtained on systems and processes/subprocesses, the auditor will typically document the information using flowcharting techniques and supporting narratives to visually portray the systems' operations. As is the case with all systems/processes, documentation is validated by walk-throughs and discussions with appropriate and knowledgeable personnel.

Upon validation of the documentation, the auditor will finalize the audit work plan to address the specific requirements for the evaluation of assessable subsystems. At this point, the auditor should have obtained sufficient information to provide the auditee with recommendations and comments. To avoid future surprises, agency management should be provided with any controls/systems recommendations or concerns as they arise.

Task 2—Execute Preliminary Risk Assessment

Upon completion of the initial planning and documentation, the auditor will proceed to develop an assessment of inherent risk and control risk.

Inherent risk is the susceptibility of information resources or resources controlled by the information system to material theft, destruction, disclosure, unauthorized modification, or other impairment (before considering related internal controls). The auditor will consider factors that may increase inherent risk, such as types of technology used (e.g., unsupported products, inherently vulnerable technologies, etc.) as well as the characteristics of transactions (e.g., nonroutine transactions, transaction volumes).

Control risk is the risk that a material misstatement in the data will not be prevented or detected and corrected on a timely basis by the entity's internal control structure. To support the assessment of control risk, the auditor will consider controls at the entity level, including control environment, internal risk assessments, information and communication, and monitoring. Other significant areas in the assessment of control risk encompass controls at the data processing level, including management processes and application processes subsystems relative to the applied information technology.

The effectiveness of an information technology supported system of internal control depends, to a large extent, on the internal control environment in which it operates. Thus, as is the case with any process, the evaluation of the internal control environment will significantly influence the auditor's conclusion on the effectiveness of information technology related internal controls. This evaluation is based on observations of actual systems processing, review of documentation, and interviews with appropriate personnel and walk-throughs. The auditor must focus on assessing management attitude, organization structure, personnel, delegation and communication of authority, policies and procedures, budgeting and reporting practices, and organizational checks and balances applicable to the system.

To streamline the process of evaluating the effectiveness of controls and compliance with a diverse collection of relevant requirements, it is useful to develop a controls and compliance requirements test matrix. This matrix should include a synthesis of Federal guidance set forth in laws, regulations, and guidance manuals such as:

- Federal Financial Management Improvement Act of 1996 (FFMIA)
- Federal Managers' Financial Integrity Act of 1982 (FMFIA)
- Federal Information Security Management Act of 2002 (FISMA)
- GAO *Federal Information System Controls Audit Manual* (FISCAM) guidelines issued by NIST (as appropriate)
- OMB Circulars (e.g., Circulars A-123, A-127, and A-130)

An evaluation of the internal control environment will permit the auditor to identify and document the specific risks, threats, and vulnerabilities of the system and its component processes and subprocesses. The auditor must then analyze each process and subprocess from origination of source documents through payment and final disposition in an attempt to isolate threats and vulnerabilities and identify mitigating controls and effectiveness of control objectives.

In general, these tasks require the auditor to identify control objectives for each relevant system process or subprocess. In this context, control objectives are the desired goals of a specific system process or subprocess. To determine whether control objectives are being met, the auditor will perform an iterative evaluation that considers, in turn:

- Threats (e.g., events which may prevent achievement of the objective)
- Vulnerabilities (e.g., whether internal control techniques are present to mitigate or negate the threat)
- Overall risk (e.g., the likelihood that a threat will occur without being prevented by the internal control):

In evaluating risk, the auditor will consider several factors, such as:

- *Efficiency:* Do the applied control techniques achieve desired results within the constraints of cost, benefit, and risk?
- *Effectiveness:* Do the applied control techniques fulfill the desired control objectives, provide the desired coverage, and operate at appropriate times?
- *Comprehensiveness:* Are applied control techniques organized and arranged in the proper sequence to ensure achievement of control objectives? Can or should other control techniques be used to reduce risk?
- *Consistency:* Are applied control techniques uniformly efficient, effective, and comprehensively practiced over extended periods of time?

Should these risk assessments identify systems weaknesses, these conditions must be reported to agency personnel and become the focus of a test plan for actual confirmation of the applied controls environment.

Task 3—Develop Test Plan

The objective of this task is to develop a logical testing approach in order to: (1) confirm that the agency's data processes conform to the understanding provided by agency management and data processing personnel (and preliminarily through auditor interviews, reviews of systems manuals, and walk-throughs); and (2) determine whether the designed and implemented controls are, in fact, being applied in practice and that the controls are functioning as intended.

In preparing the plan, the auditor will select control techniques to be tested by analyzing documentation developed in the preceding tasks, with a particular emphasis on perceived or potential system threats, deficiencies, vulnerabilities, and the existence of any compensating or mitigating controls. This analysis will serve to identify those controls which significantly contribute to control objectives. The test plan must incorporate the specific types of testing to be performed (i.e., document analyses, observation, interviews), the timing and extent of tests to conduct, expected test results, and the locations where testing will be performed.

The purpose of the testing task is to confirm or refute whether the auditor's preliminary assessment of internal controls (based on the system[s] design and documentation) is supported by practices performed and executed in the system's actual operations. That is, given the auditor earlier concluded that the system appeared to be reliable in concept, design, and description (based on manuals, systems charting, written procedures, staff training, etc.), the auditor must personally conduct independent tests to factually ascertain whether the controls upon which the earlier audit conclusions were based are being applied and complied with by agency personnel in the day-to-day operation of the system.

Phase II—Execution (Testing)

Depending on the auditor's perceptions of the nature, relative effectiveness, strengths, and weaknesses of the controls, the auditor must independently apply a variety of tests, such as:

- Inspection of documents
- Review of configuration settings
- Reperformance of calculations
- Running data analysis software
- Observation of control activities
- Processing of test data as well as software testing tools to perform vulnerability assessments.

These audit tests must be made of the agency's general and application controls.[2]

Task 1—Test General Controls

As appropriate, the auditor will apply a variety of techniques to test the *general* controls including audit software tools and, if warranted, penetration testing to validate access controls. In addition, the auditor will determine whether documented policies and procedures providing for effective controls over systems development/enhancement/changes are in place and operating as designed, and whether disaster recovery facilities are routinely tested to ensure availability and effectiveness when needed.

A test of general controls will typically cover areas of interest, such as:

- Security
- Access

---

[2] *With respect to information technology related controls, the Committee of Sponsoring Organizations (COSO)* **Internal Control—Integrated Framework,** *the model adopted by industry, government, and the auditing profession, identified two types of controls*

    (1) **General controls**—*those controls over:*
- *Data center operations (scheduling, backup, recovery procedures)*
- *Systems software controls (acquisition and implementation of operating systems)*
- *Access security*
- *Application system development and maintenance controls (acquisition and implementation of individual computer software applications)*

    (2) **Application controls**—*those controls designed to:*
- *Control information processing*
- *Help ensure the completeness and accuracy of transaction processing, authorization, validity, and effectiveness of interface of applications*

- Application software
  - Development
  - Changes
- System software
- Segregation of duties
- Service continuity

Task 2—Test Application Controls

The test of *application* controls is directed towards assuring the accuracy of the data processed by the system under review. Tests must be tailored to the characteristics of the application, paying strict attention to the methods of processing used for data origination, input, processing, and output.

Test data is constructed to allow the auditor to determine whether the application controls ensure that routine transactions are processed in a timely manner, and whether the designed and implemented application controls reject invalid transactions. Testing is also employed to determine if erroneous data is adequately controlled for correction and reentry. Tests of routine, standard, or "normal" transactions are conducted to evaluate the system's ability to establish, change, and delete records, perform calculations, and test the system's processing logic.

The objective of data origination controls is to determine the extent to which controls ensure the accuracy, completeness, and timeliness, and that data automatically proceeds through the systems application phases without loss, unauthorized addition or modification, or other errors. The testing approach must also determine the adequacy of controls over the manual preparation, collection, and processing of source documents, and evaluate the effectiveness of procedures and techniques for assuring that no data is added, lost, or altered before it is entered.

When testing data input controls, the auditor must determine the adequacy of manual and automated controls over data input to ensure accurate entry with optimum use of computerized validation and editing, and also that error handling procedures facilitate timely and accurate resubmission of corrected data. Thus, the audit focus is on data processing integrity, validation, editing, and error handling. Also of audit significance are those controls implemented and applied over files and systems which interface with the application under review.

Audit tests of data output are applied to ensure that products of the data processing results are accurate and reports are distributed to users in a timely manner. The audit test focus for output controls include data output balancing and reconciliation, output distribution, output error handling, and handling and retention of output records and accountability (e.g., audit trails) documents.

Task 3—Finalize Risk Assessment and Internal Control Evaluations

The audit test results must be compared to initial audit expectations established at the conclusion of the auditor's earlier evaluation of the system design. Test activities and results must be documented and include a description of the controls tested, the sampled population and the relationship of the sample to the overall system, a chronological record of the testing events and people involved, and a summary of test results. The test results will either validate the auditor's earlier preliminary assessment or require the auditor to revise the prior assessment and, as necessary, the overall audit approach including planned substantive testing of transactions and accounts.

Phase III—Reporting

Government Auditing Standards and OMB Circulars and Bulletins require the auditor to report findings in the auditor's report on internal control as well as in the report on compliance with laws and regulations, wherein the auditor must describe the scope of audit tests employed, describe the results of those tests and provide an audit opinion or other type of audit assurances, and, if a separate report was made with respect to these tests, to reference that report.

During this phase, the auditor will review the prior evaluation and testing efforts, and identify:

- Reportable conditions and material weaknesses to be included in the report on internal controls
- Events of noncompliance with federal guidance which need to be reported in the auditor's report on compliance with laws and regulations
- Other internal control matters and opportunities for improved efficiency which the auditor concludes should be included in the management letter (and/or reported informally to appropriate levels of federal agency management)

12 END-OF-AUDIT, QUALITY CONTROL, AND REPORTING PROCEDURES

The reporting phase will, of course, culminate with the issuance of the auditor's reports; however, prior to the issuance of the reports, a significant number of procedures requiring the involvement of the more senior members of the audit team will take place. During this phase, the auditor obtains legal and management representation letters; performs a final evaluation of audit results, including waived adjustments, and determines the types of audit assertions that the audit results support; concludes quality review procedures (including a technical review by an independent senior-level member of the audit organization such as a partner or equivalent, if a government audit team performs the audit), and issues draft and final reports.

Prior to the conclusion of the audit, a number of third-party representations from the auditee's management and legal counsel, as well as external counsel (if applicable), must be obtained. This is discussed further below.

MANAGEMENT REPRESENTATION LETTER(S)

AICPA guidance (AU 333) requires auditors to obtain management representations on all audit engagements.[1] OMB Bulletin 01-02 adopts this guidance and requires that the letter, at a minimum, address:

- Financial statements (acknowledging management responsibility for the statements and asserting that the statements were prepared in accordance with GAAP)
- Effectiveness of internal control
- Compliance with federal financial management system requirements
- Compliance with laws and regulations

More specific topics generally addressed by the letter include:

- Whether all pertinent financial records and data were made available to the auditor
- Whether all relevant data have been disclosed in the financial statements
- Management's responsibility for internal controls including fraud prevention controls
- Cases of known, suspected, and/or alleged fraud
- Related-party transactions
- Accuracy of estimates
- Contingencies

---

[1] *The citations of "AU" in this chapter refer to sections of the **Professional US Auditing Standards**, updated annually and promulgated by the AICPA, NY, NY.*

- Management plans that may affect the value of the entity's assets and/or liabilities

A management representation letter is not a substitute for audit procedures, and it is presumed that, with the exception of very subjective information such as management's future plans, the auditor has independently verified all significant assertions made by management. However, a management representation letter provides the auditor with a useful vehicle for addressing significant accounting and auditing issues by requiring management to state in writing its understanding and position on the issue, thus ensuring that the auditee and the auditor share the same understanding of complex issues. In addition to the required contents listed above, which are set forth in AU 333, the auditor should consider tailoring additional representations to the specific circumstances of the auditee.

Under AICPA guidance, referenced by OMB Bulletin 01-02, the management representation letter is an important audit procedure. Management's refusal to provide these written representations would be a limitation to the scope of the audit, sufficient to preclude issuance of an unqualified audit opinion and ordinarily would be sufficient to cause the auditor to disclaim an audit opinion (see AU 333.13). The AICPA cautions an auditor faced with this type of refusal that he or she may wish to reconsider whether to be associated with the auditee at all.

The letter is typically signed by the chief executive of the auditee and the chief financial officer. As a matter of practice, other individuals in a position to influence financial data, such as a chief accountant or controller, should also be considered. Finally, the auditor may wish to obtain specific representations from other management personnel (e.g., representation by a program manager on certain aspects of a major program for which he or she is responsible). The letter should cover all periods reported on and should be dated no earlier than the end of fieldwork to ensure the representation covers the entire period for which the auditor is responsible.

LEGAL COUNSEL REPRESENTATION LETTER(S)

Legal letters are governed by AICPA guidance (AU 337) and by OMB Bulletin 01-02. The purpose of the legal letter is to obtain information on active and/or potential litigation that may have an impact on the financial statements. According to the AICPA guidance, a lawyer's refusal to furnish the requested information, either in writing or orally, would be a limitation on the scope of the audit sufficient to preclude issuance of an unqualified audit opinion. As a general rule, the auditor will request such information from the agency's general counsel. The AICPA states that evidence obtained from inside counsel is not a substitute for information that outside counsel refuses to furnish. However, the auditor should also consider whether outside legal counsel (including the Department of Justice) has been involved in litigation and, as necessary, obtain legal letters from them.

It is important to note that the auditee's management is the primary source of information on legal matters. The legal letter provides independent evidence on the validity of management's assertion. Legal letters are requested by appropriate auditee personnel (e.g., the Chief Financial Officer) and instruct the attorney to respond directly to the auditor (with a copy to the individual making the request). In general, the letter will request information on litigation, claims, and assessments that exceed specific amounts based on the auditor's assessment of materiality and as agreed with the auditee. Legal letter content typically includes:

- Pending or threatened litigation
- Unasserted claims and assessments
- An evaluation of the two items above and likely outcome, including estimates (if possible)
- An acknowledgment from the attorney of his or her professional responsibility to disclose to the auditor matters that in his or her opinion require disclosure
- A listing of cases that have required substantial attention by the attorney
- The nature and reasons for limitations (if any) placed by the attorney on his or her representations

OMB Bulletin 01-02 provides a detailed illustration of the letter requesting a response from the attorneys. Because of the technical nature of the letter, the auditor is well advised to encourage the agency to follow the bulletin's format as closely as possible. As a practical matter, the auditor will often draft the legal letter request for the auditee's signature. Timing of the letter is critical to ensure that the date is as close as possible to the end of fieldwork and that it is received with sufficient time to meet the auditee's and the US government financial statements' reporting deadlines.

During the planning phase, the auditor will make certain assumptions (i.e., working hypotheses) to develop an audit approach that usually combines test of controls and substantive testing.

FINAL CRITIQUE OF AUDIT PLAN, PROGRAMS, AND PROCEDURES

Assuming that testing proceeded as expected (e.g., tests of controls supported the effective operation of internal controls and substantive testing resulted in no significant findings or adjustments), the auditor can conclude that the audit results support the issuance of an unqualified opinion.

In short, the audit process requires the auditor to continually reassess his or her approach and develop additional and/or alternate procedures to compensate for audit findings, audit obstacles, and other peculiar or unanticipated conditions or circumstances that were encountered in relation to the specific auditee. Given the dynamic nature of the process, it is essential that at the conclusion of testing, senior members of the audit team carefully consider the implications of the audit findings and whether the audit effort resulted in sufficient audit coverage to warrant the expression of an audit opinion, as well as what type of opinion can be issued.

In considering the sufficiency of audit coverage, the auditor will consider quantifiable findings as well as more subjective issues including financial statement exposures, accounting issues, and scope limitations (including incomplete data and limitations imposed by national security requirements).

To the extent that there is agreement with the auditee on audit adjustments and materiality, recording (or waiving, if not material) audit adjustments is a relatively straightforward process, requiring only that the auditor verify that adjustments are properly reflected in the financial statements.

Subjective issues, however, require the exercise of audit judgment in, for example, determining the reasonableness and support for estimates and contingencies (including the likelihood of occurrence in the case of contingencies), deciding on a preferred accounting principle, or considering the implications of scope limitations.

There is no simple answer or "checklist" approach to deal with issues that require the exercise of audit judgment. What is clear, however, is that these matters need to be properly documented in the workpapers. As a practical matter, the auditor will generally document this effort in written memoranda that describe the important audit and accounting issues encountered and the rationale behind his or her decisions. Thus, the auditor's conclusions regarding estimates and contingencies should carefully document all sources of information consulted and leading to his or her conclusion. Decisions regarding a choice of accounting principles should clearly identify the authoritative guidance researched by the auditor, as well as the alternatives considered.

Finally, scope limitations must be considered in light of the nature of the limitation. Limitations imposed by national security requirements usually need to be analyzed only in light of the materiality of the specific account that is affected. Limitations imposed by incomplete data (e.g., missing documentation) raise significant doubts regarding the effectiveness of internal controls and the internal control environment. Here the auditor must consider whether sufficient additional procedures were performed to overcome this situation, or whether the deficiency is significant enough to force a qualification or disclaimer of the auditor's opinion due to the lack of documentation. Finally, scope limitations that appear to be capricious in nature (e.g., an auditee's refusal to provide access to certain information or to provide requested written representations) are particularly troublesome and may force the auditor to disclaim an opinion or even refuse to be involved with the audit at all.

CLEAN OPINION NOT GUARANTEED

Although the auditor cannot guarantee the issuance of a clean opinion, the auditor has a professional responsibility to use his/her best efforts to develop an audit approach capable of compensating for existing audit obstacles. Where the auditor is unable to develop such an audit approach, he/she should provide recommendations that will enable the auditee to effectively address audit obstacles and issues to enable the issuance of an unqualified opinion in future years.

In performing the final end-of-audit evaluation of audit coverage, the auditor is also responsible for evaluating the audit team's collective professional competence. The issuance of a qualified opinion or disclaimer due to a faulty audit approach that failed to provide sufficient coverage can never justify or compensate for poor audit execution on the part of the audit team. Thus, this final assessment of audit results requires an honest evaluation of the auditor's own performance. It is the auditor's responsibility to be candid about any shortcomings in the approach or execution and attempt to resolve these matters within the contractually agreed deadlines, and/or discuss the issues, as necessary, with the auditee or other appropriate officials.

AUDIT QUALITY CONTROL REVIEW AND VALIDATION

A critical closing procedure is ensuring that the auditor has adhered to professional standards as set forth by the AICPA and GAO. It should be apparent that this final procedure cannot redress quality control issues related to the audit organization or its staff, if proper quality control was not applied throughout the audit. Thus, planning for quality control starts with the initial phase of the audit and affects every subsequent aspect. Critical quality control issues are discussed below.

AUDITOR INDEPENDENCE

AICPA and GAO general standards both address independence. CPAs performing audits for governmental units are subject to these standards, as well as the standards imposed by the applicable state commission with jurisdiction over the audit. CPAs are bound to follow, and should be aware of, all applicable standards. As a practical matter, however, the GAO standard is likely the strictest one and the one auditors involved in the execution of audits in accordance with "yellow book" standards must adhere to Paragraph 3.03 of GAO's *Government Auditing Standards* (2003 revision) states:

> *In all matters relating to the audit work, the audit organization and the individual auditor, whether government or public, should be free both in fact and appearance from personal, external, and organizational impairments to independence.*

GAO standards state that the auditor needs to consider three issues—personal, external, and organizational impairments—that may impair independence. The following considerations are derived from paragraphs 3.04 to 3.32 of GAO's *Government Auditing Standards* (2003 revision):

- *Personal impairments* encompass the individual auditor and his or her relationship to the auditee (e.g., close familial ties to auditee personnel, financial ownership/stake in the auditee, prior nonaudit services provided the auditee, etc.). Further, personal impairments also extend to the audit organization if, for example, the organization provided non–audit-related services (e.g., consulting) that constitute (or may be perceived as) a conflict of interest.
- *External impairments* revolve around outside factors that may restrict or interfere with the auditor's execution of the audit, his or her judgment, and opinions. In some respects, external impairments are similar to audit scope limitations and deal with situations where the auditor's execution of his or her responsibility is compromised by outside factors. These factors might, among other considerations, restrict funds available to pay for the audit and/or finance activities essential to the successful execution of the audit, influence the selection of audit procedures, influence the auditor's judgment through coercion (e.g., by threat of dismissal), and so on.
- *Organizational impairments* may affect governmental audit organizations and auditors employed by the federal government depending on departmental or agency organizational structure (e.g., reporting responsibilities) within which the audit organization finds itself and the extent to which the audit organization is independent of the auditee.

Organizational impairments relate to conditions affecting audit impartiality by the placement of an audit organization within a government and the structure of the government entity to which the audit organization is assigned. The "yellow book" notes that government audit organizations can meet this independence requirement in two ways.

1. A government audit organization is presumed to be independent from the audited entity if:

   a. Assigned to a level of government other than the assigned audit entity, or

   b. Assigned to a different branch of government within the same level of government as the audited entity.

2. A government audit organization is also presumed to be independent from the audited entity if the audit organization's head meets any of these criteria:

   a. Directly elected by voters of the jurisdiction being audited

   b. Elected or appointed by a legislative body and subject to removal by that body, and reports to and is accountable to that body

   c. Appointed by someone other than the legislative body as long as the appointment is confirmed by the legislature and reports to and is accountable to the legislative body

   d. Appointed by, accountable to, reports to, and can only be removed by a statutorily created governing body, the majority of whose members are independently elected or appointed from outside the organization being audited

To be considered organizationally independent under other than the structures noted above, the *Government Auditing Standards* require the government audit organization to meet all of these safeguards:

- Statutory protections that prevent the abolishment of the audit organization by the audited entity
- Statutory protections that require that if the head of the audit organization is removed from office, the head of the agency should report this fact and the reasons for the removal to the legislative body
- Statutory protections that prevent the audited entity from interfering with the initiation, scope, timing, and completion of any audit
- Statutory protections that prevent the audited entity from interfering with the reporting on any audit, including the findings, conclusions, and recommendations, or the manner, means, or timing of the audit organization's reports
- Statutory protections that require the audit organization to report to a legislative body or other independent governing body on a recurring basis
- Statutory protections that give the audit organization sole authority over the selection, retention, advancement, and dismissal of its staff
- Statutory access to records and documents that relate to the agency, program, or function being audited

There are instances where other organizations within governments, public educational institutions, and hospitals employ auditors who work for the management of those organizations, generally referred to as internal audit organizations. A governmental internal audit organization, under *Government Auditing Standards*, could be free of organizational impairment if the head of the audit organization meets all of these criteria:

- The audit head is accountable to the head or deputy head of the government entity.
- The audit head is required to report the results of the audit organization's work to the head or deputy head of the government entity.
- The audit organization is located organizationally outside the staff or line management function of the unit under audit.

The standard for auditor independence attempts to respond to the existence of real, apparent, and perceived independence or, alternatively, impairments to independence. The auditor must be independent in fact as well as appearance. Although these standards apply to external auditors, most generally CPAs, the independence standards of the profession hold all practitioners, regardless of their employer, to similar standards. For auditors employed by a government, the independence issue would not often arise with respect to most audit assignments. But, absent the "yellow book" provisions, minimal or no guidance is available to auditors employed by the government with respect to their independence.

In general, audit organizations will have developed internal quality control procedures to monitor compliance with independence rules. As a matter of practice, no audit organization will or should accept an audit engagement without first performing verification procedures to ensure that past or present endeavors and/or relationships do not compromise or appear to compromise the organization's independence. Similarly, audit staff should not be assigned to the audit without first ensuring that the individual auditors are free of independence impairments and that they remain free of impairments throughout the audit's life cycle.

Currently, many government agencies receiving audit services require that the audit organization represent that it is free of independence impairments (including an explanation of what procedures are followed to make the determination). In addition, individual representations from staff members are often required. In the interest of fully documenting the auditor's independence, quality control procedures should consider whether sufficient procedures were performed (including documentation, as discussed above) to ensure that independence requirements were complied with.

AUDIT DOCUMENTATION

Unlike the AICPA's generally accepted auditing standards (GAAS), GAO's *Government Auditing Standards* provide a separate fieldwork standard addressing the quality of audit documentation (paragraphs 4.22 through 4.26). Paragraph 4.22 states:

Audit documentation related to planning, conducting, and reporting on the audit should contain sufficient information to enable an experienced auditor who has had no previous connection with the audit to ascertain from the audit documentation the evidence that supports the auditors' significant judgments and conclusions. Audit documentation should contain support for findings, conclusions, and recommendations before auditors issue their report.

All work performed by the auditor in support of his or her assertions must be documented in the working papers to substantiate the procedures and/or tests that are performed and the conclusions reached. To facilitate the review of work performed, every work plan, procedure, step, task, and/or test is to be referenced to the work paper containing or displaying evidence of the work performed, including the initials of the individual(s) who performed the procedures and/or reviewed the work. Additionally, each work paper should stand on its own, having sufficient documentation to allow the reviewer to reach the same conclusion as the individual responsible for performing the procedure. In general, well-developed working papers that fully support the auditor's work and assertion should include:

- Workpaper reference
- Cross-reference to supporting working papers (as applicable)
- Initials of the individual responsible for performing the procedure
- Initials of the individual responsible for reviewing the workpaper
- Description of the source of the document or documents reviewed
- Purpose of the workpaper
- Procedure(s) performed
- Conclusions drawn from the work performed
- A well-thought-out indexing scheme that enables all members of the audit team, as well as the independent technical reviewer, to quickly locate specific aspects of the audit such as planning, cycle documentation, internal control assessments testing, or accounting and auditing issues

During the course of an audit, internal control issues may be uncovered that impact the audit and/or must be brought to the attention of the auditee. These issues or findings include material weaknesses, reportable conditions, and management letter comments, discussed in more detail later in this chapter. "Yellow book" standards require that the documentation of these issues include:

- *Description of the finding (condition):* A concise summary of the nature of the finding including references to supporting work papers where additional information about the finding can be found. The description of the finding includes a discussion of the condition disclosed by the audit procedures (e.g., what is wrong with the process, a description of errors found, etc.).
- *Criteria:* In general, findings such as weaknesses in internal control refer to events or conditions that violate certain rules. These rules can be as formal as specific federal internal control requirements or simply the application of common sense and some best practices. In short, the criteria explain why the condition described earlier is a problem.

- *Cause:* Typically, the cause will be the absence of effective prevention controls, clerical errors, or both. Clerical errors may be the result of a lack of training or cycle documentation, as well as carelessness or incompetence. Although the latter two may require tact when discussed with management, these conditions cannot be ignored by the auditor.
- *Effect:* A discussion of the actual and/or potential effect of the condition on the financial statements and/or the accomplishment of specific internal control objectives (e.g., safeguarding assets).

The workpaper documentation will also include the auditor's evaluation of the severity of the audit finding and whether the condition should be considered a reportable condition or a material weakness, which will need to be included in the auditor's report on internal controls.

Because reportable findings of this nature will typically require the auditor to make a special reporting or issue related documentation, the workpapers in support of the finding must also include a description of the actions the auditee should take to address the finding. To the extent that the issue has been discussed with the auditee, the auditee's response should also be documented.

STAFF ASSIGNMENT, SUPERVISION, AND COMPETENCE

GAO's general standard addressing competence (paragraph 3.39) states:

The staff assigned to perform the audit or attestation engagement should collectively possess adequate professional competence for the tasks required.

Assignments and Responsibilities

The execution of an efficient and effective audit requires a staff size and skill mix (including specialists and subject matter experts) commensurate with the requirements of the audit's magnitude, scope, and complexity. Typically, the level of individuals assigned to a specific engagement will range from junior or staff-level personnel to partner or equivalent level professionals in a governmental audit organization. The determination and assignment of the number, quality, and type of staff (including specialists and subject matter experts) required should occur as early as possible during the planning phase of the engagement.

The successful execution of an audit requires audit procedures to be delegated to auditors with the requisite skill and experience. The next summary describes responsibilities typically associated with the different levels found in an audit. The discussion addresses the traditional partner, manager, senior accountant, and staff accountant hierarchy found in most commercial firms. However, it should be understood that these titles will vary between firms. In addition, while government audit organizations will include partner-level auditors, the title "partner" is clearly not appropriate for these organizations.

- *Audit partners* or the equivalent *governmental audit directors* are responsible for overall audit management and the ultimate completion of the engagement in compliance with professional guidelines and all federal requirements. Most audit engagements should include at least one partner or governmental audit director who is responsible for audit execution and a second partner or governmental audit director (or experienced audit manager for less complex engagements) who is responsible for the performance of an independent quality control review of the audit. This latter individual should not be involved in the daily performance of the audit.

The audit partner is responsible for reviewing and approving the overall audit approach, the definition of materiality, and the identification of tolerable audit risk. As a rule, partners or governmental audit directors are involved in the development of the audit plan, the review of selected audit workpapers, and the resolution of audit and accounting issues. As needed, the partner or governmental audit director will also participate in the development and execution of audit procedures affecting the more complex areas of the audit. Finally, the audit partner or governmental audit director has the ultimate responsibility for ensuring that sufficient audit coverage was obtained to support the assertions included in the auditor's reports.

- *Audit managers* work closely with the partners or governmental audit directors in the development of the audit approach and audit plan and, as a rule, supervise the audit senior's execution of day-to-day management responsibilities. Depending on the complexity of audit procedures, audit managers will develop and/or review and approve audit programs and play a major role in the early identification and resolution of complex or significant audit and accounting issues.
- *Audit seniors* are responsible for the execution of day-to-day management activities, the development of audit programs, and the supervision of staff auditors. In most instances, an audit senior will participate in all four phases of the audit and will be involved in executing or assisting with all aspects of the audit including supervision of audit staff, workpaper documentation and review, drafting reports and findings, addressing most management and accounting/auditing issues, and the execution of complex audit procedures.
- *Staff auditors* are responsible for performing less complex procedures and tests and work under the supervision of more senior personnel.

Supervision

The second standard of fieldwork states in part, that "assistants...are to be properly supervised." Procedures must be in place to ensure that all work performed is reviewed at various stages of the audit. Although practice will vary somewhat from engagement to engagement depending on the circumstances and the competence/experience level of seniors and staff assistants, a sound supervision approach will ensure that, at a minimum, all workpapers and reports prepared by staff auditors will be reviewed by audit senior(s) and/or the audit manager. This review will take place continually, as the audit progresses, and not just at the conclusion of audit fieldwork.

Procedures should require that all workpapers prepared by the audit senior are reviewed by the audit manager and/or partner or governmental audit director and that all workpapers prepared by the audit manager are reviewed by the audit partner or governmental audit director. In addition, a second partner or governmental audit director should review all original work prepared by partners or governmental audit directors, and all work products and reports should be independently reviewed by a partner or governmental audit director with no other involvement in the audit. This same individual could also be responsible for the review of original audit workpapers developed by the partner(s) participating in the audit. Finally, it is important that workpaper documentation clearly show the review process (e.g., by requiring individuals reviewing the work to sign the workpaper and state their agreement with the conclusions reached, when applicable, and/or completeness of the procedures performed).

Continuing Professional Education

The AICPA and GAO both recognize the importance of staying abreast of developments affecting federal auditing and accounting. As a means to achieving this perpetual competence, continuing professional education requirements (CPE), beyond those contained in the AICPA's generally accepted auditing standards, have been imposed by GAO on all audits performed in accordance with "yellow book" standards. In addition, the AICPA and state agencies having jurisdiction over CPA licenses also issue CPE requirements. The auditor must be aware of these requirements and ensure compliance with both or all.

It is important that during the planning phase, the auditor consider whether all personnel assigned to the audit are in compliance with *Government Auditing Standards* (GAS) and other applicable CPE requirements (or will be by the completion of the audit). As a matter of routine, closing procedures should ensure that audit workpapers sufficiently document compliance with CPE requirements for all participating professionals subject to the requirements. In the words of GAO (paragraph 3.45 and related footnote), these continuing professional education requirements apply to all auditors performing work under GAS, including auditors planning, directing, performing fieldwork, or reporting on an audit or attestation engagement subject to the GAS. Alternatively stated, GAO's GAS state that staff members not involved in planning, directing, or reporting on the audit or attestation engagement, and who charge less than 20% annually of their time to audits and attestation engagements that are required to comply with the GAS, do not have to comply with the special 24-hour CPE requirement.

ISSUING THE INDEPENDENT AUDITOR'S REPORTS

In general, reports issued in connection with audits of federal agencies in accordance with GAO's GAS and OMB requirements, particularly its Bulletin 01-02, must include:

- The federal auditee's financial statements
- A report by the auditor on the federal auditee's internal controls
- A report by the auditor on the federal auditee's compliance with laws and regulations
- Management letters issued by the auditor to the federal auditee
- Special-purpose reports that may be required of the auditor

The appendix to this chapter provides examples of selected reports. The reports on financial statements, internal controls, and compliance with laws and regulations may be combined into one report.

Auditor's Report on Financial Statements

The auditor's report should state whether the department or agency's principal financial statements (including related notes) are fairly stated in all material respects in accordance with the GAAP, which, as noted in earlier chapters, are promulgated by FASAB. The auditor's report must comply with AICPA guidance, specifically section AU 508. The auditor's opinion or report will usually cover these principal statements:

- Balance sheet
- Statement of net costs
- Statement of changes in net position
- Statement of budgetary resources
- Statement of financing
- Statement of custodial activity (when applicable)

In addition to the above, the auditor will report on required supplementary information including:

- MD&A
- Required supplementary stewardship information (e.g., including property, plant, and equipment; investments; and social insurance information)
- Required supplementary information

Generally, contracts for audit issued by a federal department or agency will require that audit reporting procedures follow AICPA guidance set forth in AU 558 and that the reporting language conform to the guidance in AU 551.15. Unless the auditor has been engaged to audit the required supplementary information, the auditor will mention that limited procedures were performed (e.g., inquiries of management) and disclaim an opinion on the information.

Audit Opinions on Federal Financial Statements

The specific audit opinion issued on the financial statements will depend on the auditor's findings and ability to validate the implicit and explicit assertions by agency management with respect to its financial statements. An unqualified or "clean" audit opinion cannot be issued given any of these circumstances:

- If the financial statements are not prepared in accordance with applicable accounting principles, then the auditor's report should identify the GAAP departure and its effect on the financial statements. Depending on the magnitude of the departure and its subsequent effect, the auditor will qualify or issue an adverse opinion on the agency's financial statements.
- If the auditor is unable to obtain sufficient competent evidential matter to support management's assertions, he or she should disclaim an opinion, or, depending on the auditor's evaluation of the potential impact of the uncertainty

created by the lack of sufficient evidential matter, the auditor must issue a qualified (subject to) opinion. Any qualified audit opinion should explain the nature of the uncertainty. Uncertainties will arise as a result of a number of factors including:

- Externally imposed scope limitations (including limiting auditor access to data as well as inability to obtain competent evidential matter prior to reporting deadlines)
- Internal control weaknesses that cannot be overcome by performing additional or extended audit procedures
- The presence of contingencies that cannot be reasonably estimated to meet the financial statement reporting requirements set forth in the Financial Accounting Standards Board (FASB) Statement of Financial Accounting Standard 5, *Accounting for Contingencies*

Nature and Content of Audit Opinions and Federal Financial Statements

The accounting and financial reporting contained in the principal financial statements of federal departments and agencies—that is, the generally accepted accounting principles for federal entities—were initially delineated by FASAB. During the 1990s, Congress, in several laws, codified FASAB's standards and detailed other financial management requirements for examination and report during an annual audit. Soon after, OMB, by its circulars and bulletins relative to federal agency financial statements, duplicated the congressional financial reporting criteria, prescribed additional guidance, and imposed other requirements to be implemented during the annual financial reporting phase.

Federal auditing requirements—generally accepted auditing standards for federal audits—are structured in a somewhat similar fashion. The auditor of a federal entity must adhere to all of the AICPA's generally accepted auditing standards, plus the additional, broader standards required by GAO's *Government Auditing Standards*, and finally, requirements imposed on federal audits by OMB in its circulars and bulletins (of particular note is Bulletin 01-02, *Audit Requirements for Federal Financial Statements*, which imposes more detailed audit procedures and provides sample audit opinions and audit assurance requirements).

Elements of the Audit Report on Agency Financial Statements

In many ways, the auditor's report, relative to audits of federal financial statements, parallels the auditor's report on the financial statements of an organization in the private sector. However, differences do exist, and will continue to arise as Congress identifies issues that require examination and reporting. To ensure the currency of compliance with emerging federal audit requirements, auditors must annually examine OMB and GAO issuances, as well as those of agency inspectors general for emerging issues warranting audit coverage.

Introductory paragraph. The introductory paragraph of the auditor's report on financial statements for a private sector entity identifies that (1) the statements are prepared by management, (2) notes to the financial statements are management's responsibility, and (3) the auditor's responsibility is to audit the statements. All of this appears in the audit report for a federal entity, but also highlighted are the audit tasks and reporting requirements set forth in federal laws, policies, and regulations. The auditor's reporting for federal entities is more extensive than that required by the AICPA's GAAS, requiring, in addition to the audit report on the principal financial statements, an auditor's report on the results of specific tests made of controls and an auditor's report on specific tests made of compliance with laws and regulations.

Scope paragraph.　The audit of a federal entity's financial statements must comply with more than just GAAS; rather, compliance with *Government Auditing Standards* is required in addition to GAAS. Also, OMB's intermittently issued circulars and bulletins contain more guidance that must be applied when auditing a federal entity. While some of this guidance is duplicative of that required by the AICPA and GAO, much is in addition to their pronouncements.

Opinion paragraph.　To the lay reader, the opinion paragraph might not be what it appears. The auditor of a federal entity will opine that the federal agency's statements present fairly, in all material respects, "in conformity with accounting principles generally accepted in the United States of America." This reference, for a private sector entity, would typically refer to the accounting principles promulgated by the FASB. Here, however, the reference is to the accounting standards developed by the FASAB for application by federal entities, as codified in laws of Congress and defined by regulations of OMB. In this respect, the cited accounting principles are not the accounting principles generally accepted in the United States of America, but are the accounting standards prescribed by the federal government for its constituent departments and agencies.

Signature of independent auditor.　Many audits of department and agency financial statements are performed by independent auditors under contract to a federal entity, and who would qualify as the appropriate signatory for the audit report. Additionally, though, federal departments and agencies are audited by inspectors general who themselves are employed by the audited entity. The conduct of independent audits by a department's Inspector General is permitted, under certain conditions, by federal auditing guidance. As revised, the 2003 edition of GAS states that a governmental audit organization, like an Inspector General, may be presumed free of organizational impairments if the audit organization's head, among other criteria GAGAS 3.24:

> *is appointed by someone other than a legislative body so long as the appointment is confirmed by the legislative body and removal from the position is subject to oversight or approval by a legislative body, and reports the results to and is accountable to a legislative body.*

This provision of *Government Auditing Standards* essentially describes the appointment and removal process and reporting relationships for the federal government's inspectors general, as set forth in the Inspectors General Act of 1978, the founding legislation for this federal executive position.

Date of the audit report.　The date of the audit report is particularly significant to the independent auditor, legal, and otherwise. The cited date represents the end date of significant fieldwork performed for the audit being reported on. It is also the date through which the auditor's liability extends. The introductory paragraph of the audit report identifies the period, typically the 12 months of a government's fiscal year, covered by the financial statements that underwent the audit. However, if the audit report is dated three months after the fiscal year-end, the auditor is liable for financial events and reporting for the entire 15-month period: the 12 months of the fiscal year, plus the 3-month period subsequent to year-end that precedes the date on the audit report.

AUDITOR'S REPORT ON INTERNAL CONTROLS

Prior to the enactment of the Sarbanes-Oxley Act, the report on internal controls was a unique requirement of governmental auditing. GAAS only require reportable conditions (including material weaknesses) relative to internal controls to be disclosed and then only to an audit committee or, in its absence, the board of directors and/or appropriate management levels. Further, while the AICPA's GAAS state that written communication is preferable, this is not a requirement as long as the verbal communication is documented in the workpapers. Such practices, however, with respect to reporting on controls, are not acceptable when auditing a federal entity.

The second reporting standard of *Government Auditing Standards* requires that when providing an audit opinion or a disclaimer of an audit opinion on financial statements, auditors should include in their report on the financial statements either:

- A description of the scope of the auditors' testing of internal control over financial reporting and compliance with laws, regulations, and provisions of contracts or grant agreements and the results of those tests or an opinion, if sufficient work was performed.
- A reference to the separate report(s) containing that information. If auditors report separately, the opinion or disclaimer should contain a reference to the separate report containing this information and state that the separate report is an integral part of the audit and should be considered in assessing the results of the audit.

Further, OMB Bulletin 01-02 sets forth these requirements for the auditor's internal control report required in relation to a financial statements audit of a federal entity:

- The auditor's report must contain a statement that, in connection with the financial statement audit of the agency, the auditor:
  - Obtained an understanding of the design of internal controls
  - Determined whether the controls were operational and
  - Performed tests of internal controls.

- The auditor's report must contain a statement, with respect to the performance measures included in the MD&A, that the auditor obtained an understanding of the design of internal controls related to management's existence and completeness assertions and determined whether they had been placed in operation.

- The auditor's report must contain a definition of the scope of the tests performed and either an opinion on internal control or (as is the more common practice) a disclaimer of opinion and the reasons an unqualified audit opinion is not rendered.
- The auditor's report must contain a description of reportable conditions and material weaknesses identified during the audit, including the identification (if applicable) of material weaknesses that were not included in the auditee's reporting required under the Federal Managers' Financial Integrity Act.
- The auditor's report must contain a reference to the issuance of a separate management letter (if applicable).

Reportable conditions are matters coming to the auditor's attention that, in the auditor's judgment, should be communicated to management because they represent significant deficiencies in the design or operation of the internal control structure, which may adversely affect the organization's ability to meet the objectives identified in federal regulations, including OMB Bulletin 01-02.

A *material weakness* in the internal control structure is a reportable condition in which the design or operation of one or more of the internal control structure elements does not reduce to a relatively low level the risk that errors or irregularities in amounts that would be material in relation to the financial statements being audited may occur and not be detected within a timely period by employees in the normal course of performing their assigned functions.

With respect to both *reportable conditions* and *material weaknesses*, auditors must ensure that the applied definitions are required to be employed by the conditions or auditing standards noted in the audit engagement contract. At times, the applied definitions related to these circumstances have varied among Congress (in its laws), OMB (in its circulars and bulletins relating to federal audits), GAO (in its guidance and auditing standards), and the Committee of Sponsoring Organizations (COSO) *Internal Control—Integrated Framework* of the Treadway Commission, that has been adopted by the federal government as guidance for its practices.

Nature and Content of the Audit Report on Federal Agency Controls

The auditor's report on internal controls should include each of the elements discussed below.

Introductory paragraph. The initial paragraph of the auditor's report on an agency's internal controls must state that an audit was made of the agency's principal financial statements as of and for the fiscal years audited and that the auditor has issued an audit report thereon, citing the date of that audit report. The auditor must report that the audit was conducted in accordance with the AICPA's GAAS; the standards applicable to financial audits contained in *Government Auditing Standards*, issued by the Comptroller General of the United States; and the OMB's applicable circulars and bulletins.

Reference to the fact that the auditor audited the principal financial statements is necessary since the tests of controls are made in conjunction with a financial audit that must meet several other federal audit criteria, which are highlighted. In a sense, the audit report on internal controls is a by-product of tests and audit procedures employed during the overall audit of the federal entity's financial statements. It is important to understand that a separate audit was not made, nor was a separate examination undertaken of a federal entity's controls in order to comply with this Government Auditing Standard. All of GAO's standards require that there be a separate reporting on the tests conducted of controls and the results of those tests.

Scope paragraph. The auditor is required to mention that when planning and performing the financial statement audit, the agency's internal control over financial reporting was considered by (1) obtaining an understanding of the agency's internal control, (2) determining whether internal controls had been placed in operation, (3) evaluating and assessing control risk, and (4) performing tests of controls in order to determine the nature, timing, and extent of the auditing procedures applied in the audit for the purpose of expressing an opinion on the financial statements. Auditors are permitted to limit internal control testing to those controls necessary to achieve the internal control objectives described in OMB Bulletin 01-02.

Although not stated in the paragraph, these reasons for testing an agency's financial controls are the same for which controls are examined in audits that comply with the AICPA's GAAS. Also not stated in the controls report is the fact that no specific audit or special examination is required to be made of the entity's controls, separate from tests made to audit the agency's financial statements. The controls information reported on is data that is compiled in conjunction with the audit of the financial statements.

Assurance and disclaimer paragraphs. These paragraphs of the report on internal controls contain comments on limitations of tests performed and disclaimers to the effect that no audit opinion is provided on an agency's controls. Some of the more common language includes:

- We did not test all internal controls relevant to operating objectives, as broadly defined by the Federal Managers' Financial Integrity Act of 1982, such as those controls relevant to ensuring efficient operations.
- The objective of our audit was not to provide assurance on internal control, and consequently, we do not provide an opinion on internal control.
- The auditor's consideration of the internal control over financial reporting would not necessarily disclose all matters in the internal control over financial reporting that might be reportable conditions.[2]
- Because of inherent limitations in internal controls, misstatements, losses, or noncompliance may nevertheless occur and not be detected.

In these paragraphs, more than one statement is made to the effect that the current objective of testing controls is not to provide an assurance or an audit opinion on internal controls. However, if the auditor notes significant weaknesses when testing internal controls as part of the audit of the financial statements, these deficiencies must be described and reported in the auditor's report on internal controls.

---

[2] *Under standards issued by the AICPA, reportable conditions are matters coming to our attention relating to significant deficiencies in the design or operation of the internal control that, in our judgment, could adversely affect the agency's ability to record, process, summarize, and report financial data consistent with assertions by management in the financial statements.*

Government Auditing Standards require that these control deficiencies be reported, even though the conditions may have been immediately corrected by the agency. In contrast, if similar control deficiencies were noted in an audit of a private sector entity, the AICPA's GAAS would not require the auditor to make a reporting in the audit report.

As noted in earlier chapters, there is currently no requirement by Congress, OMB, or GAO that an opinion on the effectiveness of a federal agency's internal controls over financial reporting be issued. However, partly as a result of the Sarbanes-Oxley Act, this is an issue under close scrutiny by federal managers, oversight agencies, Congress, and the executive branch (see earlier discussion on revised A-123 guidance).

AUDITOR'S REPORT ON COMPLIANCE

With respect to the auditor's report on a federal agency's compliance with laws and regulations, the auditor must look to OMB, rather than the AICPA or GAO, for guidance. OMB Bulletin 01-02 sets forth these requirements for the internal control report:

- The auditor must report events of noncompliance with laws and regulations disclosed by the audit (unless deemed inconsequential by the auditor).
- The auditor must report noncompliance with federal internal control requirements including applicable provisions of the Federal Managers' Financial Integrity Act.
- The auditor must report on the scope of tests performed and provide either an audit opinion on compliance or (as is the more common practice) a disclaimer of an audit opinion.

In connection with noncompliance with the Federal Managers' Financial Integrity Act, the auditor's report should:

- Group findings together based on the three Federal Managers' Financial Integrity Act requirements that federal agencies comply with:
  - Federal financial management systems requirements
  - Federal applicable accounting standards
  - US Standard General Ledger at the transaction level
- Identify the entity or organization responsible for the noncompliance.
- Describe the noncompliance, disclosing nature, extent, probable cause of noncompliance, and relevant comments from management and other appropriate personnel.
- Provide recommendations including an implementation timetable.

AUDIT REPORT ON COMPLIANCE

Special, Additional Audit Report

An auditor's report on compliance with laws and regulations that could have a direct and material effect on the financial statements is not a requirement for conformance with the AICPA's GAAS. Like the report on internal controls, this report is another distinguishing criterion imposed by *Government Auditing Standards.* Only *Government Auditing Standards* require the auditor to report on the results of tests of compliance with laws and regulations.

The second GAGAS reporting standard states that when providing an opinion or disclaimer on financial statements, auditors should include in their report on the financial statements either:

1. A description of the scope of the auditors' testing of internal control over financial reporting and compliance with laws, regulations, and provisions of contracts or grant agreements and the results of those tests or an opinion, if sufficient work was performed

or

2. A reference to the separate report(s) containing that information. If auditors report separately, the opinion or disclaimer should contain a reference to the separate report containing this information and state that the separate report is an integral part of the audit and should be considered in assessing the results of the audit.

The standards of both the AICPA and GAO require the testing of any transaction (whether laws, regulations, contracts, grant agreements, financial covenants, etc.) that could have a direct and material effect on the financial statements. However, only GAO's *Government Auditing Standards* require the auditor to report on the fact that tests were made for compliance.

Nature of Report on Tests for Compliance

The auditor's report on compliance with laws and regulations should include each of the elements discussed below.

Introductory paragraph. Reference is made to the audited principal financial statements in the introductory paragraph, as tests for compliance with laws and regulations are typically made in conjunction with an audit of an agency's financial statements. In a sense, this audit report, like the earlier report on controls, is a by-product of tests and audit procedures employed during the overall audit of the federal entity's financial statements. To comply with *Government Auditing Standards*, a separate audit need not be made, nor a separate examination undertaken, to test a federal entity's compliance with laws and regulations that could have a direct and material effect on the financial statements. *Government Auditing Standards* require that there be a separate reporting of the tests made and of the results of those tests.

Scope paragraph. To comply with GAO's standards, the auditor must report on the tests performed relative to the entity's compliance with provisions of laws and regulations, noncompliance with which could have a direct and material effect on the determination of financial statement amounts and regulations of OMB Bulletin 01-02, as well as requirements referred to in the Federal Financial Management Improvement Act.

Assurance, disclaimer paragraphs. In the compliance report, the auditor disclaims an audit opinion and audit assurances with respect to:

- Compliance with certain provisions of laws and regulations stating that an audit opinion on compliance was not an objective of the financial statement audit.
- The auditor notes that tests were not made in compliance with all laws and regulations applicable to the federal entity.

Alternatively, though, the auditor is required to provide an audit assurance (a positive assurance) on the results of these tests. For example, this assurance might read:

*The results of our tests of compliance with the laws and regulations...disclosed no instances of noncompliance with the laws and regulations that are required to be reported under **Government Auditing Standards** and OMB Bulletin No. 01-02.*

Concurrently, though, the auditor provides a disclaimer:

Providing an opinion on compliance with certain provisions of laws and regulations was not an objective of our audit and, accordingly, we do not express such an opinion.

As a matter of practice, both the report on compliance and the report on internal control should include management's responses indicating concurrence or disagreement and, when applicable, future corrective efforts.

The issuance of a combined auditor's report encompassing all three previously discussed reports is also acceptable.

MANAGEMENT LETTERS

The management letters transmitted by the auditor to the auditee may cover any areas identified during the audit that need not be disclosed in the report on internal controls, but where in the auditor's opinion opportunities for improvements in internal controls and/or operating efficiency exist.

SPECIAL-PURPOSE REPORTS

The Department of the Treasury is responsible for the preparation of the consolidated financial statements of the executive branch of the United States Government. In July 2004, OMB amended Bulletin 01-02 to require those agencies significant to the preparation of the financial report of the US government to submit special-purpose financial statements to the Treasury Department.

The special-purpose financial statements include reclassified balance sheets, statements of net cost and changes in net position, and accompanying notes, and are designed to facilitate the government-wide financial statement consolidation process at the Treasury. The audit scope for these agencies must be designed to ensure that the statements of these agencies are reclassified in accordance with the Treasury's requirement. A sample report included in the July amendment is presented in the appendix to this chapter. The reports on financial statements, internal controls, and compliance with laws and regulations may be combined in one report.

APPENDIX

ILLUSTRATIONS OF AUDITORS' REPORTS

This appendix includes illustrations of selected auditors' reports issued in connection with audits of federal agencies. The illustration of the auditor's opinion on the basic financial statements reproduces an actual report issued to a federal agency (with the name of the agency deleted). The remaining reports were reproduced from OMB's Bulletin 01-02, *Audits of Federal Financial Statements* (as revised).

The reports are as follows:

1. Independent auditor's opinion on financial statements
2. Independent auditor's report on internal controls
3. Independent auditor's report on compliance with laws and regulations
4. Independent auditor's report special-purpose financial statements.

Illustration 1. Independent Auditor's Opinion on Financial Statements

We have audited the accompanying consolidated balance sheets of the [*agency*] as of September 30, 2004, and 2003, and the related consolidated statements of net costs, changes in net position and financing, and combined statement of budgetary resources for the year then ended. These consolidated financial statements are the responsibility of the [*agency*]'s management. Our responsibility is to express an opinion on these consolidated financial statements based on our audit.

We conducted our audit in accordance with auditing standards generally accepted in the United States of America and the standards applicable to financial audits contained in *Government Auditing Standards* issued by the Comptroller General of the United States. Those standards require that we plan and perform the audit to obtain reasonable assurance about whether the financial statements are free of material misstatement. An audit includes examining, on a test basis, evidence supporting the amounts and disclosures in the financial statements. An audit also includes assessing the accounting principles used and significant estimates made by management, as well as evaluating the overall financial statement presentation. We believe that our audit provides a reasonable basis for our opinion.

In our opinion, the consolidated financial statements referred to above present fairly, in all material respects, the financial position of the [*agency*] as of September 30, 2004, and 2003, and its net costs, changes in net position, budgetary resources, and financing for the years then ended in conformity with accounting principles generally accepted in the United States of America.

Our audit was conducted for the purpose of forming an opinion on the consolidated financial statements referred to in the first paragraph. The information in the Management's Discussion and Analysis and the Stewardship Report is not a required part of the [*agency*]'s consolidated financial statements, but is considered supplementary information required by OMB Bulletin 01-09, *Form and Content of Agency Financial Statements*. We have applied certain limited procedures, which consisted principally of inquiries of management regarding the methods of measurement and presentation of this information; however, we did not audit this information and we express no opinion on it.

In accordance with *Government Auditing Standards*, we have also issued reports dated [*report date*] on our consideration of the [*agency*]'s internal control over financial reporting and its compliance with certain provisions of laws and regulations. Those reports are an integral part of an audit performed in accordance with *Government Auditing Standards*, and should be read in conjunction with this report in considering the results of our audit.

Signed

Date [End of fieldwork date]

Illustration 2. Independent Auditor's Report On Internal Control

[*Addressee*]

We have audited the Principal Statements (hereinafter referred to as "financial statements") of [*name of federal agency*] as of and for the year ended September 30, XXXX, and have issued our report thereon dated _____. We conducted our audit in accordance with generally accepted auditing standards; the standards applicable to financial audits contained in *Government Auditing Standards*, issued by the Comptroller General of the United States; and, Office of Management and Budget (OMB) Bulletin 01-02, *Audit Requirements for Federal Financial Statements*.

In planning and performing our audit, we considered [*name of federal agency*]'s internal control over financial reporting by obtaining an understanding of the agency's internal control, determined whether internal controls had been placed in operation, assessed control risk, and performed tests of controls in order to determine our auditing procedures for the purpose of expressing our opinion on the financial statements. We limited our internal control testing to those controls necessary to achieve the objectives described in OMB Bulletin 01-02. We did not test all internal controls relevant to operating objectives as broadly defined by the Federal Managers' Financial Integrity Act of 1982, such as those controls relevant to ensuring efficient operations. The objective of our audit was not to provide assurance on internal control. Consequently, we do not provide an opinion on internal control.

Our consideration of the internal control over financial reporting would not necessarily disclose all matters in the internal control over financial reporting that might be reportable conditions. Under standards issued by the American Institute of Certified Public Accountants, reportable conditions are matters coming to our attention relating to significant deficiencies in the design or operation of the internal control that, in our judgment, could adversely affect the agency's ability to record, process, summarize, and report financial data consistent with the assertions by management in the financial statements. Material weaknesses are reportable conditions in which the design or operation of one or more of the internal control components does not reduce to a relatively low level the risk that misstatements in amounts that would be material in relation to the financial statements being audited may occur and not be detected within a timely period by employees in the normal course of performing their assigned functions. Because of inherent limitations in internal controls, misstatements, losses, or noncompliance may nevertheless occur and not be detected. However, we noted certain matters [discussed in the following paragraphs or accompanying schedule] involving the internal control and its operation that we consider to be reportable conditions [*and material weaknesses*].

> *If none of the reportable conditions is believed to be a material weakness, the report should state the following: "However, none of the reportable conditions is believed to be a material weakness."*

> *If no reportable conditions were noted during the audit, the report should state the following: "However, we noted no matters involving the internal control and its operation that we considered to be material weaknesses as defined above."*

In addition, we considered [*name of federal agency*]'s internal control over Required Supplementary Stewardship Information by obtaining an understanding of the agency's internal control, determined whether these internal controls had been placed in operation, assessed control risk, and performed tests of controls as required by OMB Bulletin 01-02 and not to provide assurance on these internal controls. Accordingly, we do not provide an opinion on such controls.

Finally, with respect to internal control related to performance measures reported in [*refer to section of financial statement or accountability report*], we obtained an understanding of the design of significant internal controls relating to the existence and completeness assertions, as required by OMB Bulletin 01-02. Our procedures were not designed to provide assurance on internal control over reported performance measures, and, accordingly, we do not provide an opinion on such controls.

> *If conditions came to the auditor's attention that in his or her judgment represent significant deficiencies in the design or operation of internal control over performance measures, which could adversely affect the agency's ability to collect, process, record, and summarize performance information and report performance measures in accordance with management's criteria, the following*

sentence should be added to the foregoing paragraph. "However, we noted certain significant deficiencies in internal control over reported performance measures [discussed in the following paragraphs or accompanying schedule] that, in our judgment, could adversely affect the agency's ability to collect, process, record, and summarize performance information and report performance measures in accordance with management's criteria."

This report is intended solely for the information and use of the management of [*name of federal agency*], OMB and Congress, and is not intended to be and should not be used by anyone other than these specified parties.

[*Signature*]
[*Date*]

Illustration 3.   Independent Auditor's Report on Compliance with Laws and Regulations

[Addressee]

We have audited the Principal Statements (hereinafter referred to as "financial statements") of [*name of federal agency*] as of and for the year ended September 30, XXXX, and have issued our report thereon dated _____. We conducted our audit in accordance with: generally accepted auditing standards; the standards applicable to financial audits contained in *Government Auditing Standards*, issued by the Comptroller General of the United States; and, Office of Management and Budget (OMB) Bulletin 01-02, *Audit Requirements for Federal Financial Statements*.

The management of [*name of federal agency*] is responsible for complying with laws and regulations applicable to the agency. As part of obtaining reasonable assurance about whether the agency's financial statements are free of material misstatement, we performed tests of its compliance with certain provisions of laws and regulations, noncompliance with which could have a direct and material effect on the determination of financial statement amounts, and certain other laws and regulations specified in OMB Bulletin 01-02, including the requirements referred to in the Federal Financial Management Improvement Act (FFMIA) of 1996. We limited our tests of compliance to these provisions and we did not test compliance with all laws and regulations applicable to [*name of agency*].

The results of our tests of compliance with the laws and regulations described in the preceding paragraph exclusive of FFMIA10 disclosed instances of noncompliance with the following laws and regulations that are required to be reported under Government Auditing Standards and OMB Bulletin 01-02, which are described below.

Describe any instances of noncompliance required to be reported and list laws and regulations for which noncompliance was disclosed exclusive of FFMIA [or provide such information in an accompanying schedule]

The results of our tests of compliance disclosed no instances of noncompliance with other laws and regulations discussed in the preceding paragraph exclusive of FFMIA that are required to be reported under *Government Auditing Standards* or OMB Bulletin 01-02.

Under FFMIA, we are required to report whether the agency's financial management systems substantially comply with the federal financial management systems requirements, applicable Federal accounting standards, and the United States Government Standard General Ledger at the transaction level. To meet this requirement, we performed tests of compliance with FFMIA section 803(a) requirements.

The results of our tests disclosed no instances in which the agency's financial management systems did not substantially comply with the three requirements discussed in the preceding paragraph.

[*If the results of tests disclosed that the agency's systems did not substantially comply with one or more of the foregoing requirements, the preceding sentence should be replaced with the following:*

The results of our tests disclosed instances, described below (or described in an accompanying schedule), where the agency's financial management systems did not substantially comply with [specify which of the three requirements where a lack of substantial compliance was found, e.g.

federal financial management systems requirements and the US Government Standard General Ledger at the transaction level].

[If the results of the audit disclosed no lack of substantial compliance with one or two of the foregoing requirements, add the following:

The results of our tests disclosed no instances in which the agency's financial management systems did not substantially comply with [specify which of the three requirements where a lack of substantial compliance was not found, e.g., applicable federal accounting standards].

In addition, when tests disclosed that the agency's systems did not substantially comply with the foregoing requirements, the auditor's report on compliance or an accompanying schedule should provide the following information as required by FFMIA and paragraph 7.c.(3)(c) of this Bulletin. Findings should be grouped together based on the requirement they relate to (i.e., federal financial management systems requirements, applicable Federal accounting standards, or the US Government Standard General Ledger).

1. *The entity or organization responsible for the financial management systems that were found not to comply with the requirements.*
2. *All facts pertaining to the noncompliance, including: (a) the nature and extent of the noncompliance, (b) the primary reason or cause of the noncompliance, and (c) any relevant comments from reporting entity management or employees responsible for the noncompliance.*
3. *Recommended remedial actions and the time frames to implement such actions.]*

Providing an opinion on compliance with certain provisions of laws and regulations was not an objective of our audit and, accordingly, we do not express such an opinion.

This report is intended solely for the information and use of the management of [*name of federal agency*], OMB and Congress, and is not intended to be and should not be used by anyone other than these specified parties.

[*Signature*]
[*Date*]

Illustration 4. Independent Auditor's Report on Special-Purpose Financial Statements

We have audited the accompanying reclassified balance sheet as of September 30, [*insert year*] and the related reclassified statements of net cost and changes in net position for the year then ended (hereinafter referred to as the special-purpose financial statements) contained in the special-purpose closing package of [*name of federal agency*]. These special-purpose financial statements are the responsibility of [*name of federal agency*]'s management. Our responsibility is to express an opinion on these special-purpose financial statements based on our audit.

We conducted our audit in accordance with auditing standards generally accepted in the United States of America and the standards applicable to financial audits contained in *Government Auditing Standards*, issued by the Comptroller General of the United States; and, Office of Management and Budget (OMB) Bulletin 01-02, *Audit Requirements for Federal Financial Statements*. Those standards require that we plan and perform the audit to obtain reasonable assurance about whether the special-purpose financial statements are free of material misstatement. An audit includes examining, on a test basis, evidence supporting the amounts and disclosures in the special-purpose financial statements. An audit also includes assessing the accounting principles used and significant estimates made by management, as well as evaluating the overall special-purpose financial statement presentation. We believe that our audit provides a reasonable basis for our opinion.

The accompanying special-purpose financial statements and accompanying notes contained in the special-purpose closing package have been prepared for the purpose of complying with the requirements of the US Department of the Treasury's Financial Manual (TFM) Volume I, Part 2, Chapter 4700, as described in note X, solely for the purpose of providing financial information to the US Department of the Treasury and US General Accounting Office to use in preparing and auditing the financial report of the US Government, and are not intended to be a complete presentation of [*name of federal agency*]'s financial statements.

In our opinion, the special-purpose financial statements referred to above present fairly, in all material respects, the financial position of [*name of federal agency*] as of September 30, [*insert year*], and its net costs and changes in net position for the year then ended in conformity with accounting principles generally accepted in the United States of America and the presentation pursuant to the requirements of the TFM Chapter 4700.

The information included in the other data is presented for the purpose of additional analysis and is not a required part of the special-purpose financial statements, but is supplementary information required by the TFM Chapter 4700. We have applied certain limited procedures, which consisted principally of inquiries of management regarding methodology and presentation of this information. We also reviewed such information for consistency with the related information presented in [*name of federal agency*]'s financial statements. However, we did not audit this information, and accordingly, we express no opinion on it.

In accordance with *Government Auditing Standards* and OMB Bulletin 01-02, we have also issued reports dated [*insert date*] on our consideration of [*name of federal agency*]'s internal control over financial reporting and its compliance with certain provisions of laws and regulations. Those reports are an integral part of an audit of general-purpose financial statement reporting performed in accordance with *Government Auditing Standards* and OMB Bulletin 01-02, and should be read in conjunction with this report in considering the results of our audit.

In planning and performing our audit of the special-purpose financial statements, we also considered [*name of federal agency*]'s internal control over the financial reporting process for the special-purpose financial statements and compliance with the TFM Chapter 4700. Management is responsible for establishing and maintaining internal control over financial reporting, including other data, and for complying with laws and regulations, including compliance with the TFM Chapter 4700 requirements.

Our consideration of internal control over the financial reporting process for the special-purpose financial statements would not necessarily disclose all matters in the internal control over the financial reporting process that might be reportable conditions. Under standards issued by the American Institute of Certified Public Accountants, reportable conditions are matters coming to our attention relating to significant deficiencies in the design or operation of the internal control over financial reporting that, in our judgment, could adversely affect the [*name of federal agency*]'s ability to record, process, summarize, and report financial data consistent with the assertions made by management in the special-purpose financial statements. Material weaknesses are reportable conditions in which the design or operation of one or more of the internal control components does not reduce to a relatively low level the risk that misstatements, in amounts that would be material in relation to the special-purpose financial statements being audited, may occur and not be detected within a timely period by employees in the normal course of performing their assigned functions.

We found no material weaknesses in internal control over the financial reporting process for the special-purpose financial statements, and our tests of compliance with the TFM Chapter 4700 requirements disclosed no instances of noncompliance that are required to be reported under *Government Auditing Standards* and OMB Bulletin 01-02. However, providing opinions on internal control over the financial reporting process for the special-purpose financial statements or on compliance with the TFM Chapter 4700 requirements were not objectives of our audit of the special-purpose financial statements and, accordingly, we do not express such opinions. This report is intended solely for the information and use of [*name of federal agency*], the US Department of the Treasury, the Office of Management and Budget and the US General Accounting Office in connection with the preparation and audit of the Financial Report of the US Government and is not intended to be and should not be used by anyone other than these specified parties.

[*Signature*]
[*Date*]

PART IV

Nature of Selected Federal Audits

13 SINGLE AUDITS

ONE AUDIT, ONCE A YEAR, BY ONE AUDITOR

Beginning in the 1950s with the growth of federal programs, problems arose involving the auditing of state and local governmental entities, academic institutions, and other organizations receiving federal financial assistance. These problems, which were cataloged in numerous reports and made the subject of several congressional hearings, led ultimately to passage of the Single Audit Act.

By the 1970s, federal agencies felt it necessary to have their own auditors perform federal audits of nonfederal organizations. Audit guides and reporting procedures proliferated to the point that a dozen federal entities had issued more than 100 separate audit guides. Finally, several governors met with the Secretary of the Treasury to protest the considerable resource costs of complying with this duplicative, overlapping, and uncoordinated federal audit approach.[1]

ATTACHMENT P AUDITS OF 1979

In response to the outcry, the Office of Management and Budget (OMB), in October 1979, issued Attachment P to OMB Circular A-102, requiring federal agencies thereafter to adhere to a program of single, organization-wide audits of any governmental entity receiving federal financial assistance. The objective of Attachment P was to significantly reduce or eliminate the thousands of duplicate audits being made on a contract-by-contract and grant-by-grant basis of organizations receiving federal monies. Despite intentions, Attachment P was only moderately successful, and many major federal organizations continued to pursue their individual agency audit practices of past years. A few years later, the GAO reported to Congress that more than 700 federal audits and examinations were conducted of the city of Indianapolis over a five-year period and that less than a half dozen complied with either generally accepted auditing standards (GAAS) or the *Government Auditing Standards*.

SINGLE AUDIT ACT 1984, AMENDED 1996

In October 1984, Congress passed the Single Audit Act, which ordered federal organizations to implement an audit concept whereby only recipients receiving $100,000 or more of federal assistance need undergo an audit each year.[2] This audit

---

[1] *The meeting was convened in November 1975 by William Simon, the then Secretary of the Treasury, with governors of six states and documented in a report entitled "A Report: Federal Government Audits: Abuses and What Corrections Are Needed," November 1975.*

[2] *This dollar threshold has been increased over the years. The most recent change (see OMB Circular, 2003 edition) now requires that only entities with federal expenditures of more than $500,000 in a year need undergo a single audit.*

would be conducted by a single auditor, and the results of this single audit would be shared with all organizations having a financial interest in that recipient. Congress declared that audits made in accordance with the Single Audit Act "shall be in lieu of any financial audit of federal awards which a non-federal entity is required to undergo under any other federal law or regulation." Within just one year, OMB reported an enormous reduction in federal audits and a change in the historical focus of federal oversight. This eliminated considerable financial and human resource costs of thousands of duplicative and uncoordinated federal audits and reviews.

By 1996, a consensus was reached: the Single Audit Act had instituted an efficient and effective audit concept, contributing to an enormous reduction in audit overlaps and duplications in comparison to the earlier federal audit approach. The Single Audit Act required a comprehensive annual audit comprised of:

- A financial statement audit of the federal recipient in its entirety
- Audit tests and reports, *entity-wide* and for *major federal programs*, on the entity's financial controls and the entity's controls to manage the federal assistance programs
- Audit tests and reports on compliance with laws and regulations *entity-wide* and separate audit opinions on compliance with laws and regulations governing *each major federal program*
- An integrated audit that complies with the GAAS of the Association of Independent Certified Public Accountants (AICPA), the *Government Auditing Standards* of the GAO, and the audit procedures and reporting requirements in OMB Circular A-133, *Audits of State and Local Governments and Nonprofit Organizations* (2003 edition), last amended in June 2003[3]

The Single Audit Act, as contemplated by Congress and as used by federal, state, and local governments, is viewed as an essential management and monitoring tool. The single audit is the only evaluation, examination, audit, and communication on performance and management that the majority of organizations that operate federal assistance programs will ever undergo.

FEDERAL AUDIT GUIDANCE: OMB REGULATIONS, COMPLIANCE SUPPLEMENT, AICPA STANDARD

The single audit is a comprehensive annual evaluation (including an audit of the annual financial statements, expenditures of federal assistance programs, and tests and reporting of compliance with laws and regulations and internal controls) of state and local governments and nonprofit organizations receiving federal financial assistance. OMB, in consultation with federal inspectors general, has provided to the audit profession extensive, detailed guidance, compiled in a single document, the

---

[3] *When first enacted, the Single Audit Act of 1984 was implemented through two separate OMB circulars: OMB Circular A-128, **Audits of State and Local Governments**, and OMB Circular A-133, **Institutions of Higher Education and Nonprofit Entities**. In 1997, OMB Circulars A-128 and A-133 were replaced and superceded by a single circular, titled OMB Circular A-133, **Audits of State and Local Governments and Nonprofit Organizations**, last amended in June 2003.*

OMB *Compliance Supplement* (hereafter called the *Supplement*). Without the *Supplement*, auditors would individually have to:

- Determine the important applicable federal audit compliance requirements.
- Research the many laws and regulations for each federal assistance program.
- "Guess" at those laws and regulations that could have a direct and material effect on each federal program.
- Identify the audit objectives and procedures to be applied.
- Define the audit report and any other reports that would best convey the results of the single audit to each report user.

OMB has decreed that the use of its *Supplement* is mandatory; adherence to its guidance will satisfy the audit requirements of OMB Circular A-133. The *Supplement* describes and defines the nature of the audit required by the Single Audit Act and OMB Circular A-133. Importantly, it includes suggested audit criteria and audit procedures for conduct of single audits.[4] The *Supplement* is a synopsis of nationwide audit requirements and other federal reporting policies (by the Congress), presidential executive orders (by the White House), government-wide regulations (by OMB), and program rules and regulations (by individual federal departments and agencies).

Auditor judgment must be applied to determine whether the audit procedures suggested in the *Supplement* are sufficient to achieve audit objectives, or whether additional or alternative audit procedures are needed. For this reason, auditors should *not* (OMB's emphasis) consider the *Supplement* to be a "safe harbor" for identifying audit procedures to apply in any particular engagement. However, OMB does state that an auditor can consider the *Supplement* to be a "safe harbor" for the identification of compliance requirements to be tested for programs included in the *Supplement* if:

- The auditor performs reasonable procedures to ensure that the requirements of the *Supplement* are current and to determine whether there are any additional provisions of the contract and grant agreements that should be covered by a single audit.
- The auditor updates or augments the requirements contained in the *Supplement*, as appropriate.

Clearly, the *Supplement* must be understood and utilized in a successful single audit. In addition, the *Supplement* provides comprehensive guidance and relevant compliance issues that must be examined during the course of the single audit. However, in the course of a comprehensive single audit or, for that matter, for audits of individual federal contracts and grants, auditors should expend the effort to acquire a working knowledge of several OMB regulations, upon which the *Supplement* guidance is based. These regulations include:

- For a detailed delineation of the single audit requirements:

---

[4] *Access to a copy of the OMB **Compliance Supplement** can be obtained via the Internet at **omb.gov**.*

- OMB Circular A-133, *Audits of States, Local Governments, and Nonprofit Organizations* (2003 edition)
- For guidance on allowable, unallowable, and indirect costs:
  - OMB Circular A-21, *Cost Principles for Educational Institutions* (2004 edition)
  - OMB Circular A-87, *Cost Principles for State, Local and Indian Tribal Governments* (2004 edition)
  - OMB Circular A-122, *Cost Principles for Nonprofit Organizations* (2004 edition)
- For identification and code of federal assistance programs:
  - OMB Circular A-89, *Catalog of Federal Domestic Assistance* (1984 edition)
- For administrative and management guidance of federal assistance programs:
  - OMB Circular A-102, *Grants and Cooperative Agreements with States and Local Governments* (1997 edition)
  - OMB Circular A-110, *Uniform Administrative Requirements for Grants and Other Agreements with Institutions of Higher Education, Hospitals and Other Nonprofit Organizations* (1999 edition)

These circulars describe selected cost items including: allowable and unallowable costs; methodologies for calculating and allocating the indirect costs of nonfederal contractors and grantees; and federal policy for the management and administration of most federal assistance programs, whether contract or grant-type programs.

This federal policy guidance is supplemented by the considerable relevant audit guidance of the AICPA in its publications, such as:

- AICPA Audit and Accounting Guide, *Audits of State and Local Governments* (GASB 34 edition), historically updated for conforming federal and other changes each June
- AICPA Audit Guide, *Audits of States, Local Governments, and Not-for-Profit Organizations Receiving Federal Awards,* historically updated for conforming federal and other changes each June

SINGLE AUDITS

The Single Audit Act established policy for audits by all federal departments and agencies for any federal financial assistance program awarded to state, local governments, the territories of the United States, Indian tribal nations, and nonprofit organizations. OMB, the delegated procedural authority for these audits, has issued considerable guidance to assist nonfederal auditors in their conduct of the desired audits.

Definitions

Congress, by the Single Audit Act, and OMB, in Circular A-133, provided several interpretative definitions on what should be audited, what should be reported, and the types of reports that should be submitted in order to comply with the Single Audit Act. Key terms and distinctions essential to understanding the single audit concept include:

- *Federal awards:* Federal financial assistance and federal cost-reimbursement contracts that nonfederal entities receive directly from federal awarding agencies or indirectly from pass-through entities
- *Federal financial assistance:* Assistance that nonfederal entities receive or administer in the form of grants, loans, loan guarantees, property, cooperative agreements, interest subsidies, insurance, food commodities, direct appropriations, or other assistance; but not amounts received as reimbursement for services rendered to individuals in accordance with guidance by OMB
- *Federal program:* Federal awards and financial assistance that have been assigned a number in the OMB *Catalog of Federal Domestic Assistance* (*CFDA*) or encompassed within a group of *CFDA* numbers
- *Audit finding:* A deficiency that the auditor is required by the act to report in the Schedule of Findings and Questioned Costs
- *Questioned costs:* A cost that is questioned by the auditor because of an audit finding:
  - That results from a violation or possible violation of a provision of a law, regulation, contract, grant, cooperative agreement, or other agreement, or document governing the use of federal funds, including funds used to match federal funds
  - Where the costs, at the time of audit, are not supported by adequate documentation or
  - Where the costs incurred appear unreasonable and do not reflect the actions a prudent person would take given the circumstances
- *Major program* (also *Type A program*): Each individual federal program whose expenditures in a single year exceed the larger of $300,000 or 3%, for those entities expending less than $100 million, of the total federal expenditures for that nonfederal entity. Generally, every major program must be audited and reported on. Other programs (Type B programs) are only required to be audited if they meet certain criteria (e.g., if classified as risk).
- *50% rule:* When the total expenditures for a nonfederal entity's Type A major programs are less than 50% of the nonfederal entity's total expenditures of all federal awards, the auditor must select, test, and report on additional programs (i.e., the Type B programs) as major programs to achieve audit coverage of at least 50% of the total federal expenditures.

  When calculating the 50% threshold, the inclusion of large loans and loan guarantees cannot result in the exclusion of other programs as Type A or major programs. That is, the distortive amounts of large loans and loan guarantees must be excluded from this calculation. However, these large loans and loan guarantees still must be audited and reported if they otherwise meet the dollar criteria of a major program.

Required Audit Reports

The Single Audit Act, in combination with *Government Auditing Standards* (which incorporate, by reference, the AICPA's GAAS) and OMB Circular A-133, the implementing regulation for the Single Audit Act, requires several audit reports if the audit is to comply with the full intent of the law. The complete report for a single audit could include a dozen or more individual reports. The list identifies the required reports.

Audit Reports for Single Audits

Two Financial Audit Reports

1. Entity-wide financial statements—an audit opinion
2. Schedule of federal expenditures—"in relation to" audit opinion

Two Internal Controls Reports

3. Narrative report—on entity-wide controls
4. Narrative report—on controls for federal programs

Two Compliance Reports

5. Entity-wide—assurance-type report on compliance
6. Federal programs—opinion compliance for each major federal award/ program

Other Reports

7. Schedule of follow-up on prior audit findings—narrative report on observations
8. Data collection form—checklist and other information OMB requires of auditor and auditee
9. Corrective action plan—prepared by auditee, submitted with other reports
10. Fraud report—if fraud is indicated or noted by the auditor
11. Schedule of findings and questioned costs
12. Management letter—if one is issued by the auditor

Annual GAAP financial statement. In order to comply with the Single Audit Act, governmental units must undergo annual audits that cover the operations of the entire nonfederal entity. The vast majority of governmental entities annually prepare basic comprehensive financial statements on the basis of generally accepted accounting principles (GAAP) (promulgated by the Governmental Accounting Standards Board) or another comprehensive basis of accounting that at times have been mandated by state law or local government statute.

If unqualified, the auditor's opinion on those statements would read, in part:

In our opinion, the financial statements referred to above, present fairly, in all material respects, the respective financial position of the governmental activities, the business-type activities, the aggregate discretely presented component units, each major fund, and the aggregate remaining fund information of the City and the respective changes in financial position and cash flows...in conformity with generally accepted accounting principles.

Schedule of expenditures of federal awards, financial statement of federal expenditures. In addition to the annual audit of the entity-wide financial statements, the Single Audit Act also states that the auditor must determine whether the schedule of expenditures of federal awards (the schedule), another report required by the act, is presented fairly in all material respects in relation to the financial statements taken as a whole. This schedule identifies each federal award program by name and the Catalog of Federal Domestic Assistance program number and reports the total year's expenditures by the nonfederal entity for each program. The federal government does not prescribe or mandate a basis of accounting for this schedule. However, if the schedule has been prepared on a basis other than that used for the financial statements, this fact must be disclosed.

If unqualified, the auditor's opinion on this schedule would read, in part:

Our audit was conducted for purposes of forming an opinion on the basic financial statements that collectively comprise the City's basic financial statements. The accompanying schedule of expenditures of federal awards is presented for purposes of additional analyses, as required by OMB Circular A-133 and is not a required part of the basic financial statements of the City. Such information has been subjected to the auditing procedures applied by us in the audit of the basic financial statements and, in our opinion, is fairly stated, in all material respects, in relation to the basic financial statements taken as a whole.

Note the auditor does not state that data on this schedule have been audited, per se, but that *in relation to* the auditing procedures applied by the auditor in the audit of the nonfederal entity's basic financial statements, the information on the schedule of expenditures of federal awards is fairly stated in all material respects.

Compliance and controls reports. The first set of compliance and controls reports imposed by the *Government Auditing Standards* require reports to be made on audit tests made of internal controls and audit tests made of compliance with laws, regulations, contracts, and grants, entity-wide, for the organization undergoing audit.

The second reporting standard of the *Government Auditing Standards* requires an auditor, when providing an audit opinion or disclaimer of opinion on financial statements, to include in the audit report either:

1. A description of the scope of the auditor's testing of internal control over financial reporting and compliance with laws, regulations, and provisions of contracts or grant agreements and the results of those tests or an audit opinion, if sufficient work was performed to render an opinion; or
2. If auditors report separately on controls and compliance, the opinion or disclaimer should contain a reference to the separate report containing this information and state that the separate report is an integral part of the audit and should be considered in assessing the results of the audit.

The third *Government Auditing Standards* reporting criteria for financial audits states that auditors should report:

- Deficiencies in internal control considered to be reportable conditions, as defined in AICPA's standards
- All instances of fraud and illegal acts, unless clearly inconsequential

- Significant violations of provisions of contracts or grant agreements and abuse
- In some circumstances, illegal acts, violations or provisions of contracts or grant agreements, and abuse directly to parties external to the audited entity

An auditor's unqualified opinion for tests of entity-wide internal controls and compliance with laws, regulations, and terms of contracts or grant agreements to comply with the *Government Auditing Standards* might read, in part:

Introductory paragraph

We have audited the financial statements of the City as of and for the year ended.... We conducted our audit in accordance with auditing standards generally accepted in the United States and standards applicable to financial audits contained in *Government Auditing Standards*, issued by the comptroller general of the United States.

Compliance report

As part of obtaining reasonable assurance about whether the financial statements are free of material misstatements, we performed tests of the City's compliance with laws, regulations, contracts, and grants, noncompliance....Providing an opinion on compliance was not an objective of our audit; accordingly we do not express an opinion on compliance. The results of our tests disclosed no instances of noncompliance that are required to be reported under *Government Auditing Standards*.

Internal control report over financial reporting

In planning and performing our audit, we considered the City's internal control over financial reporting to determine our auditing procedures for purposes of expressing our opinion on the financial statements and not to provide assurance on the internal controls. We noted no matters involving internal controls over financial reporting and its operations that we consider to be material weaknesses.

Single Audit Act reports. The Single Audit Act and the related Circular A-133 reporting requirements mandate that two types of reporting be made: (1) a report on tests of the auditee's controls related to the federal programs; and (2) a report on the auditee's compliance with laws, regulations, contracts, and grants terms applicable to federal programs:

- *Controls over federal awards.* The Single Audit Act and the related OMB Circular A-133 require the auditor to test and report on the auditee's internal controls related to the federal programs. This report must describe the scope of testing made of the internal controls over the federal awards and the results of these tests.
- *Compliance with conditions of federal awards.* For the auditee's controls pertaining to the laws, regulations, specific terms and conditions, and requirements of each major federal program, the auditor must test and report noted deficiencies during tests to:
  - Obtain an understanding of such internal controls.
  - Assess the control risks.
  - Perform tests of the controls unless the controls are deemed to be ineffective.

- Determine whether the nonfederal entity complied with the provisions of laws, regulations, and terms of contract or grants pertaining to federal awards that have a direct and material effect on *each* major program.
- Issue a report, an audit opinion, or disclaimer of an opinion on the entity's compliance with laws, regulations, and contract or grants pertaining to federal awards that have a direct and material effect on *each* major program.

If unqualified, the auditor's reports on the tests of compliance and controls, for single audit purposes, might, in part, read:

Compliance report major federal programs

We have audited the compliance of City with types of compliance requirements in the OMB Circular A-133 Compliance Supplement that are applicable to each of its major federal programs for the year ended.... We conducted our audit of compliance in accordance with the auditing standards generally accepted in the United States, the standards applicable to financial audits contained in *Government Auditing Standards*, issued by the Comptroller General, and OMB Circular A-133. In our opinion, the City complied, in all material respects with the requirements referred to above that are applicable to each of its major federal programs.

Controls report for federal programs:

The management is responsible for establishing and maintaining effective internal control over compliance with requirements of laws, regulations, contracts, and grants applicable to federal programs. In planning and performing our audit, we considered internal control over compliance with requirements that could have a direct and material effect on a major federal program, and for the purpose of expressing our opinion on compliance in accordance with OMB Circular A-133. We noted no matters involving the internal control over compliance and its operations that we consider to be material weaknesses.

Other single audit reports. As part of the report package, additional reports must be prepared by either the auditor or the auditee for an audit to meet the criteria of the Single Audit Act. Brief descriptions of these additional reports follow.

Schedule of prior audit findings. The schedule of prior audit findings is required in order to comply with the Single Audit Act, as well as the second fieldwork audit standard of GAGAS. In support of this reporting, the auditor must perform procedures to assess the reasonableness of the schedule of prior audit findings. This latter schedule, to be prepared by the auditee, is intended to be an accurate summary of prior findings and the current status of any corrective actions taken by the auditee. The auditor must then report, as a current year's audit finding, any material misrepresentations in the auditee's status of prior audit findings.

Data collection form. The auditee is required by the Single Audit Act to submit a data collection form, prepared by a senior auditee representative, summarizing a wide range of information and including representations about the auditee organization. Examples of such information include:

- Type of audit opinion received relative to the financial statements and for each of the major federal programs

- Any reportable conditions and material weaknesses relative to internal controls
- Instances of noncompliance that are material to the financial statements and to major federal programs
- Whether the auditee is a low-risk auditee, as defined by the act
- Whether there were audit findings relative to several specified types of compliance requirements
- Amount of any questioned costs associated with each finding.

The data collection form is prepared by the auditee, but the auditor must sign a statement on the form that attests to the source of the information reported by the auditee.

Corrective action plan. The Single Audit Act requires the auditee, at the completion of the audit, to prepare a corrective action plan that addresses each audit finding, outlining the action planned and the anticipated completion date.

Fraud report. For instances of known fraud, a separate reporting must be made by the auditor unless the fraud is otherwise reported as an audit finding in the schedule of findings and questioned costs.

Schedule of findings and questioned costs. This auditor-prepared schedule has three components including: (1) a summary of the auditor's reported results relative to the financial statements, including results of tests for compliance and controls; (2) findings related to the financial statements that must be reported pursuant to GAGAS; and (3) findings and known questioned costs greater than $10,000 relative to each federal program.

For this report, the auditor must attempt to quantify the *questioned costs* of each finding, which, in addition to the earlier definition, will include:

- Violations of laws, regulations, contracts, and grants related to use of federal funds
- Claimed costs are not supported by adequate documentation
- Costs incurred are unreasonable, that is, costs that would not be consistent with the actions of a prudent person under the same circumstances
- A reporting of *known questioned costs*, that is, specifically identified costs associated with a federal program that are greater than $10,000
- Consideration of the total likely questioned costs (i.e., the auditor's best estimate) when opining on an auditee's compliance with laws, regulations, contracts, and grants

Reportable elements of single audit findings. When reporting audit findings, the auditor must describe each finding in *sufficient detail* for the auditee to prepare a corrective action plan and take corrective action. OMB Circular A-133 and *Government Auditing Standards* have issued interpretative guidance regarding the desired "sufficient detail" that requires the auditor to identify and report, for each finding, the several *elements of a finding,* which include:

- Federal award or program
- Criteria violated (i.e., law, regulation, statute desired)
- Condition found, circumstances disclosed

- Cause—the persuasive evidence responsible for differences between condition and the criteria
- Questioned costs and the basis of computation
- Perspective—prevalence or consequences in relation to total universe, cases examined, dollar quantification, and so on
- Asserted effect of audit deficiency (preferably stated in quantifiable terms)
- Conclusions, when required by the audit objectives or results of the audit
- Recommendations, if warranted, by the auditor that flow logically from the reported findings and conclusions
- Views of responsible auditee officials

Management letter. A *management letter* is a separate communication from the auditor to the auditee regarding internal control issues and deficiencies that were identified during the audit and were of lesser significance than either a reportable condition or material weakness. Issuance of a management letter is the option of the auditor, as dictated by the AICPA's GAAS. However, there is a requirement under *Government Auditing Standards*, which states that a management letter must be issued and that this fact be reported to recipients of the audit report, not just the auditee. The requirement for a management letter appears in the third *Government Auditing* reporting standard:

> *Detected deficiencies, unless clearly inconsequential, in internal controls that are not reportable conditions or material weaknesses and immaterial violations of contract or grants compliance, should be communicated by the auditor in a separate management letter to officials of the auditee.*

SINGLE AUDITS: MANAGEMENT AND COMPLIANCE ASSERTIONS

The AICPA's GAAS require that auditors, in the audit of financial statements, obtain sufficient evidence to provide a reasonable basis for their audit opinion. That "sufficient evidence" is acquired by the application of audit procedures to transactions and account groups to test the five assertions management makes, explicitly or implicitly, when it presents financial statements and financial data for an audit. These five management assertions include statements regarding:

1. *Existence or occurrence:* Did the reported assets and liabilities exist as of a given date? Did the transactions occur?
2. *Completeness:* Have all incurred transactions and effected accounts been presented in the statements and financial data to be examined by the auditor?
3. *Rights and obligations:* Are the rights of the auditee and all obligations due others faithfully reflected in the financial statements or notes accompanying the statements?
4. *Valuation or allocations:* Are the asserted values and financial allocations for assets, liabilities, equity, revenue, and expenses included in the statements and provided financial data at appropriate amounts?

5. *Presentation and disclosure:* Are all components of the financial statements properly classified, described, and disclosed, and are the notes accompanying the financial statements presented in a manner that is not misleading?

Validation of these five management assertions is a requirement of any audit made of a government's financial statements. However, 14 additional management assertions apply to audits of any federal assistance program, and are described next.

Federal regulations implementing the Single Audit Act require the auditor to obtain sufficient evidence of 14 additional compliance assertions that have long been imposed by OMB to provide a reasonable basis for audit opinions and reports related to audits of federal assistance programs. Specific audit guidance is provided by OMB in the *Supplement* that outlines the 14 assertions that must be tested when applicable to the federal programs under audit. These additional federal management assertions relate to:

1. *Allowable activities:* Federal funds may be spent only for activities allowed by federal law.
2. *Allowable, unallowable, indirect costs:* Federal programs may be charged only for allowable costs, as defined by OMB in various cost circulars.
3. *Cash management:* Drawdowns of federal funds may not exceed three working days of cash.
4. *Davis-Bacon Act:* This act requires the payment of "prevailing" wages for construction work on federal programs.
5. *Eligible recipients:* Only recipients designated or identified by federal law are eligible to participate in federally funded programs.
6. *Equipment and real property:* Who holds title and when does title pass for capital assets acquired with federal monies?
7. *Matching level-of-effort contributions*: The timing, amount, type, and form of matching funds must conform to the specific program criteria.
8. *Availability of program funds:* No expenditure may be charged by the auditee to a federal program unless legally available funds are available for that program's purposes.
9. *Procurement, suspension, debarment:* No federal monies may be paid to any entity suspended or debarred by a department or agency of the federal government.
10. *Program income:* This must be deducted or added to funds used for program research or development purposes or to meet a federal fund matching requirement in strict compliance with specific award conditions.
11. Real *property and relocation assistance:* Specific federal guidelines exist with respect to length of occupancy, timing of occupancy, and comparability when federal monies are used to pay cost of relocation of personnel.
12. Reporting: Reports, financial and otherwise, submitted to federal departments and agencies must be tested by the auditor.
13. Monitoring *pass-through entity:* The auditor must determine if periodic assessments are made of nonfederal entities who receive federal funds and pass through the funds to other nonfederal entities. Recipients of "pass-

through" monies must monitor performance of their subrecipients' services, validate that audits are being made, and obtain, review, and act on reports of expenditures received from their subrecipients.

14. Special *tests, special compliance requirements:* Individual federal awardees may require that specific or more tests be made of their programs.

AUDIT METHODOLOGY FOR SINGLE AUDITS

Planning an audit that meets the criteria of the Single Audit Act and *Government Auditing Standards* is planning for an audit that differs in audit emphasis, the nature and depth of items, subjects requiring testing or audit focus, and the extensiveness of the reports that must be compiled and submitted at the conclusion of a single audit. For example, more detailed planning and audit focus is required: (1) to establish limits on what is *material*; (2) in conducting *tests for assessing compliance* with laws and regulations; (3) in testing of controls, *tests for assessing the controls* over federal programs; and (4) when reporting the audit findings under the Single Audit Act.

Exhibit 13.1 is a partial listing of the considerations necessary in the planning of a single audit in conformity with criteria of the Single Audit Act. The appropriateness and sequencing in performing listed tasks must be assessed in relation to the conditions or circumstances of each auditee required to undergo a single audit.

Level of Materiality Different under the Single Audit Concept

The key to planning an audit that conforms to the Single Audit Act is the understanding that all audit tests, audit procedures, and subsequent audit conclusions and reports must be planned in the context of a considerably lower level of materiality. To illustrate, in planning a single audit, materiality (i.e., significance) is measured in relation to the dollar value of each individual federal program. For example, for a city's federal program with expenditures of $500,000, an error or misstatement of $25,000 of that program's expenditures would be material and reportable for a federal program. However, a $25,000 error or misstatement in the citywide financial statements that report $100,000,000 of expenditures would be relatively immaterial (i.e., not significant enough to be separately highlighted in the auditor's report).

Assess Compliance with Laws and Regulations

The objective of audit tests for compliance with laws and regulations is to identify and report on instances of noncompliance that is material to affected federal program(s). *Noncompliance* is defined by the federal government as the failure to follow or the taking of an action that violates either/or:

- Any law, regulation, or policy; or
- Applicable generally acceptable accounting principle; or
- Terms and conditions of individual federal contracts and grants.

Under the Single Audit Act, compliance audits (i.e., audits to identify instances of noncompliance with laws, regulations, and other criteria) must assess compliance with the several federal policy statements noted earlier in the chapter. Specifically, those include:

Exhibit 13.1: Methodology for audits under the Single Audit Act

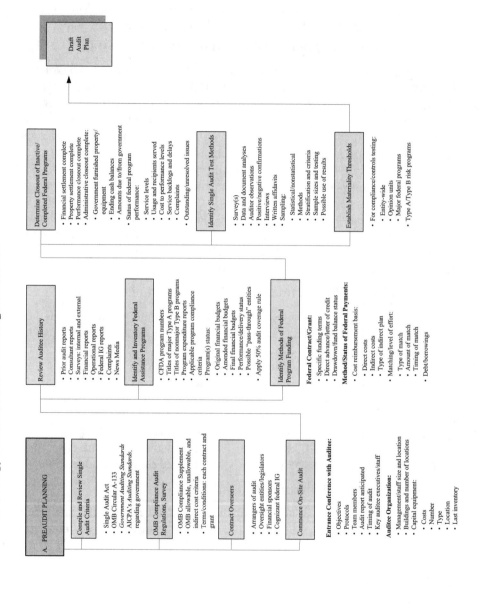

A. PREAUDIT PLANNING

Compile and Review Single Audit Criteria
- Single Audit Act
- OMB Circular A-133
- *Government Auditing Standards,* AICPA's *Auditing Standards,* regarding government

OMB Compliance Audit Regulations, Survey
- OMB Compliance Supplement
- OMB allowable, unallowable, and indirect cost criteria
- Terms/conditions: each contract and grant

Contract Overseers
- Arrangers of audit
- Oversight entities/legislators
- Financial sponsors
- Cognizant federal IG

Commence On-Site Audit

Entrance Conference with Auditee:
- Objectives
- Protocols
- Team members
- Audit report anticipated
- Timing of audit
- Key auditee executives/staff

Auditee Organization:
- Management/staff size and location
- Buildings and number of locations
- Capital equipment:
  - Costs
  - Number
  - Type
  - Location
  - Last inventory

Review Auditee History
- Prior audit reports
- Consultant reports
- Surveys: internal and external
- Financial reports
- Operational reports
- Federal IG reports
- Complaints
- News Media

Identify and Inventory Federal Assistance Programs
- CFDA program numbers
- Titles of major Type A programs
- Titles of nonmajor Type B programs
- Program expenditure reports
- Applicable program compliance criteria
- Program(s) status:
  - Original financial budgets
  - Amended financial budgets
  - Final financial budgets
  - Performance/delivery status
  - Possible "pass-through" entities
  - Apply 50% audit coverage rule

Identify Methods of Federal Program Funding

Federal Contract/Grant:
- Specific funding terms
- Direct advance/letter of credit
- Drawdown/fund balance status

Method/Status of Federal Payments:
- Cost reimbursement basis:
  - Direct costs
  - Indirect costs
  - Type of indirect plan
- Matching/level of effort:
  - Type of match
  - Amount of match
  - Timing of match
- Debt/borrowings

Determine Closeout of Inactive/Completed Federal Programs
- Financial settlement complete
- Property settlement complete
- Performance closeout complete
- Administrative closeout complete:
  - Government furnished property/equipment
  - Ending cash balances
  - Amounts due to/from government
- Status of federal program performance:
  - Service levels
  - Usage and recipients served
  - Cost to performance levels
  - Service backlogs and delays
  - Complaints
  - Outstanding/unresolved issues

Identify Single Audit Test Methods
- Survey(s)
- Data and document analyses
- Auditor observations
- Positive/negative confirmations
- Interviews
- Written affidavits
- Sampling:
  - Statistical/nonstatistical
  - Methods
  - Stratification and criteria
  - Sample sizes and testing
  - Possible use of results

Establish Materiality Thresholds
- For compliance/controls testing:
  - Entity-wide
  - Opinion units
  - Major federal programs
  - Type A/Type B risk programs

Draft Audit Plan

Exhibit 13.1: Methodology for audits under the Single Audit Act (continued)

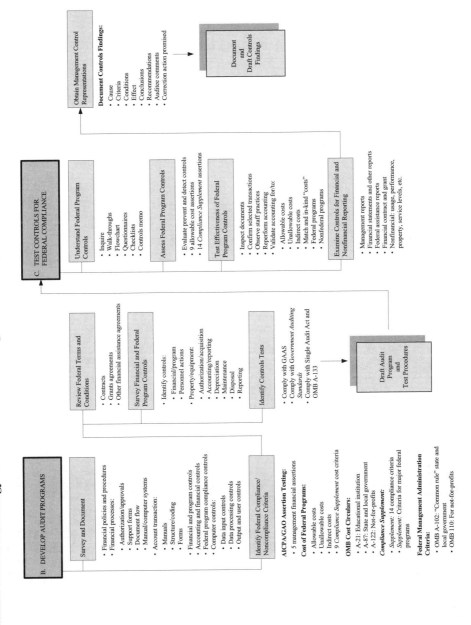

Exhibit 13.1: Methodology for audits under the Single Audit Act (continued)

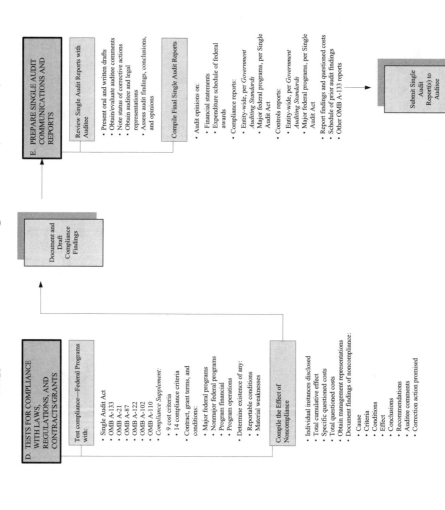

D. TESTS FOR COMPLIANCE WITH LAWS, REGULATIONS, AND CONTRACTS/GRANTS

Test compliance—Federal Programs with:

- Single Audit Act
- OMB A-133
- OMB A-21
- OMB A-87
- OMB A-122
- OMB A-102
- OMB A-110
- *Compliance Supplement:*
  - 9 cost criteria
  - 14 compliance criteria
- Contract, grant terms, and conditions:
  - Major federal programs
  - Nonmajor federal programs
  - Program financial
  - Program operations
- Determine existence of any:
  - Reportable conditions
  - Material weaknesses

Compile the Effect of Noncompliance

- Individual instances disclosed
- Total cumulative effect
- Specific questioned costs
- Total questioned costs
- Obtain management representations
- Document findings of noncompliance:
  - Cause
  - Criteria
  - Conditions
  - Effect
  - Conclusions
  - Recommendations
  - Auditee comments
  - Correction action promised

Document and Draft Compliance Findings

E. PREPARE SINGLE AUDIT COMMUNICATIONS AND REPORTS

Review Single Audit Reports with Auditee

- Present oral and written drafts
- Obtain/evaluate auditee comments
- Note status of corrective actions
- Obtain auditee and legal representations
- Assess audit findings, conclusions, and opinions

Compile Final Single Audit Reports

- Audit opinions on:
  - Financial statements
  - Expenditure schedule of federal awards
- Compliance reports:
  - Entity-wide, per *Government Auditing Standards*
  - Major federal programs, per Single Audit Act
- Controls reports:
  - Entity-wide, per *Government Auditing Standards*
  - Major federal programs, per Single Audit Act
- Report findings and questioned costs
- Schedule of prior audit findings
- Other OMB A-133 reports

Submit Single Audit Report(s) to Auditee

- OMB Circular A-133, *Audits of States, Local Governments, and Nonprofit Organizations*
- OMB *Compliance Supplement*
- OMB Cost Circulars
  - A-21, *Cost Principles for Educational Institutions*
  - A-87, *Cost Principles for State, Local, and Indian Tribal Governments*
  - A-122, *Cost Principles for Nonprofit Organizations*
- OMB Management and Administrative Circulars of federal assistance programs
  - OMB Circular A-102, *Grants and Cooperative Agreements with States and Local Governments*
  - OMB Circular A-110, *Uniform Administrative Requirements for Grants and Other Agreements with Institutions of Higher Education, Hospitals, and Other Nonprofit Organizations*

Tests for compliance require comply/noncomply decisions to be made by the auditor for each of the 14 compliance assertions. An unqualified audit opinion is possible only if there is compliance with *all 14 compliance requirements* or if the auditor is able to apply all audit procedures considered necessary for the auditee's condition or circumstances.

Assess Controls in Relation to Major Programs and OMB Supplements

For an audit to conform to policies enunciated in the Single Audit Act plus OMB Circular A-133, it is necessary that detailed audit tests, audit procedures, and audit reports be made of an auditee's controls over compliance with laws and regulations of each major federal program. These federal policies define and mandate that tests and audit reports be made of controls for single audits that are beyond and different from the audit tests necessary to conform with either the AICPA's GAAS or GAO's *Government Auditing Standards*.

Federal policy requires entities responsible for federal financial assistance programs to establish and maintain internal controls over each major federal program. These controls must provide reasonable assurance that each of the programs is managed in compliance with applicable laws, regulations, and terms and conditions of contracts, grants, and assistance agreements. To conform to federal procedural guidance and auditing guidance, the auditor must:

- *Obtain an understanding* of the controls over compliance with the major federal programs described that entail (1) identifying the compliance assertions relative to federal assistance (described earlier in the chapter) and (2) identifying the relevant controls that are supportive of these compliance assertions.
- *Assess the risk* that material noncompliance could occur in a major program and not be detected on a timely basis by the auditee. The audit assessment is the process of evaluating the effectiveness of controls in preventing or detecting material noncompliance by individual major federal programs.
- *Test the effectiveness of controls*, which may include "inquiries of the auditee's contract, grant, or other personnel; inspection of documents, reports,

electronic imaging and computer-based files; observation of application of controls by audit personnel in practice; reperformance of applied controls by the auditor."

- *Report* all instances of *reportable conditions* and *material weaknesses* related to each individual or collective major federal assistance program.

After acquiring an understanding, making an assessment of control risks, and testing controls, the auditor should prepare audit documentation that includes, at least for a large auditee:

- Systems and document flowcharts
- Internal control questionnaires
- Internal control checklists
- Decision tables and "trees" on controls
- Internal control memoranda

As noted earlier in the chapter, the Single Audit Act and the related OMB Circular A-133 require an extensive and varied report package. The submitted auditor's report may number hundreds of pages and may be presented in a single combined form or in separate reports.

14 PERFORMANCE AUDITS

The objective, purpose, and scope of performance audits vary with the parties desiring an audit. Unlike financial audits, performance audits do not have the support of 100 years of uniformity, documented precedent, precise guidance, and general acceptance. Nonetheless, performance audits are necessary and are often demanded in response to important questions left unanswered by annual financial statement audits, particularly in the public sector.

Although many assume that accountants "invented" performance auditing, this method of evaluation and analysis is practiced possibly to a greater degree in the social sciences and other disciplines. For years, scores of successful performance audits have been conducted by nonaccountants that blend the scientific research method (who, what, when, where, why, and how) with rigorous social research techniques and rather different data-gathering and documentation practices. Such approaches merge cross-disciplinary skills and practices, placing greater emphasis on current or contemplated activity and performance, in contrast to the historical emphasis of an accountant's audit of financial statements.[1]

Observers not known for their public sector involvement have without qualification concluded that service institutions, like governments, periodically need an organized audit of objectives and results in order to identify those entities no longer serving a purpose or that have proven the desired objectives are not attainable.[2]

CHANGING VIEWS

For at least 100 years, audits of financial statements validating historical data have left unanswered questions about quality of operations, competitive status, competence of management and staff, and overall effectiveness of operations. Robert Montgomery, a leader in financial auditing (and founding partner of an original Big 8 accounting firm, Lybrand, Ross Brothers & Montgomery), called attention to the need for audits with considerably different scopes from standard financial statement audits of the early 1900s. He noted that other investigations or examinations were necessary to obtain information about the affairs of and to learn the truth about alleged fraudulent transactions, infringements, rights, arbitration, or values.[3] In the 1980s, some people attempted to distinguish between "shades" of performance-type

---

[1] *Frank L. Greathouse and Mark Funkhouser, "Audit Standards and Performance Auditing in State Government,"* **Government Accountants Journal,** *Association of Government Accountants, Alexandria, VA, Winter edition, 1987, pages 56-60.*

[2] *Peter F. Drucker,* **Management: Tasks, Responsibilities, Practices** *(New York: Harper & Row, 1973), Chapter 14.*

[3] *Robert Montgomery,* **Auditing Theory and Practice** *(New York: Ronald Press Company, 1934), p. 647.*

audits. For example, Ralph Estes defined management audits, operational audits, and performance audits in this way:

- *Management audits:* Reviews and evaluations of management's performance, taking into account environmental conditions, decisions made, results obtained, and similar factors.
- *Operational audits:* The analysis and evaluation of an organization and its operations, often including reviews of structure, systems design, procedures, controls, and results. Similar to a management audit, but with more emphasis on the organization than on management.
- *Performance audits:* Reviews of a governmental program to determine whether it is effectively meeting its objectives, considering the promised benefits in relation to actual results and costs.[4]

In the 2000s, contemporary members of academe offered slightly different views of performance auditing. *Operational auditing* was defined as a subset of internal auditing (the other subsets being financial auditing, compliance auditing, and fraud auditing). Further, *management auditing* was cataloged as a subset of operational auditing that attempted to measure the effectiveness and efficiency of an entity.[5]

Another contemporary view is that an *operational audit* is one that emphasizes effectiveness and efficiency and is concerned with operating performance oriented toward the future; in contrast, financial audits are oriented to the past, with the emphasis on historical information. Although operational audits are generally understood to deal with effectiveness and efficiency, there is less agreement with the use of the term than one might expect. Many prefer to use terms such as *management auditing* and *performance auditing*, while others do not distinguish between *operational auditing*, *management auditing*, and *performance auditing*.[6]

Of more relevance to managing and overseeing the activities of public bodies, especially those of the federal government, is the recent definition of performance auditing by the GAO, appearing in its 2003 edition of the *Government Auditing Standards:*

> **Performance audits** *entail an objective and systematic examination of evidence to provide an independent assessment of the performance and management against objective criteria related to assessing (1) program effectiveness and results; (2) economy and efficiency in the acquisition, protection, and use of resources; (3) management control (i.e., programmatic, financial, and compliance controls); compliance with legal or other requirements; and (4) objectives relating to providing prospective analyses, guidance, or summary information.[7]*

---

[4] *Ralph Estes,* **Dictionary of Accounting** *(Cambridge, MA: MIT Press, 1981).*

[5] *Larry F. Konrath,* **Auditing: A Risk Analysis Approach,** *5th ed. (Mason, Ohio, Southwestern Publishing, U.S., 2002).*

[6] *Alvin Arens, James Loebbbecke,* **Auditing: An Integrated Approach,** *8th ed. (Saddle River, NJ: Prentice Hall, 2000), p. 797.*

[7] *Government Accountability Office,* **Government Auditing Standards** *(Washington, DC: GAO, 2003).*

Because each performance audit has unique objectives, the scopes of such audits must be tailored to achieve those specific desires. Thus, these audits must be conducted in conformance with criteria other than that employed for financial audits. For the most part, performance audits are the province of GAO, federal inspectors general, state and local auditors general, and governmental internal auditors. At times, however, independent accounting firms are retained under contract by a governmental entity to conduct performance audits.

PERFORMANCE AUDIT STANDARDS

More than any organization, GAO should be credited with broadening the focus of audits applied to governments, particularly to the federal government. The need for an expanded audit focus was formalized in 1972, after extensive research, by GAO in its *Government Auditing Standards*, popularly known as the yellow book. The foreword of the 1981 yellow book noted:

> *Public officials, legislators, and private citizens want and need to know, not only whether government funds are handled properly and in compliance with laws and regulations, but also whether government organizations are achieving the purposes for which programs are authorized and funded, and are doing so economically and efficiently.*

The "yellow book" foreword in the 1988 edition stated that the federal government's audit standards highlighted a demand for "full accountability by those entrusted with public funds and the responsibility for properly managing government programs and services."

To this day, *Government Auditing Standards* provide the most definitive standards for the conduct of performance audits. These auditing standards appear in the 2003 edition of the "yellow book":

- Chapter 3, *General Standards*, to be applied to the conduct of financial audits as well as performance-type audits
- Chapter 7, *Fieldwork Standards for Performance Audits*, covering planning, supervising, gathering evidence, and preparing audit documentation for performance audits
- Chapter 8, *Reporting Standards for Performance Audits*, covering performance audit report format, content, quality, and distribution.

The unique nature of each performance audit dictates that each must be planned individually. By definition, each performance audit must have different objectives, warranting different scopes of inquiry, requiring different audit skills, and resulting in a specially formatted report responsive to the specific audit objectives of only that performance audit.

GENERAL STANDARDS

Adherence to *Government Auditing Standards* is essential to ensuring the credibility of individual auditors, the competence of the audit team, and the professionalism of their audit organization. Compliance with the general audit standards described in the *Government Auditing Standards* is critical to the success of any audit. These general standards speak to such topics as:

- Auditor independence
- Exercise of experienced professional judgment
- Collective high competence of the audit team; and
- Organizational quality controls of audit organizations to ensure adherence standards

The general audit standards must be followed by:

- All auditors (public accountants and internal auditors employed by governments)
- All audit organizations (independent accounting firms, governmental inspectors, and auditors general)
- For all performance audits made of governmental (federal and other government entities) and nongovernmental entities (academic, corporations, and not-for-profits) receiving federal funding

Auditor Independence

The first general standard (GAS 3.03–3.32), on auditor independence, requires:

In all matters relating to the audit work, the audit organization, and the individual auditor, whether government or public, should be free, both in fact and appearance, from personal, external, and organizational impairments of independence.

This standard on independence is more specific than a comparable standard of the AICPA. However, Statements on Auditing Standards and additional AICPA guidance issued over the years now require that its members conform to essentially these same requirements. Where a nongovernmental auditor suffers from one or more of the cited independence impairments—personal, financial, external, or organizational—that auditor must decline to perform the work.

On the other hand, an auditor who is an employee of the federal government may not, due to legislative or other requirements, be able to decline to perform the audit. In this instance, the government employee must report the independence impairment(s) in the scope section of the audit report.

Professional Judgment

The second general standard (GAS 3.33–3.38) requires:

Professional judgment should be used in planning and performing audits and attestation engagements and in reporting the results.

GAO requires the exercise of reasonable care and diligence, the highest degree of integrity, and objectivity in applying professional judgment. This standard imposes a responsibility on performance auditors to observe *Government Auditing Standards* and to describe, justify, and disclose any departures from them.

Competence of Audit Team

The third general standard (GAS 3.39–3.48) requires:

The staff assigned to perform the audit or attestation engagement should collectively possess adequate professional competence for the task required.

By this standard, the audit organization is responsible for ensuring that, collectively, the audit team has the knowledge, skills, and experience necessary to successfully complete the performance audit. Compliance with this standard requires audit organizations to have a process for recruiting, hiring, continuous development, and evaluation of staff to ensure a continuing workforce with adequate professional competence. For performance auditing, *professional competence* refers to the knowledge, skills, and experience of the assigned audit team, and not necessarily an individual auditor.

To conduct a performance audit, an audit organization may need to employ specialists, other than auditors, who are knowledgeable, skilled, or experienced in such areas as accounting, statistics, law, engineering, health and the medicines, information technology, public administration, economics, social sciences, or actuarial science. This standard ensures that auditors and their organizations are aware that training and proficiency as an auditor only will not be adequate for performance audits requiring knowledge and skills in other fields.

GAO's interpretative guidance requires an audit staff to collectively possess the necessary technical knowledge, skills, and experience, and be competent for the type of work being performed *before* beginning the audit.

Quality Control by Auditors

The fourth general standard (GAS 3.49–3.56) requires:

Each audit organization performing audits and/or attestation engagements in accordance with GAGAS [generally accepted government accounting standards] should have an appropriate internal quality control system in place and should undergo an external peer review.

An *appropriate* internal quality control system encompasses the structure, operating policies, and procedures for monitoring, on an ongoing basis, to determine whether the policies and procedures of an audit organization are suitably designed and are being effectively applied during each audit. The internal quality control system must be documented to permit evaluation and review to assess compliance.

To conform to this standard, audit organizations, government and nongovernment, must have an external peer review of their auditing and attestation practices at least once every three years by reviewers independent of the audit organization.

FIELDWORK STANDARDS

Fieldwork audit standards provide guidance for the conduct of a performance audit in conformity with *Government Auditing Standards*.

Planning Audits

The first fieldwork performance audit standard (GAS 7.02, 7.43) requires:

Work is to be adequately planned.

The plan for a performance audit should define, to the detail possible, the audit objectives, scope, program performance criteria, and anticipated methodologies to be employed. Planning for a performance audit, even more so than a financial audit, is an iterative process that will continue to evolve over the duration of the audit. Planning for a performance audit is not a once-and-for-all task. The audit plan should be reduced to writing, becoming a part of the working papers and the audit evidence record.

Supervision of Audits

The second fieldwork performance audit standard (GAS 7.44–7.47) requires:

Staff are to be properly supervised.

The level and extent of supervision expected will vary in relation to the experience of individual team members. Those with less experience, or who are new to the audit team, would require more frequent monitoring. Evidence of supervision and review of teamwork should be documented in audit workpapers.

Audit Evidence

The third fieldwork performance audit standard (GAS 7.48–7.65) requires:

Competent and relevant evidence is to be obtained to provide a reasonable basis for the auditors' findings and conclusions.

The quality, quantity, type, reliability, and validity of evidence are all relevant to the objectives of the specific performance audit and dependent on the judgment of the auditor. Categories of evidence suggested by GAO, and considered in most performance audits include:

- *Physical evidence:* direct auditor inspection and observation of people, property, and events, documented in memoranda, photographs, charts, maps, or physical sample
- *Documentary evidence:* letters, contracts, accounting records, invoices, and management information on performance
- *Testimonial evidence:* inquiries, interviews, questionnaires, written representations
- *Analytical evidence:* as computation, comparisons, data disaggregation by components, and rational argument

GAO's "sufficiency" test stipulates that sufficient evidence must be gathered or produced to persuade a knowledgeable person of the validity of the findings. Evidence must be competent—that is, valid, reliable, and consistent with the facts reported by the audit team, which requires that the evidence be accurate, authoritative, timely, and authentic.

Audit Documentation

The fourth fieldwork performance audit standard (GAS 7.66–7.71) requires:

Auditors should prepare and maintain audit documentation. Audit documentation related to planning, conducting, and reporting on the audit should contain sufficient information to enable an experienced auditor, who has had no previous connection with the audit, to ascertain from the audit documentation, the evidence that supports the auditor's significant judgments and conclusions. Audit documentation should contain support for findings, conclusions, and recommendations before auditors issue their report.

The form, content, quantity, and type of documentation constitutes the principal record of the work performed for the audit; aids auditors in conducting and supervising the audit; and allows for a review of audit quality. Evidence of supervisory review must exist in the audit's workpapers before the audit report is issued.

REPORTING STANDARDS

The reporting standards for a performance audit provide guidance to the auditor on reporting on performance in accordance with *Government Auditing Standards*.

Written Audit Reports

The first reporting standard for performance (GAGAS 8.02–8.06) requires:

Auditors should prepare audit reports communicating the results of each audit.

A performance audit report must be written and appropriate for the report's intended use.

Content of Audit Reports

The second reporting standard for performance (GAGAS 8.07–8.37) requires:

*The audit report should include the objectives, scope, and methodology; the audit results, including findings, conclusions, and recommendation, as appropriate; a reference to compliance with **Government Auditing Standards;** the views of responsible officials; and, if applicable, the nature of any privileged and confidential information omitted. The report should describe how the audit objectives were accomplished, the evidence gathering techniques, and analysis techniques used.*

The auditor should ask legal counsel if publicly reporting certain information about potential fraud, illegal acts, violations of provisions or grant agreements, or abuse would compromise investigative or legal proceedings. Auditors should limit the extent of any public reporting to matters that would not compromise such proceedings, such as to information that is already part of the public record.

Quality of Audit Reports

The third reporting standard for performance (GAGAS 8.38–8.5) requires:

The report should be timely, complete, accurate, objective, convincing, clear, and as concise as the subject permits.

Unless prohibited, interim reporting of significant matters would be appropriate and may be oral or written, but under GAO's standards, an interim report is not a substitute for a written final report.

Distribution of Audit Reports

The fourth reporting standard for performance (GAGAS 8.38–8.53) requires:

Government auditors should submit audit reports to the appropriate officials of the auditee entity and to the appropriate officials of the organizations requiring or arranging for the audits, including external funding organizations, such as legislative bodies, unless legal restrictions prevent it. Auditors should also send copies of the reports to other officials who have legal oversight authority or who may be responsible for acting on auditing findings and recommendations, and also to others authorized to receive such reports. Unless a report is restricted by law or regulation, or contains privileged or confidential information, auditors should clarify that copies are made available for public inspection. Nongovernment auditors should clarify report distribution responsibilities with the party contracting for the audit and follow the agreements reached.

Internal auditors employed by governments should follow their audit entity's own arrangements and statutory requirements for distribution.

STRUCTURING A PERFORMANCE AUDIT

In the federal government, GAO describes program (or performance) audits in two general categories:

1. Audits and evaluations made to assess the relative economy and efficiency of an entity's operations. Suggested objectives by GAO of this type of performance audit include:

    a. Whether the appropriate type, quality, and amount of resources are procured at appropriate prices

    b. Whether an entity's assets are being properly protected, maintained, and used

    c. Whether optimum amounts of entity resources are used in producing or delivering the legislated or funded services and goods

    d. Whether an entity is complying with the laws, policies, regulations, rules, and procedures that affect the acquisition, protection, and use of government resources

    e. Whether an entity has adequate control systems for measuring, monitoring, and reporting on the relative economy and efficiency of operations

2. Audits and evaluations made to assess program results and the relative operational effectiveness, accomplishments, attained performance, goals achieved, legislated or mandated service outcomes delivered. Suggested objectives by GAO of this type of performance audit include:

    a. Whether the goals or objectives of a new or ongoing program are proper, suitable, or relevant

    b. Whether the entity is achieving the desired level of performance or program results

    c. Whether alternatives are considered for delivering program services or goods that would be more effective (i.e., is there a better way?)

    d. Whether established program/performance indicators are valid and reliable criteria of program results

    e.   Whether the program focus is on achievement of outputs and outcomes, or is limited to the measurement and reporting of inputs only

This distinction of types of performance audits is clearer in literature than in practice, wherein the relative economy, efficiency, and effectiveness are relative, interconnected, and at times not clearly distinguishable.

DIFFERENT AND ELUSIVE AUDIT CRITERIA

The accepted financial statement audit criteria is "fairness of presentation," generally defined in terms of materiality. The criterion for performance audits is not nearly as well established. At times, those arranging for a performance audit are reluctant to, cannot, or will not define or formalize measurable criteria usable in planning a performance audit, yet a performance audit is demanded. The risk of defining acceptable performance often devolves to the audit organization.

Over the years, authoritative literature relating to performance auditing has highlighted risks and other conditions needing to be addressed in planning these types of audits. Some of these include:

- *Different materiality, program significance:* A performance audit may not be directly related to dollars, but rather give greater emphasis to qualitative and other quantitative factors and place considerable weight on (a) reports in the written and electronic news media; (b) newness or changes in programs and citizen satisfaction with amounts or types of provided (or not provided) services; or (c) violations or deviations from legislated program goals and objectives.
- *No legislated performance criteria:* Some laws governing programs contain statements of objectives, goals, or desired levels of performance, including defining expected program outputs and outcomes. This information would be ideal for planning a performance audit. Absent such guidance, the auditor must conduct a survey and independently acquire a sufficient understanding of the program to design responsive, relevant program performance criteria, expected levels of program achievement, and/or desired output and outcome measures.

Concurrence of the arrangers of a performance audit to the performance measure to be examined during the audit must be obtained by the auditor at the outset of the review:

- *Minimal, no relevant program information:* Financial and operational data may not have been captured, recorded, and reported in a manner permitting program managers to effectively manage or monitor performance in strict compliance with the governing laws. Not uncommonly, performance audits require the auditor to design and build ad hoc project databases responsive to the purposes(s) of the audit.
- *Absence of consumer/customer tests:* Restrictions on what evidence an auditor should examine or to whom the auditor may speak will preclude an objective and more meaningful assessment of an auditee's performance. Limiting communication to auditee management and staff and to records and reports

compiled by the auditee may provide minimal or no information as to the relevant efficiency and effectiveness of a governmental program. "Consumer, customer, or constituent" satisfaction could be lacking concerning the types, timing, levels, delivery modes, and so on, of program services and goods. Independently compiled external data relative to program performance, achievement, and quality may be available only by the auditor conducting mailed polls or personal visit interviews with a substantial sampling of the constituents targeted by the founding law, including constituents served, those underserved, and those not served at all.

- *Outputs, outcomes not identified:* Considerable emphasis may be placed on "input" data (e.g., expenses incurred for salaries, supplies, travel, etc., but not related to levels of achievement), which is, at best, indirectly related to performance. It would be better to emphasize data on program "outputs" (e.g., goods and services provided, tons processed, numbers graduated, dollars dispersed). Still better yet would be "outcome" data (e.g., educational levels attained, vocational graduates still working two years after graduation, development of a viable alternative energy source). Defining outcomes can be controversial, heatedly disputed, and often dependent on conflicting views of affected parties. At the time the legislative branch passed enabling legislation to finance and operate a particular governmental program, even legislators may not have agreed on desired outputs, outcomes, or other achievement criteria for the program. Concurrence of the arrangers of a performance audit must be obtained by the auditor at the outset of the review.

- *Limited use of "best practices," "benchmarks":* Seek financial and operational comparisons to similar programs operated by entities external to the auditee. Seek data from external sources on relevant "best practices" and "benchmark-type" information on what and how others are performing similar activities. Performance by other governments may not have been considered or attempted, yet a "better way" may be available for the price of a phone call. There will be some governmental programs that are truly unique, never before attempted by any entity anywhere. For the most part, almost every governmental activity has a counterpart in the corporate, academic, or nonprofit world, and technical and "normative" standards may have been developed by longtime practitioners and industry trade associations with more experience than the government, particularly if the program is a new venture for the government.

- *Need "auditors" with nonaudit skills:* Government Auditing Standards emphasize the importance of collective skills, experience, and professional proficiency of the audit team with the objective of creating a multidisciplinary audit team. Experience in the fields of accounting and auditing may be only two of many skills demanded. The perceived competency of the audit team members is key to successful performance audits (i.e., an audit whose findings are accepted and that results in corrective actions). To the maximum extent, audit team members must be viewed by auditee management and staff as their professional and technical peers in every way: education, practical knowledge, applied functional skills, relevant industry experience, and general in-depth expertise.

As is evident, these conditions and circumstances require that an understanding of audit expectations be obtained from the arranger(s) of the audit before commencing. Failure to do so would result in the auditor assuming considerable risk. Arranger(s) of performance audits should examine, comment on, and agree to the evaluation criteria to apply throughout the performance audit. This cautionary measure could potentially preclude the auditee from later protesting that the performance criteria and achievement factors evaluated were "made up" by the auditor and are neither relevant nor intended by the program's legislation.

Chapter 7 of *Government Auditing Standards* contains advice and guidance to assist in the development of program performance criteria, a methodology for implying or inferring creditable, appropriate, and relevant performance criteria when possibly none was identified in law. This source should be consulted when drafting the audit program and determining the audit procedures to be applied.

OVERVIEW OF THE PERFORMANCE AUDIT PROCESS

Some forty years ago, GAO, in its earliest guidance, noted that performance audits may be conducted in uncertain environments, can have different scopes of examination, and may require audit procedures different from those used in the more common financial audits, and that the audit report may require unique tailoring to each specific audit.[8] Nonetheless, GAO outlined a process that could be applied to a performance audit, review, evaluation, or whatever title is used to describe an examination process to assure that the audit is properly planned, professionally performed, and objectively reported.

Exhibit 14.1 is a partial listing of considerations to take into account when planning a performance audit that must conform to criteria of *Government Auditing Standards*. The appropriateness, sequencing, and listed phases and tasks must be assessed in relation to the conditions or circumstances of each auditee and program to be audited. Note that there is a general scope of audit work that must be completed, a methodology that must be applied, and an objective, factually-based report that must be submitted to the arrangers of the audit.

The following sections provide an overview of that GAO guidance, some of which exists in GAO's current edition of *Government Auditing Standards*.

ORIENTATION PHASE

Performance audits should not be viewed as necessarily critical or negative. These audits can be structured to identify issues of increased staffing, modernize the equipment plant, or design new management approaches that might be required to significantly expand services and benefits to multiple locations or to several other

---

[8] Government Accountability Office, **Comprehensive Approach for Planning and Conducting a Program Results Review** *(Washington, DC: GAO, 1973).*

Exhibit 14.1: Overview of the performance process

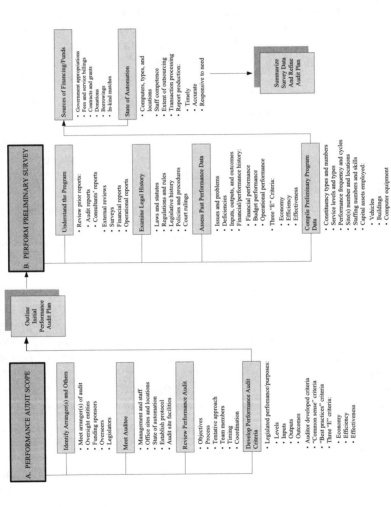

Exhibit 14.1: Overview of the performance process (continued)

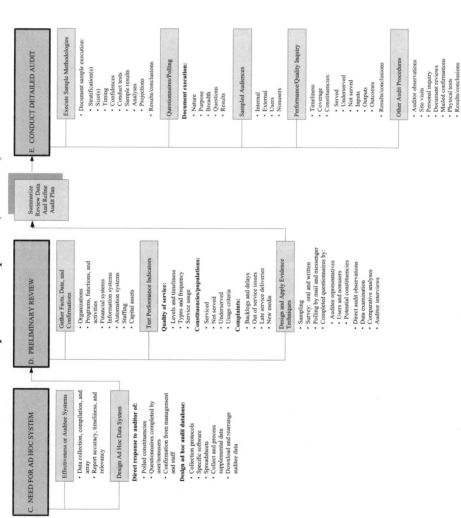

Exhibit 14.1: Overview of the performance process (continued)

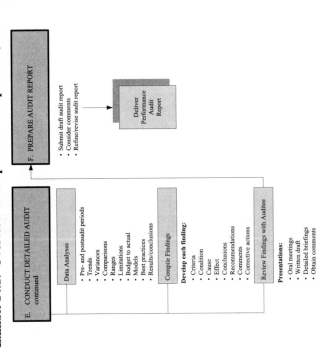

E. CONDUCT DETAILED AUDIT
continued

Data Analyses

- Pre- and postaudit periods
- Trends
- Variances
- Comparisons
- Ranges
- Limitations
- Budget to actual
- Models
- Best practices
- Results/conclusions

Compile Findings

Develop each finding:
- Criteria
- Condition
- Cause
- Effect
- Conclusions
- Recommendations
- Comments
- Corrective actions

Review Findings with Auditee

Presentations:
- Oral meetings
- Written draft
- Detailed briefings
- Obtain comments

F. PREPARE AUDIT REPORT

- Submit draft audit report
- Consider comments
- Refine/revise audit report

Deliver
Performance
Audit
Report

programs. As early as practicable, the auditor should convene separate orientation conferences with (1) arranger(s) of the audit and (2) auditee management and key staff, and these two groups may not necessarily be the same. At this time, the purpose, process, timing, and operating protocols to be applied in the audit must be discussed and agreements reached. If permitted by the arranger(s) of the audit, the nature of the "performance" that is to be examined or reviewed should be described to the auditee, before proceeding with the performance audit. There will be instances where the auditor is precluded by arrangers of the audit from discussing aspects of the audit with the auditee.

Understand the Auditee

GAO's suggested approach is to conduct a survey at the outset to assess, on a preliminary basis, whether the facts appear consistent with opinions, views, and comments provided earlier by the arranger(s) of the audit and auditee management. The tasks in this phase are directed toward acquiring, as quickly as possible, a historical perspective about the program, its constituents and their satisfaction, issues and accomplishments, extent of computerization, and knowledge of the financial, operational, and other data systems designed to support the program's management and accountability needs.

GAO described the survey as a short-duration, fast information-gathering phase; no real attempt is made to assess or "audit" the veracity of information provided by the auditee. Although it may occur, the emphasis is not on problem exploration or deficiency identification. Alternatively, the purpose of the survey is to further enhance background provided to the auditor and assist the auditor in understanding the program activities, services, functions, and constituents, each of which will be examined in greater detail as the audit progresses.

Ad Hoc Database

Depending on the nature of the performance audit, data needs could arise relative to assessing the quality of services, levels of achievement, economy and efficiency of program performance, input and output and outcome data, backlogs and bottlenecks, overruns/underruns of financial and performance budgets, trend/volume indicators, the level of user and nonuser satisfaction, and more. The typical historical accounting system will not be fully responsive to the data needs of such a performance audit. Although a management information system might have some of these data, almost no government's program data systems can address the full range of potential questions that could arise or be of concern.

The creation of an ad hoc database(s) is frequently a precedent condition to planning a performance audit. As early as possible, efforts should be made to identify where there is a shortage of information needed to address the questions and inquiries to be made in the audit. To a greater or lesser extent, ad hoc database(s) must be implemented, and will include design, drafting, and printing of data collection forms (e.g., form for surveys, polls, auditee completed questionnaires, mailed confirmations, auditor prepared inquiry forms, spreadsheets, etc.). In addition, software programs will be needed to input, process, and assist in analyzing collected data. Time devoted at the outset of the audit to brainstorming the need for ad hoc data gathering processes will be well spent.

RISKS AND ISSUES

GAO contrasts its suggested review phase with the preceding survey phase by the depth and specificity of inquiries. Also, the originally perceived program issues, problems, deficiencies, and levels of achievement may turn out to be incorrect or not relatively significant, but other more serious matters may arise or be disclosed that require a change of audit focus. Moreover, no budget would ever permit a comprehensive audit of everything. Choices must be made regarding what is to be examined, and audit focus must change as gathered facts change perceptions. Substantial, high-risk issues may require an audit of considerably greater depth than earlier planned; lesser, lower-risk issues may be dropped from the further examination.

For these reasons, the objective of the preliminary review phase is to permit an informed basis for "winnowing down" the audit scope and focusing on the most essential, important, critical, or problematic matters, and those of highest priority. Early tests must be made of known or derived performance indicators, with recognition that some known indicators may be inadequate and that other, better indicators may be needed. During the review phase, a more complete inventory will be made to confirm the skills and experiences required to competently examine the key issues and complete an assessment of the program. This phase is where more definitive conclusions must be reached concerning the relevancy, currency, accuracy, adequacy, and effectiveness of the auditee's systems, controls, accounting, and reporting (e.g., financial, operations, and management information systems). A concluding effort of the review phase must be the refinement or revision of the preliminary audit plan.

CONDUCT THE AUDIT

The detailed audit phase is concerned with obtaining facts to confirm or refute earlier hypotheses, perceptions relative to program achievement, outputs and outcomes, issues or problems and to gather evidence to permit conclusions on the operational economy, efficiency, effectiveness, and "faithfulness" of program performance and attainment of reported program results.

"Getting the facts" results from applying a variety of survey and auditing techniques, which GAO suggests could include, among other things:

- Statistical applications
- Mathematical modeling
- Auditor interview of management and staff
- Direct-mailed questionnaires and confirmations
- Direct polls of constituents, users, and nonusers of the program services
- Physical inspections by the audit team, data examination and analyses

The end game of the performance audit is to identify, develop, document, and report audit findings. A finding is defined in *Government Auditing Standards* as:

The result of information development—a logical pulling together of information to arrive at conclusions about an organization, program, activity, function, condition, or other matter that was analyzed or evaluated.

Care must be taken in any audit to ensure that the audit team does not fall victim to the "perfect vision" of hindsight. *Government Auditing Standards* include a technique requiring critical examination of the audit evidence gathered in support of what is described by GAO as the several elements of each or any audit finding:

- *Criteria:* What is the required or desired state, or what is expected from the program or operation?
- *Condition:* What did the auditor find regarding the actual situation, providing information on the scope of audit, the extent of the condition, and other comments that would provide an accurate perspective?
- *Cause:* Does the evidence provide a reasonable and convincing argument for the cause as the key factor(s) contributing to the difference between the actual condition and the desired criteria, or does evidence possibly point to flawed criteria or factors not controllable by program management?
- *Effect:* Is there a clear, logical link between what the auditor found (the observed condition) and what should be (the desired criteria) described quantitatively or qualitatively?
- *Conclusions:* Are the auditor's views clearly stated (as opposed to implied); are logical inferences about the program supportable by reported evidence, and are the reported conclusions more than just a summary of the facts?
- *Recommendations:* Does required recommendation plausibly flow from the reported findings and conclusions and identify actions that could eliminate reported deficiencies or improve programs?

The performance audit report should clearly and objectively report or comment on each of these elements for each of the reported findings.

REPORT OF AUDIT

Government Auditing Standards do not prescribe a specific form for the audit report, but require that the audit report include:

The audit's objectives, scope, and methodology; the audit results, including findings, conclusions, and recommendation, as appropriate; ...and, if applicable, the nature of any privileged and confidential information omitted.

As soon as practicable, and only when permitted by those arranging for the performance audit, information on these report content items should be provided to the auditee:

- *Objective, scope, and methodology:* This information is needed by readers and users of the report to understand: the purpose of the audit, the nature of the audit work performed, the perspective as to what is reported, and significant limitations in audit objectives, scope, or methodology.
- *Audit results:* The report on audit results should include the creditable evidence in support of each reported finding (i.e., fully report on each element of a finding).

- *Conclusions and recommendations:* Where appropriate or required, this information must flow logically from the facts in the report.

The protocol for presenting audit findings to the auditee will vary, and may even be defined by the arranger(s) of the audit. If permitted by the arrangers, the "reporting" of results of a performance audit might include an overview oral, written, or visual presentation. A written draft of each finding may be provided to the auditee with a request for auditee comments, preferably in writing. Following assessment of auditee comments and reconsideration of certain contested issues, a final audit report should be prepared and submitted to the auditee, and the final written views of the auditee will be considered.

For any audit, auditors cannot ignore the axiom: Facts not reported cannot be evaluated by readers or users of the audit report. Performance audit reports should provide sufficient information and facts to stand alone, unaided by additional oral or written supplemental testimony or explanations. A performance audit report should be sufficiently complete, in and of itself, to permit a user or reader of the report to "audit the auditor."

15 PROCUREMENT AND CONTRACT AUDITS

Contract expenditures are one of the most significant expenditures within the federal government, with obligations totaling in the trillions of dollars in any given year with individual contracts often reaching into the billions. Funds are expended under federal contracts to purchase or support a wide variety of services, purchases of equipment, and real and consumer-type properties. For many agencies, amounts spent under contracts greatly exceed amounts spent on other items in their budgets.

CONTRACTS DEFINED

Contracts are the legal obligations of the federal government, generally in writing, which obligate the government to an expenditure of money upon delivery of goods or performance of services. Federal government contracting is a preferred form of acquiring services, products, capital assets, real properties, supplies, and materials from nonfederal sources for military and civilian purposes and for use domestically or internationally.

Contracts Types

The types of federal contracts vary but may be grouped into one of two general categories, with variations in each grouping: cost-reimbursable contracts and fixed-price types of contracts.[1]

Cost-reimbursable–type contracts are used when the federal agency and contractor are not able to define the required scope of work in sufficiently definite terms, or when there is no valid basis for predicting results or performance. Also, with cost-type contracts, the financial risks are borne primarily by the governmental entity. For example:

- *Cost plus fixed fee contracts:* Reimburse the contractor for allowable costs, plus a negotiated fixed fee; maximum performance and cost risk is borne by the government; used when the scope of work is difficult to define
- *Cost plus incentive fee contracts:* Reimburse the contractor for allowable costs, plus a variable fixed fee if contract is completed within negotiated target levels; the scope of work is uncertain at the time of negotiation
- *Cost-sharing contracts:* Reimburse the contractor for allowable costs only; no fee/profit is negotiated into the contract amount since the contractor anticipates to mutually benefit from performing the scope of work

---

[1] C.E. Tierney, **Federal Financial Management: Accounting and Auditing Practices** *(New York: American Institute of Certified Public Accountants, 1976).*

- *Time and materials contracts:* Reimburse the contractor for labor and the cost of materials in a negotiated composite rate for each hour of labor worked; rate is all-inclusive of labor costs, overhead costs, and profit
- *Labor-hour contracts:* Similar to time and materials contracts; reimburse the contractor on the basis of a fixed hourly labor rate that includes the cost of labor, overhead, and a profit factor; the only variable is the number of hours provided under the contract

Conversely, when the desired results of performance can be predicted and a definite price can be determined, a *fixed-price–type contract* will be negotiated. Any costs incurred in excess of the fixed price must be borne by the contractor, provided the scope of work has remained as defined in the contract. If performance is rendered for a lesser cost than the fixed price, the contractor is entitled to the full contract amount.

- *Firm fixed-price contracts:* The contractor is paid the full amount of the contract at the time the scope of work is completed by the contractor and accepted by the government. Absent an authorized change in contract scope, the contractor may collect only the fixed contract price regardless of the cost incurred to perform. The full financial risk is with the contractor.
- *Fixed-price incentive contracts:* An alternative to the firm fixed price contract may be used when parties can agree on scope of work but cannot agree on a firm price; the contractor and the government share in cost savings, overruns, or underruns.
- *Fixed-price with escalation contracts:* These contracts reimburse the contractor for the full amount of the contract and the effect of certain risks beyond the contractor's control; escalation clauses are generally based on a predetermined price or cost index that provides for the adjustment of material and/or labor costs.
- *Purchase orders:* These are a form of firm fixed-price contracts that become effective upon the vendor/supplier's acceptance or performance of the purchase order; typically, purchase orders are for amounts not in excess of $25,000 when (1) supplies are readily available in the local area, (2) one delivery and one payment will be made, and (3) the use of a purchase order is more economical and efficient than other methods.

RESPONSIBILITY FOR CONTRACTS

Several organizations in the federal government's legislative and executive branches have the authority or responsibility for financing, negotiating, awarding, funding, administering, and settling federal contracts. The nature of authority or responsibilities exercised by these various organizations is briefly outlined next.

Congressional Responsibilities

Congress, through its authorization and appropriation committees, has the ultimate authority and responsibility for overall federal procurement and grant policies.

These policies appear in laws having government-wide applicability, and, at times, specific legislation will apply to a single, particularly significant procurement.

Cost Accounting Standards Board

The Cost Accounting Standards Board (CASB), part of the Office of Federal Procurement Policy within OMB, issues standards to achieve uniformity and consistency in the cost accounting principles adhered to by federal contractors and subcontractors.

Government Accountability Office

GAO is authorized to audit the expenditures of federal monies spent under contracts, including reviews of agency procurement systems. These reviews are made internally at the federal entity or externally at a contractor's location. GAO also has the legal authority to render binding decisions on federal entities, with respect to procurement actions, but these decisions may be appealed in the courts by a contractor.

General Services Administration

The General Services Administration (GSA) is responsible for publishing and overseeing the Federal Acquisition Regulations (FAR) that describe the terms and conditions of federal procurements. The FAR is the government-wide procurement policy. Agencies such as the Department of Defense and NASA may monitor contracts pursuant to a tailored version of the Defense Department or NASA procurement regulations, but these tailored regulations are almost identical to the FAR published by GSA.

Office of Management and Budget

The Office of Management and Budget issues government-wide regulations relating to federal procurements, the most notable of which are the OMB cost circulars that, along with provisions of various titles of the US Code, define types of allowable costs, unallowable costs, and indirect or overhead costs permitted or prohibited under federal contracts and grants.

Defense Contract Audit Agency

The Defense Contract Audit Agency (DCAA), with over 3,500 auditors at more than 300 field audit offices throughout the United States, Europe, and the Pacific, is responsible for performing all contract audits for the Defense Department as well as several hundred federal grants. These audits could include: reviews of contractor and grantee cost estimates and price proposals; audits of contractor or grantee costs for compliance with federal allowable, unallowable, and indirect costs regulations; and reviews of contractor and grantee compliance with federal cost accounting standards and other costing criteria, such as the OMB allowable and unallowable cost circulars.

Individual Contracting Agencies

Pursuant to the Budget and Accounting Procedures Act of 1950 and later laws, federal agencies must have procurement policies, procedures, and systems in place for the solicitation and evaluation of contract proposals; negotiation, award, and administration of contracts; and to account for contract performance. An agency's systems of controls, accounting, and reporting must be sufficiently precise to permit monitoring of contract obligations; liquidation of these obligations; and the costing and disbursement of contract funds.

FEDERAL PROCUREMENTS

Selected salient features of federal procurement include the responsibilities, requirements, and processes discussed in the next sections.

The Players

Not all contract award tasks or activities are resident within a single unit or function of a federal agency. The successful completion of a procurement action requires the collaboration and coordination of several various agency units. Some of these are outlined below.

Program office or allottee. The initiation or determination of need for contractor services generally originates with the responsible program management office, although functional offices (e.g., accounting, budget, data processing, human resources, and even the contracts office) might require contracted services or support. The originating office would be expected to prepare a preliminary estimate of costs, identify potential sources of supply, prepare the formal procurement request, monitor performance and accept delivery under the contract, and, at contract completion, recommend that the contractor be paid.

Contracts office or procurement section. Actual contracting activities are generally centralized in the agency's contracts function. This function often is responsible for identifying prospective contractors, issuing requests for proposals (RFPs) and invitations for bids (IFBs), conducting negotiations with prospective contractors, executing and awarding contracts, administering the contracts, and settlement and closeout upon contract completion.

Accounting section. The accounting section must confirm the availability of agency appropriations money for the contract in advance of procurement request (PR) approval. Additionally, this function would formally obligate agency funds upon notification of contract award; examine invoices related to contract terms and performance; conduct prepayment "audits" of contractor invoices; initiate formal accounting transactions to obligate, liquidate the obligations, expenditures, and payables and ultimate payment related to each awarded contract; compile internal and external financial reports on awarded contracts; prepare the schedule to request issuance of checks by the Treasury Department to the contractor; and perform the fiscal and budgetary accounting during and after expiration of the agency's appropriations.

Contractor or vendor. The contractor or vendor must first submit a proposal or bid in response to the RFP or IFB and, if successful, will negotiate contract terms and conditions and execute a contract with the federal agency. The contractor or vendor must then perform the agreed-on services or deliver the contracted goods, and complete and file end-of-contract financial, property, and performance reports for final contract settlement.

Treasury Department. Actual checks or electronic fund transfers (EFTs) in payment of invoices submitted by contractors are issued by the Treasury Department upon receiving a request from the contracting agency to initiate payment to a contractor.

The Process

As noted, many federal agencies have the authority to issue and require adherence to their policies and regulations relating to federal contracts. However, the design of a system of controls to meet the criteria of these agencies and to adequately protect the government with respect to procurements is the sole responsibility of the individual operating federal agency that issues the contract. Although the specific steps or details vary, most federal entities have established procedures requiring:

- Preparation and approval of a *procurement request or authorization*, approved by the responsible program official and annotated to show that unobligated funds exist to meet the estimated amount of the intended procurement, all of which is done before prospective contractor sources can be contacted.
- Procurements be *competitively awarded*, whether the contract is ultimately awarded through advertising or negotiation. Competition may be obtained from a variety of federal sources including electronic media (e.g., FedBizOpps).
- A *formal review process* for the objective evaluation of all proposals, solicited and unsolicited, received by the agency to ensure compliance to prescribed negotiation practices.
- Conduct of a *survey or review of contractor accounting and management controls* systems through on-site examinations of the contractors and consulting with other federal entities with whom the contractor has done business.
- The formal execution and *issuance of the contract*, with the timely notification to the agency fiscal function to permit prompt obligation of funds in an amount equal to the funded value of contracts.
- *Reporting*, on a periodic basis, of the rate of expenditures by the contractor, as well as the quality and timeliness of contractor performance or deliveries, which often includes positive confirmation of the receipt and satisfaction of service or performance.
- *Prepayment audits* of invoices to ensure that amounts, performance, and deliveries are consistent with negotiated contract terms; that prompt and accurate payment is made of properly rendered invoices; and that there is timely processing of all procurement transactions.
- Final settlement or *contract closeout* of any advanced money, government-furnished equipment, and property in a manner consistent with agency policy or contract conditions, and a final assessment of contractor compliance.

Accounting

OMB has prescribed certain agency accounting criteria for the obligation, accrued expenditure, and applied cost of contract transactions relating to the acquisition of services and goods. Except when precluded by law, the contract accounting of federal agencies must be conducted in accordance with concepts set forth in OMB Circular A-11, *Preparation, Submission, and Execution of the Budget*, and OMB Circular A-34, *Instructions on Budget Execution*.

Obligations incurred. An agency's reporting of contracted obligations incurred for contracted services or support must comply with Section 1311 of the Supplemental Appropriation Act that requires the existence of legal evidence of binding agreements, orders, or other legal liabilities prior to the recording and reporting of a contract obligation. OMB Circular A-34 sets forth the formal criteria for recognizing legal obligations. According to OMB, internal administrative commitments of funds and invitations to bid sent to prospective contractors must not be included in amounts the agency reports as obligations. These types of activities fail to meet the criteria of Section 1311 for valid obligations.

Accrued expenditures. Expenditures for printing and reproduction, contractual services, supplies and materials, and equipment will accrue when a contractor, vendor, or other party performs the service or incurs costs. Tests of *performance* may be physical receipt, passing of title, or constructive delivery. The constructive receipt criteria would apply when products or services are (1) being provided according to the federal entity specifications, and (2) the product or service is a nonstock item.

Accrued costs. The reporting of accrued costs related to contracts, orders, and agreements is similar to the reporting of accrued expenditures, with some exceptions. For instance, according to OMB

- *Applied costs* include depreciation and unfunded liabilities when such amounts are provided in the accounts of the agency.
- A net increase in inventories is an *accrued expenditure*, but would not be an applied cost until that inventory is used.
- Conversely, a net decrease in inventories is an applied cost, but not an accrued expenditure.
- For operating programs, a *change in capital assets* is not an applied cost, even though it is an accrued expenditure; the use or consumption (by depreciation or amortization) is the cost of a capital asset.

Key Forms

Within a federal entity, several forms are required to document a valid contract action. The more common forms encountered are identified next.

Procurement request and authorization. The procurement request or authorization (PR) represents the initiating document for a procurement. This record is completed by the program office determining that a need exists that cannot be met with the federal entity's existing resources. (No accounting entry results from the preparation or issuance of a PR.)

Request for proposal or bids or quotes. A request for proposal or invitation for bids should identify or describe: (1) the scope of work, (2) the period of performance, (3) the estimated level of resources required to conduct or perform the scope of work, (4) the type of contract to be awarded, (5) the special and general conditions applicable to the contract, and (6) on some occasions, the estimated amount budgeted by the entity for the specific contract action. (No accounting entry results from the preparation or issuance of an RFP/RFB/RFQ.)

Submitted proposals or bids. Interested organizations respond to the RFP/RFB/RFQ by submitting proposals or bids describing how they would undertake to perform the scope of work, the type of resources that would be required to complete the work satisfactorily, and the amount of money required to provide the goods or services. (No accounting entry results from this phase of the contractual process.)

Contract document. The award of a contract constitutes the legal binding obligation of the federal entity. The contract, signed by the contractor and agency executives, describes the negotiated scope of work, performance period, terms and conditions, amount of the contract, and the amount funded. (A formal accounting entry is made to obligate a portion of an agency's appropriation balance for the amount of the contract, or the funded amount, whichever is less.) When the amount of the contract is significantly in excess of the amount funded, the contract is said to be *incrementally funded*, limiting its liability to only the funded amount.

Financial expenditure reports and invoices. Most federal entities provide for progress or partial payments through the duration of the contract, with the amount of the payment dependent on the rate of incurred expenditures shown on periodic financial reports or invoices submitted by the contractor. (These documents are generally subjected to a prepayment "audit" and are the basis for supporting an accounting entry to liquidate the earlier obligation and record the accrued expense or costs of the contract.)

Cash advances. Certain contractors (usually nonprofit organizations and nonfederal government entities) receive an advance of funds. Advances can take one of two forms: (1) lump-sum or periodic advances, given to the contractor to cover operations for a specified time period, such as 30 or 60 days, and (2) letter-of-credit drawdowns. The letter-of-credit process is also a periodic funding that requires the existence of certain forms:

- An authorized *signature card* identifying the contractor's certifying officer, which is placed on file with the Treasury and the contractor's commercial bank or other designated disbursing organization.
- A *letter of credit* completed by the government entity and forwarded to the Treasury Department identifying the Federal Reserve Bank or Treasury disbursing agent, identifying the contractor, establishing the total amount of the letter of credit and the periodic withdrawal limits, and defining the time period for which the letter of credit will be available.
- A *request for payment* on letter of credit prepared by the contractor, consistent with the letter of credit, to withdraw funds to finance the contract scope of

work. This form requires a reconciliation of balances, withdrawals, and other letter-of-credit transactions, and an identification of the program or contract for which funds are being withdrawn.

- The issuance of an *advance* at the time of contract award or the release of funds pursuant to the submission of a request for payment on a letter of credit constitutes a disbursement of funds that is an advance which must be posted as an accounts receivable due the federal entity. These advances are a reduction in the agency's fund balance with the Treasury.

Schedule and voucher of payments. The schedule and voucher of payments, whether a hard-copy form or an electronic facsimile, is the formal request by an agency to the Treasury Department to make payment (by checks, electronic funds transfers, or direct deposits) for specific amounts to identified contractors. The Treasury Department makes no distinction between payments made for services or for advances. This accounting is a responsibility of the individual entity and the schedule represents the documentation in support of an agency's cash disbursements accounting entry.

PROCUREMENT AUDITS

A distinction generally exists between internal audits made of a federal agency's procurement functions and external audits made of the agency's contracts awarded to its contractors.

Audits of an agency's procurement functions (i.e., *internal audits*) could entail an examination of the policies, procedures, and practices by which the agency advertises, negotiates, awards, manages, monitors, finances, accounts, and ultimately closes out or settles contracts. Periodic audits of the procurement functions would more likely be made by federal inspectors general or agency internal audit staffs, but such reviews and examinations could also be outsourced to independent consulting and accounting firms.

Although larger agencies may have separate audit organizations to conduct the internal versus external audits, the internal and external audit function of smaller agencies will likely be centered in a single audit organization.

Exhibit 15.1 is a partial listing of the factors to consider in planning an audit of a federal contractor or contract. Specific conditions and circumstances related to individual federal contracts and grants may dictate that alternative tests be considered. To the extent that listed or other tasks are deemed appropriate, but circumstances will not permit performance of the tests, the auditor must reflect this fact in the audit opinion.

Audits of Procurement Process

An agency's procurement process is subjected to periodic internal audits to determine whether its program managers and contracting personnel are procuring the right services and goods at fair prices in accordance with agency policy and procedures and pursuant to the federal acquisition regulations and other laws and OMB regulations.

Exhibit 15.1. Methodology for audits for federal contracts

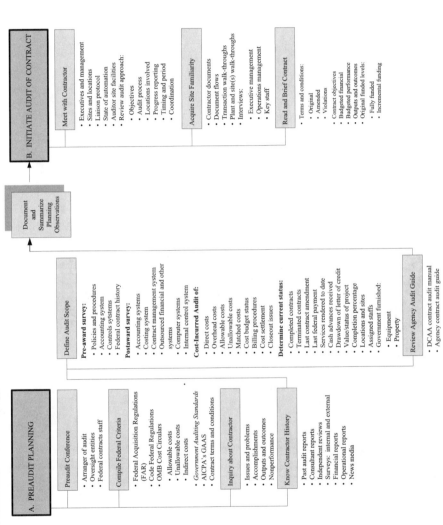

A. PREAUDIT PLANNING

Preaudit Conference
- Arranger of audit
- Oversight entities
- Federal contracts staff

Compile Federal Criteria
- Federal Acquisition Regulations (FAR)
- Code Federal Regulations
- OMB Cost Circulars
  - Allowable costs
  - Unallowable costs
  - Indirect costs
- *Government Auditing Standards*
- AICPA's GAAS
- Contract terms and conditions

Inquiry about Contractor
- Issues and problems
- Accomplishments
- Outputs and outcomes
- Nonperformance

Know Contractor History
- Past audit reports
- Consultant reports
- Independent reviews
- Surveys: internal and external
- Financial reports
- Operational reports
- News media

Define Audit Scope

Pre-award survey:
- Policies and procedures
- Accounting system
- Controls systems
- Federal contract history

Postaward survey:
- Accounting systems
- Costing system
- Contract management system
- Outsourced financial and other systems
- Computer systems
- Internal control system

Cost-Incurred Audit of:
- Direct costs
- Overhead costs
- Allowable costs
- Unallowable costs
- Matched costs
- Cost budget status
- Billing procedures
- Cost settlement
- Closeout issues

Determine current status:
- Completed contracts
- Terminated contracts
- Last contract amendment
- Last federal payment
- Services rendered to date
- Cash advances received
- Drawdown of letter of credit
- Value/status of project
- Completion percentage
- Locations and sites
- Assigned staffs
- Government furnished:
  - Equipment
  - Property

Review Agency Audit Guide
- DCAA contract audit manual
- Agency contract audit guide

Document and Summarize Planning Observations

B. INITIATE AUDIT OF CONTRACT

Meet with Contractor
- Executives and management
- Sites and locations
- Liaison protocol
- State of automation
- Auditor site facilities
- Review audit approach:
  - Objectives
  - Audit process
  - Locations involved
  - Progress reporting
  - Timing and period
  - Coordination

Acquire Site Familiarity
- Contractor documents
- Document flows
- Transaction walk-throughs
- Plant and site(s) walk-throughs
- Interviews:
  - Executive management
  - Operations management
  - Key staff

Read and Brief Contract
- Terms and conditions:
  - Original
  - Amended
  - Violations
- Contract objectives
- Budgeted financial
- Budgeted performance
- Outputs and outcomes
- Original funded levels:
  - Fully funded
  - Incremental funding

Exhibit 15.1. Methodology for audits for federal contracts (continued)

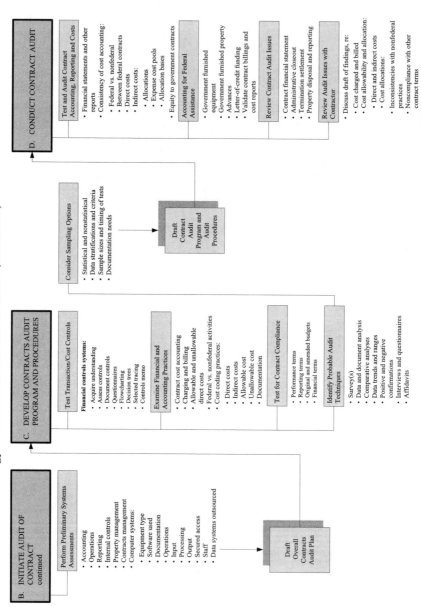

B. INITIATE AUDIT OF CONTRACT continued

Perform Preliminary Systems Assessments

- Accounting
- Operations
- Reporting
- Internal controls
- Property management
- Contracts management
- Computer systems:
  - Equipment type
  - Software used
  - Documentation
  - Operations
  - Input
  - Processing
  - Output
  - Secured access
  - Staff
  - Data systems outsourced

Draft Overall Contracts Audit Plan

C. DEVELOP CONTRACTS AUDIT PROGRAM AND PROCEDURES

Test Transaction/Cost Controls

Financial controls systems:
- Acquire understanding
- Assess controls
- Document controls
- Questionnaires
- Flowcharting
- Decision trees
- Selected tracing
- Controls memo

Examine Financial and Accounting Practices
- Contract cost accounting
- Charging and billing
- Allowable and unallowable direct costs
- Federal vs. nonfederal activities
- Cost coding practices:
  - Direct costs
  - Indirect costs
  - Allowable cost
  - Unallowable cost
  - Documentation

Test for Contract Compliance
- Performance terms
- Reporting terms
- Original and amended budgets
- Financial terms

Identify Probable Audit Techniques
- Survey(s)
- Data and document analysis
- Comparative analyses
- Data trends and ranges
- Positive and negative confirmations
- Interviews and questionnaires
- Affidavits

Consider Sampling Options
- Statistical and nonstatistical
- Data stratifications and criteria
- Sample sizes and timing of tests
- Documentation needs

Draft Contract Audit Program and Audit Procedures

D. CONDUCT CONTRACT AUDIT

Test and Audit Contract Accounting, Reporting and Costs
- Financial statements and other reports
- Consistency of cost accounting:
  - Federal vs. nonfederal
  - Between federal contracts
  - Direct costs
  - Indirect costs:
    - Allocations
    - Expense cost pools
    - Allocation bases
- Equity to government contracts

Accounting for Federal Assistance
- Government furnished equipment
- Government furnished property
- Advances
- Letter-of-credit funding
- Validate contract billings and cost reports

Review Contract Audit Issues
- Contract financial statement
- Administrative closeout
- Termination settlement
- Property disposal and reporting

Review Audit Issues with Contractor
- Discuss draft of findings, re:
  - Cost charged and billed
  - Cost allowability and allocation:
    - Direct and indirect costs
    - Cost allocations:
  - Inconsistencies with nonfederal practices
  - Noncompliance with other contract terms
- Noncompliance with other contract terms
- Contractor views and corrective actions

Exhibit 15.1. Methodology for audits for federal contracts (continued)

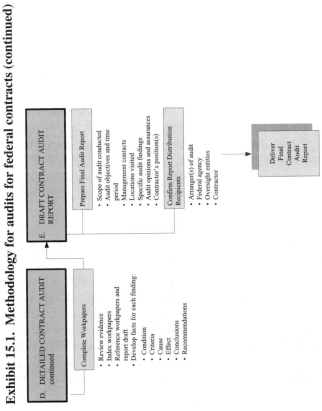

D. DETAILED CONTRACT AUDIT
continued

Complete Workpapers

- Review evidence
- Index workpapers
- Reference workpapers and
  report draft
- Develop facts for each finding:
  - Condition
  - Criteria
  - Cause
  - Effect
  - Conclusions
  - Recommendations

E. DRAFT CONTRACT AUDIT
REPORT

Prepare Final Audit Report

- Scope of audit conducted
- Audit objectives and time
  period
- Management contacts
- Locations visited
- Specific audit findings
- Audit opinions and assurances
- Contractor's position(s)

Confirm Report Distribution
Recipients

- Arranger(s) of audit
- Federal agency
- Oversight entities
- Contractor

Deliver
Final
Contract
Audit
Report

Audits with varied scopes. No uniform scope exists for internal audits of a federal agency's procurement process. Each audit is tailored to achieve the unique objectives and address the particular needs of that agency. The scope of an internal audit of a federal agency's procurement process could be broad and all-encompassing, blending aspects of a compliance audit, financial related audit, and a performance audit; or the audit scope could be limited, concentrating on a single subject or area. Most likely, the audit will concentrate on one or a few issues that concern agency management, possibly including tests of one or more of these activities to:

- Assess the effectiveness of decisions reached in determining an agency's need for services, supplies, equipment, or property.
- Examine the manner and thoroughness with which lists of prospective contractors are compiled, vetted, and solicited.
- Assure adherence to practices that will result in the maximum competition of competent, prospective contractors resulting in goods and services being procured at a competitive price.
- Test the relative completeness of bid and proposal evaluations and weightings applied in selecting the successful contractor.
- Assess the thoroughness of bid and proposal pricing reviews and cost analysis techniques.
- Review contract administration activity, including tasks to monitor contractor performance, contractor progress reports, invoice preaudits and payment approvals, controls over government furnished properties, contract closeouts, and final settlement practices.
- Assess adherence to regulations relating to contracting by small purchase orders, with particular emphasis on compliance with adherence to the dollar ceilings and repetitive award of such contracts to a single vendor.

An internal audit of a procurement process could appropriately be focused on nonfinancial administrative and management issues. Another internal audit could, with merit, be an examination of the contracting, financial, administrative and monitoring systems that support an agency's contract activities. The dollar significance of government-furnished equipment (GFE) or government-furnished property (GFP) in a contractor's possession could warrant an audit of the manner in which the GFE or GFP is procured, acquired, stored, controlled, used, and disposed of.

Internal audits are often made at the procurement function's central location, but field and site visits are not uncommon to verify or confirm the existence of a condition, possibly involving the contractor's bid, performance, or financial activities.

External Contract Audits

Audits and reviews executed in connection with federal procurements generally encompass the activities discussed below.

Contract audits. In addition to audits of an agency's procurement process (i.e., *internal audits*), audits are also made of nonfederal contractors (i.e., *external audits*). Although these audits are typically made by federal inspectors general, internal audit staffs, and the Defense Contract Audit Agency, a significant number of these audits are also performed by independent accounting firms under contract to federal and other governmental agencies.

Contract audits are made of proposals and bids from prospective contractors who desire to compete for fixed price and cost-reimbursement–type contracts. Contracts cost audits are made to test the allowability or possible unallowability of costs claimed under cost-reimbursement contracts. These audits are typically focused on assessing the adequacy of a contractor's cost accounting systems, billing procedures, and appropriateness of its cost allocations to federal and nonfederal activities.

Many audits are made of a contractor as an entity, but considerably more audits are made of individual contracts, particularly those of dollar significance, with performance scheduled over more than a single year. These federal audits could be made by agency auditors who are actually resident at the contractor's location or by a traveling federal audit team that periodically visits the contractor. The reasons for contract audits vary, but do include issues such as:

- Many contracts are awarded by negotiation, often without the benefit of competition, and result in somewhat less than a marketplace price determination.
- Cost-reimbursement contracts are audited to ensure that the contractor is reimbursed for only its actual allowable and relevant costs and to identify and restrain incurrence and billing for exorbitant costs.
- Fixed price contracts lack the right for the federal agency to audit the basic price, but such contracts often contain terms that permit reviews of price adjustments, cost escalation readjustments, and incentive compensations.
- Assessment of the quality of a contractor's property accountability policies and practices with respect to government-furnished equipment to ensure federal property is adequately safeguarded and applied only for purposes approved by the federal agency.
- Assessing the authenticity of cost or pricing data submitted by a contactor with the Truth in Negotiations Act that requires contractors to certify to the accuracy, completeness, and currency of that data.

Types of contract audits. Contract audits may be detailed, transactional-type financial audits of costs incurred and charged to a federal contract. At times, the term *contract audits* might more broadly include pricing reviews, preaward surveys, postaward surveys, and detailed audits of costs of one or more contracts.

Pricing Reviews

After proposals are received from prospective contractors, an agency may elect to have its auditors conduct a *pricing review* of elements of the proposed costs or price. A detailed pricing review might well include verification of the bidders' proposed costs for material, labor, other direct costs (i.e., travel, relocation, special equipment, computers, etc.), overhead burden, and general and administrative costs. Equally as important would be a validation of the bidders' bases for such estimates and, if possible, relating the proposed price to the bidders' performance on similar efforts.

Preaward Surveys

Should a federal agency have limited experience with a prospective contractor who is otherwise deemed to be responsive and responsible, its auditors might make a preaward survey to generally assess the prospective contractor's systems of financial accounting, cost accounting, internal controls, and project/contract management policies and procedures. Inquiries could also be made of the experiences of other federal agencies in relation to the prospective contractor.

Postaward Surveys

A postaward survey, if one is conducted, would occur within 90 days of contract award to a new contractor to ensure that the contractor has in place financial, administrative, and operational policies and procedures and that desired practices are employed for the contract.

Audits of Direct, Other Contract Costs

Contract audits are made at the conclusion of shorter-term contracts, but would be made periodically of significant contracts requiring performance over more than one year. These audits would be a blending of audit tests to assess compliance with general contract terms and conditions as well as performance, and financial terms. Although the objectives of these audits are dependent on the type of contract experience and issues or problems encountered, audits will often include audit tests of:

- Costs incurred, charged to, and later billed to the contract
- Support documents and other evidence of compliance with performance and financial terms and conditions of the contract
- Reasonableness of costs claimed in relation to the expired contract period and desired or expected contract outputs and outcomes
- Appropriateness of cost accounting and cost allocations applied to the federal contract in comparison to that employed for a contractor's nonfederal business and activities
- A comparison of proposed costs, to negotiated costs, to incurred costs to assess the overall efficacy of prices being paid by the federal agency

OMB'S COMPLIANCE SUPPLEMENT

OMB's *Compliance Audit Supplement* (the *Supplement*) provides guidance for audits of federal contracts, as well as grants and cooperative agreements.[2] Prior to the issuance of the *Supplement*, auditors of federal contracts were required to search numerous sections of the Code of Federal Regulations, OMB circulars, the federal acquisition regulations, and their agency's own procurement and contract policies in

---

[2] *The OMB **Compliance Audit Supplement** emanates from the Single Audit Act and OMB Circular A-133. The **Compliance Audit Supplement**, along with current OMB circulars, is available on the internet at **www.omb.gov.***

an effort to distill the federal contract compliance concerns into an audit program. An analysis of several OMB circulars and bulletins covering contract policies, federal laws, and regulations (the FARs, particularly) affecting the government's procurement of goods and services and the contracting policies and procedures of individual federal agencies will disclose considerable similarity, duplication, and overlap. The OMB *Supplement* is an excellent single source for identifying federal contracting policies, concerns, and issues insofar as they relate to contract audits.

OMB has stated that application of the *Supplement* will constitute a "safe harbor" for auditors with respect to the *nature* (i.e., what to audit) of audit procedures to apply. However, the *timing* (i.e., which months, periods, or accounts to test) and the *extent* (i.e., how much will be tested) depend on the auditor's judgment and on circumstances unique to the contractor or contract undergoing audit.

AUDIT ISSUES

This section focuses on audits of federal contractors and individual contracts awarded to nonfederal entities including state and local governments, corporate entities, academic institutions, utilities and authorities, and subsidiaries. Concurrent with its federal activities, a nonfederal contractor may also provide services under contract to nonfederal activities.

These conditions, relationships, and circumstances may present difficulties when undertaking an audit of individual federal contracts that could restrict the audit scope or be the basis for a qualified audit opinion. Some of these audit issues are outlined next.

Allowable, Unallowable, Indirect Costs

Uniform federal policy defines what the federal government has determined to be *allowable*, *unallowable*, and appropriate *indirect costs*. While this guidance is described in detail in OMB circulars, the same restrictions appear in laws and various sections of the Code of Federal Regulations and in the OMB *Supplement:*

- OMB A-21, *Cost Principles for Educational Institutions*
- OMB A-87, *Cost Principles for State, Local, and Indian Tribal Governments*
- OMB A-122, *Cost Principles for Non-Profit Organizations*
- 45 CFR Part 74, for public hospitals and providers of medical care

These circulars describe selected cost items, allowable and unallowable costs, and standard methodologies for calculating and allocating the indirect costs of nonfederal contractors. These cost policies are limitations on amounts that may be reimbursed or recovered under a federal contract. The cost principles articulated in each of these circulars are substantially similar, but some differences do exist, due mainly to the nature of the recipient organization, the nature of programs administered, and the breadth of services and operations of some grantees, but not others. Further, the policies closely parallel the cost provisions in the government's FARs.

A general policy relating to charges, reimbursements, billings, or payments to nonfederal contractors is that these costs must "be determined in accordance with generally accepted accounting principles (GAAP), *except* as otherwise provided for in OMB Cost Circulars." The emphasis on the word "except" is of particular significance to auditors of federal contract and grant programs because there are many significant exceptions.

Characterization of costs as allowable or unallowable does not imply that such costs are unnecessary, unreasonable, or illegal. The terms *allowable* or *unallowable* only mean that the federal government prefers not to pay a contractor for these costs. In most instances, the contractor could not function without the activities supported by the so-called unallowable costs. For example, in the case of a governmental contractor, OMB Circular A-87, *Cost Principles for State, Local, Governments*, declares general costs of a government (e.g., governors, mayors, legislative overseers, and "first-responder" costs) are unallowable as charges to federal programs.

Several policy statements (laws, regulations, OMB circulars, agency rules) detail categories of costs necessary to operate the nonfederal entity that are considered to be unallowable as a matter of declared federal policy. Some examples of costs declared as unallowable include:

- *Costs unallowed per public policy:* Write-off of uncollectible receivables; accrued cost for contingent liabilities; state and local government taxes; advertising cost; cost of idle facilities; lobbying costs; financing costs; donations; and contributions. The accounting and reporting of these costs are mandated and appropriate under GAAP but are classified as unallowable by the federal government for charges to its contracts.
- *Costs unallowed unless "funded" in advance of billing to the federal government:* All pension costs of government employees; postretirement health and other benefit costs due to government employees; and self-insured liabilities and costs are deemed unallowable until actually funded. The accounting and reporting of these incurred, but not paid, costs are required by, and appropriate under, GAAP, but are classified as unallowable by the federal government as charges to its contracts.
- *Cost unallowed unless approved in advance:* Cash drawdown in excess of three days; employee relocation costs; recruiting costs; subscriptions costs; professional membership fees; and purchase of capital assets. The accounting and reporting of these costs are mandated and appropriate under GAAP, but are classified as unallowable by the federal government for charges to its contracts, unless advance approval was obtained.

Unallowable costs may not be charged to, claimed under, or billed directly or indirectly to any federal contract, grant, or other program of federal assistance. If so done, such costs would be an audit finding reportable as a *questioned cost* by the auditor.

ALLOWABLE/UNALLOWABLE COST CRITERIA

The audit tests to assess compliance with federal procurement policy and federal allowable cost criteria require the auditor to test the direct and indirect costs charged to or claimed under a federal contract and to verify that the cost elements meet each of several allowability cost factors.

To be allowable under federal costing criteria, direct and indirect costs charged or claimed by a contractor must meet each of these criteria:

1. Be *necessary and reasonable* for the proper and efficient performance and administration of federal awards.

    Necessary costs are cost required, implicitly or explicitly, by law, regulations, and the federal contract agreement to support the program outlined in the federal contract. Necessary cost criteria should be assessed from the view of the purpose, timing, amount, authorization and approval, and the ultimate accounting of charged costs in relation to the performance period of the contract.

    Reasonable costs are costs that are *reasonable* if, in nature and amount, they do not exceed that which would be incurred by a prudent person under circumstances prevailing at the time the decision was made to incur the cost. Determination as to the reasonableness of costs must give consideration to the following questions:

    - Do the claimed costs exceed the type generally recognized as ordinary and necessary for the operation of the contractor or attainment of the performance or objectives outlined in the executed federal contract?
    - Do the claimed costs exceed restraints on spending or cost requirements imposed by sound business practices, presence of arm's-length bargaining, terms of federal and other laws, regulations, and terms, or as conditions of the federal contract?
    - Do the claimed costs exceed market prices for comparable goods or services?
    - Do the claimed costs significantly deviate from established practices in a manner that unjustifiably increases the cost to the federal contract?

2. Be *allocable* to federal awards under the provisions of OMB cost circulars.

    Allocable costs are costs that are allocable if the cost is directly allocable to a particular cost objective or if the goods and services involved are chargeable or assignable to such cost objectives in accordance with relative benefits received. OMB requires that determination of *allocability* of costs give consideration to:

    - All activities that benefit from a unit's indirect cost, including unallowable activities and services donated by third parties, receive an appropriate allocation of indirect costs.
    - Unless otherwise permitted in writing, any cost allocable to a particular federal contract or cost objective may not be charged to other federal awards to overcome fund deficiencies, to avoid restrictions imposed by law or terms of federal awards, or for other reasons.
    - Where an accumulation of indirect costs will ultimately result in charges to a federal contract, a cost allocation plan will be required, similar to those outlined in CASB standards or the appropriate OMB cost circular.

3. Be *authorized and not otherwise prohibited* under any federal, state, or local laws or regulations.

4. *Comply* with any limitations or exclusions set forth in the FARs, cost principles in OMB circulars, terms and conditions unique to the federal contract, or other governing regulations regarding types, amounts, or limits on cost items.

5. Be in *conformance with policies, regulations, and procedures* that apply uniformly to both federal and nonfederal contracts and awards and to federal and nonfederal activities of the nonfederal entity receiving assistance under a federal contract.

6. Be accorded consistent cost accounting treatment.

    Consistent cost accounting treatment means that costs may not be assigned to a federal award as a direct or indirect cost if any other cost has been incurred for the same purpose, in like circumstances, and has been allocated to the federal award directly or, in part, indirectly. The *consistency* requirement relates to the uniform accounting and charging of costs to both federal and nonfederal activities of a contractor between fiscal reporting periods.

7. Be determined in accordance with generally accepted accounting principles, *except* as otherwise provided for in OMB cost circulars.

8. Be *not* included as a cost or used to meet *cost sharing or matching* requirements of any other federal award in either the current or prior period, except as specifically provided by federal law or regulation. This restriction prohibits a contractor from claiming direct or indirect costs that were charged to the federal government under one federal agreement to meet a cost-sharing or cost matching cost requirement of another federal agreement.

9. Be net of all applicable credits.

    Net of applicable credits refers to receipts or the reduction of expenditure-type transactions that offset or reduce expense of items charged to federal contracts as direct or indirect costs (e.g., purchase discounts, rebates or allowances, recoveries or indemnities on losses, insurance refunds or rebate, or other price adjustments). In applying costs net of applicable credits, the *allocability* of net costs must give consideration to:

    • The extent that such credits relate to allowable costs, the credits must be applied to the federal award as a cost reduction or cash refund, as appropriate

    • Amounts of any credits should be recognized in determining indirect cost rates or amounts to be charged to federal awards

10. Be adequately *documented*.

    Audits of direct and indirect costs and matching contributions claimed or charged must be tested to support documentation that identifies or relates to the amount, timing, and purpose of transactions to the specific federal contract. For example, the timing of the transaction must be within the contract period. In most instances, transactions preceding or following contract award are not allowable in the absence of specific approval by the federal agency.

Supportive documentation, as defined in literature of GAO and the AICPA, includes

- *Accounting records of original entry:* for example, journals, registers, ledgers, manuals, worksheets, and support for cost allocations. Alone, though, these types of accounting data are not sufficient supporting documentation.
- *Corroborating evidence:* for example, canceled checks, invoices, contracts, grants, minutes of meetings, confirmations, and other written statements by knowledgeable personnel, information obtained by auditor inquiry, observation, inspection, personal examination, and other information developed by, or available to, the auditor.
- *Independent tests* must be made by the auditor of underlying data and records and include analyses, reviews, retracing procedural steps of the financial process, auditor recalculations, and performance of reconciliations of any cost allocations.

In audits of federal contracts, the auditor must *question* and report to the federal agency for resolution claims or charges to the contract that are not sufficiently documented or supported, or about which the auditor is unable to satisfy him- or herself by other evidential means as to the propriety and allowability of costs.

The OMB *Compliance Supplement* identifies 10 procurement compliance regulations, noncompliance with which could have a direct and material effect on the accounting, charging, and billings to federal contracts. If the contract is materially significant to the contractor, noncompliance under a federal contract might well affect overall financial statements of the contractor. Ten of the compliance policies associated with individual contracts and of importance to contract audits include:

1. *Costs charged to government: allowable, unallowable, direct, and indirect costs.* Dating to the middle of the last century, it has been federal government policy that the government will permit only certain direct and indirect costs to be claimed by and reimbursed under federal contracts. Federal money may not be claimed or paid for any direct or indirect costs defined as unallowable by federal policy. OMB has provided these definitions of direct and indirect costs:

   - *Direct costs* are those that can be identified specifically with a particular final cost objective. Typical direct costs chargeable to federal contracts include employee compensation, cost of materials, equipment, if specifically approved, and travel expenses subject to federal limits.
   - *Indirect costs* are those (a) incurred for a common or joint purpose benefiting more than one cost objective; and (b) are not readily assignable to the cost objectives specifically benefited, without an effort that is disproportionate to the results achieved. To facilitate equitable distribution of indirect expenses to the cost objectives served, it may be necessary to establish a number of pools of indirect costs within the contractor.

Indirect cost pools should be distributed to benefited cost objectives on bases that will produce an equitable result in consideration of relative benefits derived. Any direct cost of a minor amount may be treated as an indirect cost for reasons of practicality, where such accounting treatment for that item of cost is consistently applied to all cost objectives.

2. *Equipment, real property.* The title to equipment acquired by nonfederal entities with federal monies could remain with the nonfederal entity or with the federal government. Here, equipment is defined as tangible, nonexpendable property with a useful life of more than one year and an acquisition cost of $5,000 or more per unit.

3. *Matching contributions.* Matching requirements, in-kind or other, often require examination of the terms and conditions of the individual contract. Matching requirements are often specific as to the *amount*, *type*, *timing*, and *purpose* of match that is permissible. For example, if the agreed-on match was to be cash, donated labor, or any other type of contribution, free or paid, it would be unallowable. Also, there may be a requirement that the match be provided within a certain time period; compliance in a later period would have to be reported.

4. *Availability of program funds.* Legislation for all federal appropriations and other financial assistance places limits on the *amount* of funds being provided, the *purpose* for which the funds are provided, and a *time* period (or use period) after which the authority to spend the federal monies lapses. (OMB Circular A-102, the "common rule," should be consulted for additional guidance on this compliance requirement.)

5. *Procurement, suspension, debarment.* Presidential executive orders and federal regulations prohibit federal agencies from contracting with, or subcontracting to, parties who have been suspended or debarred or whose principals are suspended or debarred.

6. *Program income.* *Program income* is the gross income directly generated by the federal project, during the contract period (e.g., fees earned for services, rental income, sale of commodities or items fabricated under the program, payment of principal, and interest on loans made from federal funds). Unless otherwise specified by the federal agency, program income shall be deducted from program outlays.

7. *Reporting.* Recipients of federal contracts must use prescribed standard forms for financial, performance, and special reporting. Auditors must confirm that controls have been implemented to ensure that reports, claims for advances, and reimbursements are supported by the same books and records from which the entity's financial statements were prepared. Tests must be made to ensure submitted reports, claims for advances, and reimbursements are supported by underlying documentation and appropriate corroborating evidence.

8. *Special tests and provisions.* Laws, regulations, provisions of contracts, and grants contain requirements for special tests. The auditor must review the specific terms and conditions of the contract since the contract could contain

conditions warranting special examination. The axiom of the legal profession applies equally to contract audits: *When all else fails, read the contract.* There is no substitute for examining the terms and conditions of specific contracts, bond covenants, terms of loans, loan guarantees, and so on under which money or financial assistance is provided to support contracts to nonfederal entities.

9. *Activities: Allowable, unallowable.* Public monies may be used only for those activities allowed by law or regulation. Congress determines that certain organizations, groups, or individuals are to be beneficiaries of funding provided under particular federal legislation. The law will also define the qualifying conditions and the benefits to be conferred. Permitted and prohibited activities must be identified, and audit tests made, to ensure that federal monies are used to support only those activities permitted by law or regulation. Audit tests must be made to ensure that federal monies were used to support only those activities permitted by law or regulation.

10. *Cash management: advance funding of government programs.* For some contractors, forms of advance funding exist (e.g., lump sum or total advance of required federal funding; advances made at designated points during the contract period; or periodic drawdowns under a prearranged letter of credits procedure arranged between the contractor, the US Treasury, and a local commercial bank). Under the Cash Management Act, a contractor's procedures for drawing down federal funds must minimize the time elapsing between the transfer of funds from the US Treasury and disbursement by the contractor. Historically, the cash balance could not be in excess of three business days.

When deciding whether to test or not test a compliance requirement, the auditor must conclude: (1) whether the requirement does or does not apply to the contract, and (2) whether noncompliance with the requirement could or could not have a material effect on the contract. *Government Auditing Standards* ("yellow book") Chapter 8, Reporting Standards for Performance Audits, provides guidance for the desired narrative-type audit reports and should be consulted before undertaking an audit of federal contracts. Further, the guidance in Chapter 8 is part of the criteria used by federal inspectors general and GAO in assessing the adequacy of the contract audit.

16 GRANT AUDITS

For the federal government, expenditures under grants-in-aid are very significant. Funds are expended by grants to purchase or support a wide variety of services including purchases of equipment, real and consumer-type properties, supplies, and conduct of research, to mention a few of the purposes for which grants are issued. Amounts spent under grants greatly exceed amounts spent on other items in the budgets of many agencies. Congress will monitor major grant programs closely, agencies will track financing and operations under grant instruments, and, at times, the print and other news media will provide extensive and detailed coverage of grants, particularly if there is a hint of fraud, waste, or abuses.

GRANTS DEFINED

Since the 1960s, the definition or nature of the federal grant has evolved from an endowment or outright gift of monies, to today, where many recipients of federal grants operate programs, perform services, and render technical assistance on behalf of the federal government. Generally, a federal *grant* may be defined as:

> *money or property in lieu of money paid or furnished by the federal government to a grantee under a program that provides financial assistance to the grantee or through the grantee to a constituency defined in law by Congress. Not included in this definition would be other types of federal financial assistance, such as loans, loan guarantees, revenue sharing, and forms of insurances.*

GRANTS TYPES

In practice, the terms and conditions of grants may be indistinguishable from those of federal contracts, as both contracts and grants are legally binding instruments between the federal agency and its contractors and grantees. At times, an instrument considered to be a contract by one federal agency may be accounted for as a grant by another. A variety of descriptors are applied to grants, but some of the more common classifications have included:

- *Formula grants,* by law, have a mandated funding level for identified types of grantees only, with little or no discretion being exercised by the federal grantor, which could include allocations of money to states and their subdivisions for activities of a continuing nature, not confined to a specific project.
- *Project grants* resemble contracts because federal grantors agree to pay the grantee for services, performance, or the completion of a project. These grants for projects with fixed or known periods could include research and training grants, planning and demonstration grants, technical assistance grants, and construction grants.

- *Block grants,* which are intended to consolidate funds for broad purposes into a single funding action, are typically issued to state or local governments with minimal or less expenditure restrictions from the federal grantor.
- *Noncompetitive grants* may be awarded to all applicants meeting specified legal or other congressional criteria.
- *Competitive grants* may be awarded to a selected number of grantees having similar qualifying characteristics after an evaluation of proposals, in a manner similar to that used for competitive contract awards.

As is evident from these definitions, the categorization of grants by groups is not a mutually exclusive ranking, nor are the descriptors applied uniformly across federal agencies. In practice, a grant award could conceivably fall within two or more of these categories.

RESPONSIBILITY FOR GRANTS

Several organizations share the responsibility for award, administration, and settlement of federal grants. The nature of authority or responsibilities exercised by these organizations is outlined next.

Congressional Responsibilities

Congress, through its authorization and appropriation committees, has the ultimate authority and responsibility for federal grant policies. These policies will appear in laws having government-wide applicability, as well as specific legislation applicable to individual granting agencies. Legislation applicable to individual agencies will contain specific congressional policy and, at times, procedural directions concerning the award and administration of a grants program.

Government Accountability Office

GAO is authorized to audit the expenditures of federal monies spent under grants. In the exercise of this authority, GAO may review systems of federal agencies relating to grants award and administration and the accounting and internal controls in support of these types of agreements. These grant reviews are made both at the federal entity level and at contractor and grantee locations.

Office of Management and Budget

OMB issues government-wide regulations relating to grant awards. Most notable are the OMB circulars and various titles of the US Code, defining the types of allowable costs, unallowable costs, and indirect or overhead costs permitted or prohibited under federal governmental contracts and grants. Applicable circulars include:

- OMB Circular A-21, *Cost Principles for Educational Institutions*, setting forth the allowable, unallowable, and indirect cost principles for contracts with educational institutions

- OMB Circular A-87, *Cost Principles for State, Local and Indian Tribal Governments*, setting forth the allowable, unallowable, and indirect cost principles applicable to state and local governments
- OMB Circular A-122, *Cost Principles for Nonprofit Organizations*, setting forth the allowable, unallowable, and indirect cost principles for nonprofit organizations

Individual Federal Grantor Agencies

The Budget and Accounting Procedures Act of 1950 and later laws require the head of each federal entity to establish and maintain an adequate system of accounting and internal controls over grant assistance programs. Pursuant to the act and other legislation, federal entities have designed procedures relating to the solicitation and evaluation of grant proposals; negotiation, award, and administration of grants; and the accounting for all phases of grant performance. It is critical that an agency's systems of controls, accounting, and reporting be sufficiently precise to permit monitoring of grant obligations; liquidation of these obligations; and the costing and disbursement of funds under these agreements. The systems of controls, accounting, and reporting for contract and grant awards generally require the coordination of numerous organizations of the awarding federal agency.

Controls for Grants-in-Aid

Federal organizations such as GAO, OMB, and the General Services Administration have some authority and responsibility to issue and require adherence to their government-wide policies and regulations relating to contracts and grants. However, the actual design of systems of controls, accounting, and reporting to protect the government is the sole responsibility of individual federal granting agencies. The details will vary, but most federal entities have established operating policies and procedures requiring that:

- A grant authorization is to be approved by the responsible agency official and annotated, in advance, to show that sufficient appropriated funds exist to meet the estimated amount of the anticipated grant.
- If grants may be competitively awarded, a formal review process will exist for the objective evaluation and ranking of grant proposals received by the agency, both solicited and unsolicited.
- The issuance of a grant with the timely notification to the fiscal function permits prompt obligation of funds in an amount equal to the funded value of the grant.
- Periodic reporting of expenditures and performance must be made to grantees, with formal agency acknowledgement of grantee performance.
- Settlement by grantees of advances of money and drawdowns under letters of credit must comply with federal policy and the individual grant conditions.
- Periodic assessment of the extent to which the purpose or objective of the grant is being achieved and that the required accounting and management control systems are in place and operating effectively.

- Compliance with specific conditions and provisions for required matching or cost-sharing or in-kind contributions by grantee recipients.
- Timely payment of grant liabilities, prompt settlement and closeout, final accounting, and reporting at the conclusion or termination of the grant program.
- A final audit of the grantee must take place, with the federal agency retaining the right to recover appropriate amounts after considering audit recommendations and questioned or disallowed costs identified during the audit.

Grants-in-Aid Process

For federal agencies with the authority to operate grants-in-aid programs, the grants management process requires formal authorizations and approvals for anticipated grant awards, the execution of specific forms to document the grants award process, establishment of the controls, and performance of the accounting for each grant awarded. Identification of the types and purposes of various support documentation is essential to auditing an agency's grants-in-aid program. For example:

- An agency's grantor program office would establish operating policies and procedures to implement a grants-in-aid program to provide assistance to the eligible recipient constituency cited by Congress in the *authorization* and *appropriation* legislation for the program.
- The agency's grants director, possibly a designated *allottee*, would possess budgetary authority to approve and fund grantee selections and later execute grants.
- The responsible federal agency might issue a notification to the public in the *Federal Register* and other *announcements* describing the grants program, the eligible constituency, and the procedures for applying for the assistance to solicit applications for grants. (Some grant-in-aid processes may forgo the formal application phase, depending on the program's enabling legislation.)
- *Applications for grants assistance*, if required, would be reviewed on receipt, critiqued for compliance with law, be approved, and a formal *grant agreement* executed with grantees that is legally binding between an agency and its grantees, pursuant to Section 1311 of the Supplemental Appropriation Act.
- The receipt and acceptance of services, goods, or assistance by a grantee must often be formally monitored and acknowledged by the appropriate agency personnel.
- *Financial expenditure* and *operational reports* are provided by the grantee for reimbursement of expenses or in support of earlier advances or letters-of-credit drawdowns provided in anticipation of the reported expenditures.
- *Prepayment audits* of invoices to ensure that amounts, performance, and deliveries are consistent with negotiated grant terms; that prompt and accurate payment is made of properly rendered invoices; and that there is timely processing of all procurement transactions.
- Final settlement or *grant closeout* of any advanced money, government-furnished equipment, and property in a manner consistent with agency policy or grant conditions, and a final assessment of grantee compliance.

Not all grant award tasks or activities are resident within a single unit, function, or activity of a federal agency. Rather, the completion of a grant action requires collaboration and coordination among:

- *Grantor Program Office, Allottee.* For new programs, the federal grantor's program office is responsible for informing the congressionally-targeted constituency of the federal assistance program. This office is often responsible for conducting negotiations, when required, with prospective grantees; executing and awarding the grants; administering the grant; monitoring periodic financial and performance reports; and settlement and closeout at completion of the grant.

- *Accounting Section.* This section must confirm the availability of agency appropriations money for grants in advance of grants approval. Additionally, this function would perform the agency's accounting to record an obligation for each grant awarded, liquidate the obligation when services are performed, and process the expenditures, payables, and ultimate disbursement transactions related to each grant. The accounting section might also compile internal and external financial reports on grants; prepare the schedule to request issuance of checks by the Treasury Department to grantees; and perform the fiscal and budgetary accounting during and after expiration of the agency's appropriations.

- *Grantee.* The grantee may have to prepare and submit a grant application, negotiate terms and conditions of the prospective grant, and execute a legally binding grant with the federal agency. Federal grants could be funded by periodic advances of cash to the grantee, permitting the grantee to draw down cash under a federal letter of credit, or reimbursing the grantee on the basis of reports reporting the expenditures incurred for the federal grant program. Each grantee must perform services or operate the agreed-to grant program; periodically complete and submit financial and performance reports to the federal grantor; and compile end-of-grant financial, property, and performance reports to formally settle and close out the grant.

- *Treasury Department.* Actual checks or other types of funds transfer in payment for a grantee performance are issued by the Treasury Department upon receiving a request from the federal grantor agency that a check be issued or direct deposit made to a named grantee.

EVENTS REQUIRING ACCOUNTING ENTRIES

OMB has prescribed certain criteria for (1) the incurring of financial obligations for awarded grants, (2) the accruing of expenditures reported by grantees, and (3) the accounting for costs of grant transactions. The accounting of grants-in-aid by federal agencies must be in accordance with the concepts set forth in OMB Circular A-11, *Preparation, Submission, and Execution of the Budget*, and OMB Circular A-34, *Instructions on Budget Execution*:

- *Record only valid obligations.* An agency's reporting of obligations incurred for federal grants-in-aid programs, according to Section 1311 of the Supplemental Appropriation Act, requires that there be legal evidence of a binding agreement prior to the recording and reporting of obligations for grants. OMB Circular A-34 sets forth the formal criteria for recognizing formal grants-in-aid obligations. According to OMB, internal administrative commitments of agency funds and invitations to apply for federal assistance sent to prospective grantees are not legally valid obligations. These and other type activities fail to meet the criteria of Section 1311.

- *Accrue grant expenditures regardless of when paid.* Expenditures for grants accrue when the grantee reports performance in accordance with the terms and conditions of the grant program. The expenditures accrue and a liability to the grantee is created by the grantee's performance. The accounting for the cash disbursed in payment or reimbursement to the grantee may delay performance by weeks or even months, unless the grantee has received an advance or has withdrawn funds under a letter of credit.

The more common forms used by federal agencies when awarding and administering grant programs include several of those identified next.

Grants Authorization

The program authorization is a formal authorization for the grants program and approval to incur obligations on behalf of the federal government. Within the federal agency, this form may be executed by the head of the agency or, more often, by an official, frequently the agency's designated program *allottee*. The grants program authorization serves as the basis to allot a portion of the agency's appropriation to the grants-in-aid program.

Grant Applications

Repeat grantees of continuing grants-in-aid programs may be permitted to simultaneously submit an operating budget with the next year's financial plan, which, if approved, becomes the grantee's funding application for that year. A new grants-in-aid program might be required to request grants applications from the constituency identified by Congress in the programs authorization and appropriation legislation. Grant applications typically identify or describe: (1) the nature of the grants program, (2) the number and type of constituents to be serviced, (3) the period of performance, (4) the budget or estimated level of financial and other resources required to operate the grant program, and (5) general and special conditions applicable to the grants-in-aid program or the individual grant. (No accounting entry results from receipt of a grants application.)

Grant Agreement

The award of a grant constitutes the legally binding obligation of a federal entity. The grant agreement typically signed by a grantee and the designated agency executive describes the scope of the grant services, performance period, terms and conditions, the amount of the grant, and the amount funded. When the face amount of the grant is in excess of the amount funded by the federal agency, the contract is said to be *incrementally funded*. An incremental funding limits the federal agency's liability to the funded amount. (At this stage, an accounting entry is made to formally obligate a portion of an agency's appropriation balance for the lesser of the face amount of the grant or the incrementally funded amount.)

Expenditure Reports

Most grants-in-aid programs require that grantees submit periodic progress reports (financial and/or performance) to document grant funds received earlier as advances, letter of credit drawdowns, or requests for reimbursement of grant expenditures. (These reports are generally subjected to a prepayment "audit" and are the basis to support an accounting entry to liquidate earlier obligated amounts and record the program's accrued expense.)

Cash Advances

Most federal grantees, usually nonprofit organizations and nonfederal government entities, receive an advance of grant funds. Advances can be made in two forms: (1) lump-sum or periodic advances given to the grantee to cover operations for a specified time period, or (2) a letter of credit drawdown. The letter of credit process is a periodic funding process that requires the existence of certain forms, including:

- An authorized *signature card* identifying the grantee's certifying officer that is placed on file with the Treasury and the grantee's commercial bank or other designated disbursing organization.
- A *letter of credit*, completed by the government entity and forwarded to the Treasury, identifying the Federal Reserve Bank or Treasury disbursing agent, identifying the grantee, establishing the total amount of the letter of credit and the periodic withdrawal limits, and defining the time period for which the letter of credit will be available.
- A *request for payment* on letter of credit is prepared by the grantee, consistent with the letter of credit, to withdraw funds to finance grantee performance. The form requires the reconciliation of balances, withdrawals, and other letter-of-credit transactions and an identification of the associated grant program or grant for which funds are withdrawn.
- The issuance of an advance at the time of contract award or the release of funds pursuant to the submission of a request for payment on a letter of credit constitutes a *disbursement of funds* that is *an advance* which must be posted as an accounts receivable due the federal entity.

Schedule and Voucher of Payments

The voucher and schedule of payments, whether a hard-copy form or an electronic facsimile, is the formal request by the federal grantor agency to the Treasury Department to make payment (by checks, electronic funds transfers, or direct deposits) in specified amounts to identified grantees. The Treasury makes no distinction between payments made for performance or for advances. This accounting is a responsibility of the federal entity and the schedule merely represents the documentation in support of an agency's accounting entry for its cash disbursements.

COOPERATIVE AGREEMENTS

Cooperative agreement transactions and grants are accounted for in a similar manner. The cooperative agreement instrument was initially defined in the Federal Grants and Cooperative Agreement Act of 1977. Under this legislation, Congress attempted to distinguish among contracts, grants, and cooperative agreements by identifying the conditions under which each instrument was to be used.

- A *contract* is to be used whenever the principal purpose of the instrument is the acquisition, by purchase, lease, or barter, of property or services for the direct benefit of the government; or whenever an executive agency determines that the use of a contract is appropriate.
- A *grant* is to be used whenever the purpose of the relationship is to transfer money, property, services, or anything of value to accomplish a public purpose of support or stimulation authorized by federal statute and no substantial involvement is anticipated between the executive agency and the recipient during the performance of the contemplated activity.
- A *cooperative agreement* is to be used whenever the purpose of the relationship is the transfer of money, property, services, or anything of value to accomplish a public purpose of support or stimulation authorized by federal statute and substantial involvement is anticipated between the executive agency and the recipient during performance of the contemplated activity.

Since the cooperative agreement generally closely parallels grants and contracts, federal entities often opt to use the government's standard contract format and the applicable general contract conditions, modified to the circumstances. However, the accounting for a cooperative agreement is more similar to that performed for grant agreements.

AUDITS OF FEDERAL GRANTS

A distinction is generally made to distinguish between audits of a federal agency's grants management functions in contrast to audits of individual grantees. Audits of an agency's grants management functions (i.e., *internal audits*) could entail examination of the policies, procedures, and practices by which an agency initiates grants program outreach and generates public awareness for a new or existing grant program, and negotiates, awards, manages, monitors, finances, accounts, and ultimately closes out or settles the federal grants. Periodic audits of an agency's grants management functions are made by the agency's inspectors general or its internal audit staff. However, such reviews and examinations could also be outsourced to independent consulting and independent accounting firms.

Exhibit 16.1 is a partial listing of many factors to consider in planning an audit of a federal grantee or grant. Specific conditions and circumstances related to individual federal grants will dictate that alternative sequences testing should be considered or that additional testing should be made. To the extent the listed or other tasks are deemed appropriate, but encountered circumstances will not permit performance of those tests, the auditor must reflect this fact in the audit opinion.

Audits of Agency Management

An agency's grants management process may be subjected to periodic internal audits to determine whether program managers are awarding and managing grants in the manner required by federal law, OMB regulations, and the agency's own grants policies and procedures.

No uniform scope exists for the internal audit of a federal agency's grants management functions. Each must be tailored to the program to be audited, and, in this sense, an internal audit is somewhat similar to a performance audit. An audit of an agency's grants management functions can be broad and all-encompassing, blending aspects of a compliance audit, financial-related audit, and a performance audit. Or the audit scope could be limited, concentrating on a single subject or area of the grants function.

Most likely, the audit will concentrate on one or a few issues concerning the agency's grants management functions, possibly including tests of one or more of these activities that require the auditor to:

- Assess the decisions reached in determining if the designed grant program is the one intended by the authorization and appropriations acts of Congress.
- Assess the manner and thoroughness with which lists of prospective grantees are compiled, vetted, solicited, and, after grants award, monitored.
- Assess the relative completeness of grant applications, where such is required by, or implicit in, the grants program authorization law.
- Review the grants administration activities, including tasks to monitor grantee performance, grantee progress reports, grantee payments, controls over government-furnished properties, and end-of-grant closeout and settlement practices.

An internal audit of a grants management activity could appropriately be focused on nonfinancial or grants administrative or program management issues. Still another internal audit could, with merit, be an examination of the grant awarding, administration, financial, and monitoring processes. The dollar significance of government-furnished equipment or government-furnished property in a grantee's possession could also warrant an audit of the manner in which government equipment and property provided to a grantee was procured, acquired, stored, controlled, and transferred to grantees and used for only authorized purposes. An internal audit is typically made at the grants management program office of the agency, but field and site visits are not uncommon to verify or confirm the existence of conditions possibly involving grantee's budgets, performance, or financial activities.

AUDITS OF GRANTEES

Audits and reviews executed in connection with federal grants generally encompass the activities discussed throughout the next sections.

Although grant audits are largely made by agency federal inspectors general and internal audit staffs, many of these audits are also performed by independent accounting firms under contract to the federal and other governmental agencies.

Audits could be, and are, made of a grantee as an entity, but considerably more audits are made of individual grants, particularly those of dollar significance, with program performance scheduled over multiple years. The reasons for grantee and grant audits vary, but often include:

- Assessment of cost incurred and billed by a grantee to the federal grantor to ensure that the grantee is reimbursed for only its actual allowable and relevant costs, to identify and restrain incurrence and billing for exorbitant amounts
- Review of the quality of a grantee's administrative and property management practices, particularly if the grantee is in possession of significant amounts of government-furnished equipment and property
- Evaluations of the relative efficiency and effectiveness with which the grantee is managing and administering the federal grants-in-aid program
- Tests for compliance with federal laws, OMB regulations, and agency guidance and rules applicable to the grants program

Types of Grant Audits

Grant audits may be detailed, transactional-type financial audits of cost incurred and charged to a federal grant. At times, the term *grants audit* might more broadly include preaward surveys, postaward surveys, and audits of costs.

Preaward Surveys

Should a federal agency have limited experience with a prospective grantee who is otherwise deemed responsive and responsible, its auditors might make a *preaward survey* to generally assess the prospective grantee's systems of financial accounting, cost accounting, internal controls, and project/contract management policies and procedures. Inquiries could also be made of the experiences of other federal agencies in relation to the prospective grantee.

Postaward Surveys

A postaward survey, if one is conducted, would occur within 90 days of grant award to ensure that a new grantee has in place adequate financial, administrative, and operational policies and procedures and that desirable management practices are being employed for the contract.

Audits of Direct, Other Costs

Cost audits of grants are generally made at the conclusion of shorter-term grants but are made periodically of significant grants requiring performance over multiple years. These audits could be a blending of tests to assess the compliance with grants terms and conditions, performance achievement, and financial management. The objectives of a grant audit are dependent on the nature of the grantee, type and conditions of the specific grant, and issues or problems encountered by or with the grantee; but audits will often include tests of:

- Cost incurred, charged to, and later billed to the federal grant

- Support documents and other evidence of compliance with performance goals and objectives and with the financial terms and conditions of the grant
- Reasonableness of costs claimed in relation to the expired grant period and desired or expected grant inputs, outputs, and outcomes
- Appropriateness of cost accounting and cost allocations applied to the federal grants in comparison to those employed for a grantee's nonfederal activities
- Proposed costs in comparison to incurred costs to assess the overall efficacy of charges ultimately being paid by the federal agency

GRANT AUDIT POLICIES

OMB's *Compliance Audit Supplement* (hereafter called the *Supplement*) provides guidance for audits of federal grants and cooperative agreements.[1] Prior to issuance of the *Supplement*, auditors of federal grants were required to search countless sections of the Code of Federal Regulations, OMB circulars, and the grantor agency's own grants policies and procedures in an effort to distill the federal government's concerns into a grants audit program. The OMB *Supplement* is an excellent single source for identifying federal grant audit policies and procedures. With respect to audits of federal grants, OMB states that application of the *Supplement* will constitute a "safe harbor" for auditors with respect to the *nature* (i.e., what to audit) of audit procedures to apply. However, and reasonably so, the *timing* (which months, periods, or accounts to test) and the *extent* (i.e., how much will be tested) depend on the auditor's judgments and on the circumstances unique to the grantee or grant undergoing audit.

Audit Issues

This section of the chapter is directed toward audits of federal grantees and individual grants awarded to nonfederal grantees that could include state and local governments, academic institutions, and some utilities and authorities, plus tens of thousands of not-for-profit organizations.

Allowable, unallowable, indirect costs. Within the federal government, uniform policy exists defining what the government has determined to be *allowable*, *unallowable*, and appropriate *indirect costs* that impact the audits of every federal grant. While this guidance is described in detail in various OMB circulars, the same restrictions appear in laws and various sections of the Code of Federal Regulations and in OMB's *Supplement.*

- OMB A-21, *Cost Principles for Educational Institutions*
- OMB A-87, *Cost Principles for State, Local, and Indian Tribal Governments*
- OMB A-122 *Cost Principles for Nonprofit Organizations*
- 45 CFR Part 74, for public hospitals, providers of medical care

These circulars identify selected cost items, define those allowable and unallowable costs appropriate as charges to federal programs, and describe standard meth-

---

[1] *The OMB **Compliance Audit Supplement** emanates from the Single Audit Act and OMB Circular A-133. The **Compliance Audit Supplement,** along with current OMB circulars, is available on the Internet at **www.omb.gov**.*

odologies for calculating and allocating the indirect costs appropriate for use by non-federal grantees. These cost policies, in practice, are limitations on amounts that may be reimbursed or recovered under any federal grant. The cost policies articulated in each of these circulars are substantially similar, but some differences do exist, due mainly to the nature of the recipient organization, the nature of programs administered, and the breadth of services and operations of some grantees but not others.

Several policy statements (laws, regulations, OMB circulars, agency rules) detail categories of costs that are absolutely necessary to operate the nonfederal grantee but that are considered unallowable as a matter of declared federal policy. Some examples of costs declared as unallowable follow.

GAAP cost accounting. A general policy of the federal government relating to charges, reimbursements, billings, or payments to nonfederal grantees is that costs must:

> be determined in accordance with generally accepted accounting principles, *except* as otherwise provided for in OMB Cost Circulars.

The emphasis on the word "except" is particularly significant to auditors of federal grant programs because there are many significant exceptions to a grantee being paid when following GAAP.

The characterization of costs by the federal government as allowable or unallowable *does not* imply that such costs are unnecessary, unreasonable, or illegal. The terms *unallowable* only means that the federal government prefers not to pay a grantee for these costs. In most instances, a grantee could not function without the activities supported by many of these so-called unallowable costs. For example, in the case of a government grantee, OMB Circular A-87, *Cost Principles for State, Local, and Indian Tribal Governments*, declares that general costs of a government (e.g., cost of governors, mayors, legislative overseers, and other essential governmental expenses) are unallowable charges to federal programs.

Costs unallowed per public policy. Unallowed costs per public policy include: write-off of uncollectible receivables; accrued cost for contingent liabilities; state and local government taxes; advertising cost; cost of idle facilities; lobbying costs; financing costs; donations; and contributions. The accounting and reporting of these costs are mandated and appropriate under GAAP but are classified as unallowable by the federal government for charges to federal grants.

Costs unallowed unless "funded." All pension costs of grantee employees; postretirement health and other benefit costs due to government employees; and self-insured liabilities and costs are unallowable until actually funded. The accounting and reporting of these incurred, but not paid, costs are required by, and appropriate under, GAAP, but are classified as unallowable by the federal government as charges to federal grants.

Cost unallowed unless approved in advance. These costs include: cash drawdown in excess of three days; employee relocation costs; recruiting costs; subscriptions cost; professional membership fees; and purchase of capital assets. The accounting and reporting of these costs are mandated and appropriate under GAAP, but are classified as unallowable by the federal government as charges to federal grants, unless advance approval was obtained.

Unallowable costs may not be charged to, claimed under, or billed directly or indirectly to any other contract, grant, or program of federal assistance. If so done, such costs would be an audit finding reportable as a *questioned costs* by the auditor.

TEN ALLOWABLE COSTS CRITERIA

The audit tests to meet federal procurement policy and allowable cost criteria require the auditor to determine allowability by testing direct and indirect costs charged to, or claimed under, a federal grant and verify that the cost elements meet *each* of several defined factors of allowability. To be allowable under federal grants costing criteria, all direct and indirect costs charged or claimed by a contractor must meet *each* of these criteria:

1. Be *necessary and reasonable* for the proper and efficient performance and administration of federal awards.

   - *Necessary costs* are cost required, implicitly or explicitly, by laws, regulations, and the federal grant agreement to support the program outlined in the federal grant. The *necessary cost* criteria should be assessed from the view of the purpose, timing, amount, authorization and approval, and the ultimate accounting of charged costs in relation to the performance period of the contract.
   - *Reasonable costs* are costs that do not exceed that which would be incurred by a prudent person under circumstances prevailing at the time the decision was made to incur the cost. The determination as to the reasonableness of costs must consider these questions:

     - Do the claimed costs exceed the type generally recognized as ordinary and necessary for the operation of the grantee or attainment of the performance or objectives outlined in the executed federal grant?
     - Do the claimed costs exceed restraints on spending or cost limits imposed by sound business practices or attainable by arm's-length bargaining, terms of federal and other laws, regulations and terms, or as conditions of the federal grant?
     - Do the claimed costs exceed market prices for comparable goods or services?
     - Do the claimed costs significantly deviate from the established practices in a manner that unjustifiably increases the cost to the federal grant?

2. Be *allocable* to federal awards under the provisions of OMB cost circulars.

   Allocable costs are costs that are directly allocable to a particular cost objective or where the goods and services involved are chargeable or assignable to such a cost objective in accordance with relative benefits received. OMB requires that determinations of *allocability* of costs consider that:

- All activities that benefit from a unit's indirect cost, including unallowable activities and services donated by third parties, receive an appropriate allocation of indirect costs.
- Any cost allocable to a particular federal grant or cost objective may not, unless otherwise permitted in writing, be charged to other federal awards to overcome fund deficiencies, avoid restrictions imposed by law or terms of federal awards, or for other reasons.
- Where an accumulation of indirect costs will ultimately result in charges to a federal grant, a cost allocation plan will be required, similar to those outlined in the appropriate OMB cost circular.

3. Be *authorized and not otherwise prohibited* under any federal, state, or local laws or regulations.
4. *Comply* with any limitations or exclusions set forth in OMB circulars or the terms and conditions unique to the federal grant or other governing regulations as to types, amounts, and limits on cost items.
5. Be in *conformance with policies, regulations*, and *procedures* that apply uniformly to both federal and nonfederal grants and to federal and nonfederal activities of the nonfederal grantee.
6. Be accorded consistent cost accounting treatment.

    Consistent accounting treatment means that costs may not be assigned to a federal grant as a direct cost or indirect cost if any other cost has been incurred for the same purpose, in like circumstances, and has been allocated to the federal award directly or, in part, indirectly. The *consistency* requirement also relates to the uniform accounting and charging of costs to a grantee between fiscal reporting periods.

7. Be determined in accordance with GAAP, *except* as otherwise provided for in OMB cost circulars.
8. Not be included as a cost or used to meet *cost-sharing or matching* requirements of any other federal grant in either the current or a prior period specifically permitted by federal law or another regulation. This restriction prohibits a grantee from claiming direct or indirect costs that were charged to the federal government under one federal agreement to meet a cost-sharing or cost-matching cost requirement of another federal agreement.
9. Be net of all applicable credits.

    Net of applicable credits refers to receipts or reduction of expenditure-type transactions that offset or reduce the expense of items charged to federal contracts as either direct or indirect costs (e.g., purchase discounts, rebates or allowances, recoveries or indemnities on losses, insurance refunds or rebates, or other price adjustments). In applying costs net of applicable credits, the *allocability* of net costs must consider:

    - To the extent that such credits relate to allowable costs, the credits must be applied to the federal award as a cost reduction or cash refund, as appropriate.

- Amounts of any credits should be recognized in determining indirect cost rates or amounts to be charged to federal awards.

10. Be adequately *documented*. For audits of direct and indirect costs and matching contributions claimed or charged, there must be test support documentation that identifies or relates the amount, timing, and purpose of transactions to the specific federal grant. For example, the timing of the transaction must be within the grant period. In most instances, transactions preceding or following grant award are not allowable in the absence of specific approval by the federal agency.

    Supportive documentation, as defined in literature of GAO and the AICPA, includes:

    - *Accounting records of original entry:* for example, journals, registers, ledgers, manuals, worksheets, and support for cost allocations. Alone, however, these types of accounting data are not sufficient supporting documentation.
    - *Corroborating evidence:* for example, canceled checks, invoices, contracts, grants, minutes of meetings, confirmations, and other written statements by knowledgeable personnel, information obtained by auditor inquiry, observation, inspection, and personal examination, and other information developed by, or available to, the auditor.

The auditor must make *independent* tests of underlying data and records and include analyses, reviews, retracing procedural steps of the financial process, auditor recalculations, and performance of reconciliations of any cost allocations. In audits of federal grants, claims, or charges to the grant that are not sufficiently documented or supported, or if the auditor is unable to satisfy him- or herself by other evidential means as to the proprietary and allowability of costs, such amounts must be "questioned" and reported to the federal agency for resolution.

TEN TESTS OF FEDERAL GRANTS
COMPLIANCE POLICIES AND REGULATIONS

The *Compliance Supplement* identifies 10 procurement compliance regulations, noncompliance with which could have a direct and material effect on the accounting, charging, and billings to federal grants. If the grant is materially significant to the grantee, noncompliance under a federal grant might well affect the overall financial statements of the grantee. The 10 compliance policies frequently associated with individual contracts, and that are of importance to grants audits, include:

1. *Costs charged to government—allowable, unallowable, direct and indirect costs.* Since the middle of the last century, it has been a policy of the federal government to permit only certain direct and indirect costs to be claimed by and reimbursed under federal grants. Federal money may not be claimed or paid for any direct or indirect costs defined as unallowable by federal policy. OMB has provided these definitions of direct and indirect costs.

- *Direct costs* are those that can be identified specifically with a particular final cost objective. Typical direct costs chargeable to federal grants include employee compensation, cost of materials, equipment (if specifically approved), and travel expenses subject to any federal limits.
- *Indirect costs* are those: (a) incurred for a common or joint purpose benefiting more than one cost objective; and (b) not readily assignable to the cost objectives specifically benefited, without effort disproportionate to the results achieved. To facilitate equitable distribution of indirect expenses to the cost objectives served, it may be necessary to establish a number of pools of indirect costs within the grantee. Indirect cost pools should be distributed to benefited cost objectives on bases that will produce an equitable result in consideration of relative benefits derived. Any direct cost of a minor amount may be treated as an indirect cost for reasons of practicality.

2. *Equipment, real property.* The title to equipment acquired by nonfederal entities with federal monies could remain with the nonfederal grantee or with the federal government. Here, equipment is defined as tangible, nonexpendable property, with a useful life of more than one year and an acquisition cost of $5,000 or more per unit.

3. *Matching and in-kind contributions.* Matching requirements, in-kind or otherwise, often require examination of the terms and conditions of the individual grant. Matching requirements are often specific as to the *amount, type, timing,* and *purpose* of what match is permissible. For example, if the agreed-on match was to be cash, then donated labor or any other type of contribution, free or paid for, would be unallowable. Also, there may be a requirement dictating that the match be provided within a certain time period; compliance in a later period would have to be reported to the federal grantor.

4. *Availability of program funds.* Legislation for all federal appropriations and other laws of financial assistance place limits on the *amount* of funds being provided, the *purpose* for which the funds are provided, and a *time* period (or use period) after which the authority to spend the federal monies lapses. (OMB Circular A-102, the "common rule," should be consulted for additional guidance on this compliance requirement.)

5. *Procurement, suspension, debarment.* Presidential executive orders and federal regulations prohibit agencies and others from doing business with parties who have been suspended or debarred or whose principals are suspended or debarred under some federal grants, contracts, or other assistance program.

6. *Program income. Program income* is the gross income directly generated by the federal project during the grant period (e.g., fees earned for services, rental income, sale of commodities or items fabricated under the program, and payment of principal and interests on loans made from federal funds). Unless otherwise specified by the federal agency, program income shall be deducted from program outlays.

7. *Reporting accurately, timely, and in the prescribed form.* Recipients of federal grants must use prescribed forms for financial, performance, and special reporting. Auditors must confirm that controls have been implemented to ensure the reports, claims for advances, and reimbursements are supported by the same books and records from which the entity's financial statements are prepared. Tests must be made to ensure that submitted reports, claims for advances, and reimbursements are supported by underlying documentation and appropriate corroborating evidence.

8. *Special tests and provisions, unique requirements.* Laws, regulations, and provisions of grants contain requirements for special tests and other conditions. The auditor must review the specific terms and conditions of the grant since the grant could contain conditions warranting special examination. The axiom of the legal profession applies equally to grant audits: *When all else fails, read the grant.* There is no substitute for examining the terms and conditions of specific grants, bond covenants, terms of loans, loan guarantees, and so on, under which monies or financial assistance is provided to support grants to nonfederal entities.

9. *Activities: allowable, unallowable.* Public monies may be used for only those activities allowed by law or regulation. Congress determines that certain organizations, groups, or individuals are to be beneficiaries of funding provided under particular federal legislation. Audit tests must be made to ensure that federal monies were used to support only those activities permitted by law or regulation.

10. *Cash management: advance funding of government programs.* For some grantees, forms of advance funding exists (e.g., lump sum or total advance of required federal funding; advances made at designated points during the contract period; or periodic drawdowns under a prearranged letter of credits procedure arranged between the contractor, the Department of Treasury, and a local commercial bank). Under the Cash Management Act, a grantee's procedures for the drawing down of federal funds must minimize the time elapsing between the transfer of funds from the Department of Treasury and disbursement by the grantee. Historically, the cash balance was not to be in excess of three business days.

When deciding to test or not test a compliance requirement, the auditor must conclude: (1) whether the requirement does or does not apply to the grant, and (2) whether noncompliance with the requirement could or could not have a material effect on the grant. An audit report of a federal grantee or for an individual grant may, in addition to an audit opinion, be presented in narrative form, and supported by exhibits, tables, graphs, and illustrations that, in the auditor's judgment, are necessary to make a full reporting of the facts relative to the audited grant(s).

Chapter 8 of the *Government Auditing Standards* (the "yellow book"), Reporting Standards for Performance Audits, provides guidance for the desired narrative-type audit reports and should be consulted before undertaking an audit of federal grants. Further, the guidance in Chapter 8 is part of the criteria used by federal inspectors general and GAO in assessing the adequacy of the grants audit.

Exhibit 16.1: Methodology for audits of federal grants

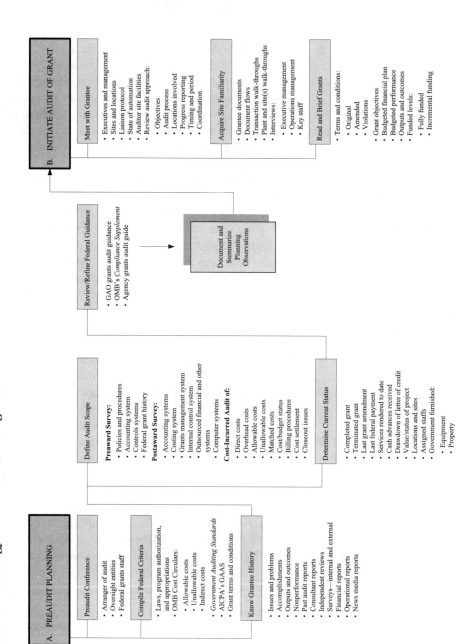

A. PREAUDIT PLANNING

Preaudit Conference
- Arranger of audit
- Oversight entities
- Federal grants staff

Compile Federal Criteria
- Laws, program authorization, and appropriations
- OMB Cost Circulars:
  - Allowable costs
  - Unallowable costs
  - Indirect costs
- *Government Auditing Standards*
- AICPA's GAAS
- Grant terms and conditions

Know Grantee History
- Issues and problems
- Accomplishments
- Outputs and outcomes
- Nonperformance
- Past audit reports
- Consultant reports
- Independent reviews
- Surveys—internal and external
- Financial reports
- Operational reports
- News media reports

Define Audit Scope

Preaward Survey:
- Policies and procedures
- Accounting system
- Controls systems
- Federal grant history

Postaward Survey:
- Accounting systems
- Costing system
- Grants management system
- Internal control system
- Outsourced financial and other systems
- Computer systems

Cost-Incurred Audit of:
- Direct costs
- Overhead costs
- Allowable costs
- Unallowable costs
- Matched costs
- Cost/budget status
- Billing procedures
- Cost settlement
- Closeout issues

Determine Current Status
- Completed grant
- Terminated grant
- Last grant amendment
- Last federal payment
- Services rendered to date
- Cash advances received
- Drawdown of letter of credit
- Value/status of project
- Locations and sites
- Assigned staffs
- Government furnished:
  - Equipment
  - Property

Review/Refine Federal Guidance
- GAO grants audit guidance
- OMB's *Compliance Supplement*
- Agency grants audit guide

Document and Summarize Planning Observations

B. INITIATE AUDIT OF GRANT

Meet with Grantee
- Executives and management
- Sites and locations
- Liaison protocol
- State of automation
- Auditor site facilities
- Review audit approach:
  - Objectives
  - Audit process
  - Locations involved
  - Progress reporting
  - Timing and period
  - Coordination

Acquire Site Familiarity
- Grantee documents
- Document flows
- Transaction walk-throughs
- Plant and site(s) walk-throughs
- Interviews:
  - Executive management
  - Operations management
  - Key staff

Read and Brief Grants
- Terms and conditions:
  - Original
  - Amended
  - Violations
- Grant objectives
- Budgeted financial plan
- Budgeted performance
- Outputs and outcomes
- Funded levels:
  - Fully funded
  - Incremental funding

Exhibit 16.1: Methodology for audits of federal grants (continued)

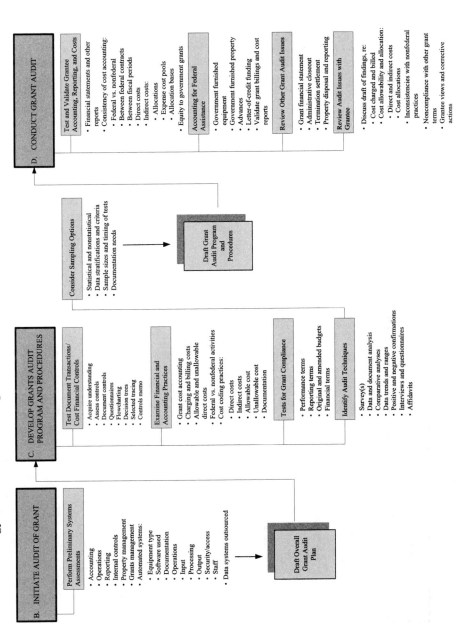

B. INITIATE AUDIT OF GRANT

Perform Preliminary Systems Assessments

- Accounting
- Operations
- Reporting
- Internal controls
- Property management
- Grants management
- Automated systems:
  - Equipment type
  - Software used
  - Documentation
  - Operations
  - Input
  - Processing
  - Output
  - Security/access
  - Staff
- Data systems outsourced

Draft Overall Grant Audit Plan

C. DEVELOP GRANTS AUDIT PROGRAM AND PROCEDURES

Test Document Transactions/ Cost Financial Controls

- Acquire understanding
- Assess controls
- Document controls
- Questionnaires
- Flowcharting
- Decision trees
- Selected tracing
- Controls memo

Examine Financial and Accounting Practices

- Grant cost accounting
- Charging and billing costs
- Allowable and unallowable direct costs
- Federal vs. nonfederal activities
- Cost coding practices:
  - Direct costs
  - Indirect costs
  - Allowable cost
  - Unallowable cost
  - Documentation

Tests for Grant Compliance

- Performance terms
- Reporting terms
- Original and amended budgets
- Financial terms

Identify Audit Techniques

- Survey(s)
- Data and document analysis
- Comparative analyses
- Data trends and ranges
- Positive and negative confirmations
- Interviews and questionnaires
- Affidavits

Consider Sampling Options

- Statistical and nonstatistical
- Data stratifications and criteria
- Sample sizes and timing of tests
- Documentation needs

Draft Grant Audit Program and Procedures

D. CONDUCT GRANT AUDIT

Test and Validate Grantee Accounting, Reporting, and Costs

- Financial statements and other reports
- Consistency of cost accounting:
  - Federal vs. nonfederal
  - Between federal contracts
  - Between fiscal periods
  - Direct costs
  - Indirect costs:
    - Allocations
    - Expense cost pools
    - Allocation bases
  - Equity to government grants

Accounting for Federal Assistance

- Government furnished equipment
- Government furnished property
- Advances
- Letter-of-credit funding
- Validate grant billings and cost reports

Review Other Grant Audit Issues

- Grant financial statement
- Administrative closeout
- Termination settlement
- Property disposal and reporting

Review Audit Issues with Grantee

- Discuss draft of findings, re:
  - Cost charged and billed
  - Cost allowability and allocation:
    - Direct and indirect costs
    - Cost allocations
  - Inconsistencies with nonfederal practices
  - Noncompliance with other grant terms
  - Grantee views and corrective actions

Exhibit 16.1: Methodology for audits of federal grants (continued)

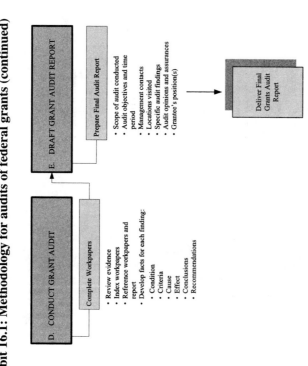

D. CONDUCT GRANT AUDIT

Complete Workpapers

· Review evidence
· Index workpapers
· Reference workpapers and report
· Develop facts for each finding:
  · Condition
  · Criteria
  · Cause
  · Effect
  · Conclusions
  · Recommendations

E. DRAFT GRANT AUDIT REPORT

Prepare Final Audit Report

· Scope of audit conducted
· Audit objectives and time period
· Management contacts
· Locations visited
· Specific audit findings
· Audit opinions and assurances
· Grantee's position(s)

Deliver Final Grants Audit Report